▶

Learning Disabilities

Related Titles of Interest

Successful Mainstreaming: Proven Ways to Detect and Correct Special Needs
Joyce S. Choate
ISBN: 0-205-14349-0

Understanding and Treating Attention Deficit Disorder
Edward A. Kirby & Liam K. Grimley
ISBN: 0-205-14391-1 Paper   0-205-14392-X Cloth

A Guide for Educating Mainstreamed Students, Fourth Edition
Philip H. Mann, Patricia A. Suiter, & Rose Marie McClung
ISBN: 0-205-13225-1

Handbook of Hyperactivity in Children
Johnny L. Matson
ISBN: 0-205-14591-4

Teaching Study Strategies to Students with Learning Disabilities
Stephen S. Strichart & Charles T. Mangrum III
ISBN: 0-205-13992-2

Assessment of Exceptional Students: Educational and Psychological Procedures, Third Edition
Ronald L. Taylor
ISBN: 0-205-14142-0

Educational Assessment of Learning Problems: Testing for Teaching, Second Edition
Gerald Wallace, Stephen Larsen, & Linda Elksnin
ISBN: 0-205-13633-8

Learning Disabilities

New Directions for Assessment and Intervention

Nancy C. Jordan
Josephine Goldsmith-Phillips
Rutgers, The State University of New Jersey

Editors

Allyn and Bacon
Boston • London • Toronto • Sydney • Tokyo • Singapore

Library of Congress Cataloging-in-Publication Data

Learning disabilities : new directions for assessment and intervention
/ Nancy C. Jordan, Josephine Goldsmith-Phillips, editors.
    p.   cm.
  Includes bibliographical references and index.
  ISBN 0-205-14124-2
  1. Learning disabled children—Education—United States.
2. Learning disabilities—United States—Diagnosis. 3. Learning
disabilities—United States—Treatment. I. Jordan, Nancy C.
II. Goldsmith-Phillips, Josephine.
LC4705.L38 1994
371.91—dc20   93-22965
                                         CIP

Papers originally presented at a conference in the fall of 1991 at the
Rutgers Graduate School of Education, New Brunswick, New Jersey.

Printed in the United States of America

10 9 8 7 6 5 4 3 2 1   97 96 95 94 93

To Michael and Len

Contents

About the Contributors

Howard S. Adelman began his professional career as a remedial teacher and went on to receive his doctorate in psychology from UCLA. As professor of psychology at UCLA and codirector of the School Mental Health Project, he and his research group have focused on youngsters who manifest learning, behavior, and emotional problems in school settings. The work resulted in a variety of publications relevant to education and mental health. His most recent book (coauthored with Linda Taylor and published by Brooks/Cole) is *Learning Problems and Learning Disabilities: Moving Forward.*

Ann L. Brown is a professor at the Graduate School of Education, University of California at Berkeley. She received her doctorate in psychology from the University of London. Her primary research interest is in promoting intentional learning and reflection in children from socioeconomic and cultural backgrounds associated with academic risk. Dr. Brown is a leading authority on child development, the psychology of reading, and metacognition. In 1991, she received the American Educational Association's Award for Distinguished Contributions to Educational Research. Recent publications have appeared in the *Journal of Learning Sciences, Cognitive Science,* and *Cognition.*

James Bryan obtained his doctorate in psychology from Northwestern University. He also is a professor at Northwestern. He has published exclusively in the area of social factors and learning disabilities. His research has been concerned with immediate impressions of students with learning disabilities, fear of failure, ingratiation tactics, and self-efficacy intervention.

Tanis Bryan obtained her doctorate in communication disorders from Northwestern University. She is professor of special education in the College of Education at the University of Illinois at Chicago. She has been involved in research in social factors in learning disabilities for several years and has published extensively in this area. With James Bryan, she coauthored the textbooks *Understanding Learning Disabilities* and *Exceptional Children*. Dr. Bryan was director and co-principal investigator of the Chicago Institute for the Study of Learning Disabilities. Recent research focuses on crime victimization of students with learning disabilities, prereferral intervention, and self-efficacy of students with learning disabilities.

Joseph C. Campione is a professor at Berkeley's Graduate School of Education. He also directs the school's joint doctoral program in special education. He received his doctorate in psychology from the University of Connecticut. His research focuses on learning strategies of educationally at-risk children, transfer of learning, metacognition, and issues of assessment and instruction. Dr. Campione has published numerous articles on these topics in journals such as the *Journal of Learning Disabilities, Intelligence,* and the *American Psychologist.*

Joanne F. Carlisle is an assistant professor in learning disabilities in the department of communication sciences and disorders at Northwestern University. She received her doctorate in special education with a concentration in learning disabilities from the University of Connecticut. Her research interests include typical and atypical patterns of acquisition of oral and written language capabilities and the assessment of reading and spelling abilities. She has published articles in journals such as *Annals of Dyslexia* and the *Journal of Educational Research.*

Jeanne S. Chall received her doctorate from the Ohio State University. She is Professor of Education Emerita at Harvard University. She directed the Harvard Reading Laboratory at the Graduate School of Education for twenty-five years. Dr. Chall has written widely on readability, reading development, methods of teaching reading, and diagnosis and remediation. Her books include *Learning to Read: The Great Debate, Stages of Reading Development, The Reading Crisis: Why Poor Children Fall Behind,* and *Should Textbooks Challenge Students: The Case for Easier or Harder Books.* Dr. Chall has received many honors and awards for educational research, including a citation of merit from the International Reading Association, the American Educational Research Association Award for Distinguished Contributions to Research in Education, the American Psychological Association's Edward L. Thorndike Award for Distinguished Contributions to Education, and a medal for Distinguished Service for Education from Teacher's College, Columbia University.

Elizabeth Dohrn is pursuing her Ph.D. in special education at the University of Illinois at Chicago. She is an instructor at UIC in the department of Special Education. She has been involved in research on self-efficacy of students with learning disabilities and their parents. Her research interests include social factors in learning-disabled and behaviorally disordered children's home–school collaboration.

Douglas Fuchs completed his doctorate in educational psychology at the University of Minnesota. He is professor of special education and a Kennedy Center investigator at George Peabody College of Vanderbilt University. His research focuses on methods that teachers can use to accommodate diverse student needs within large group contexts. His research is described in recent issues of the *American Educational Research Journal,* the *Elementary School Journal, Exceptional Children,* and *School Psychology Review.*

Lynn S. Fuchs received her doctorate in educational psychology from the University of Minnesota. She is an associate professor in the department of special education at George Peabody College of Vanderbilt University. Her research focuses on the technical development of curriculum-based measurement systems and on teachers' use of classroom methods in their instructional planning. Dr. Fuchs has published over ninety research articles in peer-review journals on these topics and is the coeditor of the *Journal of Special Education.*

Josephine Goldsmith-Phillips has two doctoral degrees from Rutgers University, one in education and one in psychology. She is an associate professor of educational psychology at Rutgers University. She has worked with reading-disabled students as a high school reading specialist, as the director of an educational opportunity fund reading program at Rutgers College, and as codirector of the Center for Cognitive Training at the Rutgers Graduate School of Education. Her research is concerned with neuropsychological test patterns in children and adults with dyslexia. She has published articles in journals such as the *Journal of Educational Psychology* and the *Elementary School Journal.*

Ann Gordon is completing her doctorate in educational psychology from the University of Illinois at Chicago. An experienced teacher, teacher trainer, and educational therapist, she has served as the lab manager for the Brown/Campione research group at UC Berkeley since 1990. Her research interests include metacognition, dynamic assessment, and reciprocal teaching.

Janellen Huttenlocher is the William S. Gray Professor of Education and Psychology at the University of Chicago. She received her doctorate in cognitive psychology from Harvard University. Her research interests include spatial cognition, memory, vocabulary development, and the development of numerical abilities. Dr. Huttenlocher has published numerous articles on these topics, some of which have appeared in *Psychological Review, Cognitive Psychology,* and *Developmental Psychology.*

George W. Hynd is a research professor of special education and clinical psychology and chairman of the Division for Exceptional Children at the University of Georgia. He is also a clinical professor of neurology at the Medical College of Georgia and directs the Center for Clinical and Developmental Neuropsychology. In addition to completing a postdoctoral fellowship in clinical neuropsychology, he was selected as a Fulbright Scholar in Child Neuropsychology and worked at the University of Jyvaskyla in Finland. He is the author of many books (e.g., *Pediatric Neuropsychology, Neuropsychological Assessment in Clinical Child Psychology*), chapters, and articles. His research and clinical interests focus primarily on the neurological basis of learning disabilities and attention-deficit disorders in children.

Nancy C. Jordan received her doctorate in human development from Harvard University. She completed a postdoctoral fellowship at the University of Chicago. She is an assistant professor in the department of educational psychology at the Graduate School of Education at Rutgers University. Dr. Jordan's research program focuses on cognitive development and learning disabilities. She has published articles in *Developmental Psychology,* the *Journal of Experimental Child Psychology,* and the *Journal of Psycholinguistic Research.*

Susan Cohen Levine received her doctorate in experimental psychology from MIT. She is an associate professor of psychology at the University of Chicago. Her research interests include developmental neuropsychology, cognitive development, and learning disabilities. Recently she has published articles in the *Journal of Experimental Child Psychology, Brain and Cognition,* and *Neuropsychologia.*

Virginia Mann is a professor in the department of cognitive sciences at the University of California, Irvine. She holds a doctorate in experimental psychology from MIT and has been a research associate at Haskins Laboratories, Inc., and a member of the psychology department at Bryn Mawr College. Dr. Mann's research interests include reading, speech perception, and sex differences in cognition. Key publications are cited in her chapter and have appeared in journals such as *Cognition,* the *Journal of Experimental Child Psychology,* and the *Journal of Learning Disabilities,* as well as in various edited volumes.

James W. Montgomery obtained his doctorate from Wichita University and completed postdoctoral fellowship at Purdue University. He is an assistant professor at the Clinical Center for the Study of Development and Learning at the University of North Carolina at Chapel Hill. His research interests are in speech perception and sentence processing of language-impaired children. Dr. Montgomery has published journal articles and book chapters on these topics. A recent publication appeared in *Applied Psycholinguistics.*

Martha Rutherford is a doctoral student in the division of language and literacy from the University of California, Berkeley. She has been part of the Brown/ Campione research group since 1991. She has taught children in both regular and bilingual classes in Oakland, California.

Margaret Semrud-Clikeman is an assistant professor of educational psychology at the University of Washington at Seattle. She worked as a school psychologist for fourteen years before pursuing her doctorate at the University of Georgia. Her doctoral dissertation received the Outstanding Dissertation National Award from the Orton Dyslexia Society. She completed a postdoctoral neuroscience fellowship at the Massachusetts General Hospital in Boston. She has published articles on neuropsychology and learning disabilities in journals such as the *Psychological Bulletin.* Dr. Semrud-Clikeman recently completed a study that utilized volumetric MRI measurements comparing attention-deficit-disordered children with matched controls. These results will be submitted for publication in the near future.

Rachel E. Stark received her doctorate from the University of Oklahoma Medical Center. She is a professor of audiology and speech sciences at Purdue University. Previously she was director of the department of communication sciences and disorders at the John F. Kennedy Institute in Baltimore. Her research interests are in infant speech development and speech processing in childhood language disorders. She has published widely in journals such as the *Journal of Speech and Hearing Disorders, Annals of Dyslexia,* and the *American Journal of Otology.*

Jill Walker has been teaching for eighteen years. She has worked in the Oakland Public Schools for nine years and is currently teaching second grade at John Swett Elementary School. She received her master's degree from the University of Northern Colorado in teaching the hearing impaired. Ms. Walker is currently collaborating with the Brown and Campione Project at UC Berkeley in developing a Community of Learners program for the second grade.

Marilyn C. Welsh received her doctorate in developmental psychology from UCLA. She is an assistant professor of psychology at the University of Northern Colorado. Dr. Welsh's research explores the nature of frontal lobe functioning in both typical and atypical children and the development of new cognitive measures to assess these functions. Her publications have appeared in *Developmental Neuropsychology, Child Development,* and *Cognitive Development.*

Series Foreword

Within the past decade, the profession of education has been challenged to respond to the crises in U.S. classrooms and the failures of American students. Critics and supporters of education alike have raised basic questions about the profession, including whether educators have satisfactorily met the challenges that students and schools present. Beginning with the highly publicized *A Nation at Risk,* seemingly endless and often contradictory criticisms, analyses, and recommendations about our educational system have appeared from virtually every segment of contemporary society.

The Rutgers Symposia on Education focus on vital issues in contemporary education in the United States. The series, now six years old, takes an interdisciplinary perspective and provides a synthesis and interpretation of high-quality educational research on topics of interest and controversy to practitioners and policymakers. The focus of each volume is upon a problem, such as teacher preparation, the structure of schools, the teaching of higher order thinking in mathematics, and learning disabilities. Each volume provides an interdisciplinary forum through which scholars can disseminate their original research and extend that work to potential applications for practice, including guides for teaching, learning, assessment, intervention, and policy formulation. We believe that the series has the potential to increase significantly perceptive analyses and have a positive impact on education in the United States.

The focus of this volume is on children with learning disabilities, who are increasing in number and representing a larger and larger proportion of all U.S. schoolchildren. Taken as a whole, the book presents an integration of current findings about learning disabilities. The work originates from a range of disciplines, including education, psychology, linguistics, and cognitive science. State-of-the-art research in attentional processes, learning, language development, cognition, neuropsychology, and social behavior is presented. Underlying each chapter is a summary of what we do know about learning disabilities. Each chapter considers implications for practice and intervention.

The editors of this volume, Nancy C. Jordan and Josephine Goldsmith-Phillips, believe as I do that teachers' adequate understanding of students with learning disabilities enhances their ability to work effectively with all children in their classrooms. It is with great pleasure that we offer this fifth volume of The Rutgers Symposia on Education. Our expectation is that this book will educate our colleagues and stimulate debate on assessment, instruction, and learning of children with learning disabilities.

> Louise Cherry Wilkinson
> Professor of Educational Psychology and Psychology
> Dean of the Graduate School of Education
> Rutgers, The State University of New Jersey

Foreword

Considerable advances in research have been accomplished over the past decade in the area of learning disabilities. With the advent of new technologies, particularly those that allow for the first time a noninvasive procedure for imaging the human brain in vivo, come new opportunities for advancing our understanding of the neural mechanisms underlying learning disabilities. New information derived from new neuromorphological studies using magnetic resonance imaging (MRI) coupled with the fine-grained behavioral information that has been accumulating from educational and psychological studies of children with learning disabilities, promises a new frontier of research in the area of developmental learning disabilities.

The ability to utilize developing technologies fully to aid in better understanding the etiology of developmental learning disabilities relies on accurate and consistent means of determining the detailed behavior profiles of learning-impaired children. Considerable research has focused on developing more detailed subgroup classifications of these children. For example, within the area of developmental reading disorders, several subclassifications have been proposed. There is now converging evidence from research laboratories around the world that upward of 80 percent of children with specific developmental dyslexia form a single subgroup that is characterized by deficits at the phonological level. Exciting new evidence now suggests that in a variety of sensory modalities (auditory, visual, tactile, cross-modal), as well as in the motor system, a pan-sensory temporal analysis deficit may directly underlie the phonological perception and production deficits of these children.

Several major longitudinal studies that have been conducted over the past decade have also recently come to fruition, adding a wealth of new information concerning the outcomes of early learning disabilities. These studies have demonstrated a potential continuum from early developmental language disorders to subsequent academic achievement disorders, as well as considerable comorbidity between developmental language disorders, reading disorders, and attention deficit disorders in school-age children. Highly significant correlations between neurodevelopmental (sensory-motor) disabilities in both language-based learning disorders and psychiatric disorders in children have also derived from these longitudinal studies. Thus, these studies have demonstrated a clear and significant link between early perceptual-motor deficits (specifically, rapid temporal analysis), phonological development, speech and language development, academic achievement disorders, and higher than expected risk for psychiatric disorders. Clearly, this cascade of events deserves a renewed focus in the development of both assessment and treatment tools for the next generation of children with learning disabilities.

The studies reported in this book are directed at integrating research findings pertaining to etiology, with new directions for assessment and intervention. In this way, they offer important direction for the future. There is a pressing need for the development of research studies specifically focused on linking outcomes from etiological research with the development of novel assessment and intervention strategies. Future advances for both assessment and intervention will be accelerated through more direct collaboration between researchers focused on etiology, assessment, and intervention.

Paula Tallal
Codirector, Center for Molecular and Behavioral Neuroscience
Professor of Neuroscience
Rutgers, The State University of New Jersey

Acknowledgments

The contributions of many people made our RISE project possible. We are grateful to Dean Louise Cherry Wilkinson, who created the RISE series as a forum for educational exchange and advancement. Our chapter authors brought original findings into a collaborative setting where teachers, researchers, and clinicians shared challenges and ideas. We also are appreciative of the guidance of insightful reviewers Elaine R. Silliman of the University of South Florida; Paulette S. Kenig, learning consultant, Palmyra School District, Palmyra, New Jersey; and Deborah Gartland of Towson State University. Kristine Spaventa undertook the demanding work of manuscript preparation with unusual skill and care, and Jane Sherwood showed extraordinary patience in shepherding all RISE correspondence. Susan Hutchinson of Allyn and Bacon was our unerring guide through the complex editorial process. We thank all of these friends and colleagues for their support and care in producing this book.

▶

Introduction

According to the Interagency Committee on Learning Disabilities' report to the U.S. Congress (1987), disorders of learning affect up to 10 percent of U.S. schoolchildren. The incidence is even higher among economically disadvantaged populations, especially children who live in the inner city. Over the next decade, the prevalence of learning disabilities may escalate further as an increasing number of children with a history of prenatal maternal substance abuse enter and progress through school. In addition, very low birth weight infants who are now being kept alive by advances in medical technology and neonatal care are at risk for future learning disabilities (Eilers et al., 1986).

Learning disabilities pose an important challenge for researchers and practitioners. They can be chronic problems with serious negative consequences. Children with such difficulties may feel a pervasive sense of failure or inadequacy. In many cases, emotional and behavioral difficulties accompany learning problems. If neglected, learning disabilities can result in poor self-esteem, academic indifference, and lifelong underachievement. Delinquency, substance abuse, school dropout and depression all are concomitants of school failure (e.g., Forness & Sinclair, 1990; Levine & Jordan, 1987; Pearl & Bryan, 1990). For these reasons, learning disabilities represent a significant risk to physical and psychological health as well as to personal life fulfillment.

Our knowledge of the causes, correlates, and behavioral manifestations of learning disabilities is expanding rapidly. Technological as well as theoretical advances in education, psychology, medicine, and linguistics have provided important insights into how children learn and why so many fail. Furthermore, new approaches to assessment and treatment are proliferating.

This book synthesizes some of the best research on learning disabilities in school-age children. It is based on original papers presented by the authors in the fall of 1991 in New Brunswick, New Jersey, at the Rutgers Graduate School of Education. The underlying theme of the book is connecting learning disabilities with assessment and practice. Many of the chapters present original research findings; others review current research to propose new techniques for assessing and treating learning disabilities. We requested that all of the authors include applications for assessment, practice, or both in their chapters, although some of the papers are inherently more applied than others.

The book begins with a chapter by Howard Adelman. Its purpose is to highlight some of the major issues in learning disabilities research, including how learning disabilities are defined, identified, and managed. Adelman emphasizes the importance of differentiating learning disabilities from other types of learning problems (e.g., problems caused by the environment). He also advocates a multidimensional approach to intervention, one that incorporates motivational and environmental as well as developmental factors. The reader should keep these basic issues in mind while reading subsequent chapters.

The remainder of the book is divided into two major sections. Part I is concerned with deficits in cognitive, developmental, and neuropsychological processes and their impact on learning. Marilyn Welsh examines the assessment of attention deficits in children from a neuropsychological perspective. She proposes that executive functions, such as planning, flexibility, and impulse control, should be considered in the evaluation of attention deficits, and she presents a battery of neuropsychological tasks that can tap these functions.

The next three chapters in this section address reading problems. Margaret Semrud-Clikeman and George Hynd examine current neuroanatomical research in dyslexia, which is likely to produce links between brain structure and reading behavior. Using current noninvasive techniques for examining the brain, such as magnetic resonance imaging (MRI), Semrud-Clikeman, Hynd, and their colleagues have found neurological differences in the brains of young children. Their studies have revealed these differences in areas involved in language processing, such as phonological coding. Virginia Mann discusses reading disabilities from a language-oriented perspective. She shows that measures of phonological awareness and phonological processing, both involving the sound patterns of language, are important predictors of early reading problems. Josephine Goldsmith-Phillips describes her recent research on developmental dyslexia. Her work shows that slowed reading time, combined with distinctive patterns of reading test scores and reading errors, differentiates children with developmental dyslexia of the phonological subtype from younger average readers. This research has useful implications for classroom assessment, since official definitions of dyslexia include few positive markers for the disorder.

The final group of chapters in Part I deal with disorders of oral language, written language, and mathematics, respectively. Rachel Stark and James Montgomery investigate rapid syllable production in children with specific language impairments. The authors show that language-impaired children perform more poorly than normal children on a task that requires rapid repetition of syllables and that difficulty on this task is related to deficits in short-term auditory memory as well as in speech-motor functioning. Joanne Carlisle presents an empirical study examining the interrelations of morphological knowledge, spelling ability, and written expression. She demonstrates that children with spelling difficulties have problems learning rule-based linguistic systems and that these problems compromise their written expression. Carlisle emphasizes the importance of considering linguistic knowledge as part of a comprehensive writing assessment. Finally, Nancy Jordan, Susan Cohen Levine, and Janellen Huttenlocher describe their research program on the development of mathematics calculation abilities in young children. They assess children's performance on both verbal and nonverbal calculation tasks. The series of studies suggests that young children with special needs may have underlying mathematical competencies that are not revealed by conventional mathematics tests.

Part II of the book emphasizes instructional issues. Jeanne Chall describes a new instrument for teachers, clinicians, and researchers who need to assess reading and related language skills. This instrument, based on the findings of Chall's extensive research on reading development and instruction, is innovative in linking reading assessment with instructional practice through both formal and informal measures. Also connecting testing with teaching, Lynn Fuchs discusses how curriculum-based measurement can guide instructional planning for students with learning disabilities. In particular, she describes procedures for integrating curriculum-based measurement with instructional activities. Douglas Fuchs describes his research program on mainstream assistance teams. This approach provides a structured method of intervention in the regular educational setting *before* underachieving students are referred for special educational services. Tanis Bryan, James Bryan, and Elizabeth Dohrn focus on the beliefs held by children with learning disabilities about their successes and failures. These authors demonstrate that attribution training, combined with specific task strategies, increases children's achievement and creates positive changes in their self-referent thoughts. In the final chapter of the volume, Joseph Campione, Martha Rutherford, Ann Gordon, Jill Walker, and Ann L. Brown describe their comprehensive classroom research project. They devised a curriculum that integrates reading, writing, and mathematics skills with the learning of scientific content. Computer technology is an integral part of the program. Their chapter focuses on the extent to which this classroom environment is responsive to children with special needs.

This book was planned to provide scholars and practitioners with recent developments in the field of learning disabilities. We selected papers representing the spectrum of issues that must be confronted in working with students with learning disabilities in classroom or research settings. Consequently, the chapters cover a wide range of issues, from questions about neurological and cognitive deficits to recommendations for tests and training programs that address individual differences.

Given the recent changes in state and federal laws, the responsibility for educating students with learning disabilities will be shared by many teachers without special training or the opportunity for advanced preparation. It is our hope that this book will be useful for these professionals as well as for specialists and researchers who seek an update and current perspective on the quandaries posed by children who are not learning.

REFERENCES

Eilers, B. L., Desai, N. S., Wilson, M. A., et al. (1986). Classroom performance and social factors of children with birth weights of 1,250 grams or less: Follow-up at 5 to 8 years of age. *Pediatrics, 77,* 203–208.

Forness, S., & Sinclair, E. (1990). Learning disabilities in children with clinical depression. In H. L. Swanson & B. Keogh (Eds.), *Learning disabilities: Theoretical and research issues* (pp. 315–332). Hillsdale, NJ: Erlbaum.

Interagency Committee on Learning Disabilities (1987). *Learning disabilities: A report to the U.S. Congress.* Washington, DC.

Levine, M. D., & Jordan, N. C. (1987). Neurodevelopmental dysfunction: Their cumulative interactions and effects in middle childhood. In J. J. Gallagher & C. T. Ramey (Eds.), *The malleability of children* (pp. 141–154). Baltimore, MD: Paul H. Brooks.

Pearl, R., & Bryan, T. (1990). Learning disabled adolescents' vulnerability to crime victimization and delinquency. In H. L. Swanson & B. Keogh (Eds.), *Learning disabilities: Theoretical and research issues* (pp. 139–154). Hillsdale, NJ: Erlbaum.

► 1

Learning Disabilities
On Interpreting Research Translations

HOWARD S. ADELMAN
University of California, Los Angeles

Abstract

As an aid in evaluating research applications to learning disabilities practice, this chapter highlights concerns about the lack of clarity surrounding research samples and the narrowness of intervention approaches studied. Specifically emphasized with respect to research samples is the tendency not to differentiate learning disabilities from other types of learning problems. Toward countering this trend, a framework is presented for conceiving learning disabilities as one type of learning problem. With respect to intervention, the trend is seen as one of narrowly focusing on remediation of developmental problems. To provide a broader perspective for intervention research and practice, comprehensive and multifaceted approaches are outlined.

When a group of talented researchers focus on learning disabilities (LD) in translating their research into practice, the effort cannot help but advance knowledge. At the same time, such translations inevitably raise concerns. The purpose of this chapter is to present some perspectives for evaluating research applications to learning disabilities practice. My intent is not to criticize but to provide a framework for understanding contributions and concerns and to highlight additional directions for research and practice.

Evaluating any effort to apply research to interventions for learning disabilities requires a perspective on the fundamental questions confronting learning disability practitioners. Stated simply, those questions are:

Who is it that we are talking about?
What should be done to help those with learning disabilities?

What follows is an attempt to underscore some fundamental concerns related to these matters and to highlight some concepts that may help address these concerns.

WHO IS IT THAT WE ARE TALKING ABOUT?

This is not the place to reiterate all the arguments about prevailing conceptual and operational definitions of learning disabilities. Suffice it to say that both as a concept and as a diagnostic classification, LD has been used indiscriminately (e.g., see Chalfant, 1985; Kavale & Forness, 1985; Siegel, 1989; Rispens, van Yperen, & van Duijn, 1991). As a result, almost any individual with a common learning problem stands a good chance of being diagnosed as having a learning disability, a reading disability, dyslexia, or something of the sort. Such labels, of course, both reflect and perpetuate psychological and sociopolitical tendencies to view most learning problems as if their cause was due to some form of internal pathology. This state of affairs has limited investigation of the role played by teaching and learning environments in causing the majority of learning problems and has hindered research and practice related to the relatively few who truly have learning disabilities.

Assessment and Sample Classification

Assessment, of course, is central to diagnostic classification (Adelman & Taylor, 1991). That is, providing data for classifying the nature of a learning problem is one of the various practical functions assessment serves (see Figure 1-1). Moreover, on the basis of assessment of various correlates, subgroups of learning problems have been described with the intention of differentiating subtypes of learning disabilities.

It is well to remember, however, that individuals classified as LD may not have been labeled through a formal differential diagnostic process. That is, classification often is an informal by-product of research, program planning, or evaluation activity. For example, if researchers or practitioners believe cognitive deficiencies are linked fundamentally to reading problems, they will look for and then discuss findings in terms of such deficiencies. In the process, they refer to those assessed as having a reading disability—although the data they have gathered are insufficient for making a diagnosis that implies the problem stems from internal pathology.

Whether a label is the product of formal diagnostic assessment findings or is inferred from other data, it also is important to keep in mind that the

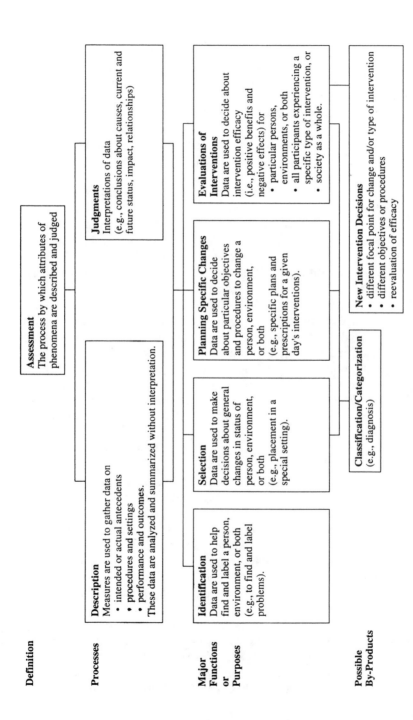

FIGURE 1-1 **Assessment process and purposes**

Source: H. S. Adelman & L. Taylor, *Learning Problems and Learning Disabilities: Moving Forward* (Pacific Grove, CA: Brooks/Cole, 1993), Figure 2-1. Reprinted by permission of Brooks/Cole Publishing Company.

classification of someone as having a learning disability currently is based on observable behaviors. That is, cognitive variables or causal factors may be referred to, but one does not observe constructs such as intelligence, perception, phonological processing, memory, attention, or minor central nervous system (CNS) dysfunctioning. One sees (or receives reports about) response or nonresponse to stimuli. Even then, one obtains only a limited sample of information. Furthermore, data indicating poor performance may be due to low or negative (avoidance) motivation resulting from high anxiety or negative attitudes—especially among populations with problems. For these reasons, interpretations concluding that assessment findings indicate specific academic or social deficiencies often are in error.

Because so many factors can negatively affect assessment, a variety of methods are used to minimize errors. These include accounting for contaminants in interpreting findings; improving task content, context, and administration to reduce biasing conditions; and going beyond standardized administration to assess how much more the individual can do (see Adelman & Taylor, 1993; Salvia & Ysseldyke, 1991; Swanson, 1991). Taking a step further, highly interventionist approaches have been developed (e.g., dynamic assessment, assisted assessment) involving comprehensive strategies to prompt, teach, and motivate (see Campione et al., Chapter 13, this volume; Lidz, 1987). An appreciation of all this provides a critical perspective for evaluating the adequacy of data, the validity of interpretations, and the appropriateness of conclusions and recommendations. In general, an understanding of the major applied purposes of assessment and the range of factors that can influence findings and their interpretation provides an essential foundation for evaluating the appropriateness of any research translation.

To Whom Does the Research Apply?

In part because of the limitations of current assessment practices, there has been a widespread failure to differentiate learning disabilities from other types of learning problems—particularly with respect to cause. The result of this failure has been that those found in most programs and research samples range from individuals whose learning problems were caused primarily by environmental deficiencies to those whose problems stem from internal disabilities. This source of sample variability confounds efforts to compare findings from sample to sample, limits generalization of findings, and makes practical translations tenuous.

Because of the classification problem, a large proportion of research purporting to deal with LD samples has more to say about learning *problems* in general than about learning *disabilities.* In this regard, failure to differentiate underachievement caused by neurological dysfunctioning from that caused by other factors has been cited specifically as a major deterrent to important lines of research and theory and is certainly a threat to the very integrity of the LD field (National Joint Committee on Learning Disabilities, 1989).

With respect to intervention practice and research, failure to differentiate learning problems in terms of cause contributes to widespread misdiagnosis and to prescription of unneeded specialized treatments (i.e., individuals who do not have disabilities end up being treated as if they do). In turn, this leads to profound misunderstanding of which interventions do and do not have unique promise for learning disabilities. In general, the scope of misdiagnoses and misprescriptions in the field has undermined prevention, remediation, research, and training and the policy decisions shaping such activity.

Keeping LD in Proper Perspective

Given that the concept of LD is poorly defined and differentiated and results in overdiagnosis and inflated prevalence and incidence figures, it is not surprising that those so diagnosed have become the largest percentage in special education programs. It also is not surprising that the LD field has experienced a significant backlash in the form of criticism of current practices and policies, such as the Regular or General Education Initiative (see discussion by Fuchs & Fuchs, 1991; Kauffman, 1989). In its extreme form, this backlash questions whether there is such a thing as a learning disability (e.g., Ysseldyke & Algozzine, 1983). The danger in this position, of course, is that we lose sight of learning problems caused by internal pathology such as minor CNS dysfunction (see Chapter 2 in this volume by Welsh, Chapter 3 by Semrud-Clikeman and Hynd, and Chapter 5 by Goldsmith-Phillips).

In an effort to reduce the confusion caused by varying definitions and criteria, some have recommended that specific "markers," such as demographic, personality, and programming variables, be reported on every LD sample (e.g., Keogh, Major-Kingsley, Omori-Gordon, & Reid, 1982). This recommendation, however, along with efforts to identify "LD" subtypes (e.g., Lyon & Flynn, 1991; McKinney, 1988; Rourke & Strang, 1983), overlooks the confusion caused by accepting current LD samples as validly diagnosed. That is, by starting with a group already diagnosed as having LD, the researchers skip over the more fundamental classification problems of differentiating LD from other learning problems. Such a practice works against conceptual clarity and colludes with trends to treat all learning problems as if they were learning disabilities.

The key to identifying learning problems caused by minor neurological dysfunctions—that is, learning disabilities—is to assess CNS dysfunctioning. Unfortunately, available methodology precludes doing this in a valid manner; that is, existing procedures for assessing neurological correlates of learning problems lack validity for making a differential diagnosis of learning disabilities. Indeed, in most cases, there can be no certainty about the primary instigating factor causing an individual's learning problem. As a result, persons currently diagnosed with learning disabilities have been so labeled mainly on the basis of assessment of relatively severe underachievement—the causes of which remain undetermined (cf. Chalfant, 1985; Coles, 1987).

Obviously, then, the fact that someone has been assigned the LD label is not sufficient indication that the individual has an underlying dysfunction. Still, it remains scientifically valid to conceive of a subgroup (albeit a small subset) whose learning problems are neurologically based and to differentiate this subgroup from those with learning problems *caused* by other factors. A useful perspective for doing this is provided by a reciprocal determinist or transactional view of behavior. (Note that this view goes beyond emphasizing the importance of environmental variables and an ecological perspective.)

The trend toward understanding behavior from a reciprocal determinist or transactional perspective has a distinguished history (cf. Bandura, 1978). Over the last twenty-five years, the usefulness of such a perspective has been discussed with respect to the causes and correction of learning problems in general and learning disabilities in particular (e.g., Adelman, 1970–1971, 1971; Adelman & Taylor, 1983, 1986a; Coles, 1987; Sameroff, 1978; Smith, 1991).

A transactional perspective subsumes rather than replaces the idea that some learning problems stem from neurological dysfunction and differences. As elaborated by Adelman and Taylor (1983, 1986a), a transactional view acknowledges that there are cases in which an individual's disabilities predispose him or her to learning problems even in highly accommodating settings. At the same time, however, such a view accounts for instances in which the environment is so inadequate or hostile that individuals have problems despite having no disability. Finally, it recognizes problems caused by a combination of person and environment factors. The value of a broad transactional perspective, then, is that it shifts the focus from asking whether there is a neurological deficit causing the learning problem to asking whether the causes are to be found *primarily* in one of the following:

- The *individual* (e.g., a neurological dysfunction; cognitive skill and/or strategy deficits; developmental and/or motivational differences)
- The *environment* (e.g., the primary environment, such as poor instructional programs, parental neglect; the secondary environment, such as racially isolated schools and neighborhoods; or the tertiary environment, such as broad social, economic, political, and cultural influences)
- The reciprocal *interplay of individual and environment*

Type I, II, and III Learning Problems

As the foregoing discussion suggests, a classification scheme is needed that puts learning disabilities into perspective vis-à-vis other learning problems, and a transactional view of causality clarifies the parameters for such a scheme. Of course, no simple typology can do justice to the complexities involved in classifying learning problems for purposes of research, practice, and policymaking. However, even a simple conceptual classification framework based on a transactional view can be heuristic. My colleagues and I, for example, have found it extremely valuable to use such a model to differentiate types of learning problems along a causal continuum (e.g., Adelman & Taylor, 1986b).

To illustrate: Think about a random sample of students whose learning problems are not due primarily to major physical, affective, or cognitive deficits (i.e., the learning problem is not the result of visual or hearing impairments, severe mental retardation, severe emotional disturbance, or autism). What makes it difficult for them to learn? Theoretically, it is reasonable to speculate that a *small group* may have a relatively minor internal disorder causing a minor CNS dysfunction that makes learning difficult even under good teaching circumstances. As suggested by proposed LD definitional changes, these are individuals for whom the term *learning disabilities* was created (e.g., NJCLD, 1989). In Figure 1-2, these individuals are represented as part of the group designated Type III—those whose problems, in theory, are caused by factors within the individual. At the other end of the continuum are those with problems caused by factors outside the individual, such as inadequacies in the environment in which learning takes place (Type I problems). In the middle are those whose problems stem from a relatively equal contribution by both sources (Type II problems). This group includes persons who do not learn or perform well in situations in which their individual differences and vulnerabilities are

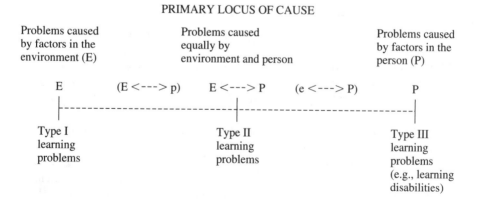

PRIMARY LOCUS OF CAUSE

Problems caused by factors in the environment (E)	Problems caused equally by environment and person	Problems caused by factors in the person (P)

E (E <---> p) E <---> P (e <---> P) P

Type I learning problems	Type II learning problems	Type III learning problems (e.g., learning disabilities)

FIGURE 1-2 **A continuum of learning problems reflecting a transactional view of the locus of primary instigating factors**

Source: H. S. Adelman & L. Taylor, *Learning Problems and Learning Disabilities: Moving Forward* (Pacific Grove, CA: Brooks/Cole, 1993), Figure 3-3. Reprinted by permission of Brooks/Cole Publishing Company.

poorly accommodated or are met in a hostile fashion. That is, they have some internal factor that can predispose them to a learning problem in certain but not all learning and teaching situations. The learning and performance problems (and many behavior problems) of such persons are truly the reciprocal product of individual predispositions *and* the nature of the environment in which they must learn and perform. At points along the continuum, the degree of variance accounted for, respectively, by person and environment variables shifts.

After Type I, II, and III problem groupings are identified, subtypes can be formulated. For example, subtypes Type III might include not only learning disabilities but also learning problems arising mostly from other internal disorders, such as serious behavioral or emotional disabilities or developmental disruptions. In formulating subtypes, basic dimensions such as problem severity, pervasiveness, and chronicity obviously play an important role.

There are tremendous practical problems to be overcome before differential diagnoses can be made along such a continuum. This fact, however, does not preclude the use of such a conceptual classification scheme as an aid in understanding (1) the variety of learning problems that confront practitioners and researchers and (2) concerns that have arisen because of failure to differentiate among learning problems. Differentiating among learning problems seems particularly crucial to improving research and its practical applications; failure to do so can be seen as high among the factors that result in a waste of the limited resources available for intervention and research.

BROADENING INTERVENTION RESEARCH AND PRACTICE

For decades, practical implications for LD derived from the research literature have focused almost exclusively on *remedies* for *developmental* problems. Moreover, the remedies have focused primarily on assessing and fixing individuals rather than in assessing and fixing teaching and learning environments. Many of the practical implications discussed in the chapters of this book continue along these same lines.

Unfortunately, the weight of available evidence indicates that most interventions for learning disabilities have had only limited efficacy (e.g., Horn, O'Donnell, & Vitulano, 1983; Kavale & Forness, 1985; cf. Torgesen & Wong, 1986). In understanding why this has been the case and in judging the potential value of proposals to translate recent research into practice, one needs to adopt a broad perspective regarding intervention. Such a perspective suggests there has been an underemphasis on multifaceted approaches and an overemphasis on developmental remediation of individual problems.

Overcoming learning problems in general and learning disabilities in particular warrants a comprehensive, multifaceted, societal approach. That is, significant improvements in intervention efficacy probably require a full continuum of programs, ranging from prevention to treatment of chronic problems (see Figure 1-3), and procedures that tie the programs together so they function in a coordinated and integrated way.

With respect to instructional programs, the overemphasis on remedying an individual's problems or accommodating disabilities appears to have had the effect of narrowing the curriculum. Today's complex world requires more than reading, writing, and arithmetic; additional "basics" are needed, such as the ability to solve problems and to interact effectively with others (see chapters in this volume by Campione et al.; Welsh; and Bryan, Bryan, and Dohrn). That is, the need is for a comprehensive curriculum. Figure 1-4 presents a matrix outlining three general dimensions that are of concern in designing a comprehensive curriculum (and related assessment procedures).

Good teaching, of course, requires more than having a comprehensive curriculum. It also involves strategies that make skill learning meaningful, as well as the ability to bring subject matter to life. Moreover, individuals with learning problems need instruction that accounts for their strengths, weaknesses, and limitations. For a classroom teacher, this means accommodating a wide range of individual and subgroup differences. More specifically, good teaching related to learning problems should encompass such ideas as matching both motivation and development, enhancing and expanding intrinsic motivation, overcoming avoidance motivation, and using the least intervention needed. In our work, my colleagues and I have incorporated such ideas into a two-step model that emphasizes first personalizing classroom instruction and then approaching remediation from a hierarchical perspective (see Figure 1-5).

Personalized, Sequential, and Hierarchical Teaching

A transactional perspective suggests that prevention and remediation of many learning problems (e.g., Type I) primarily require general changes in systems and learning environments, such as modifying approaches to schooling and instruction. In particular, it seems likely that major benefits would accrue from modifying current instructional practices to better match individual differences not only in developmental capability, but also in motivation. Indeed, a systematic emphasis on motivation, especially *intrinsic* motivation, probably needs to be given primary emphasis (Deci & Chandler, 1986).

The theoretical concept of the *match,* as advocated by leading scholars such as Piaget (see Furth & Wachs, 1974), Bruner (e.g., 1966), Vygotsky (e.g., 1978), and J. McVickers Hunt (1961) reflects a transactional view of learning and learnng problems. All individualized and personalized interventions can be seen as based on this concept. The major thrust in most *individualized* approaches, however, is to account for individual differences in capability, whereas *personalization* has been defined as accounting for individual differences in both

Intervention Continuum	Types of activities

Prevention ↑

1. Primary prevention to promote and maintain
   * safety
   * physical and mental health
     (beginning with family planning)

Early-age Intervention

2. Preschool programs
   * day care
   * parent education
   * early education
     (encompassing a focus on psychosocial and mental health problems)

3. Early school adjustment
   * personalization in primary grades
   * parent participation in problem solving
   * comprehensive psychosocial and mental health programs
     (school-based)

Early-after-onset Intervention

4. Improvement of ongoing regular support
   * specified remedial role for regular classroom teachers
   * parent involvement
   * comprehensive psychosocial and mental health programs
     (school-based — all grades)

5. Augmentation of regular support
   * academic (e.g., reading teachers, computer-aided instruction, volunteer tutors)
   * psychosocial (e.g., staff and peer counselors, crisis teams)

6. Specialized staff development and interventions prior to referral for special education and other intensive treatments
   * staff training/consultation
   * short-term specialized interventions

Treatment for Chronic Problems ↓

7. System changes and intensive treatment
   * rehabilitation of existing programs
   * special education services
   * referral to and coordination with community mental health services

FIGURE 1-3   From prevention to treatment: A continuum of programs for learning, behavior, and socioemotional problems

Source: H. S. Adelman & L. Taylor, *Learning Problems and Learning Disabilities: Moving Forward* (Pacific Grove, CA: Brooks/Cole, 1993), Figure 10-5. Reprinted by permission of Brooks/Cole Publishing Company.

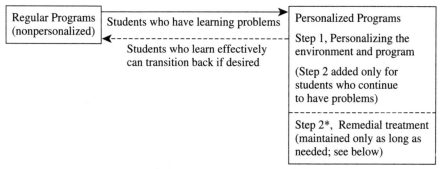

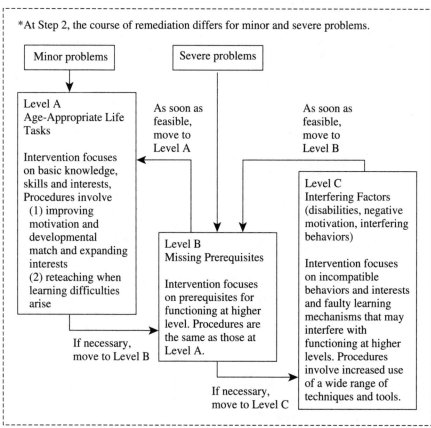

FIGURE 1-4 **Curriculum areas, levels, and types of content**

Source: H. S. Adelman & L. Taylor, *Learning Problems and Learning Disabilities: Moving Forward* (Pacific Grove, CA: Brooks/Cole, 1993), Figure 10-6. Reprinted by permission of Brooks/Cole Publishing Company.

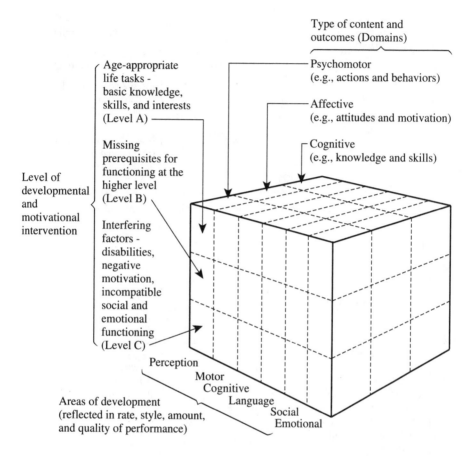

FIGURE 1-5 **A sequential and hierarchical approach**

Source: H. S. Adelman & L. Taylor, *Learning Problems and Learning Disabilities: Moving Forward* (Pacific Grove, CA: Brooks/Cole, 1993), Figure 13-2. Reprinted by permission of Brooks/Cole Publishing Company.

capability and motivation (for an extensive discussion and specific examples, see Adelman, 1971; Adelman & Taylor, 1983, 1986a, 1990, 1993).

Personalization represents an application of the principles of normalization and least intervention needed (which encompass the concept of "least restrictive environment"). Furthermore, personalization can be treated as a psychological construct if the *learner's perception* is viewed as the critical factor in defining whether the environment appropriately accounts for his or her interests and abilities (cf. Lazarus, 1991). In emphasizing learners' perceptions of teaching and learning environments, my colleagues and I have tried to highlight the importance of placing equal and perhaps primary emphasis on assessing an individual's interests as well as abilities.

Properly designed and carried out, personalized programs should reduce the need for remediation. That is, maximizing motivation and matching developmental capability should be a sufficient condition for learning among those who have no internal disability (i.e., Type I learning problems), thereby minimizing the need for remedial intervention. Thus, personalized programs represent the type of program regular classrooms need to implement in order to improve significantly the efficacy of mainstreaming and prereferral interventions (see D. Fuchs, Chapter 11, this volume; also see Chalfant, Van Dusen Pysh, & Moultrie, 1979; Graden, Casey, & Christenson, 1985; Johnson & Pugach, 1991).

Once a personalized program is properly implemented, it is to be expected that, though mobilized to try harder, some students will continue to have significant learning problems (e.g., those in the Type III category). From this perspective, a personalized program can be seen as the first step in assessing who does and does not require more than appropriate accommodation of individual differences in order to learn effectively. Those who do need more, of course, are candidates for the full range of remedial interventions.

Depending on problem severity and pervasiveness, remediation involves one (or more) of three hierarchical levels, ranging from a focus on observable problems to one on underlying problems (Adelman, 1989a, Adelman & Taylor, 1986a). Level A focuses on age-appropriate life tasks (basic knowledge, skills, and interests), level B on missing prerequisites for learning, and level C on factors interfering with learning (disabilities, negative motivation, interfering behaviors).

Decisions about general curriculum goals are based on assessment of the individual's interests and abilities. The level of remediation on which to focus with respect to any curricular goal is determined by assessing an individual's responses to daily instruction. Specific remedial objectives are formulated initially through dialogue with the learner to generate processes and outcomes that are valued and that he or she perceives as attainable. General goals and specific objectives are modified through ongoing dialogues informed by analyses of task performance, supplemented with formal assessment devices when necessary (as reflected in most of the chapters in this book).

Procedures used for personalization and remediation should reflect a primary, systematic focus on motivation. In particular, they should emphasize (a) assessing motivation, (2) overcoming negative attitudes, (3) enhancing motivational readiness for learning, (4) maintaining intrinsic motivation throughout the learning process, and (5) nurturing the type of continuing motivation that results in the learner engaging in activities away from the teaching situation. Attending to these matters is seen as essential to maximizing maintenance, generalization, and expansion of learning. Failure to attend systematically and comprehensively to these matters means approaching passive (and often hostile) learners with methods that confound diagnostic and research efforts and that may just as readily exacerbate as correct learning and behavior problems (Adelman & Taylor, 1990).

Beyond having potential for preventing and correcting a full range of learning problems, the personalized, sequential, and hierarchical approach outlined here is seen as having promise for identifying different types of learning problems and for detecting errors in diagnosis. For example, when only personalization based on capability and motivation is needed to correct a learning problem, it seems reasonable to suggest that the individual does not have a learning *disability*. At the same time, when a highly mobilized individual still has extreme difficulty in learning, the hypothesis that the person has a disability seems safer. (In our work, personalization is seen as a necessary step in facilitating valid identification of Type I, II, and III learning problems.)

From the foregoing perspective, concerns arise about research applications that encourage an overemphasis on narrowly focused assessment and remedial approaches in efforts to correct the wide range of learning problems found in public schools. For example, applied ideas for assessing and fostering development of language and cognitive abilities (e.g., phonological, executive function, writing, and mathematics skills) are appropriate and invaluable; however, an overemphasis on remedying these areas of development could have the same unfortunate consequences as the historic overemphasis on remedying problems related to visual-spatial abilities. That is, when specific areas for remediation are overstressed, other areas tend to be deemphasized, resulting in a narrowing of curriculum and a fragmentation of instruction.

The roots of the problem of overemphasis (as well as the problem of premature application) are to be found in the actions of both researchers and practitioners. Researchers who focus on learning disabilities have immersed themselves in studies of cognitive and language development and assessment and teaching approaches that are oriented primarily to direct instruction of observable skills. As a result, other potentially important areas of study are receiving little attention. For example, there has been relatively little research on environmental causes of learning problems and on motivation as a readiness, process, and outcome concern in preventing and correcting learning problems (see Lovitt, 1989; Stipek, 1988). Not surprisingly, what is studied dominates new directions for practical applications. Researchers also contribute to the problem by (1) not being proactive enough in emphasizing limitations with respect to the meaning and generalizability of their findings and (2) not taking the time to place their findings into a broad intervention perspective. Practitioners collude with all this by uncritically accepting proposed applications, usually because of the pressure to come up with something new to replace currently unproductive approaches.

A Societal Approach to Intervention

Beyond the classroom, an even broader perspective is evolving regarding research and practice for problems related to learning and behavior. Policymakers increasingly are recognizing the importance of multifaceted approaches that account for social, economic, political, and cultural factors. The potential array of preventive and treatment programs is extensive and promising. The range can be appreciated by grouping them on a continuum from prevention through treatment of chronic problems (see Figure 1-3). Categorically, the activities encompass (1) primary prevention to promote and maintain safety and physical and mental health (beginning with family planning), (2) preschool programs, (3) early school adjustment programs, (4) improvement of ongoing regular support, (5) augmentation of regular support, (6) specialized staff development and interventions prior to referral for special help, and (7) system change and intensive treatments. Examples of relevant interventions in each category are cited in Figure 1-3.

Unfortunately, implementation of the full continuum of programs with an extensive range of activities does not occur in most communities. Moreover, what programs there are tend to be offered in a fragmented manner.

Policymakers are coming to see the relationship between limited intervention efficacy and the widespread tendency for complementary programs to operate in isolation. For instance, physical and mental health programs generally are not coordinated with educational programs; a youngster identified and treated in early education programs who still requires special support may or may not receive systematic help in the primary grades; and so forth. Failure to coordinate and follow through, of course, can be counterproductive (e.g., undermining immediate benefits and working against efforts to reduce subsequent demand for costly treatment programs). Limited efficacy seems inevitable as long as interventions are carried out in a piecemeal fashion. Thus, there is increasing interest in moving beyond piecemeal strategies to provide a comprehensive, integrated, and coordinated programmatic thrust (e.g., Hodgkinson, 1989; Kagan, 1990; Kean, 1989).

The range of programs cited in Figure 1-3 can be seen as integrally related, and it seems likely that the impact of each could be exponentially increased through integration and coordination. Indeed, a major breakthrough in the battle against learning and behavior problems may result only when the full range of programs are implemented in a comprehensive and coordinated fashion.

As I have proposed previously (Adelman, 1989a, 1989b), it is time to determine the efficacy of a comprehensive, societal approach through a demonstration project. This kind of project will require a consortium to develop, coordinate, and evaluate *in one catchment area* an integrated set of programs encompassing the entire continuum outlined in Figure 1-3. The findings of such a project should have preventive and corrective implications for a wide range of learning and behavior problems. Such a project could help address the concerns surrounding the Regular or General Education Initiative (Fuchs & Fuchs, 1991; Kauffman, 1989; Will, 1986). That is, the data could have major cost-benefit and policy implications for decisions about how to reverse the current overemphasis on special education programs so that the limited resources available can be reserved for students who manifest severe and pervasive psychoeducational problems.

CONCLUDING COMMENTS

From the foregoing perspective, then, proposed translations of research into practice should be evaluated in terms of whether they are appropriate for Type I, II, or III learning problems and where they fit into a comprehensive scheme of intervention needs.

Turning the matter around, researchers primarily concerned with application (i.e., improving intervention for those with learning problems) must at the very least broaden their view of teaching; optimally, they need to expand their view of intervention beyond teaching. With respect to the former, my colleagues and I have argued that it seems particularly important to focus on motivation as a primary intervention concern and, in doing so, to pursue personalized, sequential, and hierarchical teaching strategies. Beyond teaching, it is important to think in terms of a societal approach encompassing an integrated continuum of preventive and treatment services. There is a considerable agenda of research that warrants attention related to these ideas.

As the world around us is changing at an exponential rate, so must the way we approach learning problems. Over the coming decade, we all will be called upon to play a role in doing something about the many individuals who have trouble learning academic skills. In responding to this call, it will be essential to have a broad understanding of what causes learning problems (including learning disabilities) and what society in general and schools in particular need to do to address such problems. Anyone concerned with research applications must evaluate them within a broad context—not just from the narrow perspective of specific assessment practices or direct instruction of observable skills. To do less is to risk too much.

REFERENCES

Adelman, H. S. (1970–1971). Learning problems: Part I. An interactional view of causality. *Academic Therapy, 6,* 117–123.

Adelman, H. S. (1971). The not so specific learning disability population. *Exceptional Children, 8,* 114–120.

Adelman, H. S. (1989a). Prediction and prevention of learning disabilities: Current state of the art and future directions. In L. Bond & B. Compas (Eds.), *Primary prevention in the schools* (pp. 106–145). Newbury Park: Sage.

Adelman, H. S. (1989b). Toward solving the problems of misidentification and limited intervention efficacy. *Journal of Learning Disabilities, 22,* 608–612, 620.

Adelman, H. S., & Taylor, L. (1983). Learing disabilities in perspective. Glenview, IL: Scott, Foresman.

Adelman, H. S., & Taylor, L. (1986a). *An introduction to learning disabilities.* Glenview, IL: Scott, Foresman.

Adelman, H. S., & Taylor, L. (1986b). The problems of definition and differentiation and the need for a classification schema. *Journal of Learning Disabilities, 19,* 514–520.

Adelman, H. S., & Taylor, L. (1990). Intrinsic motivation and school misbehavior. *Journal of Learning Disabilities, 23,* 541–543.

Adelman, H. S., & Taylor, L. (1991). Issues and problems related to the assessment of learning disabilities. In H. L. Swanson (Ed.), *Handbook on the assessment of learning disabilities: Theory, research, and practice* (pp. 21–44). Austin, TX: Pro-Ed.

Adelman, H. S., & Taylor, L. (1993). *Learning problems and learning disabilities: Moving Forward.* Pacific Grove, CA: Brooks/Cole.

Bandura, A. (1978). The self system in reciprocal determinism. *American Psychologist, 33,* 344–358.

Bruner, J. S. (1966). *Toward a theory of instruction.* Cambridge, MA: Belknap Press.

Chalfant, J. C. (1985). Identifying learning disabled students: A summary of the National Task Force Report. *Learning Disabilities Focus, 1,* 9–20.

Chalfant, J. C., Van Dusen Pysh, M., & Moultrie, R. (1979). Teacher assistance teams: A model for within-building problem solving. *Learning Disability Quarterly, 2*(3), 85–96.

Coles, G. (1987). *The learning mystique: A critical look at "learning disabilities."* New York: Pantheon Books.

Deci, E. L., & Chandler, C. L. (1986). The importance of motivation for the future of the LD field. *Journal of Learning Disabilities, 19,* 587–594.

Fuchs, D., & Fuchs, L. S. (1991). Framing the REI debate: Abolitionists v. conservationists. In J. W. Lloyd, N. N. Singh, & C. Repp (Eds.), *The Regular Education Initiative: Alternative perspectives on concepts, issues, and models* (pp. 241–255). Sycamore, IL: Sycamore.

Furth, H. G., & Wachs, H. (1974). *Thinking goes to school.* New York: Oxford University Press.

Graden, J. L., Casey, A., & Christenson, S. L. (1985). Implementing a prereferral intervention system: 1. The model. *Exceptional Children, 51,* 377–387.

Hodgkinson, J. L. (1989). *The same client: The demographics of education and service delivery systems.* Washington, DC: Institute for Educational Leadership/Center for Demographic Policy.

Horn, W. F., O'Donnell, J. P., & Vitulano, L. A. (1983). Long-term follow-up studies of learning disabled persons. *Journal of Learning Disabilities, 16,* 542–555.

Hunt, J. McV. (1961). *Intelligence and experience.* New York: Ronald Press.

Johnson, L. J., & Pugach, M. C. (1991). Peer collaboration: Accommodating students with mild learning and behavior problems. *Exceptional Children, 57,* 454–461.

Kagan, S. L. (1990). *Excellence in early childhood education: Defining characteristics and next-decade strategies.* Washington, DC: Office of Educational Research and Improvement, U.S. Department of Education.

Kavale, K., & Forness, S. (1985). *The science of learning disabilities.* San Diego: College-Hill Press.

Kauffman, J. M. (1989). The Regular Education Initiative as Reagan–Bush education policy: A trickle-down theory of education of the hard-to-teach. *Journal of Special Education, 23,* 256–277.

Kean, T. H. (1989). The life you save may be your own: New Jersey addresses prevention of adolescent problems. *American Psychologist, 44,* 828–830.

Keogh, B. K., Major-Kingsley, S., Omori-Gordon, H., & Reid, H. P. (1982). *A system of marker variables for the field of learning disabilities.* Ithaca, NY: Syracuse University Press.

Lazarus, R. S. (1991). Cognition and motivation in emotion. *American Psychologist, 46,* 352–367.

Lidz, C. S. (Ed.). (1987). *Dynamic assessment: An interactional approach to evaluating learning problems.* New York: Guilford Press.

Lovitt, T. C. (1989). *Introduction to learning disabilities.* Boston: Allyn and Bacon.

Lyon, G. R., & Flynn, J. M. (1991). Assessing subtypes of learning abilities. In H. L. Swanson (Ed.), *Handbook of assessment of learning disabilities: Theory, research, and practice* (pp. 59–74). Austin, TX: Pro-Ed.

McKinney, J. D. (1988). Research on conceptually and empirically derived subtypes of specific learning disabilities. In M. C. Wang, H. J. Walberg, & M. C. Reynolds (Eds.), *The handbook of special education: Research and practice* (pp. 268–282). Oxford: Pergamon Press.

NJCLD (1989). *Letter from National Joint Committee on Learning Disabilities to member organizations.* Topic: Modifications to the NJCLD definition of learning disabilities.

Rispens, J., van Yperen, T. A., & van Duijn, G. A. (1991). The irrelevance of the IQ to the definition of learning disabilities: Some empirical evidence. *Journal of Learning Disabilities, 24,* 434–438.

Rourke, B. P., & Strang, J. D. (1983). Subtypes of reading and arithmetical disabilities: A neuropsychological analysis. In M. Rutter (Ed.), *Developmental neuropsychiatry* (pp. 473–488). New York: Guilford Press.

Salvia, J., & Ysseldyke, J. E. (1991). *Assessment,* 5th ed. Boston: Houghton Mifflin.

Sameroff, A. (1978). Transactional risk factors and prevention. In J. Steinberg & M. Silverman (Eds.), *Preventing mental disorders: A research perspective* (DHHS Publication No. ADM 87-1492, pp. 74–89). Washington, DC: U.S. Government Printing Office.

Siegel, L. S. (1989). Why we do not need intelligence test scores in the definition of learning disabilities. *Journal of Learning Disabilities, 22,* 514–518.

Smith, C. R. (1991). *Learning disabilities: The interaction of learner, task, and setting,* 2nd ed. Boston: Little, Brown.

Stipek, D. J. (1988). *Motivation to learn: From theory to practice.* Englewood Cliffs, NJ: Prentice-Hall.

Swanson, H. L. (Ed.). (1991). *Handbook on the assessment of learning disabilities:*

Theory, research, and practice. Austin, TX: Pro-Ed.

Torgesen, J. K., & Wong, B. Y. L. (Eds.). (1986). *Psychological and educational perspectives on learning disabilities.* Orlando, FL: Academic Press.

Vygotsky, L. S. (1978). *Mind in society: The development of higher psychological processes.* Cambridge, MA: Harvard University Press.

Will, M. (1986). *Educating students with learning problems: A shared responsibility.* Washington, DC: U.S. Department of Education.

Ysseldyke, J. E., & Algozzine, B. (1983). LD or not LD: That's not the question! *Annual Review of Learning Disabilities, 1,* 26–28.

▶ 2

Executive Function and the Assessment of Attention Deficit Hyperactivity Disorder

MARILYN C. WELSH
University of Denver

Abstract

This chapter proposes that the cognitive domain of executive function is an important area of functioning to consider when evaluating the cognitive strengths and weaknesses of children with attention problems. Executive functions are necessary for goal-directed behavior and include the skills of planning, working memory, organized search, flexibility, and impulse control. This set of cognitive skills is thought to be mediated by the frontal cortex of the brain. A battery of tasks that has been selected to tap executive functions will be presented, as will the difficulties inherent in the measurement of this construct. Next, the clinical, neurobiological, and cognitive evidence supporting the hypothesis that executive function impairments are characteristic of attention deficit hyperactivity disorder (ADHD) is reviewed. Finally, the limitations of current executive function tasks, as well as the practical applications of this construct to assessment and management strategies, are discussed.

The objective of this chapter is to describe the cognitive construct of executive function, with an emphasis on its relevance to understanding both brain function and behavior. This is followed by a review of several lines of evidence that together suggest an executive function impairment in children diagnosed with attention deficit hyperactivity disorder (ADHD). Finally, the practical implications of the executive function construct will be discussed in terms of the current limitations, as well as the potential applications to the development of more effective teaching and management strategies for children with ADHD.

GENERAL ISSUES REGARDING EXECUTIVE FUNCTION

Definition of the Construct

Executive function represents a domain of cognition unlike any other. Its critical importance to everyday functioning means that it is painfully evident when executive function skills fail. It is, however, a set of skills that are equally difficult to define and a definite challenge to measure well. Identifying executive function is somewhat like defining pornography. As the old saying goes, "I don't know what it is, but I know it when I see it."

Traditional categories of cognition, such as attention, memory, language, and visual-spatial skills, have long been thought of as relatively discrete, well-defined, and independent processes. In contrast, executive function is an overarching concept that transcends these traditional modules of cognition. Executive function regulates, integrates, and coordinates these various cognitive processes in the service of goal-directed behavior. Whenever a future-oriented goal presents itself that requires some degree of novel problem solving and strategizing, executive function skills are recruited. This future goal could be 20 seconds or, theoretically, 20 years in the future. Most instances of future-oriented behavior demanded of children in school, for example, would fall within the time frame of minutes to days.

What specific cognitive skills are subsumed under the rubric of executive function? We have integrated theories from both cognitive psychology (Neisser, 1967) and neuropsychology (Luria, 1973) to develop a working list of executive function skills that is fluid and dynamic in light of ongoing research in the area. Elsewhere (Welsh & Pennington, 1988) we have defined executive function as set maintenance required to achieve a future goal. This "set" would include the requisite skills of planning, organization, inhibition of maladaptive responses, self-monitoring, and flexibility of strategies contingent on feedback. There is a definite overlap with the concept of metacognition (Brown, 1978; Flavell & Wellman, 1977): it is not "knowing," per se, but "knowing" or "knowing how to know."

What would the behavior of a child with executive function impairments look like, and how would he or she perform in school? Let's use the example of an 8-year-old boy, Robert, in the fourth grade. This child may have difficulty sitting still in class and focusing on the teacher's long list of instructions for an upcoming project. While other children in the class are reflecting on the project and generating plans for how they will attack it, Robert doesn't have a way to organize the information into strategic plans of action. Once the project begins, he has difficulty monitoring the effectiveness of his work: Is he following the instructions correctly? Has he encountered obstacles? Is he on the right track? Even if he realizes he is off track, Robert cannot flexibly modify his strategies to be more effective. Instead, he may impulsively try new approaches in a trial-and-error manner. He appears to be unable to keep all of the relevant information (e.g., goals, subgoals, primary and secondary plans) in mind as he works, and he may need constant reminders and assistance from the teacher.

Implicit in our definition of executive function is the importance of mental representation. The cognitive set generated to accomplish a future goal involves mental representation of several key features: the goal and embedded subgoals, the planned sequence of actions, the potential implications of such actions, and backup plans if required. Goldman-Rakic (1990) has expanded on the importance of mental representation to executive function by suggesting that this domain of cognition can best be thought of as working memory. She proposes that a novel future-oriented problem requires the representation of relevant information "on line" in working memory; such representations are dynamic integrations of both current external stimulation and past ideas and experiences from long-term memory. It is, perhaps, our most crucial cognitive skill because it allows us to respond effectively and flexibly to ever-changing stimulus contingencies to achieve necessary goals. It is not clear, however, whether the concept of working memory alone adequately covers the full spectrum of behaviors necessary for executive function.

Psychological and Neuropsychological Implications

The executive function domain has captured a great deal of scientific interest in the past few years because of its many points of intersection with other areas of psychology. For example, developmental psychologists are clearly interested in the developmental course of executive function skills, which may manifest in a rudimentary form as early as infancy (Diamond, 1988; Haith, Hazan, & Goodman, 1988; Welsh & Pennington, 1988) and grow in sophistication over the school years (Brown, 1978; Flavell & Wellman, 1977). Cognitive psychologists have sought to delineate the basic component processes of executive function skills (Carpenter, Just, & Shell, 1990; Dehaene & Changeux, 1991) and how these differ from, as well as interact with, other cognitive abilities. Individual difference researchers may be exploring various features of executive function in their studies of the variability in fluid intelligence across individuals (Horn, 1985).

There are several reasons that educators and educational psychologists should be interested in executive function. First, any academic task that is novel to the student and requires critical thinking, judgment, planning, and self-monitoring will tap executive function skills. That is, rote drills on spelling and multiplication tables will not emphasize executive function to the degree that writing a book report or carrying out a science experiment will. Second, because these skills change quantitatively and qualitatively with age, the nature of the executive function demands placed on the student in school must be age-appropriate. For example, in the preschool and early elementary school years, the most critical executive function skills might be those of impulse control and flexibility, which allow the child to concentrate on the teacher's instructions before responding and to move easily from task to task. In contrast, older children will utilize the more sophisticated executive function skills of planning, organization, and self-monitoring to deal effectively with the complex demands of designing experiments, writing compositions, and studying for exams. Across a large age range, however, executive functions are crucial to effective learning by providing structure and systematic strategies for acquiring new knowledge and skills. Third, there are most likely individual differences in executive function skills across normally functioning children, as well as special impairments in these skills in certain populations of children with learning disabilities. Unfortunately, a large database addressing these issues is not yet available to the educator, but it is slowly being built through current research efforts.

The most interesting implications for executive function research may be for the field of psychology that investigates brain–behavior relations, that of neuropsychology. An extensive literature based on case studies of adults with brain damage and experimental lesion work with animals has explicated the cognitive and behavioral functions subserved by many cortical structures. Decades of research suggest that executive function skills, as described here, are mediated by the frontal lobes of the human brain, more specifically the prefrontal section of this lobe. The symptoms exhibited by adult patients following frontal lobe damage suggest that this brain structure (in coordination with other brain systems) is uniquely dedicated to the important human abilities of insight, anticipation, planning, self-evaluation, flexibility, and general goal-directedness (Damasio, 1985; Fuster, 1980; Luria, 1973; Stuss & Benson, 1984). Whereas persons with frontal damage may have relatively intact intellectual capacity and may execute well-practiced established routines with ease, their impairments will manifest themselves when any degree of novel planning and shifts in these plans are required. Just as a frontal-lesioned monkey cannot shift search strategy as the hiding place of an object is changed (Jacobsen, 1935), a frontal-damaged human cannot shift strategies on various sorting and naming tasks (Milner, 1963). There is now substantial evidence that the neural architecture underlying these skills involves the prefrontal cortex as a major coordinating center of the system (Goldman-Rakic, 1988).

Measurement of Executive Functions

What are important characteristics of tasks designed to tap executive functions in children? Clearly, the task should involve goal-directedness and some degree of novel problem solving; however, in light of the range of skills included within the executive function construct, a given task may involve only a subset of these behaviors. One task may demand planning and working memory abilities but may not emphasize flexibility of strategies. In contrast, another task may encourage flexibility of thought and action but relatively little planning and working memory.

The traditional neuropsychological tests with documented sensitivity to the prefrontal cortex appear to fall into this second category. For example, the Wisconsin Card Sorting Test (WCST; Grant & Berg, 1984) has been considered the "gold standard" in the assessment of frontal lobe executive functions since the pioneering work of Milner (1963, 1964) with adult lesion cases. A recent task-analytic study suggests that this test assesses flexibility and responsiveness to feedback to a greater degree than it does planning and working memory skills (Dehaene & Changeux, 1991). The task involves four standard cards displaying unique combinations of three categorical stimuli (e.g., number, shape, and color are represented by one card as two green stars, by another as three yellow crosses, etc.). The subject is instructed to sort the cards in his deck of 164 according to a rule of his choosing (e.g., sort by color). The experimenter has the correct current rule in mind and gives the subject accuracy feedback after each sort. Once the subject has made ten correct consecutive sorts, the experimenter changes the sorting rule without warning. The most informative behavior measured in this task is whether the subject can effectively switch to the new sorting rule (i.e., can the person flexibly shift mental sets?) The dependent measure of perseveration is operationalized as continuing to sort to the previous rule (or other incorrect rule) in the face of negative feedback. Perseveration indicates a lack of cognitive flexibility and has been found by Milner and others (Drew, 1975; Goldberg & Tucker, 1979; Heaton, 1981; Stuss & Benson, 1984) to be a prevalent symptom following frontal lobe damage. In addition, perseveration on the WCST has been observed in clinical conditions thought to involve a frontal dysfunction secondary to a neurochemical perturbation, such as Parkinson's disease and schizophrenia (Bilder & Goldberg, 1987; Saint-Cyr, Taylor, & Lang, 1988; Weinberger, Berman, & Zec, 1986).

Although tasks of executive function in adults have evolved from the neuropsychological literature primarily on a post hoc basis (i.e., documented sensitivity to frontal lobe damage), tasks for children are scarce for several reasons. First and foremost, the case studies of focal frontal damage in children needed for classic neuropsychological investigations are limited because children are rarely the victims of localized trauma such as stroke and gunshot wounds. A second, related problem is that to describe and measure frontal skills in children is to get caught in a huge tautological web: Executive function tasks measure frontal skills in children, and frontal processes in children are what the executive function tasks measure. Thus, our best guess regarding the functions of the frontal cortex in children comes from case studies of adults with frontal damage or dysfunction. Tests are extrapolated from those sensitive to frontal damage in adults, and these are sometimes (though not frequently enough) modified to be age-appropriate for children. The implicit, albeit critical, assumption in this process is that the frontal lobes subserve similar skills in adults and children. There is an assumption of some degree of continuity of frontal or executive processes in the developing human, such that similar tasks will tap these functions across the lifespan. However, without independent validation of the effectiveness of the child tests (i.e., sensitivity to documented frontal lobe dysfunction in children), the relation between performance on the executive function tasks to be described and the operation of the prefrontal cortex remains an empirical question. In the last section of this chapter, methods of dealing with this validity problem will be discussed.

The Executive Function Battery for Children

This section will focus on an executive function battery developed in our laboratory in order to contribute to the sparse literature on frontal assessment tools for children. The battery was designed to tap various executive function skills, including planning, working memory, and flexibility. Developed by Welsh, Pennington, and Groisser (1991), it represents a combination of tasks from clinical neuropsychology and traditional developmental psychology, as shown in Table 2-1. Visual Search (VS), Verbal Fluency (VF), and Motor Sequencing (MS) represent tasks from the neuropsychological literature that appear to have documented sensitivity to frontal lesions in adults, and these were modified to be age-appropriate for children 3 to 12 years of age. The WCST was adopted unchanged from the neuropsychological literature for children 7 years and older. Two tasks, the Matching Familiar Figures Test (MFFT) and the Tower of Hanoi (TOH), were drawn from the developmental psychology literature on the basis of their compatibility with the executive function construct.

The MFFT is a visual search task that requires the child to select the one of six similar variants that exactly matches the standard picture. Accuracy on the MFFT demands organized search strategies, and a latency measure assesses impulse control. The TOH task requires that a configuration of disks be transformed into a predetermined goal pattern (i.e., the tower) by moving the disks according to a set of specified rules. The child must generate a sequence of disk moves that achieves the goal but also adheres to the following constraints: (1) a larger disk cannot be placed on a smaller disk, (2), only one disk can be moved at a time, and (3) disks must be held on one of three pegs at all times. Because of these constraints, the task demands covert planning to generate the optimal sequence of moves. In addition, working memory skills are tapped as subgoals, and "chunks" of move sequences are held on line during problem solving.

This battery of six executive function tasks was explored in a study of 110

TABLE 2-1 **Tasks in the Executive Function Battery**

Task	Description and References	Ages Tested
VS	A task that requires the child to search for 8 randomly placed targets embedded in disractors. Assesses *organized search* and *flexibility* (Teuber, Battersby, & Bender, 1955.	3–12 years and adults
VF	A task that requires the child to name as many items as possible in 4 semantic categories. Measures *organized search* and *flexibility* (McCarthy, 1972).	3–12 years and adults
MS	A finger-sequencing (finger-to-thumb) task that taps *fine motor planning* (Golden, 1981).	3–12 years and adults
WCST	A card-sorting task that measures *rule learning* and *flexibility* of strategies (Milner, 1963, 1964; Heaton, 1981).	7–12 years and adults
TOH	A disk-transfer task that assesses *planning* and *working memory* skills (Simon, 1975; Borys, Spitz, & Dorans, 1982).	3–12 years and adults
MFFT	A matching task that taps *impulse control, hypothesis testing,* and *organized search* (Kagan, Rosman, Day, Albert, & Phillips, 1964).	7–12 years and adults

normally functioning subjects ranging in age from 3 to 12 years ($N = 10$; Welsh et al., 1991). Three issues were addressed by this study: (1) the factor structure of the battery, (2) the association of executive function skills with general intelligence, and (3) the developmental trends in performance across tasks. First, three factors emerged representing speeded responding (VS, VF, and MS), set maintenance (WCST, MFFT), and planning (three- and four-disk TOH). Second, performance on most of the executive function tasks was uncorrelated with general intelligence as measured by a standardized group-administered IQ test. Third, adult-level performance was achieved at three different ages depending on the executive function tasks: visual search and simple planning on the three-disk TOH matured by age 6 years, optimal performance on the MFFT and the WCST was observed by age 10 years, and complex planning (four-disk TOH), verbal fluency, and motor sequencing appeared to continue developing into adolescence, as 12-year-olds were significantly poorer in these skills than adults. On some of these tasks, however, possible ceiling effects may have obscured additional developmental progressions.

The results of this study converge with those of other research programs exploring frontal lobe functions in children. For example, Passler, Isaac, and Hynd (1985) developed a frontal battery for children based on the work of Luria (1966, 1973) and Christensen (1975). Unlike the broad range of skills tapped in the Welsh et al. battery, this set of tasks focused on inhibition and perseveration in both verbal and nonverbal domains. Normal male and female children in four age groups from 6 through 12 years were tested and, as was also true for the Welsh et al. study, a multistage pattern of development emerged. Significant improvements in performance occurred at ages 6, 8, and 10 years. For instance, by age 10 years, perseveration and impulse control problems on their measures virtually disappeared. In another study, Chelune and Baer (1986) gathered normative data on the WCST from a sample of children 6 through 12 years of age. The Welsh et al. results replicated their finding that adult-level performance on the task was attained by age 10. Because the WCST has long been considered the quintessential measure of frontal lobe function in adults, such a finding has been used to support the assumption that the frontal cortex does not become functional until preadolescence (Golden, 1981). However, the studies discussed above, as well as others (Diamond, 1988; Willatts, in press) clearly demonstrate the existence of rudimentary executive function skills in younger children. In fact, a later analysis of perseverative responses on the VS and VF tasks from the Executive Function Battery (Cuneo & Welsh, 1992) found that perseveration decreased significantly from 3 to 7 years of age. In general, it appears that, given appropriate problem-solving tasks, very young children and even infants (Haith et al., 1988) can display effective executive function skills. On the other hand, adults may manifest executive function impairments when the task is sufficiently novel, challenging, and complex.

EXECUTIVE FUNCTION DEFICITS IN ATTENTION DEFICIT HYPERACTIVITY DISORDER

Symptoms of ADHD

Over the past several decades, a subgroup of children has been identified by parents, teachers, and physicians as manifesting attention problems despite normal intelligence and benign family circumstances. Through the years, the diagnostic label for this disorder has ranged from "minimal brain dysfunction" to "hyperactivity" to "attention deficit disorder," reflecting the particular surface symptoms that were the focus of identification and treatment. For example, the label "hyperactivity" described a childhood disorder in which motor activity, restlessness, and distractibility were the most salient features. However, research in the 1960s and 1970s targeting these characteristics found that it was not the quantity but the quality of activity that distinguished these children from controls (Cromwell, Baumister, & Hawkins, 1963). That is, the children's behavior was often inappropriate for the situation, impulsive, and disorganized, all of which gave the false impression of overactivity. In light of these research findings, the focus of investigation shifted from activity level to the cognitive deficits that may underlie the overt display of poor attention and impulse control.

Today, the diagnosis of ADHD is based on the existence of particular core symptoms that fall into three categories: inattention, impulsivity, and hyperactivity. According to the *Diagnostic and Statistical Manual of Mental Disorders,* third edition, revised (DSM-III-R; American Psychiatric Association, 1987), a majority of symptoms should be present for a period of at least 6 months and should manifest prior to age 7. Many of the symptoms of ADHD conform to a hypothesized executive function impairment. The poor concentration, distractibility, inhibition problems, and pursuit of dangerous activities without consideration of future consequences all could be interpreted as a failure of the planning, set maintenance, and organization mechanisms of the executive function system. The ADHD child frequently comes to clinical attention during the school years because of behavior problems that conflict with the demands of the classroom environment. Examples of these behavior problems include talking excessively, squirming and having difficulty remaining seated, blurting out answers to the teacher's questions without waiting one's turn, and having problems finishing assignments. The diagnosis of ADHD is usually made if the child has a history of these and related behavioral impairments in the early school years and if these problems cannot be attributed to extraneous causes, such as closed head injury or chaotic family circumstances (Pennington, 1991).

Neurobiological Mechanisms

In addition to the surface similarity between the symptoms of ADHD and those of an executive function disorder, the brain mechanisms hypothesized to underlie this condition also support this characterization. That is, much of the recent evidence points to a possible frontal lobe dysfunction explanation of ADHD, most likely the consequence of a neurochemical perturbation in this region.

Neurological substrates of ADHD can be explored on two global levels: structure (anatomy) and function (physiology). To date there is no clear evidence of neuroanatomical abnormalities in the brains of ADHD children based on computerized tomography (CT) scans (Harcherik et al., 1985; Shaywitz, Shaywitz, Cohen, & Young, 1983). However, Hynd, Semrud-Clikeman, Lorys, Novey, and Eliopulas (in press) recently reported the absence of the typical right frontal lobe size advantage in ADHD children as observed on magnetic resonance imaging (MRI) scans.

The investigations of brain function using electrophysiology, regional cerebral blood flow, and neurochemistry have proved more fruitful in revealing differences between ADHD children and controls. The findings of electrophysiological studies indicate the existence of CNS underarousal in at least a subgroup of hyperactive children (Ferguson & Rappaport, 1983). Decreased cerebral blood flow was evident in the frontal lobes of ADHD children, and Ritalin treatment was associated with a corresponding increase (Lou, Henriksen, & Bruhn, 1984). Ritalin is known to release stored dopamine from neurons, suggesting that the increased function in the frontal cortex was neurochemically mediated. In a follow-up study, Lou, Henriksen, Bruhn, Borner, and Nielsen (1989) replicated this result on a larger sample of children with ADHD, highlighting the basal ganglia as the locus of the diminished blood flow. The basal ganglia is a subcortical structure that is rich in dopamine receptors and that has connections with the frontal lobe. It is the neurological structure that is presumed to mediate motor planning. Zametkin et al. (1991) studied the parents of ADHD children, who themselves had the residual form of the condition. Using the positron emission tomography (PET) scan technique, they found reduced glucose utilization in the right frontal lobe and increased utilization in posterior brain regions. Glucose utilization indicates cerebral activation, and this lack of activation in the frontal lobes of the adults with residual-type ADHD is consistent with the CNS underarousal found in the electrophysiological research (Pennington, 1991).

Finally, the majority of neurochemical research with humans (Shaywitz, Cohen & Bowers, 1977) and with animals (Shaywitz et al., 1983) indicates that a depletion of the catecholamine, dopamine, underlies some attention deficits. Dopamine is the neurochemical that is most highly represented in the frontal cortex. Consistent with these findings is the fact that Ritalin, a frequently prescribed stimulant medication for children diagnosed with ADHD, is known to release stored dopamine and has been found to decrease motor activity and to facilitate sustained attention in at least a subgroup of persons with this clinical condition (Barkley, 1977). Currently, however, it is unclear whether Ritalin has a specific positive effect on the executive functions described here. An noteworthy alternative view proposes that the attention deficits are the result of decreased levels of norepinephrine in the right posterior cortex (Posner & Petersen, in press).

Although the neurobiological evidence to date is not unequivocal, much of it presents a picture of a frontal lobe dysfunction in the form of underarousal. The diminished function is reflected in reduced cerebral blood flow in the frontal cortex and may be mediated by lowered dopamine levels. The frontal dysfunction hypothesis is further supported by the generally positive behavioral impact of Ritalin treatment in at least a subgroup of ADHD children, given that this medication increases functional levels of this neurochemical. Therefore, both the overt symptoms of ADHD and the emerging neurophysiological evidence converge on a frontal cortex locus of dysfunction. The following section reviews empirical evidence of specific executive function deficits in this disorder.

Empirical Studies of Cognitive Performance

With the shift in emphasis from motor overactivity to attentional processes, researchers investigating the behavioral problems of ADHD children have traded in their pedometers for vigilance and reaction time tasks. Although these latter measures vary in their demands, the general requirement is for the child to respond as quickly as possible to target stimuli while inhibiting responses to nontarget items. In the more difficult version of the Continuous Performance Test (CPT; Rosvold, Mirsky, Sarason, Bransome, & Beck, 1956), the subject must respond to the target stimulus only when it is preceded by another specified stimulus. Thus, attentional set must be maintained between this warning signal and the subsequent target, and responses to the target in isolation (not preceded by the warning signal) must be inhibited.

A large body of literature demonstrates that children with ADHD exhibit deficits on vigilance tasks like the CPT (Barkley, 1977; Douglas, 1972; Douglas & Peters, 1979; Ross & Ross, 1976; Sykes, Douglas, & Morgenstern, 1973; Sykes, Douglas, Weiss, & Minde, 1971; Whalen, 1983). They make more errors of commission and omission, have slower and more variable reaction times, and perform particularly poorly on tasks that include a preparatory interval prior to the target (Douglas, 1983). Although these tasks were originally developed to measure the global construct of attention, it is clear that subprocesses are also tapped, including maintenance of effortful information processing over time and inhibition of irrelevant and impulsive responding. Thus, the performance impairments observed on these attention tasks may also reflect executive function deficits.

During the past two decades, the emphasis of ADHD research has been on the core cognitive deficits that may underlie these problems in sustained attention. Douglas (1983, 1988) has reviewed the empirical evidence for a set of specific cognitive impairments in ADHD. She points out that these children perform poorly on monitoring tasks like the CPT (Dykman, Ackerman, Clements, & Peters, 1971), visual search tasks such as the MFFT (Parry, 1973), reasoning tasks that require matrix solution and rule learning (Tant & Douglas, 1982), and motor-planning and visuomotor tasks such as the Porteus Mazes (Parry, 1973). In addition, ADHD children exhibit impairments on measures of prefrontal function, including the WCST (Chelune & Baer, 1986; Parry, 1973; Pennington, Groisser, & Welsh, in press), the TOH planning task (Pennington et al., in press; Welsh, Wall, & Towle, 1989), and motor conflict tasks such as the "go–no go" paradigm (Douglas, 1988; Luria, 1973). In contrast, children with ADHD perform normally on various tasks of verbal memory, such as digit span (forward), paired associate learning, and story recall, as well as on tasks of visual memory, such as recurring figures and spatial position recall (Douglas, 1988). It is important to note that ADHD performance deficits can be found in any information-processing domain, including memory, given task conditions that stress the executive function system.

In fact, Douglas (1983, 1988) concludes from her review of the cognitive research that ADHD children manifest a deficit in self-regulation that affects the organization of information-processing strategies, the recruitment of attention and effort during information processing, and the inhibition of inappropriate responding that would interfere with information processing. In Douglas's (1983, 1988) model, the organization component involves such skills as planning, metacognition (i.e., understanding and controlling cognition), set maintenance, modulation of arousal and attention, and self-monitoring. Mobilization of attention includes its appropriate deployment to meet task demands and its maintenance over time. The inhibition component reflects the ability to control interference from response patterns, stimuli, and reinforcers that are irrelevant to the task at hand but that nevertheless have a prepotent pull on the child's attention. Douglas proposes that ADHD children demonstrate specific cognitive impairments in these three components that bear a striking resemblance to the domain of executive function as described here.

Studies exploring executive function deficits in ADHD children are a relatively recent phenomenon, and the results to date are somewhat mixed. Across studies, the way in which executive functions are conceptualized, operationalized, and measured will vary and may contribute to these conflicting findings. Research from our laboratory has employed the Executive Function Battery described earlier that taps the efficiency and organization of visual and semantic search, planning ability (TOH), flexibility of strategies (WCST), and impulse control (MFFT, CPT). In one study, 5- to 9-year-old children presenting to a child evaluation clinic with attention problems were compared with age- and IQ-matched clinical control children presenting with speech and language difficulties without attention deficits (Welsh et al., 1989). The latter group was impaired on a speech and language screening test, whereas the former group was not. The attention problem group demonstrated less efficiency in visual search, more perseveration on the verbal fluency test, and poorer planning skills on the TOH than did the language problem group, which did not differ in performance from age-appropriate norms (Welsh et al., 1991).

In a second study, two well-defined, independent groups of children (mean age of 9 years) with ADHD only and with dyslexia only were compared on a set of executive function tasks and a set of discriminant phonological tasks (Pennington et al., under review). The ADHD group, but not the dyslexic group, was significantly impaired on the executive function tasks compared to normal controls. Conversely, the dyslexic group was alone in exhibiting significant deficits on the phonological tasks. These two studies together suggest that, in their "pure" forms, language-related disorders (e.g., dyslexia) are neuropsychologically independent from executive function disorders (e.g., ADHD) with regard to the core cognitive deficits and the underlying brain mechanisms involved.

In summary, recent research investigating the specific cognitive impairments associated with ADHD converges on the domain of executive function as a likely candidate. The evidence for specificity of cognitive disability is not as clear as it is for other learning disabilities, such as dyslexia and its concomitant phonological impairment. However, as further research is conducted to test this executive function hypothesis of ADHD, a more complete understanding of the core neuropsychological deficit should be forthcoming.

APPLICATIONS OF THE EXECUTIVE FUNCTION CONSTRUCT

The first two sections of this chapter argued for the importance of the executive function construct in the assessment of cognitive abilities in children, especially those identified with attention deficits. Although current research is responsible for developing potentially valuable assessment tools, these should not yet be considered clinical instruments for detecting frontal lobe dysfunction in children. This section of the chapter discusses several limitations of the executive function tasks described earlier. With these caveats in mind, some ideas regarding the relevance of the executive function construct to the development of assessment and management strategies for children with attention problems will be offered.

Psychometric and Validation Issues

If performance on the executive function tests is to become an integral part of the diagnostic process when evaluating children with possible frontal cortex dysfunction, then the psychometric properties must be substantiated. That is, the reliability and validity of these tasks must be established, standardized procedures for administration must be set up, and normative data on various age groups must be gathered. A test that contains a great deal of measurement error and that is an equivocal reflection of the psychological construct of interest cannot be used as an aid to diagnosis with any level of confidence. Assuming that the necessity of identifying executive function deficits in children with ADHD and other clinical conditions is accepted, the next wave of research should focus on refining these tasks so that they meet the basic standards for good psychological tests.

The reliability of a test refers to the repeatability, dependability, and consistency of the results (Kaplan & Saccuzzo, 1989), and it is inversely related to the amount of measurement error contributing to the test scores. Clearly, if one is to utilize the executive function tests as diagnostic tools, it is critical that they be reliable and provide a veridical reflection of the person's true level of these skills. With regard to clinical instruments, an adequate level of test–retest reliability is particularly essential when interventions and follow-up testing are involved. For example, in the case of ADHD it would be important to assess whether executive function performance improves subsequent to Ritalin treatment. If the executive function tasks lack adequate test–retest reliability, changes in performance after treatment could not be unequivocally attributed to the effects of medication.

Thus, the test–retest reliability of the executive function measures must be explored in future studies. However, there is one problem associated with this type of research that is due to the unique nature of the executive function construct. Because novel problem solving is an important attribute of executive function tests, repeated testing may compromise this novelty and the degree to which executive skills are elicited. This problem may be circumvented if testing is repeated only after a long enough interval or if parallel forms of the tests can be constructed. Related to this problem is the fact that specific executive function tasks, like the WCST, rely on "surprises" to which the child must flexibly adjust. Once the test has been administered and the surprise revealed, the test no longer taps the executive function skills needed to adjust flexibly to changing environmental contingencies.

Reliability of a test is no guarantee of its validity. The validity of a test refers to the meaning of the test results; do these results reflect the psychological processes the test was constructed to measure? If a test is valid, then certain inferences about the individual's ability can be made from her performance. That is, the investigator is confident that the test measures the psychological construct that it was intended to measure. The establishment of construct validity is a necessary first step that must be taken for newly identified constructs for which there is neither a universally accepted criterion nor a domain of content (Cronbach & Meehl, 1955). Through the process of construct validation, the investigator simultaneously formulates a definition and creates the tools to measure the construct. This systematic investigation involves the gathering of both convergent and divergent evidence so that a more complete understanding of the construct is derived.

One line of convergent evidence for construct validity comes from studies examining the performance of clinical groups that are believed to manifest a prefrontal cortex dysfunction on the basis of surface symptoms and neurobiological evidence. Studies from our own laboratory have found executive function deficits in children with early-treated phenylketonuria (PKU; Welsh, Pennington, Ozonoff, Rouse, & McCabe, 1990), ADHD (Pennington et al., in press; Welsh et al., 1989), high-functioning autism (Ozonoff, Rogers, Pennington, 1991), and preterm birth (Welsh & Towle, 1991). Importantly, these deficits are found on a variety of executive function tasks cutting across the three independent components of the battery, and this contrasts with normal performance on tests of other cognitive processes (e.g., memory). Therefore, although all of the executive function tasks do not converge in the strictest sense by intercorrelating, they do "hang together" as an impaired performance domain for certain clinical groups.

The second method of assessing construct validity is by gathering discriminant evidence. This process involves identifying the unique aspects of behavior that are assessed by the new measure (Kaplan & Saccuzzo, 1989). In our research, the executive function tests as a set can be discriminated from tests of other cognitive processes, such as recognition memory (Welsh et al., 1990; Welsh et al., 1991) and language (Pennington et al., in press). Moreover, evidence for discriminant validity also can be derived by comparing the performance of clinical groups. We have found that two clinical conditions with different putative neurological substrates, ADHD and dyslexia, exhibit very different patterns of performance on executive function tasks (Pennington et al., under review).

Thus, the importance of establishing the reliability and validity of executive function measures prior to incorporating them into diagnostic batteries should be clear. Although there are reliability and validity data on some of the more well established tasks (e.g., WCST, MFFT), there is very little psychometric information regarding many of the other tests. Moreover, standardized administration procedures and an extensive normative database are also necessary for these tasks to serve as useful clinical instruments.

In addition to the lack of psychometric information on the executive function tasks, a second limitation is the fact that studies documenting the neurological sensitivity of the tests to frontal function in children are rare. As discussed earlier in the chapter, to avoid the tautological reasoning typical of this type of research, one needs independent criteria of frontal lobe dysfunction in the particular clinical group studied. Once this is established, one can infer that impaired performance on the executive function tasks may be a reflection of this brain anomaly. These independent criteria can come in the form of neurochemical, neurophysiological, and neuroanatomical indices. In order to achieve neurological validation of the executive function tasks, studies exploring these parameters concurrently with executive function performance in a variety of clinical groups must be conducted. One study (Welsh et al., 1990) from our laboratory pursued this approach by assessing the relationship between executive function performance and biochemical functioning in early-treated PKU. There is a suspected frontal lobe dysfunction in this condition because the inability to metabolize phenylalanine (Phe) reduces the functional level of tyrosine, the rate-limiting step in the production of dopamine. Given tht the highest concentration of dopamine is found in frontal cortex, depletion of this neurochemical would be most likely to have a negative impact on this brain region. Welsh et al. (1990) found 4- to 5-year-old PKU children to be impaired on several executive function skills (e.g., planning, flexibility) compared with an age- and IQ-matched unaffected control group. More important, the degree of executive function deficit within the PKU group was correlated with the serum level of Phe concurrent with testing. Higher Phe levels have found to be associated with lower dopamine levels (Krause, et al., 1985), and, therefore, these results suggest that the executive function tasks may be sensitive to perturbed dopaminergic functioning in the frontal cortex.

It is important to note that the results of Welsh et al. (1990) provide only *indirect* evidence of an association between executive function performance and frontal lobe functioning. The cognitive performance was correlated with a biochemical index that is still several steps away from neurological function. A somewhat more direct approach would be to correlate cognitive performance with the dopamine metabolite homovanillic acid (HVA); this has been pursued in the study of children with ADHD, with some success (Shaywitz et al., 1983). The least ambiguous criterion for frontal lobe dysfunction is provided by neurological imaging techniques that reveal anomalies in structure (CT and MRI scans) and function (PET scans, regional cerebral blood flow, electrophysiology). Unfortunately, several of these techniques are still quite invasive, precluding their routine use in studies of children. Lou and colleagues (Lou et al., 1984; Lou et al., 1989) did find cerebral blood flow abnormalities in the frontal cortex of children with ADHD, who also exhibited deficits on sustained attention tasks. Initial validation of these executive function measures could be pursued by examining whether neurophysiological function in the frontal cortex correlates with performance in *adult* subjects. Such a connection has been documented for the WCST (Berman, Zec, & Weinberger, 1986; Weinberger et al., 1986). However, it is important to consider that brain–behavior associations found in adult subjects may not replicate in child populations and that empirical validation must still be pursued.

Practical Applications

Once the executive function measures have been refined and adequate psychometric properties established, these are potentially valuable tools for the assessment of children with behavior, attention, and learning problems. It is painfully clear to practitioners in the field of child assessment that good measures of skills such as planning, working memory, and flexibility are lacking. In general, traditional measures of intelligence and achievement provide the kind of external structure that obviates the need for novel problem-solving and, hence, executive function skills. The subtests of IQ measures such as the WISC-R are overdetermined in terms of the cognitive skills required and, therefore, do not always discriminate well between clinical groups of children with specific processing deficits. In contrast, a range of studies in our laboratory and in others have found that many experimental executive function tasks are sensitive to the types of cognitive deficits that may reflect a subtle frontal cortex dysfunction. This chapter has focused on the proposition that ADHD, in particular, is a clinical condition that is likely to manifest executive function impairments.

How would one incorporate the assessment of executive function into a typical evaluation of a child's cognitive strengths and weaknesses? Ideally, executive function (or some variation on this construct) should be acknowledged as a substantive cognitive domain that will be one target of the evaluation.

That is, along with the more traditional cognitive domains of language, spatial skills, and memory, a set of executive function measures should be included. It is probably the case that measures of the more traditional cognitive domains vary in terms of the executive function demands placed on the child. For example, a relatively "pure" spatial task such as mental rotation (Cooper & Shepard, 1973) will tap executive function to a lesser degree than would a complex figure-copying task like the Rey-Osterrith Figure (Waber & Holmes, 1985) that requires planning and organizational skills. Therefore, a child might perform relatively poorly in the spatial domain as a result of a primary executive function impairment and *not* because of a specific deficit in spatial skills. In addition to selecting more "pure" measures of each cognitive domain, independent assessment of the child's executive functions would make it possible to tease out the core cognitive deficit contributing to poor performance.

With regard to the assessment of children with attention problems, executive function measures clearly are relevant. Currently, diagnosis of ADHD in a child evaluation clinic is based on extensive parent interviews, behavior problem checklists and questionnaires completed by the parents and teacher, and IQ and achievement testing to look for performance patterns thought to typify this clinical condition. Less commonly, experimental measures of attention and impulse control such as the CPT and the MFFT are included in the evaluation. It is proposed here that measures specifically targeting the executive functions of planning, working memory, impulse control, and flexibility be incorporated into the assessment process. In this way, the executive function deficits that have been observed clinically and in educational settings can be documented, quantified, and clarified.

One goal of assessment is to describe precisely the nature of the cognitive impairment interfering with the child's learning and performance. A second objective is to utilize the information from the assessment to develop an appropriate intervention plan. In the case of the child diagnosed with ADHD, a description of the executive function deficits as well as the more traditional attentional parameters should contribute to more relevant, complete, and effective educational and treatment programs. Recall that an executive function impairment manifests as an inability to generate an organized, systematic plan of action to accomplish future goals. This goal-directed behavior requires that inappropriate impulses are controlled and strategies are monitored and flexibly modified. Given specific deficits in these cognitive skills, an intervention program can be developed to help the child compensate for weaknesses in this domain.

For example, the learning disability specialist would provide the structure and organization for goal-directed behavior that the child cannot provide for himself or herself. The child can be taught methods for controlling impulsive actions that are maladaptive, generating future-oriented plans, monitoring the effectiveness of these plans, and flexibly shifting these strategies in response to feedback. The child's deficiencies in these areas will require that external cues, structure, and scaffolds be provided by the teacher, parent, and therapist. The working assumption is that the intervention program must bolster the weak frontal cortical system of the child. This intervention plan is reminiscent of suggestions made by Douglas (1972) two decades ago in her classic "Stop, Look, and Listen" paper in which she described the need to teach hyperactive children to pause, reflect on, and monitor their actions. However, it is important to keep in mind that there likely will be limitations in the child's learning, integration, and transfer of these strategies given the presumed core executive function deficit. Therefore, another approach may be to steer the child toward educational activities characterized by minimal executive function demands.

SUMMARY

The domain of executive function is a relatively new construct developed to describe the cognitive functions ascribed to the frontal cortex of the human brain. Executive function refers to the set maintenance required for goal-directed behavior and includes such skills as planning, organized search, flexibility of strategies, impulse control, and self-monitoring. This is an overarching construct that intersects with more traditional modules of cognition, such as memory, visuospatial skills, and language.

Executive functions are difficult to measure well, and only recently have tasks been developed for children. The battery developed in our laboratory includes measures incorporated from both the developmental and neuropsychological literatures, and these tasks have proved sensitive to the cognitive deficits in several clinical conditions of childhood. Specifically, there is reason to hypothesize that children with ADHD may exhibit executive function deficits on the basis of clinical, neurobiological, and cognitive evidence.

Although the executive function tasks have been successful in revealing specific cognitive impairments in certain clinical groups, these measures cannot be considered diagnostic instruments because of several limitations. Further research is needed to establish the psychometric properties, cognitive demands, and neuropsychological sensitivity of these measures before they can contribute meaningfully to the identification of learning and behavior problems of children. In light of this research, assessment of executive function skills should be included in evaluations of the cognitive functioning of children thought to have ADHD and other learning and behavior disorders.

REFERENCES

American Psychiatric Association. (1987). *Diagnostic and statistical manual of mental disorders,* 3rd ed., revised. Washington, DC: Author.

Barkley, R. A. (1977). The effects of methylphenidate on various types of activity levels and attention in hyperkinetic children. *Journal of Abnormal Child Psychology, 5,* 351-369.

Berman, K. F., Zec, R. F., & Weinberger, D. R. (1986). Physiologic dysfunction of dorsolateral prefrontal cortex in schizophrenia: II. Role of neuroleptic treatment, attention, and mental effort. *Archives of General Psychiatry, 43,* 126-135.

Bilder, R., & Goldberg, E. (1987). Motor perseveration in schizophrenia. *Archives of Clinical Neuropsychology, 2,* 195-214.

Borys, S. V., Spitz, H. H., & Dorans, B. A. (1982). Tower of Hanoi performance of retarded young adults and nonretarded children as a function of solution length and goal state. *Journal of Experimental Psychology, 33,* 87-110.

Brown, A. L. (1978). Knowing when, where and how to remember: A problem of metacognition. In R. Glaser (Ed.), *Advances in instructional psychology* (pp. 77-165). Hillsdale, NJ: Erlbaum.

Carpenter, P. A., Just, M. A., & Shell, P. (1990). What one intelligence test measures: A theoretical account of the processing in the Raven Progressive Matrices Test. *Psychological Review, 97,* 404-431.

Chelune, G. J., & Baer, R. L. (1986). Developmental norms for the Wisconsin Card Sorting Test. *Journal of Clinical and Experimental Neuropsychology, 8,* 219-228.

Christensen, A. L. (1975). *Luria's neuropsychological investigation.* New York: Spectrum.

Cooper, L. A., & Shepard, R. N. (1973). Chronometric studies of the rotation of mental images. In W. G. Chase (Ed.), *Visual information processing.* New York: Academic Press.

Cromwell, R., Baumister, A., & Hawkins, W. (1963). Research in activity level. In N. Ellis (Ed.), *Handbook of mental deficiency* (pp. 632-663). New York: McGraw-Hill.

Cronbach, L. J., & Meehl, P. E. (1955). Construct validity in psychological tests. *Psychological Bulletin, 52,* 281-302.

Cuneo, K. M., & Welsh, M. C. (1992). Perseveration in young children: Developmental and neuropsychological perspectives. *Child Study Journal, 22,* 73-92.

Damasio, A. R. (1985). The frontal lobes. In K. M. Heilman & E. Valenstein (Eds.), *Clinical neuropsychology* (pp. 339-376). New York: Oxford University Press.

Dehaene, S., & Changeux, J. (1991). The Wisconsins Card Sorting Test: Theoretical analysis and modeling in a neuronal network. *Cerebral Cortex, 1,* 62-79.

Diamond, A. (1988). Differences between adult and infant cognition: Is the crucial variable presence or absence of language? In L. Weiskrantz (Ed.), *Thought without language* (pp. 337-370). New York: Oxford University Press.

Douglas, V. I. (1972). Stop, look, and listen: The problem of sustained attention and impulse control in hyperactive children. *Canadian Journal of Behavioural Science, 4,* 259-282.

Douglas, V. I. (1983). Attentional and cognitive problems. In M. Rutter (Ed.), *Developmental neuropsychiatry* (pp. 280-329). New York: Guilford Press.

Douglas, V. I. (1988). Cognitive deficits in children with attention deficit disorder with hyperactivity. In L. M. Bloomingdale & J. Sergeant (Eds.), *Attention deficit disorder: Criteria, cognition, intervention. A book supplement of the Journal of Child Psychology and Psychiatry* (No. 5). New York: Pergamon Press.

Douglas, V. I., & Peters, K. G. (1979). Toward a clearer definition of the attentional deficit of hyperactive children. In G. A. Hale & M. Lewis (Eds.), *Attention and cognitive development* (pp. 173–247). New York: PLenum Press.

Drew, E. A. (1975). Go-no go learning after frontal lobe lesions in humans *Cortex, 11,* 8–16.

Dykman, R. A., Ackerman, P. T., Clements, S., & Peters, J. E. (1971). Specific learning disabilities: An attentional deficit syndrome. In H. R. Mykelbust (Ed.), *Progress in learning disabilities* (Vol. 2, pp. 56–93). New York: Grune & Stratton.

Ferguson, H. B., & Rappaport, J. L. (1983). Nosological issues and biological validation. In M. Rutter (Ed.), *Developmental Neuropsychiatry* (pp. 369–384). New York: Guilford Press.

Flavell, J., & Wellman, H. (1977). Metamemory. In R. V. Kail & J. Hagen (Eds.), *Perspectives on the development of memory and cognition* (pp. 3–33). Hillsdale, NJ: Erlbaum.

Fuster, J. M. (1980). *The prefrontal cortex.* New York: Raven Press.

Goldberg, E., & Tucker, D. (1979). Motor perseveration and long-term memory for visual forms. *Journal of Clinical Neuropsychology, 1,* 273–288.

Golden, C. J. (1981). The Luria-Nebraska Children's Battery: Theory and formulation. In G. W. Hynd & J. E. Obrzut (Eds.), *Neuropsychological assessment and the school-age child* (pp. 277–302). New York: Grune & Stratton.

Goldman-Rakic, P. S. (1988). Topography of cognition: Parallel distributed networks in primate association cortex. *Annual Review of Neuroscience, 11,* 137–156.

Goldman-Rakic, P. A. (1990). Cellular and circuit basis of working memory in prefrontal cortex of nonhuman primates. *Progress in Brain Research, 85,* 325–336.

Grant, D. S., & Berg, E. A. (1948). A behavioral analysis of degree of reinforcement and ease of shifting to new responses in a Weigl-type card sorting problem. *Journal of Experimental Psychology, 321,* 404–411.

Haith, M. M., Hazan, C., & Goodman, G. S. (1988). Expectation and anticipation of dynamic visual events by 3.5-month-old babies. *Child Development, 59,* 467–479.

Harcherick, D. F., Cohen, D. J., Ort, S., Paul, R., Shaywitz, B. A., Volkman, F. R., Rothman, S. L. G., & Leckman, T. F. (1985). Computed tomographic brain scanning in four neuropsychiatric disorders of childhood. *American Journal of Psychiatry, 142,* 731–737.

Heaton, R. K. (1981). *Wisconsin Card Sorting Test manual.* Odessa, FL: Psychological Assessment Resources.

Horn, J. (1985). Remodeling old models of intelligence. In B. Wolman (Ed.), *Handbook of intelligence: Theories, measurements, and applications* (pp. 267–300). New York: Wiley.

Hynd, G. W., Semrud-Clikeman, M., Lorys, A. R., Novey, E. S., & Eliopulas, D. (in press). Brain morphology in developmental dyslexia and attention deficit disorder/hyperactivity. *Archives of Neurology.*

Jacobsen, C. F. (1935). Functions of the frontal association area in primates. *Archives of Neurology and Psychiatry, 33,* 558–569.

Kagan, J., Rosman, B. L., Day, L., Albert, J., & Phillips, W. (1964). Information processing in the child: Significance of analytic and reflective attitudes. *Psychological Monographs, 78,* Whole No. 578.

Kaplan, R. M., & Saccuzzo, D. P. (1989). *Psychological testing: Principles, applications, and issues.* Pacific Grove, CA: Brooks/Cole.

Krause, W. L., Halminski, M., McDonald, L., Dembure, P., Salvo, R., Freides, D., & Elsas, L. J. (1985). Biochemical and neuropsychological effects of elevated plansma phenylalanine in patients with treated phenylketonuria: A model for the study of phenylalanine and brain function in man. *Journal of Clinical Investigation, 75,* 40–48.

Lou, H. C., Henriksen, L., & Bruhn, P. (1984). Focal cerebral hypofusion and/or attention deficit disorder. *Archives of Neurology, 41,* 825–829.

Lou, H. C., Henriksen, L., Bruhn, P., Borner, H., & Nielsen, J. B. (1989). Striatal dysfunction in attention deficit and hyperkinetic disorder. *Archives of Neurology, 46,* 148–152.

Luria, A. R. (1966). *Higher cortical functions in man.* New York: Basic Books.

Luria, A. R. (1973). *The working brain.* New York: Basic Books.

McCarthy, D. (1972). *Manual for the McCarthy Scales of Children's Abilities.* New York: Psychological Corporation.

Milner, B. (1963). Effects of different brain lesions on card sorting. *Archives of Neurology, 9,* 90–100.

Milner, B. (1964). Some effects of frontal lobectomy in man. In J. M. Warren & K. Akert (Eds.), *The frontal granular cortex and behavior* (pp. 313–334). New York: McGraw-Hill.

Neisser, U. (1967). *Cognitive psychology.* New York: Appleton-century-Crofts.

Ozonoff, S., Rogers, S. A., & Pennington, B. F. (1991). Asperger's syndrome: Evidence of an empirical distinction from high-functioning autism. *Journal of Child Psychology and Psychiatry, 32,* 1107–1122.

Parry, P. A. (1973). *The effect of reward on the performance of hyperactive children.* Unpublished doctoral dissertation, McGill University.

Passler, M. A., Isaac, W., & Hynd, G. W. (1985). Neuropsychological development of behavior attributed to frontal lobe functioning in children. *Developmental Neuropsychology, 1,* 349–370.

Pennington, B. F. (1991). *Diagnosing learning disorders: A neuropsychological framework.* New York: Guilford Press.

Pennington, B. F., Groisser, D. B., & Welsh, M. C. (in press). Contrasting neuropsychological profiles in children with attention deficit hyperactivity disorder vs. reading disbility. *Developmental Psychology.*

Posner, M. I., & Petersen, S. E. (in press). The attention system of the human brain. *Annual Review of Neuroscience.*

Ross, D. M., & Ross, S. A. (1976). *Hyperactivity: Research, theory and action.* New York: Wiley.

Rosvold, H. E., Mirsky, A. F., Sarason, I., Bransome, E. D., & Beck, L. H. (1956). A continuous performance test of brain damage. *Journal of Consulting and Clinical Psychology, 20,* 343–352.

Saint-Cyr, J. A., Taylor, A. E., & Lang, A. E. (1988). Procedural learning and neostriatal dysfunction in man. *Brain, 111,* 941–959.

Shaywitz, B. A., Cohen, D. J., & Bowers, M. B. (1977). CSF monoamine metabolites in children with minimal brain dysfunction: Evidence for alteration of brain dopamine. *Journal of Pediatrics, 90,* 67–71.

Shaywitz, S. E., Shaywitz, B. A., Cohen, D. J., Young, J. G. (1983). Monoaminergic mechanisms in hyperactivity. In M. Rutter (Ed.), *Developmental neuropsychiatry* (pp. 340–347). New York: Guilford Press.

Simon, H. A. (1975). The functional equivalence of problem solving skills. *Cognitive Psychology, 7,* 268–288.

Stuss, D. T., & Benson, F. (1984). Neurophysiological studies of frontal lobes. *Psychological Bulletin, 95,* 3–28.

Sykes, D. H., Douglas, V. I., & Morgenstern, G. (1973). Sustained attention in hyperactive children. *Journal of child Psychology and Psychiatry, 14,* 213–220.

Sykes, D. H., Douglas, V. I., Weiss, G., & Minde, K. K. (1971). Attention in hyperactive children and the effect of methylphenidate (Ritalin). *Journal of Child Psychology and Psychiatry, 12,* 129–139.

Tant, J. L., & Douglas, V. I. (1982). Problem solving in hyperactive, normal, and reading disabled boys. *Journal of Abnormal Child Psychology, 10,* 285–306.

Teuber, H. L., Battersby, W. S., & Bender, M. B. (1955). Changes in visual searching performance following cerebral lesions. *American Journal of Physiology, 159,* 592.

Waber, F. P., & Holmes, J. M. (1985). Assessing children's copy productions of the Rey-Osterrieth Complex Figure. *Journal of Clinical and Experimental Neuropsychology, 7,* 264–280.

Weinberger, D. R., Berman, K. F., & Zec, R. F. (1986). Physiologic dysfunction of dorsolateral prefrontal cortex in schizophrenia: I. Regional cerebral blood flow evidence. *Archives of General Psychiatry, 43,* 114–124.

Welsh, M. C. (1991). Rule-guided behavior and self-monitoring on the Tower of Hanoi disk-transfer task. *Cognitive Psychology, 6,* 59–76.

Welsh, M. C., & Pennington, B. F. (1988). Assessing frontal lobe functioning in children: Views from developmental psychology. *Developmental Neuropsychology, 4,* 188–230.

Welsh, M. C., Pennington, B. F., & Groisser, D. B. (1991). A normative-developmental study of executive function: A window on prefrontal function in children. *Developmental Neuropsychology, 7,* 131–149.

Welsh, M. C., Pennington, B. F., Ozonoff, S., Rouse, B., & McCabe, E. R. B. (1990). Neuropsychology of early-treated phenylketonuria: Specific executive function deficits. *Child Development, 61,* 1697–1713.

Welsh, M. C., & Towle, P. O. (1991, February). *Executive functions and associations with perinatal variables in premature children.* Paper presented at the annual conference of the International Neuropsychological Society, San Antonio, Texas.

Welsh, M. C., Wall, B. M., & Towle, P. O. (1989, April). *Executive function in children with attention deficit: Implications for a prefrontal hypothesis.* Paper presented at the biennial meeting of the Society for Research in Child Development, Kansas City, Missouri.

Whalen, C. K. (1983). Hyperactivity, learning problems, and the attention deficit disorders. In T. H. Ollendick & M. Hersen (Eds.), *Handbook of child psychopathology* (pp. 151–199). New York: Plenum Press.

Willatts, P. (in press). Development of problem solving. In A. Slatert & J. G. Bremner (Eds.), *Infant development.* Hillsdale, NJ: Erlbaum.

Zametkin, A. J., Nordahl, T. E., Gross, M., King, A. C., Semple, W. E., Rumsey, J., Hamburger, S., & Cohen, R. M. (1991). Cerebral glucose metabolism in adults with hyperactivity of childhood onset. *The New England Journal of Medicine, 323,* 1361–1366.

▶ 3

Brain–Behavior Relationships in Dyslexia

MARGARET SEMRUD-CLIKEMAN   GEORGE W. HYND
University of Washington   University of Georgia

Abstract

The purpose of this chapter is to review and examine current neuroanatomical research in dyslexia. The neurobiological theory of dyslexia is briefly reviewed, with attention to its relation to current research. Research findings from CT, MRI, metabolic, and postmortem studies are discussed. Although several studies found differences in asymmetry of the planum temporale in dyslexia, inconsistencies were found as to whether the planum temporale showed symmetry or reversed asymmetry. Differences in measurement may contribute to these varying findings. Two studies found relationships between phonological coding and asymmetry differences in the planum for dyslexia. This finding is important, as it is evidence of a link between pathoanatomic structure and dysfunction in reading processes. Finally, this chapter provides suggestions for extension of the current research as well as avenues for further exploration of brain–behavior relationships.

The evidence for the presumed relationship between reading disability and brain dysfunction has historically come from correlational and/or behavior research (Golden, 1982; Taylor & Fletcher, 1983). In addition, an understanding of possible localization of deficient brain organization in dyslexia has been adapted from studies of adult brains with lesions and the resulting behavioral changes (Geschwind & Galaburda, 1985; Filipek, Kennedy, & Caviness, 1991). For example, if a child showed poor reading comprehension with coincident language difficulties, dysfunction would be hypothesized to be present in the left superior temporal lobe. Given the difference between an established and a developing nervous system, it is not clear that localization findings from adults with asphasia (Damasio & Damasio, 1989) directly relate to the developing brains of children with learning disorders.

Until recently, there were few vehicles for directly relating dysfunctional learning with pathoanatomic development. Studies of adults with dyslexia that utilized autopsy findings or computed tomography (CT) studies have provided useful, though limited, information. CT involves the use of small amounts of radiation, which can then be pictured to reflect densities of tissues. Magnetic resonance imaging (MRI) techniques, now make it possible to provide evidence for deviations in structural variation in the brains of living persons with developmental dyslexia. MRI involves the use of magnetic fields that image structures of the brain and produce a photographic image. This development is important in order to provide an empirical underpinning for the currently prevailing definition of dyslexia as "intrinsic to the individual and presumed to be due to central nervous system dysfunction" (Wyngaarden, 1987, pp. 62082–62085). In addition, such empirical verification may well shed light on the etiology of dyslexia and provide important information for possible prevention and appropriate interventions at earlier ages than is currently possible.

The purpose of this chapter is twofold. The first purpose is to review the current research findings from CT, MRI, metabolic, and postmortem studies. Second, this chapter will attempt to extend the current research and suggest avenues for further exploration of brain–behavior relationships. In order to put such research into a theoretical framework, however, the neurobiological theory of dyslexia will first be discussed, followed by a review of the relevant procedures.

NEUROBIOLOGICAL THEORY

Initial efforts at localizing function were aimed at demonstrating the existence of specific centers for higher level cognitive activities such as reading. These efforts arose from the finding that speech, vision, and auditory comprehension were localized to various centers of the brain. Reasoning from these data, it was thought that reading, arithmetic, writing, and other higher level cognitive skills would likewise be localizable. This reasoning was later empirically discounted as too simplistic.

Current neurobiological theory suggests that the complex behaviors of reading and writing arise from the interaction of functional systems (Luria, 1980). In this sense, areas that are responsible for various sensory inputs are combined into units that allow for higher level and dynamic processing of information. For example, the auditory system has a direct sensory component, a secondary component that further analyzes sensory data, and a tertiary component that integrates the sensory input with past learning. in this type of functional system, one can see the ability of the system to change dynamically in organization, depending on input and experience as well as over the range of development.

In order for a neurobiological theory to be useful, it needs to predict the systems that are crucial for normal reading acquisition. Furthermore, these systems need to be demonstrated to be disrupted in children with dyslexia (Jorm, 1979). For example, it is reasonable to speculate that different pathoanatomic variations may contribute to varying types of reading disorders. For example, differences in organization and development in the superior temporal and inferior parietal regions of the brain including the area known as the angular gyrus, planum temporale, and insular region may result in difficulties in phonemic coding and reading comprehension (Figure 3-1 presents a simplified version of the reading process) (Claiborne, 1906; Herman, 1959; Geschwind, 1965, 1974). In contrast, children with visual-spatial deficits may show other areas of

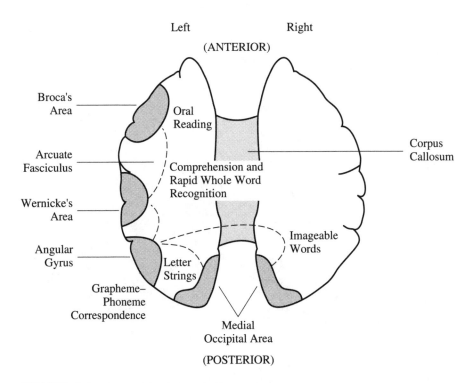

FIGURE 3-1 **A model of the reading process**
Reprinted by permission of G. W. Hynd.

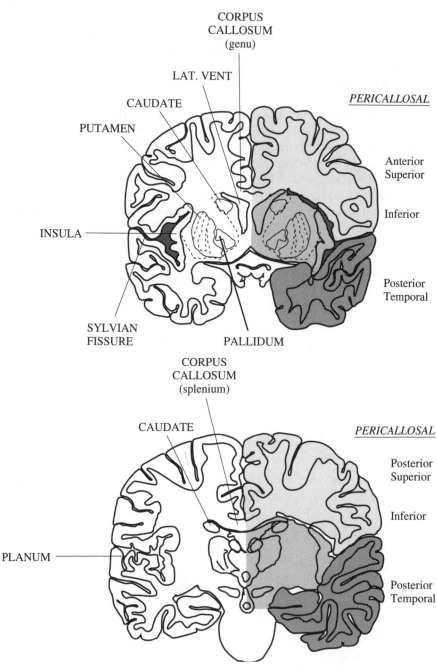

CORPUS
CALLOSUM
(genu)

LAT. VENT

CAUDATE

PUTAMEN

PERICALLOSAL

Anterior
Superior

Inferior

INSULA

Posterior
Temporal

SYLVIAN
FISSURE

PALLIDUM

CORPUS
CALLOSUM
(splenium)

CAUDATE

PERICALLOSAL

Posterior
Superior

Inferior

PLANUM

Posterior
Temporal

FIGURE 3-2 **Brain geography**

Source: P. A. Filipek, P. N. Kennedy, & V. S. Cavines, Neuroimaging in child neuropsychology. In F. Boller & J. Graham (Eds.), *Handbook of Neuropsychology* (Amsterdam:
Elsevier Science Publishers in press). Reprinted by permission of Elsevier Science Publishers.

pathoanatomic development. Moreover, this conceptualization appears to be consistent with information-processing paradigms of the reading process (LaBerge & Samuels, 1974; Newcombe, Phil, & Marshall, 1981). Though speculative at this time, these hypotheses may be empirically tested through recently introduced techniques.

Differences in size and pattern of asymmetry or symmetry of structures may be implicated in dyslexia. Figure 3-2 presents the pertinent brain geography. In order to understand abnormal anatomical development, it is first important to explore normal patterns of asymmetry. The following section briefly reviews current knowledge of normal patterns of cerebral asymmetry.

CEREBRAL ASYMMETRIES

Asymmetries have been found in normal brains through the use of postmortem and CT studies. Asymmetry refers to a larger area/volume of a structure on one side of the brain. Using postmortem methods, larger volume asymmetry of the right anterior and the left occipital lobe in adult and fetal brains at 20 weeks' gestation was found. This result suggests an embryologic basis for lateralized cerebral functions (Weinberger, Luchins, Morihisa, & Wyatt, 1982).

An asymmetry of the planum temporale has been found, with approximately 66 percent of normal brains showing longer left plana temporale and left posterior regions than right (Geschwind & Levitsky, 1968; LeMay, 1981; Rubens, Mahuwold, & Hutton, 1976; Teszner, Tzavaras, Gruner, & Hecaen, 1972; Weinberger et al., 1982; Witelson, 1983). This finding is important in that the planum temporale contains auditory association cortex, which is intimately involved in language (Galaburda & Sanides, 1980; see Figure 3-2).

The majority of infant brains studied (40 to 70 percent) were found to have left < right planum temporale asymmetry (Wada, Clarke, & Hammn, 1975; Witelson & Pallie, 1973). Fetal brains have been found to show planum asymmetry by the thirty-first week of gestation (Chi, Dooling, & Giles, 1977), which is shortly after cerebral cortex neuronal migration has ended (Sidman & Rakic, 1973). It has been speculated that the proportions of asymmetrical infant and fetal brains may vary compared to adult brains as a result of environmental factors, differential survival rates, and/or postnatal changes (such as pruning of the right planum not taking place after birth) that affect the resulting percentages in favor of left-sided asymmetry (Galaburda, Rosen, & Sherman, 1991). It has also been found that the region of the angular gyrus generally is asymmetric to the left side, and the magnitude of this asymmetry is highly correlated with left plana asymmetry (Eidelberg & Galaburda, 1984).

This finding is very exciting, as both regions are involved in the language system. The fact that the magnitude of asymmetry is highly correlated suggests a systematic link to language processing for these areas (Galaburda et al., 1991).

Therefore, these particular areas would be important to investigate for possible differences in brain morphology in persons with dyslexia compared to normal readers.

CT AND POSTMORTEM STUDIES

Until recently, most studies had utilized CT scans and used adult populations. CT has been criticized for its poorer gray/white matter structure resolution and its limitation to the transaxial plane (Filipek et al., 1991). However, CT studies have provided evidence for deviations in brain asymmetry in the brains of persons with dyslexia. Whereas 66 percent of normal brains show L > R posterior asymmetry (LeMay, 1981), 10 to 50 percent of brains of persons with dyslexia show this asymmetry pattern on the basis of CT/MRI results (Haslam, Dalby, Johns, & Rademaker, 1981; Hier, LeMay, Rosenberger, & Perlo, 1978). Most of the CT studies evaluated the presence of obvious neurostructural abnormalities and/or deviations in normal patterns of left greater than right parieto-occipital asymmetry. Of the seven CT studies, five found significantly less L > R parieto-occipital asymmetry with increased symmetry (Haslam et al., 1981; Hier et al., 1978; Leisman & Ashkenazi, 1980) or reversed symmetry of this area (LeMay, 1981; Rosenberger & Hier, 1980). The sole MRI study conducted during this time period also found parieto-occipital symmetry (Rumsey, Dorwart, Vermess, Denckla, Kruesi, & Rapoport, 1986). An average of 58 percent of these with dyslexia were found to show symmetry of this region. One of the remaining CT studies did not evaluate the parieto-occipital asymmetry (Denckla, LeMay, & Chapman, 1985).

Parkins, Roberts, Reinarz, and Varney (1987) found reversed asymmetry/symmetry present only in left-handed subjects. There appears to be consistency of findings that persons with dyslexia may evidence some symmetry of the posterior cortex. However, the effect of handedness on this symmetry is not clear and may have confounded several of the studies that did not control for handedness. Although there may be a relationship between handedness and posterior symmetry, only one study supports such a hypothesis. A more complete review of the limitations of the CT/MRI studies can be obtained in Hynd and Semrud-Clikeman (1989).

Two studies reported anterior asymmetries in their dyslexic subjects (Haslam et al., 1981; Parkins et al., 1987). LeMay (1976) provided evidence from normal subjects that in approximately 75 percent of the population, the volume of the right anterior cortex exceeds that of the left anterior cortex. Although Haslam et al. (1981) did not appear to present significant findings of anterior area asymmetry in persons with dyslexia compared to control subjects, proportionately more children with dyslexia were found to evidence equivalent anterior hemispheres than would be expected from LeMay's data. The original data were not provided, so it was impossible to determine whether Haslam et al.'s (1981) finding is statistically significant. Parkins et al. (1987) found no significant differences in anterior measures in their sample with dyslexia.

None of the CT studies examined planum temporale patterns of asymmetry, possibly because of the difficulty in visualizing this structure on CT. Postmortem studies have found symmetrical plana temporale (Galaburda & Kemper, 1979; Galaburda, Sherman, Rosen, Aboitiz, & Geschwind, 1985). These researchers attribute the planum temporale symmetry to a larger right plana. Focal dysplasias were found to be more prevalent in the left anterior, left perisylvian, and right anterior regions.

The conclusions from the CT and postmortem studies are that the dyslexic brains showed differences from the controls in parieto-occipital reversed asymmetry or symmetry. Postmortem results showed planum temporale abnormalities, with significantly larger right plana temporale in brains of persons with dyslexia than in normal brains. Although anterior areas were not studied in most of the CT studies, postmortem studies show abnormalities in dyslexic brains, with disordered cells and misplaced layers occurring in this region.

MAGNETIC RESONANCE IMAGING FINDINGS

The recent development of magnetic resonance imaging (MRI) has yielded the opportunity to visualize structures in living subjects with comparatively clarity compared to postmortem methods and without the radiation involved with CT (Filipek et al. 1991). This advance has made possible several studies that utilized the MRI technology with child populations. At present, we know of only four published MRI studies using children with dyslexia. The results from these studies are detailed next.

University of Georgia Study

An investigation that utilized carefully diagnosed pediatric dyslexics compared linear MRI brain morphology measures with a clinic control group (attention deficit disorder/hyperactivity; ADD/H) and a normal control group (Hynd, Semrud-Clikeman, Lorys, Novey, & Eliopulus, 1990). No significant differences were found in brain area or left/right asymmetry among the three groups. Moreover, the common finding of posterior reversed asymmetry/symmetry in persons with dyslexia was not found by these investigators. However, they suggest that this aberrant finding was due to the measuring of more posterior regions (a line drawn horizontally from the posterior tip of the splenium) than in the CT scans and, therefore, not directly comparable.

Reversed or symmetrical planum temporale for the dyslexic group (90 percent with L < R plana asymmetry) was significantly different when compared to the normal rate of 70 percent L > R asymmetry found in the clinic and normal control groups (see Figure 3-3). These results were due to a smaller left planum, whereas the right planum length did not differ from the control groups.

Bilaterally smaller insular regions were found for those with dyslexia compared to the other two groups. This study found that in areas previously hypothesized to be implicated in the reading processes (planum temporale and insular region), brains of those with dyslexia were significantly morphologically different from normal readers and were unique when compared to those of normal readers with attentional deficits.

The anterior region was measured using a line drawn horizontally across the posterior tip of the genu (the most anterior portion of the corpus callosum) to the outside of the hemisphere. The width of the anterior region was found to be symmetrical for the dyslexic group; the control groups showed the expected R > L width differential. The ADD/H group also showed smaller anterior cortices. Pairwise comparisons found that both the dyslexic and the ADD/H children differed in right anterior region widths, but not on the left anterior region width. Therefore, the group differences would appear to be due to smaller right anterior width measures for both the dyslexic and the ADD/H children in comparison to the wider right anterior region of the normal sample. Only the dyslexic group showed symmetry of this region and thereby provided a different pattern from the expected L < R asymmetry of this region present in the normal and ADD/H groups.

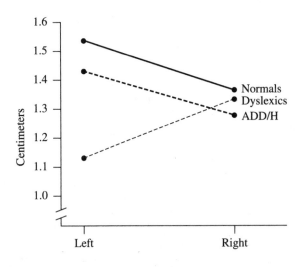

FIGURE 3-3 **Group differences in plana length**

Duara et al. (1991) Study

This study compared linear measures in men and women with dyslexia with those of male and female normal adult controls. They divided the brain into six segments, each with a left and right component. In addition, they compared measures of the corpus callosum among their four groups. Total brain area was found to differ significantly between the groups and therefore was used as a covariate. The right midposterior region was found to be significantly larger (including the angular gyrus region) than the left in adults with dyslexia compared to the symmetry of this area in the normal readers. Moreover, a significant relationship was found between the severity index of dyslexia and the area of the right posterior polar region. Thus, the larger the right posterior side, the more severe the dyslexia.

Although this study did not directly study the planum temporale measure, the area which included most of this structure was found to be symmetrical with no group difference (measure of 11.3 + 1.0 for the dyslexics vs. 11.2 + 0.7 for the normal readers). Because there was no direct measure of the planum temporale, it is impossible to compare these results to those of the University of Georgia study. It is entirely possible to have area measures that are nonsignificant paired with regional areas that do differ.

The corpus callosum data showed a larger splenium (most posterior region of the corpus callosum) present in the dyslexic sample, with dyslexic females possessing the largest splenium, followed by dyslexic males. Conclusions from this study were that, given that the transcallosal pathways connecting the right and left angular gyri connect through the splenium, an anatomic abnormality was felt to exist in the angular gyrus region for dyslexic subjects. These researchers hypothesized that more communication takes place between the right and left angular gyri regions in dyslexic subjects. Therefore, the portion of the corpus callosum connecting such regions would also need to be larger.

Norway Study

A study by Larsen, Hoien, Lundberg, and Odegaard (1990) compared MRI morphometry between developmental dyslexics and normal-reading adolescents. Seventy percent of the dyslexics were found to have symmetrical plana, while 70% of the normals were found to have the expected asymmetry of L > R. This research team concluded that the symmetrical plana for the dyslexics was the result of a larger right planum rather than a smaller left planum. This result is similar to the findings of the postmortem studies.

San Diego Study

An MRI study using language- and learning-impaired children was conducted by Jernigan, Hesselink, Sowell, and Tallal (1991). No significant gross neurological differences were found. Hemispheric volumes as well as cerebral asymmetries were measured in six cerebral regions. The language- and learning-impaired children showed significantly smaller left posterior perisylvian region volume compared to the normal control subjects. Anterior asymmetry was found to be reversed (L > R) for the learning- and language-impaired subjects compared to the normal controls, with the left volume measure more decreased than the right.

This group also found significantly reduced volume in the left posterior perisylvian region for the dyslexic sample. The right volume of this area was also nearly as reduced as the left for the dyslexics. This area included the planum temporale and, although this was not directly measured, this structure plus others showed less volume on the left than the right relative to controls.

Conclusions

In summary, MRI studies of dyslexics have found morphological differences in the regions of the planum temporale, insula, and inferior parietal area of the angular gyrus. Not all studies used the same selection methods of their dyslexic subjects, and most included persons with other diagnoses in their samples, which may cloud the results. For example, language-impaired subjects (but not necessarily dyslexic subjects) were included in the Jernigan et al. (1991) study; dyslexic subjects with attention deficit disorders were included in the Duara et al. (1991) study. Moreover, the studies varied in their measurement procedures of the MRI scans. It is not clear at present whether the consistent finding of planum temporale differences is due to a larger right or a smaller left planum. The Hynd et al. (1990) finding of a smaller left planum measure, with no right planum difference from normal brains, is consistent with Witelson's (1983) findings, whereas the Larsen et al. (1990) finding is consistent with the 1987 findings of Galaburda, Corsiglia, Rosen, and Sherman of a larger right planum temporale. These opposing findings may be due to measurement procedures or subject selection differences (possible use of different subtypes of dyslexia, use of different determination of dyslexia, or use of adults rather than children). Additional studies are warranted to resolve this discrepancy. However, the aforementioned studies do reflect the existence of a morphology difference in dyslexic brains, underscoring the validity of the central nervous dysfunction assumption inherent in many definitions of dyslexia.

Although it is important to determine brain morphologic differences in dyslexic brains, it seems equally imperative to begin gathering data concerning the effects of these brain differences on neuropsychological performance. As these types of studies are just beginning to shed light on this linkage, it is important to summarize currently available findings that dynamically link structure and function.

MRI AND NEUROLINGUISTIC FUNCTIONING

There are few studies available that link MRI morphometry with neurolinguistic functioning. Larsen et al. (1990) found that dyslexics with symmetrical plana showed phonological deficits, whereas normal controls with L > R plana asymmetry showed no phonological deficits. In addition, of the three normal controls with symmetrical plana, two showed phonological deficits. This finding is important in that it shows that symmetrical plana place a child at risk for phonological deficits. The authors do not discuss why the two "normal" subjects with symmetrical plana and phonological deficits did not develop dyslexia.

In our study (Semrud-Clikeman, Hynd, Novey, & Eliopulus, 1991), we compared the neurolinguistic functioning to brain morphology measurements and group membership. A clinic control group of attention deficit disorder/hyperactivity (ADD/H) without learning deficits and a normal control group were used. The dyslexic group showed significant deficits on measures of phonological coding, reading comprehension, rapid naming abilities, and confrontational naming skills compared to the other two groups. There were no group differences in receptive or expressive language skills or visual-motor abilities. A central question was how these neuropsychological weaknesses related to morphological differences.

Reading comprehension was found to be directly related to magnitude of the right anterior width. Dyslexic subjects with smaller right anterior width measures performed significantly more poorly than any of the other subjects. Furthermore, they performed more poorly than did dyslexic subjects with less symmetric anterior widths. Figure 3-4 shows this relationship. Similarly, dyslexic subjects with smaller right anterior area measures performed more poorly on phonological coding tasks than did dyslexics with larger right anterior measures or subjects in the two comparison groups. Figure 3-5 illustrates this interaction.

In our study, the direction for the asymmetry of the plana temporale was not able to be related to neurolinguistic measures because of the lack of dyslexic subjects with normal asymmetry (L > R). When group membership was not used, however, subjects with reversed or symmetrical plana (L < R) showed lowered scores on the verbal comprehension factor of the WISC-R. This finding is consistent with Rosenberger and Hier's (1980) finding of lowered verbal IQ in subjects with reversed planum asymmetry. Taken together, then, these results strongly suggest that the plana is a major language-processing center. Figure 3-6 illustrates this relationship.

To evaluate further the role of the plana in reading and language processing, our sample was divided into L > R planum temporale and L < R. This procedure is similar to that used in previous studies (Galaburda & Kemper, 1979; Galaburda et al., 1985; Hier et al., 1978). There were 15 subjects per group, with the majority of dyslexics (9 of 15) in the reversed and symmetrical plana group. No IQ differences were found, but significant differences in performance

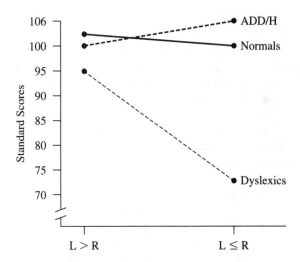

FIGURE 3-4 **Interaction between anterior width asymmetry and performance on passage comprehension**

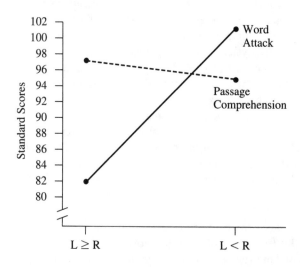

FIGURE 3-5 **Interaction between anterior area asymmetry and performance on word attack and passage comprehension**

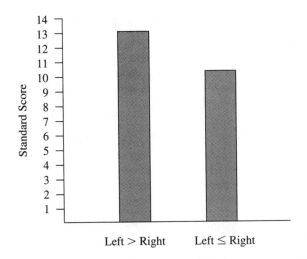

FIGURE 3-6   **Plana asymmetry and performance on the Verbal Comprehension factor of the WISC-R**

was found on four of the five neurolinguistic measures. Because of the loading of dyslexics into the reversed asymmetry or symmetrical plana group, the clinic control and normal control groups were split into two groups by a process similar to the foregoing procedure. Because this resulted in two groups of 6 (3 clinic and normal controls each in the groups), inferential statistics were not appropriate. Upon examination of the means, however, these groups were found to be in the same direction as shown by Table 3-1. Again, those subjects with reversed or symmetrical plana performed more poorly on all neurolinguistic tasks than did those subjects with the expected asymmetry.

It is reasonable to speculate that the ability to encode letters, colors, numbers, and words is impaired by morphological differences that are present at birth and place the child at risk for the development of dyslexia. When several morphological differences are present, the child may well experience reading deficits while also developing intact cognitive and visual-motor abilities. It is not immediately clear whether it is truly the degree of asymmetry or the smaller size of crucial areas that produces poorer neurolinguistic development. Certainly the reduced area and width of the right anterior area reduced the dyslexic person's ability to comprehend reading passages or perform phonological coding.

It is important to note that both the study by Larsen et al. (1990) and our study (Semrud-Clikeman et al., 1991) found that "normal" subjects with differing asymmetry or symmetry of the plana temporale showed deficits on specific tasks. Therefore, it may well be the pattern of deviant brain asymmetry/

TABLE 3-1   **Means on Neurolinguistic Measures for Direction of Plana Asymmetry (L > R and L < R)**

Measure	L > R	L > or = R
Word attack	115.00	107.00
Passage comprehension	108.16	105.00
Boston Naming Test	51.17	45.17
Rapid Naming Total − Error	.83	1.83
Rapid Naming Total-Time	191.67	219.83

symmetry rather than the specific deviation that contributes to dyslexia. For some of our subjects, the only brain morphological difference they possessed was that of the plana temporale. These subjects achieved lower scores compared to ability (while still in the average range) on phonological coding and naming tasks. It is important to emphasize that these lowered abilities did not significantly interfere with performance in areas of reading comprehension. Thus, it appears that the brain is far more resilient in its ability to compensate for developmental differences than was previously thought. It may also be that those subjects with differing asymmetry found other neurological connections to facilitate their reading performance. These questions are still to be resolved, and, as large-scale studies of normal brains have found, 30 percent of the population evidences such reversed asymmetry and yet appears to have had no history of reading problems. Thus, the question of what else is needed to produce dyslexia remains open.

Although MRI is quickly developing, it is only a static representation of the brain. New techniques such as spectroscopy are beginning to allow for the use of MRI and dynamic picturing of brain activity to be overlaid and perhaps shed further light on just what is happening in the dyslexic brain. At this point, no spectroscopy study has been completed on adults or children with dyslexia. This type of study plus studies done with three-dimensional MRI are just beginning to be utilized. Currently, dynamic studies of the brain have been limited to positron emission tomography and evoked potential/EEG studies. These areas will be discussed briefly below.

METABOLIC DIFFERENCES IN DYSLEXIA

Positron emission tomography (PET) scans require the use of a radioactive isotope. Therefore, PET scans are conducted using adult volunteers, and the following data are from adults. PET scans are used to evaluate metabolic activity during a cognitive task. It has been found that dyslexic adults differ from nondyslexics in the distribution of cerebral metabolic activity during a reading task (Gross-Glenn, Lewis, Smith, & Lubs, 1985). Metabolic activity was found to be bilaterally lower in the temporal regions (particularly the insula) and anterior regions in the dyslexics, with activation in the visual centers similar to that of the control subjects. Moreover, the dyslexic adults were found to use different cognitive strategies to solve reading problems than did adults without a history of reading difficulties (Olson, 1985, 1988).

Regional cerebral blood flow has further substantiated these findings. Flowers, Wood, and Naylor (1991) found increased activation of the posterior temporoparietal area for adults with a history of reading problems, whereas normal readers showed higher activation in the superior temporoparietal area (Wernicke's). They hypothesized inefficient neural processing in dyslexic brains, possibly as a result of structural displacement during cortical migration at approximately 5 to 7 months of gestation. Moreover, it is possible that poor readers have compensated for their inefficient neural connections through the development of other regions.

It has been demonstrated in cats (Hubel & Wiesel, 1959) that when connections are prevented from forming between areas that are normally linked, these connections will be established at alternative areas. These resulting connections may not be as well suited to the functions assigned them and therefore may show anomalous activation in dyslexics (Flowers et al., 1991). It may well be that cortical migration is disrupted for those with dyslexia in such a way that neural connections are formed that are anatomically deviant from those of normally developing brains. It can be speculated that familial dyslexia is due to disruption in the genetic blueprint for just such connections. Such hypotheses are exciting and are just beginning to be able to be tested empirically.

To provide an empirical test of the hypothesis of differential neural connectivity, Gross-Glenn et al. (1991) utilized PET scans with normal-reading adults and familial adult dyslexics. These subjects were asked to read high-frequency words. Only the normal controls showed left greater than right hemispheric values. In comparison, those with dyslexia showed symmetrical values. The metabolic pattern in the anterior regions was also found to be symmetrical for those with dyslexia and asymmetric (favoring the right anterior region) for the normal readers. Moreover, those with dyslexia were found to show increased activation of the pathway from the primary visual cortex to the temporal lobe compared to the normal controls, perhaps implicating inefficient word processing. Conclusions were that those with dyslexia have compensated for tasks usually subsumed in the superior temporal area through the use of complementary regions not normally associated with these type of tasks. Thus, these connections must not only work harder but also adjust to tasks not normally relegated to them.

If, in fact, there is inefficient processing of visual information in persons with dyslexia, possibly involving subcortical as well as anterior connections, then the ability to interpret visual symbols would be impaired. Behavioral data are consistent with this hypothesis. Those with dyslexia experience difficulty in reading simple nonsense words; find high-imagery words easier to read than low-imagery words (e.g., *in, the, is*); and have a tendency to make visual errors in reading (Guthrie, 1973; Jorm, 1977; Patterson & Marcel, 1977; Shallice & Warrington, 1975; Warrington, Logue, & Pratt, 1971). Evidence for a morphometric basis of difficulty with visual material comes from a study by Semrud-Clikeman (1990). When children with dyslexia were asked to name colors, letters, and numbers quickly, they made far more errors and required a longer time to complete the task compared to age-matched normal and clinic controls. In addition, their longer time for naming was related to a smaller left anterior width measure (see Figure 3-6). Thus, the dyslexic group as a whole evidenced poorer automatic naming skills, which were related to symmetrical anterior widths. It is noteworthy that the anterior region was found by Galaburda et al. (1985) to be at high risk for disordered cells and layers and by Hynd et al. (1990) and Duara et al. (1991) to be symmetrical in those with dyslexia.

The right prefrontal region has been hypothesized to be involved in sustained attention and receives inputs from visual and auditory association areas (Mesulam, 1985). Semrud-Clikeman et al. (1991) found deficient phonological coding and reading comprehension skills in those with dyslexia who had a smaller right anterior region. Given the frequent finding of visual inaccuracy in persons with dyslexia, it may well be that the difficulty in decoding nonsense words is related to visual information–processing problems, lack of attention to detail, and auditory-processing inefficiencies.

To investigate empirically the relationship between visual processing and dyslexia, Livingstone, Rosen, Drislane, and Galaburda (1991) recently published evoked potential results showing that those with dyslexia experience difficulty distinguishing between closely related visual signals. Livingstone et al. (1991) also evaluated autopsied brains of dyslexics and found differences at the magnocellular layer. The lateral geniculate is intimately involved with the visual system and the magnocellular portion of the lateral geniculate has been found to have a role in the interpretation of spatial orientation (Livingstone & Hubel, 1988). They concluded that persons with dyslexia may well show difficulty in interpreting visual information because of thalamic morphological differences. These findings coincide with the findings of Gross-Glenn et al. (1991) of disrupted activation of the visual cortex. There are rich connections between the visual system, the thalamus, and anterior regions of the brain (Mesulam, 1985). Therefore, it is reasonable to speculate that disruption of the subcortical pathways from the visual cortex to the corticothalamic pathway is implicated in dyslexia.

The foregoing section demonstrates the beginning efforts to relate brain structure to neurolinguistic functioning. Applications of such research are just beginning to be discussed. It is fruitful to relate such investigations not only to current functioning but also to possible changes in brain activity following interventions. The following section explores some of the possibilities these findings have for the development of educational and clinical interventions.

IMPLICATIONS OF BRAIN MORPHOLOGY RESEARCH FOR EDUCATIONAL INTERVENTIONS

The foregoing research has several implications for educators. A few precautions are necessary before examining these possibilities. First and foremost, the utility of these various measures needs much more development before a direct relevance to education is to be found. Second, the PET and regional cerebral blood flow data are generated from adults and so can only be used as suggestive as applied to children. Given these precautions, however, it is certainly appropriate to speculate as to what the future may bring and how it can be helpful to the educator, clinician, parent, and child.

The aforementioned studies and the data from the research of Semrud-Clikeman et al. (1991) and Larsen et al. (1990) suggest a relationship between anomalies in brain structures and deficits in reading skills. Reversed or symmetrical planum temporale was highly correlated with phonological deficits. It is important to note that both of these research teams found such deficits in normals and clinic controls who otherwise had normal reading functioning. Moreover, deficits were also found in the automatic naming of overlearned objects (colors, numbers, and letters), which was also highly correlated with smaller right anterior area for the dyslexic population only. Anterior width asymmetry was highly correlated with deficient performance on passage comprehension and anterior area asymmetry with poorer phonological coding skills.

These results point to the interaction of systems in the brain that contribute to the reading process. In addition, these systems appear to occur in deviant patterns and in more areas of the brain in children with dyslexia. The involvement of the anterior area in reading and attention found in evoked potential and PET research indicates a close tie between reading, attention, and efficient visual processing. Data are just beginning to suggest that there may be ineffectual connections between the visual and auditory systems in the thalamus to primary sensory areas and anterior regions. Thus, a breakdown may well be present not only in the metabolic activity but also in basic structural differences, which are laid down during gestation and are possibly due to genetic deviances in the case of those with familial dyslexia.

In the future, the use of MRI systems to understand dyslexia may also be a more culture-free way to identify children with dyslexia. At present there is no reason to believe that ethnicity would interact with brain structure. Current psychometric measures are heavily weighted with cultural information and thus may inappropriately identify those of various ethnicities as having dyslexia. Moreover, the use of MRI to compare various cultures eliminates the language barrier usually found between behavioral measures. Thus, it may well be possible to compare brain morphometry of persons with dyslexia in countries using pictorial systems (e.g., Japan) and those using Arabic systems (e.g., United States).

Most exciting is the possibility of using MRI to identify dyslexia in high-risk populations for early interventions. Although this situation is in the future if the MRI promise bears out, it will be helpful in identifying children of parents with dyslexia who are at high risk for developing reading difficulties and beginning interventions with them in infancy and toddlerhood. In this manner, early language and visual stimulation as well as social interaction could be taught to these parents and in order to give these children a head start on learning. If school was a difficult place for parents, it may be difficult for them to avail themselves of services. These early interventions may prompt these parents to use the services they deserve and to be an integral part of their child's program. Moreover, teachers appear interested in learning how children's brain structures may interact with their learning abilities. This type of understanding will allow teachers to put their considerable talents into developing programs that teach to children's strengths and help them learn compensatory tactics.

Finally, given the lack of side effects from the use of MRI, it may well be possible to study families with dyslexia and to determine empirically characteristics that are common in dyslexia across generations. At this point, we know little about the developing brain of a child with dyslexia, about how the brain differentially adapts to its environment, or whether there are longitudinal differences among childhood, adolescent, or adult brains of those with dyslexia. This type of study could compare the brains of those with dyslexia at various ages with the brains of normal-reading subjects. To our knowledge this study has yet to be conducted.

FUTURE DIRECTIONS

Exciting future developments in MRI technology are anticipated. The senior author is currently involved in a project that uses three-dimensional MRI to evaluate the full volume of brains. Various structures can now be measured in three dimensions, with less brain structure volume lost than when measures are made linearly. Rather than using a few thicker slices, three-dimensional MRI allows for measurement of thinner slices additively. Moreover, whole-brain and various structure-derived volume has been found to be closely concordant with the volume of postmortem fresh brains (Filipek et al., 1989).

We hope that the volumetric analysis of MRI can also allow for analysis of the shape of various structures (Filipek, et al. 1991). This advice will allow for structures such as the caudate, which may have the same volume whether it is spherical or football-shaped, to be analyzed according to shape as well as volume.

Another interesting development is the use of spectroscopy with MRI. This technique allows for the dynamic analysis of task performance coupled with the MRI overlay of brain structures. In other techniques (PET, rCBF, EEG), brain activity is analyzed and interpolated to the areas of various structures. The use of spectroscopy to view brain activity is an exciting advance. Currently this technique is experimental and has been applied only to adults. Now, however, some centers are beginning to develop protocols for children that utilize this method (Ronald Steingard, 1991, personal communication). In the future it may be possible to obtain baseline data, provide intensive intervention, and then remeasure the brain's activity to determine if changes in activation are present. Given theories presented by Gross-Glenn et al. (1991) that persons with dyslexia develop other routes for processing, it would be instructive not only to test this hypothesis, but also — if this indeed occurs — to determine how and where these alternative connections are made.

Finally MRI needs to be applied to various populations. Consistent with an article by Shaywitz, Shaywitz, Fletcher, and Escobar (1990) that found underidentification of females with reading delays, it appears appropriate to begin to study females. Comparisons with males as well as with normally developing females may help to determine whether a sex difference exists in the morphometric expression of dyslexia. Although Hynd et al. (1990) did not find a sex difference, their numbers were very small and not definitive. Moreover, the question of handedness has not been answered. Do left-handers with dyslexia differ from left-handed normal readers? Or do left-handed readers differ qualitatively from right-handed readers? Finally, do left-handers with dyslexia differ from right-handers with dyslexia? Some speculate that left-handed children with no history of familial left-handedness may have experienced early brain insult that changed their handedness (Satz, Orsini, Saslow, & Rolando, 1985). This hypothesis has yet to be tested morphologically.

Given the various subtypes of dyslexia, it may also be possible to compare the person with auditory/language dyslexia to the one with visual/perceptual dyslexia to the person with the mixed type to see if morphological differences are present. Are there differences in expression of dyslexia due to brain structure differences, and, if so, when would these pathoanatomic differences happen? Some researchers have also suggested that children with arithmetic disabilities but without reading disturbances represent a subset of children with learning disabilities due to different neurological wiring (see Semrud-Clikeman & Hynd, 1990).

It is important that these technological advances go hand in hand with

theoretical development about dyslexia. Unless the relation between brain structure and function is theoretically linked, morphometry may become similar to
phrenology in its place in history. With such a theoretical basis, however, the
etiology of dyslexia can be a fruitful and advantageous avenue of research and
concurrent development of interventions.

REFERENCES

Chi, J. G., Dooling, E. C., & Giles, F. H. (1977). Gyral development of the human
brain. *Annals of Neurology, 1,* 86–93.

Claiborne, J. H. (1906). Types of congenital symbol amblyopia. *Journal of the American
Medical Association, 47,* 1813–1816.

Damasio, H., & Damasio, A. R. (1989). *Lesion analysis in neuropsychology.* New York:
Oxford University Press.

Denckla, M. B., LeMay, M., & Chapman, C. A. (1985). Few CT scan abnormalities
found even in neurologically impaired learning disabled children. *Journal of Learning Disabilities, 18,* 132–135.

Duara, R., Kushch, A., Gross-Glenn, K., Barker, W. W., Jallad, B., Pascal, S., Loewens-
tein, D. A., Sheldon, J., Rabin, M., Levin, B., & Lubs, H. (1991). Neuroanatomic
differences between dyslexic and normal readers on magnetic resonance imaging
scans. *Archives of Neurology, 48,* 410–416.

Eidelberg, D., & Galaburda, A. M. (1984). Inferior parietal lobule: Divergent architec-
tonic asymmetries in the human brain. *Archives of Neurology, 41,* 843–852.

Filipek, P. A., Kennedy, D. N., & Caviness, V. S. (1991). Neuroimaging in child neuropsychology. In I. Rapin & S. Segalowitz (Eds.), *Child Neuropsychology* (Vol. 6,
pp. 200–263). Amsterdam: Elsevier.

Filipek, P. A., Kennedy, D. N., Caviness, V. S., Rossnick, S. L., Spraggins, T. A.,
& Starewicz, P. M. (1989). Magnetic resonance imaging–based brain morphometry:
development and application to normal subjects. *Annals of Neurology, 25,* 61–67.

Flowers, D. L., Wood, F. B., & Naylor, C. E. (1991). Regional cerebral blood flow
correlates of language processes in reading disability. *Archives of Neurology, 48,*
637–643.

Galaburda, A. M., Corsiglia, J., Rosen, G. D., & Sherman, G. F. (1987). Planum temporale asymmetry: Reappraisal since Geschwind and Levitsky. *Neuropsychologia,
25,* 853–868.

Galaburda, A. M., & Kemper, T. L. (1979). Cytoarchitectonic abnormalities in
developmental dyslexia: A case study. *Annals of Neurology, 6,* 94–100.

Galaburda, A. M., Rosen, G. D., & Sherman, G. F. (1991). Cerebrocortical asymmetry.
In A. Peters & E. G. Jones (Eds.), *Cerebral cortex: Normal and altered states of
function* (Vol. 9, pp. 263–277). New York: Plenum Press.

Galaburda, A. M., & Sanides, F. (1980). Cytoarchitectonic organization of the human
auditory cortex. *Journal of Comparative Neurology, 190,* 597–610.

Galaburda, A. M., Sherman, G. F., Rosen, G. D., Aboitiz, P., & Geschwind, N. (1985).
Developmental dyslexia: Four consecutive patients with cortical anomalies. *Annals
of Neurology, 18,* 222–233.

Geschwind, N. (1965). Disconnection syndromes in animals and man. *Brain, 88,* 237–294.

Geschwind, N. (1974). The development of the brain and the evolution of language. In N. Geschwind (Ed.), *Selected papers on language and the brain* (pp. 314–353). Dordrecht, The Netherlands: D. Reidel.

Geschwind, N., & Galaburda, A. M. (1985). Cerebral lateralization: Biological mechanisms, associations, and pathology: I. A hypothesis and program for research. *Archives of Neurology, 42,* 428–459.

Geschwind, N., & Levitsky, W. (1968). Human brain: Left–right asymmetries in temporal speech region. *Science, 161,* 186–187.

Golden, G. S. (1982). Neurobiological correlates of learning disabilities. *Annals of Neurology, 12,* 409–418.

Gross-Glenn, K., Duara, R., Barker, W. W., Lowenstein, D., Chang, Y. J., Apicella, A. M., Pascal, S., Boothe, T., Sevush, S., Jallad, B. J., Novoa, L., & Lubs, H. A. (1991). Positron emission tomographic studies during serial word-reading by normal and dyslexic adults. *Journal of Clinical and Experimental Neuropsychology, 13,* 531–544.

Gross-Glenn, K., Lewis, D. C., Smith, S. D., & Lubs, H. A. (1985). A phenotype of adult familial dyslexia: Reading of visually transformed texts and nonsense passages. *International Journal of Neuroscience, 28,* 49–59.

Guthrie, J. T. (1973). Reading comprehension and syntactic responses in good and poor readers. *Journal of Educational Psychology, 65,* 294–299.

Haslam, R. H., Dalby, J. R., Johns, R. D., & Rademaker, A. W. (1981). Cerebral asymmetry in developmental dyslexia. *Archives of Neurology, 38,* 679–682.

Herman, K. (1959). *Reading disability.* Copenhagen: Munkgaard.

Hier, D. B., LeMay, M., Rosenberger, P. B., & Perlo, V. P. (1978). Developmental dyslexia: Evidence for a subgroup with a reversal of cerebral asymmetry. *Archives of Neurology, 35,* 90–92.

Hubel, D. H., & Wiesel, T. N. (1959). Receptive fields of single neurons in the cat's striate cortex. *Journal of Physiology, 148,* 574–591.

Hynd, G. W., & Semrud-Clikeman, M. (1989). Dyslexia and brain morphology. *Psychological Bulletin, 106,* 447–482.

Hynd, G. W., Semrud-Clikeman, M., Lorys, A. R., Novey, E. S., & Eliopulos, D. (1990). Brain morphology in developmental dyslexia and attention deficit disorder/hyperactivity. *Archives of Neurology, 47,* 919–926.

Jernigan, T. L., Hesselink, J. R., Sowell, E., & Tallal, P. A. (1991). Cerebral structure on magnetic resonance imaging in language- and learning-impaired children. *Archives of Neurology, 48,* 539–545.

Jorm, A. F. (1977). Effect of word imagery on reading performance as a function of reader ability. *Journal of Educational Psychology, 69,* 46–54.

Jorm, A. F. (1979). The cognitive and neurological basis of developmental dyslexia: A theoretical framework and review. *Cognition, 7,* 19–33.

LaBerge, D., & Samuels, S. J. (1974). Toward a theory of automatic information processing in reading. *Cognitive Psychology, 6,* 293–323.

Larsen, J. P., Hoien, T., Lundberg, I., & Odegaard, H. (1990). MRI evaluation of the size and symmetry of the planum temporale in adolescents with developmental dyslexia. *Brain and Language, 39,* 289–301.

Leisman, G., & Ashkenazi, M. (1980). Aetiological factors in dyslexia: IV. Cerebral hemispheres are functionally equivalent. *Neuroscience, 11,* 157–164.

LeMay, M. (1976). Morphological cerebral asymmetries of modern man, fossil man, and nonhuman primates. *Annals of the New York Academy of Science, 280,* 349–366.

LeMay, M. (1981). Are there radiological changes in the brains of individuals with dyslexia? *Bulletin of the Orton Society, 31,* 135–141.

Livingstone, M., & Hubel, D. (1988). Segregation of form, color, movement, and depth: Anatomy, physiology, and perception. *Science, 240,* 740–749.

Livingstone, M., Rosen, G. D., Drislane, F. W., & Galaburda, A. M. (1991). Physiological and anatomical evidence for a magnocellular defect in developmental dyslexia. *Proceedings of the National Academy of Science, USA, 88,* 7943–7947.

Luria, A. R. (1980). *Higher cortical functions in man,* 2nd ed. New York: Basic Books.

Mesulam, M.-M. (1985). Patterns in behavioral neuroanatomy: Association areas, the limbic system and hemispheric specialization. In M.-M. Mesulam (Ed.), *Principles of behavioral neurology* (pp. 135–176). Philadelphia: F. A. Davis.

Newcombe, F., Phil, D., & Marshall, J. C. (1981). On psycholinguistic classifications of the acquired dyslexias. *Bulletin of the Orton Society, 31,* 29–46.

Olson, R. K. (1985). Disabled reading and cognitive profiles. In D. B. Gray & J. F. Kavanagh (Eds.), *Biobehavioral measures of dyslexia* (pp. 215–243). Parkton, MD: York Press.

Olson, R. K. (1988). Sources of heritable variance in adult dyslexia: A twin and family study. *Journal of Clinical and Experimental Neuropsychology, 10,* 65.

Parkins, R., Roberts, R. J., Reinarz, S. J., & Varney, N. R. (1987, January). *CT asymmetries in adult developmental dyslexics.* Paper presented at the annual convention of the International Neuropsychological Society, Washington, DC.

Patterson, K. E., & Marcel, A. J. (1977). Aphasia, dyslexia, and the phonological coding of written words. *Quarterly Journal of Experimental Psychology, 29,* 307–318.

Rosenberger, P. B., & Hier, D. B. (1980). Cerebral asymmetry and verbal intellectual deficits. *Annals of Neurology, 8,* 300–304.

Rubens, A. B., Mahuwold, M. W., & Hutton, J. T. (1976). Asymmetry of the lateral (sylvan) fissures in man. *Neurology, 26,* 620–624.

Rumsey, J. M., Dorwart, R., Vermess, M., Denckla, M. B., Kruesi, M. J. P., & Rapoport, J. (1986). Magnetic resonance imaging of brain anatomy in severe developmental dyslexia. *Archives of Neurology, 43,* 1045–1046.

Satz, P., Orsini, D. L., Saslow, E., & Rolando, H. (1985). The pathological left-handedness syndrome. *Brain and Cognition, 4,* 27–46.

Semrud-Clikeman, M. (1990). *Dyslexia and brain morphology: Contributions to disturbances in phonological coding, naming, and reading.* Unpublished dissertation, University of Georgia, Athens.

Semrud-Clikeman, M., & Hynd, G. W. (1990). Right hemispheric dysfunction in nonverbal learning disabilities: Social, academic, and adaptive functioning in adults and children. *Psychological Bulletin, 107,* 196–209.

Semrud-Clikeman, M., Hynd, G. W., Novey, E. S., & Eliopulos, D. (1991). Dyslexia and brain morphology: Relationships between neuroanatomical variation and neurolinguistic tasks. *Learning and Individual Differences, 3,* 225–242.

Shallice, T., & Warrington, E. K. (1975). Word recognition in a phonemic dyslexic patient. *Quarterly Journal of Experimental Psychology, 27,* 187–189.

Shaywitz, S. E., Shaywitz, B. A., Fletcher, J. M., & Escobar, M. D. (1990). Prevalence of reading disability in boys and girls: Results of the Connecticut Longitudinal Study. *Journal of the American Medical Association, 264,* 998–1002.

Sidman, R. L., & Rakic, P. (1973). Neuronal migration, with special reference to developing human brain: A review. *Brain Research, 62,* 1–35.

Taylor, H. G., & Fletcher, J. M. (1983). Biological foundations of "specific developmental disorders": Methods, findings, and future directions. *Journal of Clinical Child Psychology, 12,* 46–65.

Teszner, D., Tzavaras, A., Gruner, J., & Hecaen, H. (1972). L'Asymetrie droite–gauche du planum temporale: A propos de l'étude anatomique de 100 cerveaux. *Revue Neurological, 126,* 444–449.

Wada, J. A., Clarke, R., & Hamm, A. (1975). Cerebral hemispheric asymmetry in humans. *Archives of Neurology, 32,* 239–246.

Warrington, E. K., Logue, V., & Pratt, R. T. C. (1971). The anatomical localization of selective impairment of auditory verbal short-term memory. *Neuropsychologia, 9,* 377–387.

Weinberger, D. R., Luchins, D. J., & Morihisa, J., & Wyatt, D. (1982). Asymmetrical volumes of right and left frontal and occipital regions of the human brain. *Annals of Neurology, 11,* 97–100.

Witelson, S. F. (1983). Bumps on the brain: Right–left anatomic asymmetry as a key to functional lateralization. In S. J. Segalowitz (Ed.), *Language functions and brain organization* (pp. 117–144). New York: Academic Press.

Witelson, S. F., & Pallie, W. (1973). Left hemisphere specialization for language in the newborn: Neuroanatomical evidence of asymmetry. *Brain, 96,* 641–646.

Wyngaarden, J. E. (1987). *Learning disabilities: A report to the U.S. Congress.* Washington, DC: National Institutes of Health, Interagency Committee on Learning Disabilities.

▶ 4

Phonological Skills and the Prediction of Early Reading Problems

VIRGINIA MANN
University of California, Irvine

Abstract

This chapter views early reading problems from a language-oriented perspective, presenting evidence that phonological awareness and certain phonological processing skills are a key to understanding why poor readers become poor *readers*. A justification of this perspective is followed by a review of the language problems that distinguish poor readers from children who read well, and then by a presentation of the author's research on the language problems that predict reading problems. Final sections discuss some plausible origins and characterizations of the problems of poor readers, and a few remarks about methods of instruction that might be particularly effective

READING PROBLEMS AND LANGUAGE PROBLEMS

Within this century, psychologists, educators, and medical doctors have all been baffled by the problem of "unexpected" reading problems. In fact, the

Much of the research herein described was funded by NICHD Grant HD-01994 and BRS Grant 05596 to Haskins Laboratories, Inc. Many of the same points were made in two technical papers, Mann (1986) and Mann and Brady (1988) and in Mann (1991). The data and methodology are described more fully in Mann (1993).

67

"unexpected" aspect of the problem is at the core of the definition of dyslexia. Of the many who have tried to explain dyslexia, most, like the blind men with the elephant, have been guided by a premature assumption of one sort or another. For example, some researchers assumed that poor readers were "dumber" than other children and that reading problems were due to a lack of intelligence. A low IQ canot be the sole basis of reading problems, however, because some children are deficient in reading ability but average in intelligence (Rutter & Yule, 1973). Also, poor readers can perform as well as good readers on certain intellectual tasks (for reviews, see Mann, in press; Stanovich, 1982a, 1982b; Vellutino, 1979). Another example comes from researchers who assumed that poor readers were less able to make "cross-modal" integration of sound and sight (Birch & Belmont, 1964; see reviews by Benton, 1975; Rutter & Yule, 1973). Here, more careful examinations of children's behavior showed that, when visual–auditory integration problems were present, so were auditory–auditory ones and visual–visual ones. Ultimately, the poor readers' problems with visual–auditory integration came to be viewed as one of the many consequences of a more general linguistic coding problem that hurts integration within modalities as well as between them (see Vellutino, 1979, for a review.)

Perhaps the best theory of dyslexia assumed that reading is first and foremost a complex visual skill that demands differentiation and recognition of the letter forms. This perspective led researchers to blame early reading difficulty on some problem in the visual domain, such as reversals of sequence and form. Yet much research has shown that visual skills do not reliably distinguish between children who differ in reading ability (see Rutter, 1978; Stanovich, 1982a; and Vellutino, 1979, for reviews). Although it is true that all young children tend to confuse spatially reversible letters such as *b, d, p,* and *q* until they are 7 or 8 years old (Gibson, Gibson, Pick, & Osser, 1962), letter and sequence reversals actually account for only a small proportion of the reading errors that children make—even children who have been formally diagnosed as dyslexic (Fisher, Liberman, & Shankweiler, 1977). Also, kindergartners identified as having deficient visual perception and/or visuomotor coordination skills show no more instances of reading difficulty at age 8 to 9 than do matched controls who possess no such deficits (Robinson & Schwartz, 1973). All in all, visual problems would not seem to be a primary causé of many instances of reading problems.

Any successful account of reading disability must explain the paradox that poor readers equal good readers on some tasks yet perform poorly on others. In the next several pages I hope to show that certain language skills are the key to understanding what poor readers can and cannot do. They are also a key to predicting which children will encounter reading problems. That language problems and reading problems should be related follows from certain evidence about how reading depends on spoken language. A brief review of this evidence will be the starting point of this chapter.

WHY SPOKEN LANGUAGE IS SO CRUCIAL TO READERS

Reading involves the processes of perceiving, recognizing, remembering, and interpreting the various letter shapes and the words and sentences that they form. Although we should consider certain aspects of these processes as "visual," others are clearly "linguistic" in that writing systems write *language.*

One linguistic aspect of the reading process involves the linguistic units that the writing system represents. An awareness of these units will be an important key to decoding the relation between a grapheme, word, or character and its spoken language counterparts (for discussion, see Hung & Tzeng, 1981; Liberman, Liberman, Mattingly, & Shankweiler, 1980). Alphabets represent phonemes, the small, meaningless linguistic units that distinguish the words *cat* and *cap,* and make *pin* a longer word than *in.* Alphabets have the advantage of being economical, rule-governed, and highly productive (for further discussion, see Liberman et al., 1980; Mann, 1991). Nonetheless, they pose an obstacle because they cannot be used effectively unless one is sensitive to the fact that words can be broken down into phonemes. This sensitivity, termed *phoneme awareness,*[1] is not required for the normal activities of speaking and hearing, although it can play a role in certain secondary language activities such as appreciating verse (e.g., alliteration), making jokes (e.g., "Where do you leave your dog?" "In a barking lot."), talking in secret languages (e.g., Pig Latin) — and reading an alphabetic orthography such as the English writing system.

A second linguistic aspect of reading involves the use of language-processing skills to recover the message conveyed by sentences and paragraphs. The question of whether or not written words must be recorded into some type of silent speech has been a topic in much of the research on the psychology of skilled reading. One could debate the role of speech or phonetic recoding in individual word recognition, but from the point of word perception onward, reading is quite parasitic on phonetic representation. In part, this is because skilled readers rely on a temporary or short-term memory that holds printed material in a phonetic representation. Studies of memory show that this type of representation is used whether the reader is remembering isolated letters, printed nonsense syllables or printed words. Both the nature of the errors, and the experimental manipulations that help or hurt memory performance have shown that readers remember a sequence of letters in terms of the letter names, rather than the visual shape of the letters and the same goes for a sequence of written words and even the words of a sentence (cf., e.g., Baddeley, 1978; Conrad, 1964, 1972; Levy, 1977). Research has further shown that the comprehension of written sentences and paragraphs requires readers to rely on phonetic representation in short-term memory. This is true not only for alphabetic writing systems (Kleiman, 1975; Levy, 1977; Slowiaczek & Clifton, 1980), but for logographic ones as well (Tzeng, Hung, & Wang, 1977).

Thus we may point to two linguistic aspects of reading, the requirement of phoneme awareness and the requirement of certain language-processing skills. Realization of this fact offers a perspective on the language skills that children must have if they are to learn to read: If children are to make any real sense of the way in which the alphabet works, they will need to achieve phoneme awareness; if they are to understand what they read — and if they are to perceive and understand the teacher's spoken language instructions — they will also need certain language-processing skills. It also raises the possibility that a problem with one or both of these language skills could be a cause of reading problems.

THE LANGUAGE PROBLEMS ASSOCIATED WITH READING PROBLEMS

Since the mid-1970s, there have been considerable discoveries about the associates of early reading problems and study after study has demonstrated that good and poor readers are distinguished by their performance on linguistic tasks. It has also been shown that good and poor readers who differ in language skills do not necessarily differ in performance on comparably demanding non-linguistic skills (as shown by Brady, Shankweiler, & Mann, 1983; Katz, Shankweiler, & Liberman, 1981; Liberman, Mann, Shankweiler, & Werfelman, 1982; Swanson, 1978). For example, poor readers are just as able as good readers to see the visually based similarities between two objects, but they cannot as readily see the phoneme-based similarities between two words (e.g., Mann, Tobin, & Wilson, 1987); they can remember as many faces or nonsense drawings as good readers, but not as many spoken words (e.g., Liberman et al., 1982). Considered broadly, the problems of poor readers tend to be language problems and to fall within the two categories of phoneme awareness and language processing. A brief survey of the literature will support this point.

Oral reading errors are among the most important sources of evidence about the problems of poor readers. Analysis of these errors shows that, rather than reversing letters and sequences, all children, including those with dyslexia, do something else. They tend to mispronounce the middle and final letters of a word and to have more difficulty with vowels than with consonants. Those who have considered this pattern have argued that a lack of phoneme awareness is responsible. For more detailed presentation of this point, the reader is referred to papers by Shankweiler and Liberman (1972) and Fisher et al. (1977).

Further confirmation about the link between deficient phoneme awareness and reading problems has come from tasks that measure phoneme awareness directly. These tasks require children to play language games that manipulate phonemes in one way or another: counting them, deleting them, choosing words that contain the same phoneme, and so on. The use of these tasks in numerous experiments involving widely diverse subjects, school systems, and measurement devices has revealed that phoneme awareness develops later than either phoneme perception or the use of phonetic representation, and can be a chronic problem for those individuals who are poor readers (see, e.g., Alegria, Pignot, & Morais, 1982; Fox & Routh, 1976; Liberman et al., 1980; Perfetti, 1985; Yopp, 1988). Yet this same body of research shows that poor readers can perform just as well as good readers when they are asked to count the visual aspects of a drawing, delete a note from a sequence of tones, and so on (see Mann, 1986; Morais, Cluytens, & Alegria, 1984).

Complementing the research on phoneme awareness is a growing body of evidence that language-processing problems are also associated with reading problems. That evidence comes from a variety of studies whose techniques range from speech perception to spoken sentence comprehension. For example, a study of speech perception by Brady et al. (1983) indicated that poor readers made almost 33 percent more errors than good readers when they were they asked to identify spoken words under a "noisy" listening condition. Yet these same poor readers were just as accurate as the good readers when asked to identify environmental sounds heard under "noisy" conditions. There are also some indications that reading problems are related to spoken vocabulary and to "naming" or "productive vocabulary" problems in particular (see, e.g., Katz, 1986; Denckla & Rudel, 1976). Recognition vocabulary has been related to early reading comprehension ability (see Stanovich, Cunningham, & Feeman, 1984) but not always to decoding ability (see Mann, 1991).

One of the best researched problems of poor readers concerns their use of phonetic representation in short-term memory. It has often been noted that poor readers tend to perform less well on the digit span test and are deficient in the ability to recall strings of letters, nonsense syllables, or words in order. This is true whether the stimuli are read silently or heard aloud. Yet poor readers can do just as well as good readers when they are asked to remember a set of faces, a series of nonsense doodle drawings, or a block design (see Jorm, 1979; Mann & Brady, 1988; and Mann, Liberman, & Shankweiler, 1980, for references to these effects). Liberman, Shankweiler, and their colleagues (Shankweiler, Liberman, Mark, Fowler, & Fisher, 1979) were the first to note that the short-term memory difficulties of poor readers were unique to linguistic material, and it was their hypothesis that the problem involved use of phonetic representation in working memory. Several experiments have now supported this hypothesis, using the same analyses of error patterns and manipulations that first illuminated the use of phonetic representation by adult readers (e.g., Brady et al., 1983; Byrne & Shea, 1979; Mann et al., 1980; Mann & Liberman, 1984; Shankweiler et al., 1979).

Aside from their problems with recalling strings of letters and nonsense syllables, poor readers also fail to recall the words of spoken sentences as accurately as good readers do. This particular observation has provoked questions about whether they have problems with sentence comprehension and such "higher level" language skills as the understanding of syntax (i.e., grammar). It has now been shown that poor readers do, in fact, have comprehension problems, but only for certain types of sentences (see Mann, Cowin, & Schoenheimer, 1989, for a review). They have problems with spoken sentences that contain relative clauses such as "The dog jumped over the cat that chased the monkey" (Mann, Shankweiler, & Smith, 1985) and with some of the longer instructions from the "Token Test" (Spellacy & Spreen, 1969) such as "Touch the small red square and the large blue triangle" (Smith, Mann, & Shankweiler, 1986). They also are less able to distinguish between the meanings of spoken sentences like "He showed her bird the seed" and "He showed her the birdseed" that use the stress pattern of the sentence (its prosody) and the position of the article *the* to mark the boundary between the indirect object and the direct object. The search to explain these and other sentence comprehension problems has yielded little evidence that poor readers have trouble with the syntactic structures being used in the sentences. Instead, the evidence suggests that the problems are due to a bottleneck in short-term memory. It seems that poor readers are just as sensitive to syntactic structure as good readers; they fail to understand sentences because they are less able to hold the sentence in working memory (for discussion, see Mann et al., 1985; Mann et al., 1989; Shankweiler & Crain, 1986).

LANGUAGE PROBLEMS AS PREDICTORS OF READING PROBLEMS

Having reviewed some of the differences between good and poor readers, which can be characterized in terms of deficient phoneme awareness and language-processing problems on the part of poor readers, let me now turn to the matter of predicting reading problems. There are both theoretical and practical issues when we ask whether language problems predict reading problems. Not only may we establish the direction of causality, we may also learn about the hallmarks of children at risk. In this section I will focus on various tests that my colleagues and I have been using to assess phonological skills in young children.

The relation between deficient phoneme awareness and future reading problems has been the most intensely researched topic in this area. Liberman and her colleagues were among the first to show that phoneme segmentation had some power to presage first-grade reading ability, offering evidence from a longitudinal follow-up of kindergarten children who performed a phoneme counting game (reported in Liberman, Shankweiler, Fisher, & Carter, 1974). Since that time many researchers have confirmed that individual differences in phoneme awareness are a hallmark of future differences in reading ability. Even when we recognize that the experience of learning to read can promote children's awareness of phonemes, we still find that phoneme awareness can presage future reading ability.

My own research on the importance of phoneme awareness as a predictor of reading ability involves several longitudinal studies of kindergarten and first-grade children. The first of these (Mann & Liberman, 1984) concerned a series of linguistic and nonlinguistic tests that were given to group of kindergartners unable to read at the time of testing (December of the kindergarten year). One of the linguistic tests was a phoneme awareness test that asked the child to reverse phonemes (i.e., "How do you say *mo* backwards?" *"Om."*), and it proved a significant predictor of first-grade reading ability. At about the same time, research by other experimenters showed that a kindergarten battery of individually administered tests that assessed phoneme awareness accounted for 66 percent of the variance in children's first-grade reading ability (Stanovich, Cunningham, & Cramer, 1984).

More recently, I have been working to develop other tests of phoneme awareness that can be administered to a small group of children instead of one on one. One of these tests is a phoneme segmentation task that requires a child to decide which of four pictures starts with a different sound. It was inspired by some of the research of Stanovich, Cunningham, and Cramer (1984a), who tested phoneme awareness by presenting a child with four words and asking him or her to repeat the word that started with a different sound. It was my intent to reduce the memory load of the task—since we know that short-term memory can pose a problem for some poor readers—by having pictures accompany the words. This also permitted group testing, because children could silently mark the picture instead of repeating the word. Thus far, the results are quite promising. In my first study, correlations between kindergarten scores and various measures of first-grade reading ability were as high as $r = .65$. Some of the data from that study are summarized in Table 4-1, which compares the average percentage of correct responses made by kindergartners who became poor readers with that of those who became good readers.

Table 4-1 contains a partial summary of the data from my most recent study of a group of 100 public school pupils (for presentation of the complete data base, see Mann, 1993). The table compares the kindergarten performance of 21 poor readers and 24 good readers who were identified by their teachers' ratings at the end of the first grade (using a four-point scale). It is interesting to note that, on the Metropolitan Achievement Test, all of the good readers had fallen within the top 90 percent and all of the poor readers had fallen within the bottom 50 percent of the standard distribution. The scores are from a battery of four tests that was given at the end of kindergarten. (Because the raw test values vary in magnitude, scores appear in terms of the percentage of the maximum possible value.) A series of *t*-tests indicate that good and poor readers differed significantly on the three language tests (the phoneme segmentation test, the invented spelling test, and the sentence comprehension test) but not on the Beery-Buktenica test (graphomotor skills).

The second test of phoneme awareness that I have been developing is an

TABLE 4-1 **Predictors of Reading Ability: Scores Obtained by Kindergarten Children Grouped According to Their First-Grade Teachers' Ratings**

	First Graders Whom Teachers Rate as:	
	The Worst Readers in Class (*N* = 21)	The Best Readers in Class (*N* = 24)
In Kindergarten, Averaged		
Phoneme segmentation	52%	95%
Invented spelling	23%	57%
Beery-Buktenica	72%	79%
Sentence comprehension	69%	83%

invented spelling test. As Charles Read (1986) first noted, preschoolers often "invent" spellings in their first attempts to write words, and although their spellings may not follow the conventional orthography, they do exhibit certain regularities that reflect knowledge of letter names and sounds and an ability to analyze the phonological structure of words (see Mann, Tobin, & Wilson, 1987, for a review and further discussion). Using a system for scoring the phonetic accuracy of invented spellings, Isabelle Liberman and I have each shown that differences in invented spelling relate to differences in phoneme awareness (Liberman et al., 1985; Mann, Tobin, & Wilson, 1987; Mann & Balise, in press). My students and I have also shown that differences in the phonetic accuracy of invented spellings are not readily ascribed to differences in IQ, visual perception, or graphomotor ability. Most important, we have shown that the invented spelling scores achieved by kindergarten children are very effective predictors of first-grade reading ability, with correlations as high as .70 (Mann et al., 1987; Mann & Ditunno, 1990; Mann & Balise, in press). Some scores on this test appear in Table 4-1, and they indicate that the good readers surpassed the poor readers in kindergarten ability to give phonetically accurate spellings. On the Beery-Buktenica test, the future good and poor readers were quite similar in graphomotor ability.

Although phoneme awareness has been the most widely studied predictor of reading, there is also a growing body of evidence about the predictive power of linguistic-processing skills. My first research on this topic was conducted in collaboration with Isabelle Liberman in a study that examined kindergarten children's ability to repeat sequences of words as a measure of their linguistic short-term memory (Mann & Liberman, 1984). We also studied nonlinguistic short-term memory and IQ, and we assessed phonological awareness by way of a test of syllable awareness. Our results successfully established that the measure of linguistic short-term memory could predict future reading ability, considerably more so than IQ or nonlinguistic short-term memory. We also uncovered a relationship between syllable segmentation and linguistic short-term memory and some evidence that each of these language skills makes a unique contribution to future reading ability. Two subsequent studies have confirmed these results (Mann, 1984; Mann & Ditunno, 1990).

About the same time I also began to consider the relation between sentence comprehension problems and future reading problems. My first study on this topic yielded a null result, most likely because it used passive sentences that were not very demanding (Mann, 1984). More recently, I have been working on a new test of sentence comprehension which presents two of the types of sentences that have distinguished good and poor readers (relative clause constructions from Mann et al., 1985, and double-object constructions from Mann et al., 1989). In this test, which also appears in Table 4-1, children listen to a sentence and choose which of four pictures illustrates its meaning. We are finding that this test predicts future reading ability with correlations as high as $r = .5$. The future good readers chose the correct picture more often than the future poor readers did.

Short-term memory and sentence comprehension have been the primary concern of my research into the relation between language-processing problems and future reading problems. However, my students and I have sometimes included a test of letter-naming ability in the battery of tests we give to kindergarten children (Mann, 1984; Mann & Ditunno, 1990). We have consistently found that kindergartners who take longer to name a randomized array of the capital letters are significantly more likely to become poor readers in first grade. We have also shown that present letter-naming ability in kindergarten predicts reading ability in first grade far more consistently than kindergarten reading ability predicts first-grade letter-naming ability (for relevant evidence, see Mann & Ditunno, 1990; also see Stanovich, Nathan, & Zolman, 1988). These results are in agreement with other indications that naming ability (i.e., productive vocabulary) is an effective predictor. For example, performance on the Boston Naming Test (a measure of word retrieval skill) has been found to be a significant predictor of both the word recognition and the reading comprehension ability tht kindergarten children will achieve in first grade (see Wolf, 1984; Wolf & Goodglass, 1986).

All in all, there do appear to be certain hallmarks of future reading problems: deficient phonological awareness and deficient phonological processing skills. Measures of phonological awareness and certain measures of language-processing ability have predicted future reading ability to a greater and more consistent degree than have IQ tests, tests of visual perception, nonverbal memory, and the like. Other reviews of this body of research are offered by

Stanovich, Cunningham, and Cramer (1984), by Wagner et al. (1987), by Wagner and Torgesen (1987), as well as in Mann and Brady (1988), and in articles by Bradley and Bradley (1991) and by Lundberg (1991).

SOME PLAUSIBLE ORIGINS OF THE LANGUAGE PROBLEMS THAT LEAD TO READING PROBLEMS

Having made the point that deficiencies in phoneme awareness and in certain language-processing skills both associate with and predict reading problems, let me now turn to some speculations about the origins of those deficiencies. In principle, the deficiencies could be based in the classroom or home environment, brain structure, genetic makeup, or rate of physical development. Most likely they represent an interaction of complex factors.

There is a wealth of evidence about the role of the environment — the educational environment — in the development of phoneme awareness. This evidence informs us that not only may phoneme awareness be important for the acquisition of reading, being taught to read may help to develop phoneme awareness (see, e.g., Alegria, Pignot, & Morais, 1982; Liberman, Liberman, Mattingly, & Shankweiler, 1980; Morais, Cary, Alegria, & Bertelson, 1979). It would seem that awareness of phonemes is particularly enhanced by methods of reading instruction that direct the child's attention to the phonetic structure of words (Alegria et al., 1982).

However, inadequate experience cannot be the only factor behind some children's failure to achieve phoneme awareness. This is aptly shown by a comparison between a group of 6-year-old skilled readers and a group of 10-year-old disabled readers who were matched for reading ability. The disabled readers performed significantly worse on a phoneme awareness task, even though they would be expected to have had more reading instruction than the younger children (Bradley & Bryant, 1978). Here it could be argued that some intrinsic factor limited the disabled readers' ability to profit from instruction, and thus limited their attainment of phonological sophistication. Indeed, Pennington and his colleagues (Pennington, Van Orden, Kirson, & Haith, 1991) have offered some new and interesting evidence that deficient phoneme awareness is the primary trait of individuals with "familial" dyslexia.

That reading problems and language problems do tend to run in certain families was first noted by Thomas (1905) and has received considerable attention in recent literature as well (see, for example, Owen, 1978; Owen, Adams, Forrest, Stolz, & Fischer, 1971; Rutter, 1978). In fact, whether or not a child comes from a family including other individuals with dyslexia is one of the most important factors to consider when attempting to predict that child's likelihood of becoming a poor reader (see Scarborough, 1988). Further evidence about genetically based dyslexia has become available through the use of linkage analysis (see DeFries, Fulker, & LaBuda, 1987; Smith, Kimberling, Pennington, & Lubs, 1983).

Neuropsychological accounts of dyslexia have been historically popular and continue to be so. These attempt to place the cause of the problem within the brain structure of the affected child. One of the first neuropsychological accounts was offered by Orton (1937) in his now famous theory of "strephosymbolia" and incomplete hemispheric dominance. All in all, the data on hemispheric dominance are not particularly supportive of Orton's thesis (see Fennell, Satz, & Morris, 19083; McKeever & van Deventer, 1975; Rutter, 1978). Yet, Orton may still have been correct in the spirit, if not the letter, of this explanation; the cerebral hemispheres may hold an answer. Given that the left hemisphere is the mediator of language processing in the majority of individuals, we might suppose that poor readers have some anatomical or neurochemical abnormality within that hemisphere. This is the position taken in a theory by Geschwind and Galaburda (1987) that views developmental dyslexia as a consequence of slowed development of the left hemisphere due to prenatal exposure/sensitivity to testosterone.

Another, somewhat related explanation is prompted by the observation that poor readers' language abilities are not so much deviant as delayed relative to those of good readers. This raises the possibility of a maturational lag in development (Fletcher, Satz, & Scholes, 1981) that may be specific to language development (Mann & Liberman, 1984), especially in the case of children with dyslexia (Stanovich, 1988). Maturational lag has been offered to explain the poor readers' word-decoding problems (Stanovich, 1988), their speech perception difficulties (Brandt & Rosen, 1980), their problems with phonetic representation in temporary memory and phonological awareness (Mann & Liberman, 1984), and their sentence comprehension problems (Mann et al., 1989). Such theories also provide an interesting account of adolescent learning disability (Wong, Wong, & Blenkinsop, 1989). The primary difficulty with the concept of maturational lag is that it is not yet able to explain why the language difficulties of poor readers tend to be predominantly phonological. Perhaps we might want to conceive of a maturational lag that is confined to phonological skills. We might also want to recognize that the language-processing skills of poor readers may never really catch up to those of good readers (Russell, 1982; Scarborough, 1984).

SUMMARY AND CONCLUDING REMARKS

This chapter has proceeded from a consideration of the linguistic aspects of reading, to a survey of evidence that good and poor readers differ in certain language skills, to evidence that problems with these same skills can actually predict future reading problems, and finally to a consideration of some origins of these problems. Poor readers—and children who are likely to become poor readers—tend to have problems with phoneme awareness and also with certain language-processing skills. As a concluding comment, let me now point out the common trait that exists among the language problems associated with reading problems. All of them somehow involve the sound pattern of language, its phonological structure. Accordingly, we may speculate that the cause of many instances of reading disability is some problem within the phonological system (Mann, 1986), something that has been referred to as a phonological core deficit (Stanovich, 1988).

In the future we might hope to achieve an increasingly accurate description of the phonological core deficit and its role in the reading problems of various children. Phonological problems seem to be a common trait of both garden-variety poor readers and so-called dyslexic children (see Stanovich, 1988); yet there could be different clusters of problems for different types of poor readers. For example, Pennington and his colleagues have noted that the language problems of adults from families with dyslexia in their members tend to be restricted to phoneme awareness, whereas those of individuals from "nondyslexic" families demonstrate problems with linguistic short-term memory as well as problems with phoneme awareness (Pennington et al., 1991).

As we come closer and closer to understanding the phonological problems associated with reading problems, we might also aspire to develop more effective procedures for remediation of those problems—if not prevention altogether. For example, if a maturational lag in language development is the cause of reading difficulty, we should identify children at risk for such a lag. Research could then be conducted to determine whether delaying beginning reading instruction is advantageous. But such research should bear in mind the paradox of what poor readers can and cannot do. It should also bear in mind the option of remediation as opposed to retention.

Certainly the brightest prospects for remediation are offered by research showing that various types of training can facilitate phoneme awareness. Some very interesting and very practical advice is available on how to facilitate phoneme awareness and have it promote reading (Bradley & Bryant, 1985; Goswami & Bryant, 1990; Liberman, 1982; Liberman, Shankweiler, Blachman, Camp, & Werfelman, 1980). Let me conclude this chapter by mentioning some of the research of Blachman and her colleagues and of Cunningham.

Blachman and her colleagues have been developing some very clever ways of promoting phoneme awareness. For a presentation of this work, see Blachman (1984, 1989). Teachers of preschool children as young as age 3 will find that Blachman makes some interesting observations about how word play with nursery rhymes can help to promote phoneme awareness. Kindergarten and first-grade teachers and reading specialists will be interested in the variety of tasks that Blachman is using to promote phoneme awareness and ultimately link it to reading. One that I find particularly appealing is a progressive series of "say-it-and-move-it" segmentation activities. In this series, the children learn to use disks to represent each of the phonemes in a word and ultimately learn to connect the sound segments represented by the disks to the letters of the alphabet.

That we should pay attention not only to the activities but also to the type of instruction that we use is the very important point made by Cunningham and illustrated in one of her most recent studies (Cunningham, 1990). In her view, activities that encourage phoneme awareness will be the most beneficial to reading when the children learn *how* these activities are beneficial to reading. The validity of this view is illustrated with a study in which Cunningham compared two groups of kindergarten and first-grade children who were taught phoneme segmentation and blending tasks. Relative to children who did not learn such tasks, the children who received a "skill-and-drill" approach to learning had some advantage in learning to read. However, the greatest advantage was seen when children received a method of instruction that helped them to appreciate the value, application, and utility of phoneme awareness in reading.

NOTE

1. The term *phoneme awareness* has been used interchangeably with several other terms — *phonological awareness, metalinguistic awareness,* and *linguistic awareness,* to name a few. As I confined myself to sensitivity about phonemes, I have used the term *phoneme awareness* throughout this chapter. Some other authors use *phonemic awareness* in an equivalent manner — for example, Cunningham (1990).

REFERENCES

Alegria, J., Pignot, E., & Morais, J. (1982). Phonetic analysis of speech and memory codes in beginning readers. *Memory and Cognition, 10,* 451–456.

Baddeley, A. D. (1978). The trouble with levels: A reexamination of Craik and Lockhardt's framework for memory research. *Psychological Review, 85,* 139–152.

Benton, A. (1975). Developmental dyslexia: neurological aspects. In W. J. Freelander (Ed.), *Advances in neurology* (Vol. 7, pp. 1–47). New York: Raven Press.

Birch, H. G., & Belmont, L. (1964). Auditory–visual integration in normal and retarded readers. *American Journal of Orthopsychiatry, 34,* 825–861.

Blachman, B. (1984). Relationship of rapid naming and language analysis skills to kindergarten and first-grade reading achievement. *Journal of Educational Psychology, 76,* 610–622.

Blachman, B. (1989). Phonological awareness and word recognition: Assessment and intervention. In A. G. Kamhi & H. W. Watts (Eds.), *Reading disabilities: A developmental language perspective* (pp. 133–158). Boston: College Hill.

Bradley, L., & Bradley, P. (1991). Phonological skills before and after learning to read.

In S. Brady & D. Shankweiler (Eds.), *Phonological processes in literacy* (pp. 37–45). Hillsdale, NJ: Erlbaum.

Bradley, L., & Bryant, P. E. (1978). Difficulties in auditory organization as a possible cause of reading backwards. *Nature, 271,* 746–747.

Bradley, L., & Bryant, P. (1985). *Rhyme and reason in reading and spelling.* Ann Arbor: University of Michigan Press.

Brady, S., Shankweiler, D., & Mann, V. (1983). Speech perception and memory coding in relation to reading ability. *Journal of Experimental Child Psychology, 35,* 345–367.

Brandt, J., & Rosen, J. J. (1980). Auditory phonemic perception in dyslexia: Categorical identification and discrimination of stop consonants. *Brain and Language, 9,* 324–337.

Byrne, B., & Shea, P. (1979). Semantic and phonetic memory in beginning readers. *Memory and Cognition, 7,* 333–338.

Conrad, R. (1964). Acoustic confusions in immediate memory. *British Journal of Psychology, 55,* 75–84.

Conrad, R. (1972). Speech and reading. In J. F. Kavanaugh & I. G. Mattingly (Eds.), *Language by ear and by eye: The relationships between speech and reading.* Cambridge, MA: MIT Press.

Cunningham, A. E. (1990). Explicit versus implicit instruction in phonemic awareness. *Journal of Experimental Child Psychology, 50,* 429–444.

DeFries, J. C., Fulker, D. W., & LaBuda, M. C. (1987). Evidence for a genetic etiology in reading disability of twins. *Nature, 329,* 537–539.

Denckla, M. B., & Rudel, R. G. (1976). Naming of object drawings by dyslexic and other learning-disabled children. *Brain and Language, 3,* 1–15.

Fennell, E. B., Satz, P., & Morris, R. (1983). The development of handedness and dichotic ear assymetries in relation to school achievement: A longitudinal study. *Journal of Experimental Child Psychology, 35,* 248–262.

Fisher, F. W., Liberman, I. Y., & Shankweiler, D. (1977). Reading reversals and developmental dyslexia: A further study. *Cortex, 14,* 496–510.

Fletcher, J. M., Satz, P., & Scholes, R. (1981). Developmental changes in the linguistic performance correlates of reading achievements. *Brain and Language, 13,* 78–90.

Fox, B., & Routh, D. K. (1976). Phonemic analysis and synthesis as word-attack skills. *Journal of Educational Psychology, 69,* 70–74.

Geschwind, N., & Galaburda, A. M. (1987). *Cerebral lateralization.* Cambridge, MA: Bradford Books.

Gibson, E. J., Gibson, J. J., Pick, A. D., & Osser, R. (1962). A developmental study of the discrimination of letter-like forms. *Journal of Comparative and Physiological Psychology, 55,* 897–906.

Goswami, U., & Bryant, P. (1990). *Phonological skills and learning to read.* East Sussex: Lawrence Erlbaum Associates Ltd.

Hung, D. L., & Tzeng, O. J. L. (1981). Orthographic variations and visual information processing. *Psychological Bulletin, 90,* 377–414.

Jorm, A. F. (1979). The cognitive and neurological basis of developmental dyslexia: A theoretical framework and review. *Cognition, 7,* 19–33.

Katz, R. B. (1986). Phonological deficiencies in children with reading disability: Evidence from an object naming task. *Cognition, 22,* 225–257.

Katz, R. B., Shankweiler, D., & Liberman, I. Y. (1981). Memory for item order and

and phonetic recoding in the beginning reader. *Journal of Experimental child Psychology, 32,* 474-484.

Kleiman, G. (1975). Speech recoding in reading. *Journal of Verbal Learning and Verbal Behavior, 14,* 323-339.

Levy, B. A. (1977). Reading: Speech and meaning processes. *Journal of Verbal Learning and Verbal Behavior, 16,* 623-638.

Liberman, I. Y. (1982). A language-oriented view of reading and its disabilities. In H. Mykelburst (Ed.), *Progress in learning disabilities* (Vol. 5). New York: Grune and Stratton.

Liberman, I. Y., Liberman, A. M., Mattingly, I. G., & Shankweiler, D. (1980). Orthography and the beginning reader. In J. Kavanaugh & R. Venezky (Eds.), *Orthography, reading and dyslexia* (pp. 137-154). Baltimore: University Park Press.

Liberman, I. Y., Mann, V. A., Shankweiler, D., & Werfelman, M. (1982). Children's memory for recurring linguistic and non-linguistic material in relation to reading ability. *Cortex, 18,* 367-375.

Liberman, I. Y., Rubin, H., Duquès. S., & Carlisle, J. (1985). Linguistic abilities and spelling proficiency in kindergarten and adult poor spellers. in D. B. Gray and J. F. Kavanagh (Eds.), *Biobehavioral measures of dyslexia* (pp. 163-176). Parkton, MD: York Press.

Liberman, I. Y., Shankweiler, D., Blachman, B., Camp, L., & Werfelman, M. (1980). *Steps towards literacy.* Report prepared for Working Group on Learning Failure and Unused Learning Potential. President's Commission on Mental Health, November 1, 1977. In P. Levinson & C. H. Sloan (Eds.), *Auditory processing and language: Clinical and research perspectives* (pp. 189-215). New York: Grune & Stratton.

Liberman, I. Y., Shankweiler, D., Fisher, F. W., & Carter, B. (1974). Explicit syllable and phoneme segmentation in the young child. *Journal of Experimental child Psychology, 18,* 201-212.

Lundberg, I. (1991). Phoneme awareness can be developed without reading instruction. In S. Brady & D. Shankweiler (Eds.), *Phonological Processes in Literacy* (pp. 47-53). Hillsdale, NJ: Erlbaum.

Mann, V. A. (1984). Longitudinal prediction and prevention of early reading difficulty. *Annals of Dyslexia, 34,* 117-136.

Mann, V. A. (1986). Why some children encounter reading problems: The contribution of difficulties with language processing and linguistic sophistication to early reading disability. In J. K. Torgesen & B. Y. Wong (Eds.), *Psychological and educational perspectives on learning disabilities* (pp. 133-159). New York: Academic Press.

Mann, V. A. (1991). Language Problems: A key to early reading problems. In B. Y. Wong (Ed.), *Learning about learning disabilities* (pp. 130-161). San Diego: Academic Press.

Mann, V. A. (1993). Phoneme awareness and future reading ability, *Journal of Learning Disabilities, 25,* 259-269.

Mann, V. A., & Balise, R. R. (in press). Predicting reading ability from the invented spellings of kindergarten children. To appear in W. Watt (Ed.), *Written language and cognition.* Amsterdam: Kluver Publishing.

Mann, V. A., & Brady, S. (1988). Reading disability: The role of language deficiencies. *Journal of Consulting and Clinical Psychology, 56,* 811-816.

Mann, V. A., Cowin, E., & Schoenheimer, J. (1989). Phonological processing, language comprehension and reading ability. *Journal of Learning Disabilities, 22,* 76–89.

Mann, V. A., & Ditunno, P. (1990). Phonological deficiencies: Effective predictors and further reading problems. In G. Pavlides (Ed.), *Perspectives on dyslexia: Cognition, language and treatment* (Vol. 2; pp. 105–131). New York: Wiley.

Mann, V. A., & Liberman, I. Y. (1984). Phonological awareness and verbal short-term memory: Can they presage early reading success? *Journal of Learning Disabilities, 17,* 592–598.

Mann, V. A., Liberman, I. Y., & Shankweiler, D. (1980). Children's memory for sentences and word strings in relation to reading ability. *Memory and Cognition, 8,* 329–335.

Mann, V. A., Shankweiler, D., & Smith, S. T. (1985). The association between comprehension of spoken sentences and early reading ability: The role of phonetic representation. *Journal of Child Language, 11,* 627–643.

Mann, V. A., Tobin, P., & Wilson, R. (1987). Measuring phonological awareness through the invented spellings of kindergarten children. *Merrill-Palmer Quarterly, 33,* 365–391.

McKeeever, W. F., & van Deventer, A. D. (1975). Dyslexic adolescents: Evidence of impaired visual and auditory language processing associated with normal lateralization and visual responsivity, *Cortex, 11,* 361–378.

Morais, J., Cary, L., Alegria, J., & Bertelson, P. (1979). Does awareness of speech as a sequence of phonemes arise spontaneously? *Cognition, 7,* 323–331.

Morais, J., Cluytens, M., & Alegria, J. (1984). Segmentation abilities of dyslexic and normal readers. *Perceptual and Motor Skills, 58,* 221–222.

Orton, S. T. (1937). *Reading, writing and speech problems in children.* New York: Norton.

Owen, F. W. (1978). Dyslexia—Genetic aspects. In A. L. Benton & D. Pearl (Eds.), *Dyslexia: An appraisal of current knowledge* (pp. 265–284). New York: Oxford University Press.

Owen, F. W., Adams, P. A., Forrest, T., Stolz, L. M., & Fischer, S. (1971). Learning disorders in children: Sibling studies. *Monographs of the Society for Research in Child Development, 36.* Chicago: University of Illinois Press.

Pennington, B. F., Van Orden, G., Kirson, D., & Haith, M. (1991). What is the causal relation between verbal STM problems and dyslexia? In S. Brady & D. Shankweiler (Eds.), *Phonological processes in literacy* (pp. 173–186). Hillsdale, NJ: Erlbaum.

Perfetti, C. A. (1985). *Reading ability.* New York: Oxford Press.

Read, C. (1986). *Children's creative spelling.* London: Routledge & Kegan Paul.

Robinson, M. E., & Schwartz, L. B. (1973). Visuo-motor skills and reading ability: A longitudinal study. *Developmental Medicine and Child Neurology, 15,* 280–286.

Russell, G. (1982). Impairment of phonetic reading in dyslexia and its persistence beyond childhood—Research note. *Journal of Child Psychology and Child Psychiatry, 23,* 459–475.

Rutter, M. (1978). Prevalence and types of dyslexia. In A. L. Benton & D. Pearl (Eds.), *Dyslexia: An appraisal of current knowledge* (pp. 3–28). New York: Oxford Press.

Rutter, M., & Yule, W. (1973). The concept of specific reading retardation. *Journal of Child Psychiatry, 16,* 181–198.

Scarborough, H. S. (1984). Continuity between childhood dyslexia and adult reading. *British Journal of Psychology, 75,* 329–348.

Scarborough, H. S. (1988). *Early language development of children who became dyslexic.* Paper presented to the New York Child Language group.

Shankweiler, D. C., & Crain, S. (1986). Language mechanisms and reading disorder: A modular approach. *Cognition, 24,* 139–168.

Shankweiler, D. C., & Liberman, I. Y. (1972). Misreading: A search for the causes. In J. F. Kavanaugh & I. G. Mattingly (Eds.), *Language by ear and by eye: The relationships between speech and reading* (pp. 293–318). Cambridge, MA: MIT Press.

Shankweiler, D. C., Liberman, I. Y., Mark, L. S., Fowler, C. A., & Fisher, F. W. (1979). The speech code and learning to read. *Journal of Experimental Psychology: Human Perception and Performance, 5,* 531–545.

Slowiaczek, M. L., & Clifton, C. (1980). Subvocalization and reading for meaning. *Journal of Verbal Learning and Verbal Behavior, 19,* 573–582.

Smith, S. D., Kimberling, W. J., Pennington, B. F., & Lubs, H. A. (1983), Specific reading disability: Identification of an inherited form through linkage analysis. *Science, 219,* 1345–1347.

Smith, S. T., Mann, V. A., & Shankweiler, D. C. (1986). Spoken sentence comprehension by good and poor readers: A story with the Token Test. *Cortex, 22,* 627–632.

Spellacy, F. J., & Spreen, O. (1969). A short form of the Token Test. *Cortex, 5,* 390–399.

Stanovich, K. (1982a). Individual differences in the cognitive processes of reading: I. Word decoding. *Journal of Learning Disabilities, 15,* 485–493.

Stanovich, K. (1982b). Individual differences in the cognitive processes of reading: II. Text-level processes. *Journal of Learning Disabilities, 15,* 549–554.

Stanovich, K. (1988). Explaining the differences between the dyslexic and the garden-variety poor reader: The phonological-core variable difference model. *Journal of Learning Disabilities, 21,* 590–604.

Stanovich, K. E., Cunningham, A. E., & Cramer, B. B. (1984). Assessing phonological awareness in kindergarten children: Issues of task comparability. *Journal of Experimental Child Psychology, 38,* 175–190.

Stanovich, K. E., Cunningham, A. E., & Feeman, D. J. (1984). Intelligence, cognitive skills and early reading progress. *Reading Research Quarterly, 14,* 278–303.

Stanovich, K. E., Nathan, R. G., & Zolman, J. E. (1988). The developmental lag hypothesis in reading: Longitudinal and matched reading-level comparisons. *Child Development, 59,* 71–86.

Swanson, L. (1978). Verbal encoding effects on the visual short-term memory of learning-disabled and normal children. *Journal of Educational Psychology, 70,* 539–544.

Thomas, C. C. (1905). Congenital "word blindness" and its treatment. *Opthalmoscope, 3,* 380–385.

Tzeng, O. J. L., Hung, D. L., & Wang, W. S.-Y. (1977). Speech recoding in reading Chinese characters. *Journal of Experimental Psychology: Human Learning and memory, 3,* 621–630.

Vellutino, F. R. (1979). *Dyslexia: Theory and research.* Cambridge, MA: MIT Press.

Wagner, R., Balthazor, M., Hurley, S., Morgan, S., Rashotte, C., Shaner, R., Simmons, K., & Stage, S. (1987). The nature of prereaders' phonological processing abilities. *Cognitive Development, 2,* 355–373.

Wagner, R. K., & Torgesen, J. K. (1987). The nature of phonological processing and its causal role in the acquisition of reading skills. *Psychological Bulletin, 101,* 192–212.

Wolf, M. (1984). Naming, reading and the dyslexias: A longitudinal overview. *Annals of Dyslexia, 34,* 87–115.

Wolf, M., & Goodglass, H. (1986). Dyslexia, dysnomia and lexical retrieval: A longitudinal investigation. *Brain and Language, 28,* 159–168.

Wong, B. Y. L., Wong, R., & Blenkinsop, J. (1989). Cognitive and metacognitive aspects of learning-disabled adolescents' composing problems. *Learning Disability Quarterly, 12,* 300–322.

Yopp, H. K. (1988). The validity and reliability of phonemic awareness tests. *Reading Research Quarterly, 23,* 159–177.

▶ 5

Toward a Research-Based Dyslexia Assessment
Case Study of a Young Adult

JOSEPHINE GOLDSMITH-PHILLIPS
Rutgers, The State University of New Jersey

Abstract

This chapter presents three characteristics of dysfunctional reading in children with phonological dyslexia. In a recent study, students with dyslexia in grades 4 through 7 showed slowed word recognition latencies compared to normally achieving third-grade readers. Additionally, those with dyslexia produced a greater proportion of whole words as error responses in reading both pseudowords and words. Finally, dyslexics showed a distinctive distribution of reading test scores. Error analyses suggest that these students suffer from a deficit that prevents them from remembering the precise sound segments which correspond to letter clusters in words. The case study of a 29-year-old dyslexic illustrates a shift to a more semantic search strategy hypothesized to develop in adulthood. Applications of these findings to classroom assessment are made.

The identification of children with developmental dyslexia remains an elusive goal and, in practice, a controversial enterprise. This chapter will approach the

A grant from the Rutgers University Council provided support for the preparation of this chapter. The writer expresses appreciation to the administrators, teachers, and children in the districts of South Brunswick, West Windsor, and New Egypt, New Jersey, who participated in the study. Thanks are due to Angela O'Donnell for her salient editorial comments.

identification problem by proposing characteristics of dysfunctional reading found in young children with phonological dyslexia as assessment guidelines. A case study will illustrate these reading patterns in an adult whose dyslexia was unrecognized in childhood and who now shows characteristics of deep dyslexia, as described by Coltheart (1980a, 1980c).

CHARACTERISTICS OF PHONOLOGICAL DYSLEXIA

Phonological dyslexia will be defined as a deficit in the ability to produce the sounds that correspond to letter clusters in words. Problems with phonology that lead to a failure to master decoding are the most frequently cited and analyzed difficulty experienced by young disabled readers (Kamhi, 1992; Liberman, Shankweiler, Fisher, & Carter, 1974; Mann & Liberman, 1984; Stanovich, 1988; Vellutino, 1979). People with dyslexia characteristically produce many reading errors, particularly on unfamiliar words.

Typologies of reading disability that classify persons with dyslexia typically include a phonological subgroup (Bakker, Licht, & van Strien, 1991; Boder, 1973; Doehring, 1985; Lyon & Flynn, 1991; Mattis, French, & Rapin, 1975). In contrast to poor word reading, comprehension is often in the average range when text is read aloud to the child. Typically, children read longer imageable words (e.g., *elephant*) more accurately than shorter function words, which are often confused with other high-frequency words. For example, *then* may be read as *when* and *though* as *through*. These errors are highly resistant to remediation (Goldsmith, 1981).

Various labels have been used to describe the difficulty in word reading, including *phonological dyslexia* (Desrouesne & Beauvois, 1979; Shallice & Warrington, 1980), *specific reading retardation* (Rutter, 1978), language disorder (Mattis et al., 1975, *dysphonetic dyslexia* (Boder, 1973), and *P-type dyslexia* (Bakker et al., 1991).

The cognitive characteristics of children experiencing this problem have been explored in depth (Bakker et al., 1991; Lyon & Flynn, 1991; Vellutino, 1979). Tasks that require phoneme perception have been shown to be difficult for disabled readers. These include recovering phonemes from printed words (Liberman & Shankweiler, 1979) and memory for printed nonsense syllables as opposed to faces and abstract drawings (Liberman, Mann, Shankweiler, & Werfelman, 1982). Mann and Liberman (1984; also see Mann, Chapter 4, this volume) found that kindergarten children who had difficulty with phonological awareness were at risk for later reading problems. Tallal (1980) reported that the rate and redundancy of the context in which phonemes are embedded are the major predictors of perceptual accuracy. These studies point to a disruption in one or more stages of the processes that converts print to language sounds.

Decoding ability is relatively independent of intelligence and rapidly becomes automatic in children without reading disabilities.

THE NEED FOR BEHAVIORAL DESCRIPTION

Definitions in federal and state law do not specify the characteristics that could identify persons with dyslexia. Official definitions are largely exclusionary, stating all the conditions which must be ruled out or excluded before a reading problem can be identified as dyslexia. For example, subaverage intelligence, severe emotional disturbance, visual or auditory problems, or lack of opportunity to learn to read disqualify a reading-disabled person from the dyslexia label. Dyslexia becomes the diagnosis for a "leftover" group of children and adults whose reading disability resists both explanation and remediation.

One of the most specific of the exclusionary definitions is found in the *Diagnostic and Statistical Manual of Mental Disorders,* third edition — revised (American Psychiatric Association, 1987), which states that "The essential feature of this disorder is marked impairment in the development of word recognition skills and reading comprehension that is not explainable by Mental Retardation or inadequate schooling and that is not due to a visual or hearing defect or a neurologic disorder" (p. 43). Although this definition incorporates a reference to reading skills, it still leaves researchers and educators in the frustrating situation of being required to diagnose and treat a disorder without clearly specified symptoms (Kamhi, 1992). The situation becomes more confusing because researchers have found that several subtypes exist (Bakker et al., 1991). Additionally, there is a current interest in developing criteria to distinguish children with developmental dyslexia from those with less severe and chronic reading problems, the "garden variety" reading-disabled (Stanovich, 1988).

A STUDY OF READING BEHAVIOR IN DYSLEXIA

A recent study (Goldsmith-Phillips, 1991) investigated reading speed as a discriminator of dyslexia in children. The word-reading latencies of 16 disabled readers in grades 5 to 9 were compared to latencies of 36 average readers in grade 3. Those suspected of having dyslexia met the exclusionary criteria in that their problems with reading could not be explained by low intelligence, history of brain trauma, sensory deficits, emotional disorders, or lack of opportunity to learn. All students in the sample with dyslexia had a history of difficulty in basic word reading that persisted despite several exposures to remedial programs. Additionally, each dyslexic scored two years under age expectancy on an average of three subtests of the Woodcock Reading Mastery Tests — Revised (Woodcock, 1987): Word Attack, Word Identification, and Passage Comprehension.

Each student read three passages aloud from a computer screen. One passage consisted of random words, another was composed of randomly ordered sentences, and the third had normal context. Latency, the time needed for lexical access, was defined as the interval from the appearance of the word on the computer screen to initiation of the child's voice, which cut off the timing mechanism. Time was measured in one-hundredths of a second. Details of design and presentation are described in the 1991 study. The hypothesis of this study was that reduced speed of word reading represented a basic deficit that would continue to differentiate disabled readers from younger achieving peers. Additionally, clinically relevant data on the types of errors made by each group and the patterns of reading test scores were examined.

This comparison fits the comprehension-level match design (Stanovich, 1988). Stanovich suggests that the finding of a match in comprehension ability between average readers and those with dyslexia, combined with differences in subskills would allow us to conclude that dyslexics reached their comprehension scores using different subroutes or compensatory processes. That finding would constitute evidence that dyslexics are a cognitively different group, a notion that is disputed by some educators (Coles, 1978, 1989; Spache, 1981).

Developmental Difference versus Delay
The comprehension-level match design also allows us to address the issue of whether the difficulties seen in young impaired readers are best conceptualized as a developmental difference or a delay. If the major problem of reading-disabled children is that they take longer to learn the reading code, then they should eventually master sound–symbol correspondences and become indistinguishable from their normally achieving peers. That situation would represent a developmental delay. If, in contrast, children with reading disabilities are cognitively and/or neurologically different (i.e., dyslexic), their deficits would not disappear over time but would continue to show in lower achievement and slowed word reading as compared to average peers. This situation would represent a developmental difference. Findings of such differences would imply that young children with dyslexia are a distinct group and that developmental dyslexia is a phenomenon worth study.

THREE CHARACTERISTICS OF DYSLEXIC READING

The 1991 study showed evidence of three differences in reading behaviors between the younger average readers and older dyslexics:

1. *Those with dyslexia access words more slowly than younger achieving readers.* Results showed that dyslexics who were, on average, three years older than the control children, read significantly more slowly in all context conditions. These findings demonstrate a continuing difficulty with word access that has not disappeared despite an average of three years of opportunity for additional practice. Although the average difference between dyslexic and control groups was small (approximately one-third second) it still reflects a disruption in word-reading automaticity. Such delays would produce a strain on working memory and consequently hamper comprehension (LaBerge & Samuels, 1974).

Dyslexics showed a higher error rate and a wider standard deviation for latency, which points to the possibility of a selective disruption of word reading depending on word characteristics. Such disruptions have been documented in subtypes of brain-injured alexics who read imageable (e.g., *tent*) and phonologically regular words (e.g. *thank*) more accurately than abstract (e.g., *though*) or irregular words (e.g. *thought*) (Shallice & Warrington, 1980). Evidence that developmental dyslexics show reading patterns similar to those of adults who lost their reading ability after suffering a brain insult would strengthen the argument for a innate, possibly biological basis to the disorder. The persistent slowness found in these dyslexics supports the premise of Liberman et al. (1974) that reading-disabled children of average intelligence are deficient in a specific biologically endowed system that translates between print and speech, allowing phonetic units to be perceived and remembered.

2. *Dyslexics make more whole word errors in reading lists and texts.* The numbers of whole words given as error responses were found to be greater (compared) for the dyslexics than for average readers. This comparison was motivated by a curiosity about two questions. First, do persons with dyslexia use the same or different strategies to access words as do younger average readers? The second question was the extent to which young dyslexics make semantic errors of the type described by Coltheart (1980b) as a marker of deep dyslexia.

Coltheart (1980a, 1980b, 1980c) studied adult alexics – individuals who virtually lost their ability to read as a consequence of a documented brain insult such as a stroke. He found that a subgroup of these individuals, labeled deep dyslexics, retained a remarkable capacity to produce words that were semantically related, even virtually identical in meaning to the word in text, although they were unable to read the actual printed word. (e.g., *thermos* read as *flask; blowing* as *wind* (Coltheart, 1980b, p. 147). Whereas such errors are made by young children in reading text, the person with deep dyslexia makes them in reading lists, where the only context must be supplied by the reader. The production of such an error suggests that meaning is accessed but that the phonetic realization cannot be achieved. Although this syndrome is found largely in brain-injured adults, cases of children who fit the pattern have also been reported (Marshall, 1985). Occurrence of semantic errors would suggest that the young children with dyslexia showed a type of aphasic response, whereas whole word errors that did not reflect this pattern would indicate a more straightforward difficulty in mastering phonology.

To address this question, the numbers of errors in three categories were compared. These were (*a*) errors that were phonological fragments — for example, *yacht* read as *yectic* and *hysterical* as *hysticle;* (*b*) errors that were whole words that had a strong phonological similarity to the target word but little semantic similarity — for example, *bragging* read as *bargaining, chair* as *cheer;* and (*c*) words that retained the meaning of the word in the text but presented it in a different visual and phonological form — for example, *child* read as *girl, era* as *time* (Coltheart, 1980a, p. 32).

Results showed that those with dyslexia produced significantly more whole words as error responses than the younger average readers (Goldsmith-Phillips, in preparation). This pattern was found both for responses to words in the Word Identification subtest and to pseudowords in the Word Attack subtest.

Readers who were adept at use of a phonological route — in this case, the third-grade children — apparently used the more time-efficient strategy of sounding out the word. These fluent readers would be more likely to produce a stream of phonemes, making errors of type *a* as they attempted to read unfamiliar words. Dyslexic readers, who are typically unsuccessful at decoding, appeared to respond on the basis of their memory of other words that shared visual features, such as the same initial letter or letter clusters in common. A failure in phonology, without the aphasic component of deep dyslexia, would be likely to result in words that are visually rather than semantically related.

An earlier developmental study of average readers in grades 2, 4, and 6 (Goldsmith-Phillips, 1989) found that sixth-grade students made more phonological substitutions than children in grades 2 or 4. Children in grade 2 produced more whole word responses that were semantically appropriate than did children in either of the upper grades. These trends are consistent with reports by Biemiller (1970) and Weber (1970) that associate a phonological strategy with more developed reading, whereas the production of whole word responses is characteristic of beginners.

Almost without exception, whole word responses in the 1991 study for both average readers and those with dyslexia fell into category *b*. Errors in both groups were phonologically but not semantically similar to the word the child was attempting to read. Whole word errors made by third-graders on the Word Identification test included *mathematician* read as *merchant, cologne* as *colony,* and *twilight* as *twiddling light.* Examples of dyslexics' whole word errors were *moustache* as *mustard, receive* as *recover,* and *expert* as *exposed.*

The reading test patterns and errors of the present group with dyslexia indicate a pattern similar to phonological dyslexia, an impairment of the phonological route without the semantic error pattern that characterizes deep dyslexia (Coltheart, 1980a). The three errors made by children in the dyslexic group that could be characterized as semantic in Coltheart's terms were *stir* read as *stove, hurry* as *hunger,* and *twilight* as *twinkle.* These errors also show considerable phonological similarity. These dyslexic children did not produce errors with heavy semantic similarity and low sound relationships to the words they attempted to read. Overall, the pattern is that of a reader struggling with inept phonological skills, and eager to produce a whole word unit with reasonable similarity to the target word.

Explanations of the problems in word reading as a failure to learn basic rules of sound–symbol correspondence do not precisely capture the qualities of the dyslexics' error responses. Although those with dyslexia show difficulty in retrieving and confusions in discriminating the correct sounds of words, they do show evidence of phonological knowledge. For example, dyslexics invariably respond by giving a phonologically legal segment, a consonant cluster preceded and/or followed by vocalic separations (Gibson, 1977). Moreover, many errors show strong phonological similarity to the word in text. For example, *stigma* read as *sticker* and *fairness* as *furnace* share a high proportion of phonological units. These errors are also typical in demonstrating preference for a higher frequency word in the child's lexicon, and for one that is more concrete. The child, E, who made these errors was a 9-year-old girl, the youngest in the sample. Her receptive language quotient on the Peabody Picture Vocabulary Test (PPVT; Dunn & Dunn, 1981) was 112 (mean = 100). Older dyslexics also demonstrate reliance on morphemes. An example is found in C, a 12-year-old male (PPVT 98) who read *mechanic* as *magnetic; artesian* as *artisan,* and *causation* as *caution.* Individual style also appears, as in the somewhat less analytic errors of T, an 11-year-old female (PPVT 99) who produced *urgent* as *urge,* *mechanic* as *medicine, relativity* as *reality, causation* as *caution, naive* as *native,* and *vehicle* as *Vaseline.* The difficulty seems to be a failure to store or retrieve the sequence of phonological elements in the correct order.

3. *Those with dyslexia show a distinctive distribution of reading test scores.* The distribution of reading scores was examined for the children participating in the word latency study described earlier (Goldsmith-Phillips, 1991). Those with dyslexia showed their highest score on the Passage Comprehension subtest, their lowest score on Word Attack, and a score at an intermediate level on Word Identification. Comparisons with the control group showed significantly higher scores on both Word Attack and Word Identification subtests for younger average readers. In contrast, there were no significant differences between dyslexics and controls on Passage Comprehension scores. The Passage Comprehension subtest requires students to read short passages and answer comprehension questions using a cloze procedure. Given their word-reading difficulties, dyslexics must have skipped or misread many of the words. They were, in effect, attempting to comprehend distorted texts. In this situation their true comprehension ability was probably underrated. Results on any comprehension task requiring silent reading must be regarded with suspicion for this group.

These data suggest a dissociation between the ability to read words and the ability to comprehend in average younger readers versus older children with dyslexia. Control group students in third grade showed the highest performance in Word Attack, the subskill that was the lowest for the group with dyslexia. Insignificant differences between the two groups on Passage Comprehension scores suggests that cognitive abilities may have put a ceiling on comprehension for the third-grade controls, whereas problems with decoding may have limited the comprehension of older dyslexics. These findings support the existence of differences in the ability to process written language that do not disappear with experience or instruction.

PROPOSED COGNITIVE DEFICITS IN PHONOLOGICAL DYSLEXIA

The central deficit, underlying the three reading behaviors outlined above, appears to be a virtual inability to overlearn the phonological correspondences of letters and letter clusters.

Gibson's Components of Reading Competence
Gibson (1977) proposed three stages of reading development based on "perceptual trends" or cognitive skills. The first is "succession," the ability to remember and order items in a temporal sequence. The second, and perhaps most complex, is the ability to recode stimuli into subordinate and superordinate structures. In terms of phonological development, this could be translated into recoding of letters into cluster and morpheme units, a necessary skill for the development of reading fluency. The final skill, described as more speculative, is "attention," by which Gibson indicates the ability to select cues that result in the most efficient performance of a perceptual task. Gibson proposed that beginning readers attend to the semantic aspects of words. In the period from grades 2 to 4, the focus shifts to the structural properties of words and then refocuses on meaning at approximately sixth grade. Chall's testing procedures (Chapter 9, this volume) reflect a similar stage model.

The reading behaviors of those with dyslexia suggest an arrest at the semantic stage described by Biemiller (1970), in which children lean on meaning cues and tend to make whole word responses. Using Gibson's model, the difficulty can be placed at the initial sequencing stage and perhaps the final attentional stage. Young children with dyslexia do not experience gross deficits in the second stage of subordination of letters into phonological clusters and morphemes, because these units appear in their errors. Their difficulty appears to lie at some stage in the process of discriminating and sequencing.

The developmental explanation is supported by the appearance of word errors in the younger average reading controls. Several of these were identical. For example, both dyslexic and average children read the nonword *wrey* as *weary,* whereas dyslexics produced the additional responses *worry* and *rare.* Additional support for the view that a shift from semantic to phonological errors represents normal reading development is found in Goldsmith-Phillips (1989). The issue of metacognitive monitoring in these children would be a profitable one to pursue. Several children gave an incorrect response, then changed it to a correct one and changed back to the error as a preferable answer. One of the children stated that he was "never sure" which of his choices was correct, so that the selection of his final answer became a game of chance. The extent to which these children might fail to self-monitor, and whether monitoring could be effective in the face of the decoding deficit, would be interesting questions to study in future research.

STUDY OF AN ADULT DYSLEXIC: THE CASE OF ANTHONY

The following case study illustrates the effects of phonological dyslexia in the life of a young adult. Although Anthony showed some variations from the patterns discussed here, his presentation was typical in the patterns of reading scores and the major life disruptions caused by dyslexia.

This client produced semantic errors in lists, cited by Coltheart (1980b) as the characteristic sign of a deep dyslexia. The appearance of these errors, which did not occur in the reading of younger dyslexics reviewed earlier, allows speculation as to their association with the increased verbal experience of adults.

Referral

Anthony was referred by his immediate supervisor at the telephone company, where he was employed. He presented as a white male, age 29, who had been suffering from a long-standing intransigent reading disability, which now was preventing job promotion.

Test Data

Testing with the Wechsler Intelligence Test — Revised (Wechsler, 1981) revealed IQ in the lower end of the average range (Verbal IQ = 90; Performance IQ = 85, Full Scale IQ = 86). Analysis of scaled score scatter demonstrated a moderately flat profile. However, two significant discrepancies were found on subtests measuring different components of the IQ scores. The client showed a significantly higher score, or strength, in the Similarities subtest and one weakness in Coding. The strength in the Similarities subtest shows above-average potential on a test measuring verbal conceptualization. This test requires the client to state the similarity between two different objects or concepts (e.g., *horse* and *camel* or *loyalty* and *honesty*). The Coding subtest requires the client to write symbols paired with numbers under timed conditions, with the correct combinations listed in a key at the top of the page. Average performance on this subtest, in contrast to difficulty on a task requiring sequencing and memory, is typical of a dyslexic profile.

History

Anthony's memories of early schooling illustrate the major learning difficulties plus the inevitable discouragement and hurt encountered by young children with dyslexia. He remembered that subjects became more difficult as a function of the amount of reading involved. He reported that "Math I took to real easy . . . reading was hard." Second, his spontaneous comments indicated that comprehension was intact when material was read aloud but became a major problem when he was required to read the words (i.e., in silent reading). "I noticed that, as a little guy — had tremendous memory. If I had stuff read to me . . . could say it right back . . . I start reading, come to words I can't make out . . . feel like I'm making it up as I go along." Negative feelings about school are reflected in memories of being "left back" in grade 1, and "yelled at" by the teacher, and by his statement, "I never was into school."

Anthony attended parochial school for two months, then attended three public schools in grade 1. He recalls being "in therapy" to correct the reading problem and experiencing behavioral difficulties, fighting with the other children. He was tutored in reading "constantly" until eighth grade. During that time he remembered that he had never been able to complete a basal reader. The sole "whole book" that he read was a children's story whose name was still salient to him, *A Pony for Juan*. After he had completed eighth grade, his parents were advised to send him to vocational school, which he described as the "last stop before reform school."

Anthony attended two vocational schools, where he studied plumbing. He characterized his vocational education as "good training in shops" but not in academics. English class was "mostly crossword puzzles." He dropped out of school in eleventh grade and took the job with the telephone company. He received several promotions, which he attributed to hard work. Now, as a candidate for chief technician, he found that the reading disability stood in the way of advancement. Another strong motivating force was that Anthony had become a father and wanted to read stories to his little son. He told the examiner that books "talked to" other people, but never to him. "I want to have a book talk to me."

Consistency with the phonological dyslexia profile. Anthony's errors, a sample of which are shown on Table 5-1, show his reading to be consistent with the profile of phonological dyslexia (Shallice & Warrington, 1980). He makes identification errors both on individual graphemes (*bed* read as *ded*) and on syllables (*departure* read as *departed*). His error patterns were consistent with the

TABLE 5-1 **Anthony's Errors**

I. Derivational

Word in Text	*Response*		*Word in Text*	*Response*
laughing	⟶ landing	⟶ laying	exist	⟶ exceed
design	⟶ decision		departure	⟶ departed
meaning	⟶ meeting			

II. Lexicalizations of Nonwords

sloy	⟶ slow		hets	⟶ hats
tash	⟶ test		laip	⟶ lip

III. Reversals/Inversions

bim	⟶ dim		bed	⟶ ded
ab	⟶ ed		tab	⟶ tod
nudd	⟶ nub		we	⟶ me

IV. Semantic Errors in Lists

need	⟶ eat		again	⟶ whip
me	⟶ I		clothes	⟶ coats

V. Semantic Errors in Context

Text	*Response*
village common	⟶ village cannon
a dog that bites is sick	⟶ a dog that bites a stick

three characteristics that discriminated those with dyslexia from younger average readers from the 1991 study described above.

1. *Decreased reading speed associated with a decoding deficit.* Anthony was seen before the computerized word-reading test had been developed. However, clinical observation showed that his word reading was hesitant and slowed to the point where the intonation patterns characteristic of normal speech were missing.

Anthony made numerous word-reading errors. A sample of these is shown on Table 5-1. Many of his responses illustrate the error pattern originally interpreted by Orton (1937) as reversals (e.g., *bed* as *ded*; *tab* as *tod*). There is also one error that could have been regarded as an inversion (*nudd* read as *nub*). Liberman et al. (1982) later showed that poor readers did not differ from good readers in memory for faces or nonsense designs, only for letter sequences within syllables. Apparently, the supposed reversals are the result of a specific problem in remembering material that must be coded phonetically.

2. *Words as error responses.* Anthony showed the tendency toward whole word errors noted in the young dyslexic group. Typically for someone with dyslexia, he showed virtual inability to read nonwords and substituted whole words for many of these. He read *tash* as *test, hets* as *hats,* and *sloy* as *slowly.*

His error responses for whole words in text and lists appeared to rely less on combinations of visual and phonological match than those of the school-aged children with dyslexia. The strong semantic similarity of many of his errors to the word in text, contrasted to low phonological similarity, suggests the deep dyslexia syndrome described by Coltheart (1980a, 1980b, 1980c). His reading of *I* for *me* and *eat* for *need* evokes Shallice and Warrington's (1980) suggestion that semantic errors made by those with phonological dyslexia show that the process of reaching the correct semantic network is intact, but the phonological difficulty results in the selection of an incorrect word.

These errors are significant only in lists. When the student is reading connected text, the context is the reasonable basis for errors that continue text meaning but often have little formal relationship to the word being read. In contrast, when lists are read, all semantic context must come from the reader. Anthony's semantic errors in lists suggest such a process. The substitution of *whip* for *again* appears to refer to past experience. Other examples are shown less dramatically in the substitution of *eat* for *need* and of *coats* for *clothes,* examples in which some phonological transcribing could have contributed to the responses.

The question remains as to why Anthony's errors were more like those of the deep dyslexics than the errors of younger dyslexics reported above. The explanation could be in an idiosyncratic pattern in his reading or a developmental shift that might occur in dyslexics' word reading over time. Shifts in the characteristics of dyslexic reading overdevelopment have not been specified and remain a rich area for further study.

3. *Patterns of reading test scores.* Grade Equivalent scores on the Woodcock Reading Mastery Tests — Revised (Woodcock, 1987) showed Word Attack at 2.1, Word Identification at 2.9, and Passage Comprehension at 5.9. These scores match the predicted pattern found in the latency data reviewed earlier. Anthony's Word Attack is the lowest, followed by Word Identification, which is somewhat higher. Typically for a person with phonological dyslexia, the more cognitively based Passage Comprehension score exceeds those on the phonologically based reading tasks. A discrepancy between his ability to express his ideas and his ability to comprehend was captured in his statement, "Sometimes it comes to me so fast that it's like — caught. I can't tell the person — It's in my head. I know what's happening. I can't get it out. I get all frustrated and mad. It's so bottled up." This statement suggests that Anthony's reading disability, like that of many people with dyslexia, may be associated with a range of subtle linguistic disabilities.

APPLICATIONS TO ASSESSMENT

The patterns of dyslexic reading reviewed here suggest that several assessment strategies could be added to a test battery when a dyslexia is suspected. These are as follows.

1. *A measure of reading speed.* In the study described here, reading time was a significant discriminator of the dyslexic group. Although the method of timed reading used in the study was a specialized experimental technique, reading speed could be measured on a standardized reading test. Further, school or district norms for graded passages could be developed. It should be noted that many of the widely used standardized reading tests do not include a measure of reading speed.

2. *Analysis of errors.* The second discriminator discussed in this chapter was the propensity for those with dyslexia to make whole word errors, suggesting that they do not analyze words phonetically. Because automatic phonological decoding is characteristic of older and, therefore, more developed readers (Goldsmith-Phillips, 1989) whole word substitutions may be a compensatory strategy used when decoding systems fail. A tendency of children in grades 4 and above to rely on semantic associations in their error responses would be a corrobating sign of dyslexia in a reading-disabled child who showed the other patterns discussed here.

3. *Patterns of reading test scores.* The patterns of reading test scores found in this study were strong discriminators of developmental dyslexia. This contrast between the three abilities (i.e., word attack, word identification, and comprehension measures) reflects the patterns of cognitive strength and weakness found in phonological dyslexia. These students will have the greatest difficulty with reading nonwords and the most success with passage comprehension, which is a more cognitively loaded task. The task of word identification will be at an intermediate level because the words may have been learned by Gestalt processing.

A CAUTIONARY NOTE ON SILENT READING TESTS

The patterns of test scores suggested here are most validly measured in an individually administered test with oral responses, such as the Woodcock Reading Mastery Tests — Revised (Woodcock, 1987), used in the 1991 study (also see Chall, Chapter 9, this volume). Translation of these measures to a silent reading group test often changes the tasks so that they overestimate word attack ability and underestimate comprehension, as will be discussed.

1. *Word attack measured in a silent reading task.* One well-reviewed and widely used silent reading test uses items that ask the child to choose one word out of three — for example, *hammer, hate,* and *party* — that matches the sound of *a* in a key word, such as *start.* This test is labeled as measuring word attack ability. However, the child has already overlearned many of the words, including their component sounds. The task then becomes one of auditory discrimination, not phonological decoding. Any task that purports to measure word attack should use nonwords.

2. *Tests of silent reading comprehension.* These tests will also handicap a person with dyslexia because many errors will be made in reading the words, giving a different conception of the text. Additionally, these tests typically have time limits, and it has been demonstrated that speed of reading is a significantly slowed for those with dyslexia. Children with a reading disability should be tested with a listening comprehension procedure where passages are read aloud and oral responses accepted. In fact, a higher score on such a listening procedure would provide one important bit of evidence to support the assessment of a dyslexia.

REFERENCES

American Psychiatric Association. (1987). *Diagnostic and statistical manual of mental disorders,* 3rd ed. revised. Washington, DC: Author.

Bakker, D. J., Licht, R., & van Strien, J. (1991). Biopsychological validation of L and P-type dyslexia. In B. P. Rourke (Ed.), *Neuropsychological validation of learning disability subtypes* (pp. 124–139). New York: Guilford Press.

Biemiller, A. (1970). The development of the use of graphic and contextual information as children learn to read. *Reading Research Quarterly, 6,* 75–96.

Boder, E. (1973). Developmental dyslexia: A diagnostic approach based on three atypical reading patterns. *Developmental Medicine and Child Neurology, 15,* 663–687.

Coles, G. S. (1978). The learning-disabilities test battery: Empirical and social issues. *Harvard Educational Review, 48,* 313–340.

Coles, G. S. (1989). Excerpts from The Learning Mystique: A critical look at "learning disabilities." *Journal of Learning Disabilities, 22,* 267–273, 277.

Coltheart, M. (1980a). Deep dyslexia: A review of the sundrome. In M. Coltheart, K. Patterson, & J. C. Marshall (Eds.), *Deep dyslexia* (pp. 22–47). London: Routledge & Kegan Paul.

Coltheart, M. (1980b). Reading, phonological recoding and deep dyslexia. In M. Coltheart, K. Patterson, & J. C. Marshall (Eds.), *Deep dyslexia* (pp. 197–226). London: Routledge & Kegan Paul.

Coltheart, M. (1980c). The semantic error: Types and theories. In M. Coltheart, K. Patterson, & J. C. Marshall (Eds.), *Deep dyslexia* (pp. 146–159). London: Routledge & Kegan Paul.

Desrouesne, J., & Beauvois, M. F. (1979). Phonological processing in reading: Data from alexia. *Journal of Neurology, Neurosurgery and Psychiatry, 42,* 1125–1132.

Doehring, D. G. (1985). Reading disability subtypes: Interaction of reading and nonreading deficits. In B. P. Rourke (Ed.), *Neuropsychology of learning disabilities: Essentials of subtype analysis* (pp. 133–166). New York: Guilford Press.

Dunn, L. M., & Dunn, L. M. (1981). *Peabody Picture Vocabulary Test—Revised.* Circle Pines, MN: American Guidance Service.

Gibson, E. J. (1977). How perception really develops: A view from outside the network. In D. LaBerge & S. J. Samuels (Eds.), *Basic processes in reading: Perception and comprehension.* (pp. 155-173). Hillsdale, NJ: Erlbaum.

Goldsmith, J. S. (1981). Decoding re-examined. *The Elementary School Journal, 82,* 153-159.

Goldsmith-Phillips, J. (1989). Word and context in developmental reading: A test of the interactive–compensatory hypothesis, *Journal of Educational Psychology, 81,* 299-305.

Goldsmith-Phillips, J. (1991). *Word reading latency in developmental dyslexia: A test of cognitive difference versus delay.* Unpublished dissertation, Rutgers University, New Brunswick, New Jersey.

Goldsmith-Phillips, J. (in press). Are developmental dyslexics neurologically different? *Reading and Writing Quarterly.*

Goldsmith-Phillips, J. (in preparation). *Reading time and error patterns in phonological dyslexia.*

Kamhi, A. G. (1992). Response to historical perspective: A developmental language perspective. *Journal of Learning Disabilities, 25,* 48-52.

LaBerge, D., & Samuels, S. J. (1974). Toward a theory of automatic information processing in reading. *Cognitive Psychology, 6,* 293-323.

Liberman, I. Y., Mann, V. A., Shankweiler, D., & Werfelman, M. (1982). Children's memory for recurring linguistic and nonlinguistic material in relation to reading ability. *Cortex, 18,* 367-375.

Liberman, I. Y., & Shankweiler, D. P. (1979). Speech, the alphabet and teaching to read. In L. Resnick & P. Weaver (Eds.), *Theory and practice of early reading* (pp. 127-152). Hillsdale, NJ: Erlbaum.

Liberman, I. Y., Shankweiler, D., Fischer, F. W., & Carter, B. (1974). Explicit syllable and phoneme segmentation in the young child. *Journal of Experimental Child Psychology, 18,* 201-202.

Lyon, G. R., & Flynn, J. M. (1991). Educational validation studies with subtypes of learning-disabled readers. In B. P. Rourke (Ed.), *Neuropsychological validation of learning disability subtypes* (pp. 233-242). New York: Guilford Press.

Mann, V. A., & Liberman, I. Y. (1984). Phonological awareness and verbal short-term memory. *Journal of Learning Disabilities, 22,* 592-598.

Marshall, J. C. (1985). On some relationships between acquired and developmental dyslexias. In F. H. Duffy & N. Geschwind (Eds.), *Dyslexia: A neuroscientific approach to clinical evaluation.* (pp. 55-66) Boston: Little, Brown.

Mattis, S., French, J. H., & Rapin, I. (1975). Dyslexia in children and young adults: Three independent neuropsychological syndromes. *Developmental Medicine and Child Neurology, 17,* 150-163.

Rutter, M. (1978). Prevalence and types of dyslexia. In A. L. Benton & D. Pearl (Eds.), *Dyslexia: An appraisal of current knowledge* (pp. 5-42). New York: Oxford University Press.

Shallice, T., & Warrington, E. K. (1980). Single and multiple component central dyslexic syndromes. In M. Coltheart, K. Patterson, & J. C. Marshall (Eds.), *Deep dyslexia* (pp. 119-145). London: Routledge & Kegan Paul.

Spache, G. D. (1981). *Diagnosing and correcting reading disabilities.* Boston: Allyn and Bacon.

Stanovich, K. E. (1988). Explaining the differences between the dyslexic and the garden-variety poor reader: The phonological-core variable-difference model. *Journal of Learning Disabilities, 21,* 590–604, 612.

Tallal, P. (1980). Auditory temporal perception, phonics and reading disabilities in children. *Brain and Language, 9,* d182–198.

Vellutino, F. R. (1979). *Dyslexia: Theory and research.* Cambridge. MA: MIT Press.

Weber, R. (1970). A linguistic analysis of first grade reading errors. *Reading Research Quarterly, 5,* 547–551.

Wechsler, D. (1981). Wechsler Adult Intelligence Test—Revised. New York: Psychological Corporation.

Woodcock, R. W. (1987). Woodcock Reading Mastery Tests—Revised. Circle Pines, MN: American Guidance Service.

▶ 6

Rapid Syllable Production in Specifically Language-Impaired Children

RACHEL E. STARK
Purdue University

JAMES W. MONTGOMERY
University of North Carolina at Chapel Hill

Abstract

Rapid production of two- and three-syllable sequences, an equal number of which did and did not constitute meaningful words, was contrasted in specifically language-impaired (SLI) and language normal (LN) children. Twenty SLI and 20 LN subjects, matched for age and Performance IQ, participated. It was found that: (1) accuracy of production of the LN children was superior to that of the SLI children overall; (2) both SLI and LN children were more accurate in producing meaningful word than nonword sequences; (3) syllable duration was not significantly different for words and nonwords in either group, nor across subject groups; (4) syllable duration was different across sequences comprising different consonants; this effect also differed across word and nonword sequences. These results suggest that auditory-vocal learning is involved in rapid syllable production, not motor skills only. Implications for the role of short-short memory in naming, word recall, and word finding in SLI children are discussed.

In a study of 35 carefully selected specifically language-impaired (SLI) children, Stark and Tallal (1988) set out to discover if earlier reports of rapid rate auditory processing deficits in SLI children (Tallal & Piercy, 1974, 1975) could be replicated. They also asked if rate of movement was affected in these same children. Specific language impairment has been defined by exclusion as language impairment in the absence of mental retardation, hearing loss, frank neurological deficit, or emotional or behavioral disturbance (Benton, 1964). Many SLI children go on to manifest reading impairment (Stark, Bernstein, Condino, Bender, & Tallal, 1984), and reading-impaired and SLI children have been found to share many characteristics (Kamhi & Catts, 1989). Thus, questions about rapid-rate auditory deficits and rate-of-movement deficits may have relevance for both groups.

Stark and Tallal (1988) were able to replicate the finding of rapid-rate auditory processing deficit in their studies and also showed that these deficits were highly correlated with level of receptive language (Tallal, Stark, & Mellits, 1985). In addition, they found that SLI children's performance on motor tasks that involved the speech musculature and the limbs of both the right and left sides of the body, and that were both fine and gross in nature, was less efficient at rapid rates than for matched normal (LN) children (Stark & Tallal, 1981; Johnston, Stark, Mellits, & Tallal, 1981). With respect to speech motor tasks, where children in both groups were asked to produce polysyllabic words (e.g., television, cafeteria) as fast as possible three times each, the SLI children made many errors of substitution, deletion, and addition of syllables, even when they could produce the target word correctly in isolation and at a slower rate; the normal children made significantly fewer errors.

In subsequent discriminant function analyses that included a subset of children from both groups, it was found that performance on the rapid speech production task was more highly predictive of group membership (LN or SLI) than any other experimental variable included in the study — for example, speech perception variables or demographic variables (Tallal, Stark, & Mellits, 1985). This finding did not permit the authors to conclude that rapid syllable production would discriminate SLI children from all other groups of children with developmental speech and language disorders, but it did suggest that this form of speech breakdown under testing might be highly characteristic of SLI children.

The present study was designed to test for replication of this effect, and to examine its nature more closely if it should be replicated, in a study of SLI and LN children. Specifically, we were interested in addressing the question: Is difficulty with rapid syllable production in SLI children based primarily on speech motor difficulties (i.e., difficulty in controlling movements of the speech musculature when these have to be performed rapidly) or on more complex auditory-motor processes affecting speech output? Such processes might include auditory recall of the sequence of syllables to be produced, or auditory monitoring of the accuracy of production.

The children were asked to repeat both meaningless (nonword) and meaningful (word) sequences rapidly. These sequences were matched for number of syllables and resembled one another in the consonant types predominating. However, the syllable structure was simpler for the nonword sequences and more complex for the word sequences. Both speech motor deficits (Katz, Curtiss, &

Tallal, 1991) and short-term auditory memory deficits (Gathercole & Baddeley, 1990) have been proposed as giving rise to difficulty in word repetition in SLI children. It was hypothesized that, if the SLI children had a speech motor difficulty or a difficulty in monitoring the accuracy of their performance through tactile and kinesthetic means primarily, they would make more errors on the complex real word sequences (e.g., on *skirt* in *miniskirt*). If, on the other hand, they had difficulty primarily in remembering the sequences to be produced and/or with auditory monitoring (i.e., checking output against remembered sequence), they would make more errors on the simpler but unfamiliar nonword sequences (e.g., bədəgə).

METHODS

Subjects

Twenty SLI and 20 LN subjects were included. There were 13 males and 7 females in the SLI group and 10 males and 10 females in the LN group. The predominance of males in the SLI group is typical (Stark, Tallal, & Mellits, 1983). A closer match in sex ratio was sought between the two groups. However, potential male subjects were more likely to be excluded because they did not meet criteria for the LN group than were potential female subjects, and it became too time-consuming to achieve the desired match. In addition, previous work had revealed no sex differences on rapid movement tasks (Johnston et al., 1981).

All subjects were required to have a Performance IQ on the Wechsler Intelligence Scale for Children — Revised (Wechsler, 1974) ranging between 80 IQ and 126 IQ, and to have normal hearing as tested by hearing screening bilaterally at 20 dB across the frequencies 250 through 8 KHz (American National Standards Institute, 1969). A recent history of recurring otitis media was grounds for exclusion, as was emotional or behavioral disturbance requiring specific intervention. Children were also excluded if they had oral structural or functional deviation as revealed by the Robbins and Klee (1987) protocol. The SLI children were required to score below the 25th percentile on the Clinical Evaluation of Language Functions — Revised (CELF-R; Semel, Wiig, & Secord, 1987), and/or to show at least a 15-point difference between Performance IQ and Verbal IQ, with Performance IQ being the higher. In addition, they each had to have been identified as sufficiently language-impaired by the speech-language pathology staff in the child's school system to receive some form of speech-language intervention. The LN children were required to score at or above the 25th percentile on the CELF-R and to have no history of intervention in their school system for a speech, hearing, or language disorder. One LN child scored at the 13th percentile on the CELF-R, but this child was a speaker of Black English. When scoring was adapted to take his dialect into account, he satisfied the percentile criterion. In addition, the LN children were excluded if they showed a 15-point difference between Performance and Verbal IQ, with Performance IQ being the higher.

The two groups did not differ significantly with respect to age or Performance IQ (Mann-Whitney U; Siegel, 1956). The Verbal IQ, and hence the Full Scale IQ scores of the SLI children, were significantly lower than those of the LN children, as expected (*p* < .001; Mann-Whitney U; Siegel, 1956).

Procedures

The children in both groups were asked to repeat the ten polysyllabic words shown in Table 6-1 in isolation and, subsequently, three times in rapid succession. They did so in response to a tape recording of a male speaker, who also spoke the words in isolation and then three times rapidly. The children's attempts were tape-recorded for later auditory analysis. The total possible score was 30 words correct. Two listeners scored each production attempt as correct or, if it was incorrect, provided a broad phonetic transcription of the child's response. Agreement between the listeners was 95 percent for the judgment of correct versus incorrect. The mean score for the LN children was 29.15 words correct (± 1.46). For the SLI children, the mean score was 21.95 words correct (± 6.82). The scores of the two groups were found to be significantly different (*p* < .001; Mann-Whitney U; Siegfel, 1956). Thus, the difficulty shown by SLI children in rapid production of polysyllabic words was replicated.

In order to examine this difficulty further, the subjects were then asked to repeat three-syllable sequences in response to a tape-recorded stimulus. Again, the production of the stimulus sequences was modeled in isolation, three times slowly and three times rapidly, by a male speaker on this tape recording. In each case the child was required to repeat the sequence once in isolation, three times in succession at a normal to slow rate, and finally three normal to slow rate, and finally three times in rapid succession. The single sequence and three

TABLE 6-1 **Polysyllabic Words Produced at a Rapid Rate by the SLI and LN Subjects**

3 Syllables	4 Syllables	5 Syllables
gingerbread	television	cafeteria
bicycle		refrigerator
tomato		
animal		
carefully		
forgotten		
handkerchief		

normal to slow sequences were designed as training. Thus, each child experienced the same amount of training and practice on this task before engaging in rapid repetition. Rapid rate of production has been used by a number of investigators to stress the subject and thus yield a maximum number of errors of sequencing, which was our aim in the present study.

All attempts at repetition were tape-recorded for later auditory and acoustic analysis. Four of the three-syllable sequences were nonwords; consonants were stops, nasals, and fricatives; the vowels were / Ǝ / or a schwa /ə/ throughout, depending on the syllable stress applied by the "model" speaker. The remaining four three-syllable sequences were meaningful words. All of the children had some familiarity with these words. The consonant sequences were similar to those found in the nonword items, but included syllable-final consonants and consonant clusters not present in the nonword sequences. The vowels were also more varied in the word than in the nonword items. The meaningful words were of greater phonetic complexity than the nonword items and thus could be considered more difficult to repeat rapidly. On the other hand, the children had heard the meaningful words before and were likely to have produced them in various contexts previously. In addition, the greater variety of vocalic components has the effect of introducing acoustic redundancy (Tallal & Stark, 1981) and could have conferred a perceptual advantage upon the meaningful items. All three-syllable items are shown in Table 6-2.

In preliminary work, it was determined that two-syllable items were easier for normal children to produce rapidly than three-syllable items (see also Gathercole, Willis, Emslie, & Baddeley, 1991). In the present study, children were asked to respond to two-syllable sequences only if they failed to repeat at least three word and three nonword three-syllable sequences correctly at the rapid rate. There were six nonword two-syllable sequences, in which each syllable was a consonant (stop, nasal, or fricative affricate), followed by / Ǝ/ or /ə/ vowel depending on syllable stress, and six two-syllable words, in which the consonant sequences were the same as for the nonword items but the vowels showed

TABLE 6-2 **Three-Syllable Meaningless Nonword Items and Familiar, Meaningful Words Repeated by the SLI and LN Subjects in Training (in Isolation and in Three-Item Sequences at a Normal to Slow Rate) and in Testing (Three-Item Sequences at a Rapid Rate)**

Nonword Sequences	Word Sequences
p Ǝtəkə	prettycat
b Ǝ dəgə	buttercup
m Ǝ nətʃə	miniskirt
f Ǝ ʃəsə	fish 'n' chips

somewhat greater variation. No final consonants or consonant clusters were present in the 2-syllable words. All two-syllable items are shown in Table 6-3. The responses of children in both groups were scored as correct or incorrect. Incorrect responses were transcribed in broad phonetic transcription. Intrajudge reliability was established for the primary listener (RES). Interjudge reliability was established by having a second listener judge 50 percent of the responses, chosen randomly from each subject group. Both were found to be satisfactory (interjudge reliability: LN children = 96 percent; SLI children = 91.7 percent; intrajudge reliability: LN children = 97 percent; SLI children = 94.1 percent). The number of two-syllable and three-syllable sequences produced correctly was derived for the normal to slow and rapid-rate conditions. Accuracy of repetition for word and nonword three-syllable sequences was compared across the two groups of children. In addition, measures of sequence duration were made and compared across groups for both the word and nonword three-syllable sequences.

It was noted from review of the transcriptions of these sequences that SLI children frequently deleted syllables or added them. Sometimes they produced four rather than three sequences, presumably because of self-correction on one item (e.g., pɘkɘtɘkɘ for pɘtɘkɘ). In addition, children in both groups were observed to make false starts, followed by correct production. Because of the unequal numbers of syllables and sequences resulting, it was decided (1) to submit only the first three sequences produced by the child to auditory analysis; (2) to make duration measurements only for the first three sequences produced; and (3) to derive mean syllable duration for each sequence rather than total duration. If a syllable was omitted or added, the sequence on which the omission/addition was observed was judged to be in error. If children made a consonant error in producing test syllables that was characteristically present in their spontaneous speech also (e.g., /s/ for /ʃ/ as in shoe), the relevant sequences

TABLE 6-3 **Two-Syllable Meaningless Nonword Items and Familiar, Meaningful Words Repeated by All Subjects Failing to Meet Criteria for Repetition of the Three-Syllable Sequences**

Meaningless Sequences	Meaningful Words
pɘtɘ	putty
tɘkɘ	taco
dɘgɘ	doggy
mɘnɘ	money
fɘʃɘ	fishy
nɘtʃɘ	nacho

Note: The two-syllable items shown were employed in training (in isolation and in three-item sequences at a normal to slow rate) and testing (three-item sequences at a rapid rate).

were also judged, for the purpose of the present study, to be in error. This strategy was adopted partly because the children's speech motor control was of interest to the authors and would presumably be reflected in their errors of sponataneous speech, and partly because one subject was highly unintelligible, and it was not always possible to derive the phoneme he intended to produce.

The duration measures were made by means of a Bruel and Kjaer Sound Level Recorder Model 2307. The settings employed were: paper speed, 3 cm/sec; drive shaft speed, 3 to 6 rpm; lower limiting frequency, 200 Hz. Measurements were made from the point where the recording trace at the beginning of the first three-syllable sequence rose above the level of background noise to the point where the trace at the end of the third sequence dropped below that level. Number of silent pauses between sequences was also recorded for each subject. Pauses were recorded where an ongoing trace dropped below the level of background noise. Measures of pause duration were not attempted. Duration measures could not be made for six children (three LN and three SLI subjects) because of high levels of background noise or partial erasure of the original recording. Intrajudge reliability for duration measures was examined by having the first judge remeasure 20 percent of the responses of the LN and the SLI children, and interjudge reliability by having a second judge measure a different set of 20 percent of these responses. The majority (91 percent) of the repeated duration measurements, (i.e., those repeated by a single judge and those made by two judges independently) were in 5 percent to 10 percent agreement with one another.

RESULTS

Responses to Training

We first asked whether the children in both groups could repeat the sequences presented to them at a normal to slow rate. It was found that the LN children could repeat all meaningful three-syllable sequences (familiar words) at this rate with no more than a single error (mean words correct 11.5 [±.76] of 12). They were only slightly less successful in repeating the nonword three-syllable sequences at normal to slow rates (mean sequences correct 11.10 [±1.33] of 12). Six normal children were required to repeat the two-syllable sequences because their performance did not meet criterion for performance on the three-syllable sequences at the rapid rate. All were able to repeat the two-syllable meaningful words with no more than a single error, and the two-syllable nonword sequences with at most two errors (of a possible 18).

The SLI children in the present study were not as successful in repeating three-syllable sequences at a normal to slow rate as were the LN children. Mean words correct was 9.40 (±2.62) of 12. Mean nonword sequences correct was at a somewhat lower level (7.40 [±2.70] of 12). Only one SLI child was unable to repeat at least some three-syllable sequences correctly.

Eighteen SLI children had to repeat the two-syllable sequences because their performance did not meet the criterion at the rapid rate for three-syllable sequences. The majority of these SLI children were able to repeat the two-syllable meaningful words at a normal to slow rate with no more than two errors (mean words correct 16.78 [±3.06] of 18). One child made six errors, and a second (the subject unable to repeat any three-syllable sequences correctly) made 12 errors. These SLI children's attempts to repeat nonword two-syllable sequences were at a somewhat lower level than for words (15.78 [±3.77] sequences correct of 18). These results suggested that the children in both groups understood the task and were able in every case to repeat at least some items correctly at a normal to slow rate in training.

Responses to Test Sequences: Accuracy of Syllable Repetition

The overall performance of the SLI children in rapid repetition of the three-syllable sequences was significantly poorer than that of the LN children. For both groups of children, rapid repetition of three-syllable words was significantly more accurate than that of the nonword three-syllable sequences. The difference in performance for these two sequence types was more marked for the SLI than for the LN children (see Figure 6-1). The performance of the majority of the SLI children on two-syllable sequences was more accurate than their performance on three-syllable sequences. Rapid repetition of meaningful two-syllable words was not more accurate than that of nonword two-syllable sequences.

The data for number of sequences correct were analyzed by means of a repeated measures two-way analysis of variance (ANOVA), with subject group and sequence type as factors. There was a significant group effect, with the LN children performing significantly more accurately (10.85 ± 1.39 words correct and 9.45 ± 1.43 nonwords correct) than the SLI children (8.75 ± 3.06 words correct and 5.05 ± 2.93 nonwords correct) ($F = 25.51$; df 1,38; $p < .0001$). Sequence type was also a significant effect, with meaningful words being produced more accurately overall than meaningless (nonword) sequences ($F = 48.69$; df 1,38; $p < .0001$). In addition there was a significant group by sequence type interaction ($F = 9.9$; df 1,38; $p < .003$). The SLI children showed a significantly greater advantage in sequence accuracy in response to meaningful words (as compared with nonword sequences) than did the LN children.

Stops were produced more accurately than fricatives. Mean number of sequences correct for "pətəkə" and "bədəgə" was 5.30 for the LN children and 2.95 for the SLI children; and for "prettycat" and "buttercup" it was 5.85 for the LN and 4.65 for the SLI children (out of a possible total of 6 sequences correct). Mean number correct for "f ∃ ʃəsə" was 1.05 for the LN children and

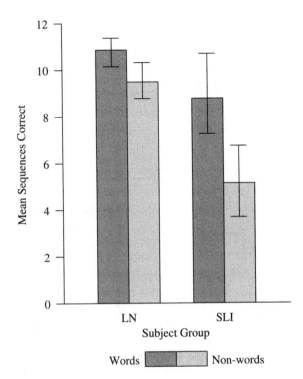

FIGURE 6-1 **Mean number of word and
nonword sequences produced correctly by the
LN and SLI children**

.15 for the SLI children; for "fishnchips" it was 2.3 for the LN children and
1.35 for the SLI children (out of a possible of three sequences correct). Because
m ∋ nət∫ə" and "miniskirt" incorporate both nasals and fricatives/affricates,
with respect to stops and fricatives these sequences were not included in the
manner of articulation observations. The finding with respect to stops and
fricatives is not surprising. Stops are acquired earlier than fricatives and require
less articulatory control in production.

The sequence errors on the two-syllable sequences produced by the 18 SLI
children who failed to meet criterion at the three-syllable level were compared
across word and nonword sequences by means of the Wilcoxon Matched Pairs,
Signed Ranks Test (Siegel, 1956). No significant difference in number of sequences correct was found for these two-syllable sequence types.

Responses to Test Items: Syllable Duration

For both groups of children, mean syllable duration (i.e., rate of syllable production) was greatest for the word and nonword sequences that comprised fricatives and least for those that comprised stops. Syllable duration for the sequences that included both nasals and fricatives ("m ∋ nətʃə" and "miniskirt") was intermediate between the rates for the stop and the fricative sequences in both subject groups. A similar pattern may be observed in the syllable duration data obtained from the adult who provided the model for the children. Syllable duration was not significantly greater for the phonetically more complex word sequences than for the simpler nonword sequences. It was not significantly different across subject groups, although this difference did approach significance.

Mean syllable duration is shown for word and nonword sequences for both subject groups in Table 6-4. A three-way ANOVA was run with subject group, sequence type (word versus nonword) and word/nonword items as factors. A $1/y$ transformation was applied to the raw duration data to correct for lack of homogeneity in the raw duration data. Mean syllable duration was found to be significantly different across word and nonword items comprising different consonants (primarily stops, nasals, or fricatives) ($p < .0001$). This finding is predictable; stops are characterized by an abrupt release followed by voicing in the vowel portion of a consonant-vowel (CV) or consonant-vowel-consonant (CVC) syllable, whereas nasals and fricatives are continuants and are prolonged to a certain extent before transition into the following vowel. There was, in addition, a significant interaction between sequence items and sequence type ($p < .005$). In other words, for both groups, sequences comprising fricatives showed the opposite effect; that is, they were produced at a lower rate in words than in nonwords. Sequences comprising nasals primarily did not appear to differ in rate across word and nonword sequences.

Mean syllable duration was not found to be significantly different across subject groups, although this effect approached significance. Mean syllable duration across sequence type (words versus nonwords) was not significantly different, and there was no group by sequence type interaction.

DISCUSSION

Two types of deficit have been proposed as having an influence on rapid rate syllable production, namely a speech motor deficit and a deficit in short-term memory for phonemes and syllables. In addition, the effect of knowledge of words and their structure on repetition of word or wordlike sequences had been investigated. These functions are presented in a tentative model of speech production in children in Figure 6-2. In this model, the Production Plan refers to

TABLE 6-4 Mean Syllable Duration for Word and Nonword Sequences Produced by the Model Speaker, and the LN and SLI Children

ID	Nonword Sequences				Word Sequences			
	p ɔ təkə	b ɔ dədgə	m ɔ nətʃə	f ɔ ʃəsə	prettycat	buttercup	miniskirt	fishnchips
Model	.186	.188	.216	.216	.188	.193	.203	.214
LN	.238(±.10)	.235(±.03)	.238(±.05)	.305(±.08)	.216(±.02)	.218(±.03)	.260(±.06)	.347(±.06)
SLI	.265(±.08)	.279(±.09)	.301(±.11)	.330(±.17)	.227(±.05)	.243(±.05)	.287(±.06)	.376(±.12)

111

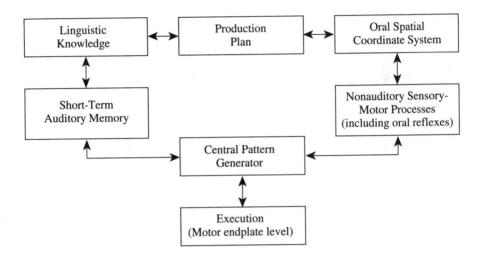

FIGURE 6-2 **A tentative model of the processes involved in rapid syllable production in children**

the general intention to perform a speech task, in this study one of rapid syllable production. Linguistic knowledge includes the semantic representations and structural features (syllabic and phonological features) of established lexical entries that are stored in long-term memory and can be transferred temporarily to short-term memory. The short-term memory component includes immediate memory for phonological and syllable structure. The oral spatial coordinate system is made up of a map of the vocal tract, including tongue, lips, jaw, and soft palate in relation to the hard palate; and of the larynx and related structures in relation to one another and to the vocal tract above the larynx. The nonauditory sensory-motor information includes local tactile and kinesthetic information and oral reflex mechanisms. The central pattern generator denotes the central executive function controlling speech motor output. Peripheral sensory-motor effector mechanisms are located at the motor endplate level. Note, however, that with the exception of the motor endplate, no location within the nervous system is proposed for the components in Figure 6-2. It will be observed that interactions between and among all the components of this model are proposed.

Katz, Curtiss, and Tallal (1991) suggest that an underlying motor deficit in SLI children is a general one, not limited to speech. They found that rapid automatized naming (RAN; Denckla & Rudel, 1976), tested longitudinally in language-impaired children, was significantly poorer than in a matched group of normal children. The language-impaired children also performed more poorly than controls on a manual (mimed) version of the RAN test. Higher correlations between RAN scores and tests of reading ability were observed for the SLI children at 8 years of age than for their matched controls. The authors conclude that the SLI children's deficits in rapid sequential processing are not limited to oral responses but, rather, generalize to other motoric domains.

Recall that there is considerable overlap of characteristics between SLI and reading-impaired children. It is therefore of interest that Wolff, Michel, and Ovrut (1990) have reported deficits in rapid rate speech production in adolescents and adults with developmental dyslexia. These authors had their subjects repeat nonword (meaningless) two- and three-syllable sequences only, in time to four different metronome speeds. The dyslexic subjects were not able to maintain the prescribed rates of production for these three-syllable sequences; they repeated syllables too slowly at all metronome speeds. In addition, they made more errors in accuracy of production of three-syllable sequences than either normal controls or learning-disabled controls without dyslexia. The dyslexic subjects were comparable to the control groups in rate and accuracy of performance on two-syllable sequences.

Repetition rate in the Wolff et al. (1990) study was found to modify the sequencing errors, but these authors regarded the two types of deficit as somewhat independent. For example, sequencing errors were also present at the slowest repetition rates. The authors interpret their findings in terms of a motor speech deficit and suggest it may be "one outward manifestation of a more general impairment of motor timing control that distinguishes dyslexic students from adequate readers and learning-disabled students without reading difficulties" (p. 33).

Catts (1989) has shown that adults with dyslexia also produce familiar simple and complex phrases at a significantly slower rate than normal, and that they make significantly more errors than normal in production of complex phrases. Most of the errors of production were context-conditioned slips of the tongue; thus, Catts concluded that they might reflect difficulty in planning serial movements for speech. He proposes that lack of fluency in oral reading might, in fact, be the consequence of a deficit in speech production.

A speech motor deficit in SLI children might imply immaturity or malfunction in components D and E of the model in Figure 6-2. Malfunction in component C would give rise to oral apraxia and, in component F, to weakness of the speech musculature. In either case, the child would fail the Robbins and Klee (1987) procedure and would thus have been excluded from the present study. It will be recalled, however, that both the LN and the SLI children made a significantly greater number of errors on nonword than on word sequences. This effect was more marked for the SLI than the LN children. Yet the word sequences were more complex in syllable structure and presumably demanded greater articulatory motor skill in production than did the nonword sequences.

Unfortunately, at present there is no generally accepted theory of the nature of speech motor control in normal children or adults—hence the tentative nature of the model in Figure 6-2. It is widely agreed that central representations play an essential role in the generation of speech movements, but there is no agreement with respect to the locus or nature of the central pattern generator. Kelso and Tuller (1983), for example, have proposed a dynamic pattern theory in which coordinative structures within the central nervous system (the central pattern generator) provide for the regulation of speech behavior without the need for on-line sensory information. Others (e.g., Lindblom, Lubker, & Gay, 1979) have argued that the changing contexts of segmental speech production in terms of stress, rate, loudness, and pitch, require sensory input. The work of Smith and her colleagues (Smith & Luschei, 1983; Smith, McFarland, Weber, & Moore, 1987) suggests that the integration of orofacial reflexes, with their afferent components, may be important for control of speech production. Smith (1992) also points out that afferent-based flexibility and continuous sampling of sensory input may be more important in the period of development of speech than for speech motor control in the mature speaker. Language-impaired and dyslexic children might show difficulty in rapid production of speech because of lack of oral reflexes. Indeed, Wood and Smith (1991) have suggested on the basis of preliminary evidence that speech-impaired children may show delayed development of oral reflex responses when compared with children who have no speech-language impairments. In such a case the deficit might be in component D, Figure 6-2.

One of the most important sensory feedback systems for speech development, however, is the auditory system. Speech sound discrimination, identification of segments and syllables of speech, and short-term memory for segments of speech may all be important for production. Deficits have been found in SLI as compared with normal children in fine-grained speech discrimination (Elliott & Hammer, 1988; Elliott, Hammer, & Scholl, 1989), identification of, and short-term memory for, CV syllables (including stops and fricatives; Tallal & Piercy, 1975; Tallal & Stark, 1981; Stark & Tallal, 1981) and short-term memory for syllables (phonological memory; Gathercole & Baddeley, 1990). These deficits might relate to immaturity or malfunction in component B of Figure 6-2. In this respect, it is important to consider the significantly greater difficulty demonstrated by both groups of children in repeating unfamiliar as compared with familiar syllable sequences; and, in addition, their greater difficulty with longer (three-syllable) as compared with shorter (two-syllable) sequences. It will be recalled that the unfamiliar three-syllable nonword sequences were simpler in phonetic structure than the familiar three-syllable word sequences, yet the SLI children were better able to generate the three-syllable words than the nonword sequences at both slow and rapid rates. This finding suggests that they were able to take advantage of a stored representation for meaningful words but had to depend on their ability to store the nonword sequences in short-term auditory memory as they were presented, and to retrieve them shortly afterward for the purposes of the production task.

It has been suggested that accuracy of repetition of nonword sequences included might be influenced by linguistic knowledge as well as phonological memory; (Gathercole, Willis, Emslie, & Baddeley, 1991). In this case, the deficit might be located in component A of Figure 6-2. Gathercole et al. did not require their subjects to repeat at a rapid rate. They found, however, that repetition accuracy in normal children decreased with the length (in number of syllables) of the sequences to be repeated, as in the present study. One linguistic factor (wordlikeness in the nonword test item) was also associated with repetition accuracy, but articulatory accuracy was not.

In the present study, the poor performance of the SLI as compared with LN children on repetition of meaningful words might suggest that the semantic and/or the syllabic and phonological representations of familiar words encoded in long-term memory (component A) were impoverished. On the other hand, their significantly poorer performance on repetition of nonwords than on words would implicate impaired short-term phonological memory in component B.

Gathercole and Baddeley (1990) also compared language-disordered and LN children's performance on their normal-rate nonword repetition task. The language-disordered children made more errors on this task than did younger normal children matched with them for vocabulary recognition scores. The authors concluded that vocabulary knowledge did not influence repetition performance. They suggested that, instead, the impaired phonological memory of the language-disordered children affected their nonword repetition. It should be pointed out, however, that word recall is impaired in SLI children to a significantly greater extent than is word recognition (Stark, Bernstein, Condino, Bender, & Tallal, 1984). If the two groups of subjects in the Gathercole and Baddeley study had been matched for vocabulary of recall scores, a significant association with nonword repetition performance might have been discovered.

Yet another hypothesis has been advanced by Wolff et al. (1990) to account for the correlation they report in their study between the dyslexic subjects' performance on the syllable repetition task and their reading test scores. They point out that the rate at which normal children repeat multisyllablic words increases with age. Repetition rate is also quite highly correlated with the normal child's short-term memory for word lists (Hulme, Thomson, Muir, & Lawrence,d 1984). The latter effect is mediated by rehearsal strategies, the success of which appears to depend on the amount of material that can be rehearsed in a given period of time (1 to 2 seconds), and hence on both rate of speech production and stimulus word length (see also Baddeley, Thomson, & Buchanan, 1975). Thus, reduced rate of production in rehearsal could effectively impair short-term memory. In such a case we might propose that immaturity or malfunctioning in components D or E of Figure 6-2 reduces the efficiency of storage in component B.

It will be recalled that the SLI and LN children did not differ significantly from one another in syllable duration for words or nonwords. Duration was lowest for fricative sequences, highest for stop sequences. It might therefore be supposed that rehearsal would be less efficient in the case of fricative than stop sequences, and that accuracy would be lowest for fricative sequences and highest for stop sequences as a result. This order of accuracy across consonant types was indeed found for both subject groups in the present study. A Spearman correlation coefficient (Siegel, 1956) was calculated for duration and accuracy on words and nonwords for both subject groups. For the LN children, there was a negative correlation between accuracy and duration (i.e., the more accurate the repetition, the shorter the mean syllable duration) for real words ($r_s = -.46$). For nonwords, the negative correlation approached but did not attain significance ($r_s = -.39$) for these children. For the SLI children, there was no significant correlation between accuracy and duration on nonwords ($r_s = .33$) or words ($r_s = -.12$). These findings might suggest that, when short-term memory for a series of syllables is within the subject's capacity, speed of production in rehearsal may have a significant effect on accuracy of recall. Where short-term memory for syllables is the primary impairment, however, speed of rehearsal may not be an important factor in recall. On the other hand, correlations between rate and accuracy of production may not implicate rehearsal in the LN children. Fricatives are acquired later than stops by normally developing children, presumably because they require greater precision of articulatory placement. This effect may be indirectly related to the differences in duration between stops and fricatives, but not through the mediation of rehearsal.

SUMMARY

The results of this study suggest that accuracy in the rapid syllable production task may be related in part to speech motor functioning, in part to deficits in short-term auditory memory. The fricative sequences, which demand greater articulatory precision in production, were repeated less accurately by children in both subject groups than were the stop sequences, which demand less articulatory precision. Accuracy appears to be related also to efficiency of short-term memory. Longer sequences were produced less accurately than shorter sequences of both words and nonwords by the SLI children and, it is assumed, by the LN children also. Familiar words were also repeated more accurately than unfamiliar nonword sequences, although the articulatory complexity required in production of the word sequences was greater than for the nonword sequences. This effect was significantly greater for the SLI than the LN children.

These findings suggest that adequacy of representation in short-term memory is an important factor, although retrieval from short-term memory may also be implicated. Sensory and motor factors may contribute, however, to both articulatory precision and the functioning of short-term memory. Perception and production must interact at many different levels within the central nervous system, as suggested in Figure 6-2, in performance on a rapid speech production task. Rapid-rate syllable production in children may involve a number of specific auditory-vocal motor circuits. Such a conclusion is consistent with the results of the anatomic studies of Semrud-Clikeman and Hynd (Chapter 3, this volume), namely that children with dyslexia typically show dysplasias and ectopias in left presylvian locations that support both auditory and speech motor areas; and those of Tallal, Sainburg, and Jernigan (1991) that report similar conclusions for language-impaired children.

In summary, the learning of phoneme and syllable sequences may be impaired primarily as a result of immature or defective short-term memory functioning. However, auditory and motor control components and also the integration of these components may be immature or malfunctioning in affected children. All such effects are likely to impair word learning and word recall. Impoverishment of the SLI child's vocabulary of recall may well be a factor in word finding in oral reading, where auditory (phonological) and motor processing are again involved.

IMPLICATIONS FOR ASSESSMENT AND INTERVENTION

Difficulty with word recall and confrontation naming is commonly found in SLI children and in children with developmental dyslexia. It is suggested that these children should routinely receive a test of vocabulary of recall—for example, the Expressive One-Word Picture Vocabulary Test (Gardner, 1991), the Boston Naming Test (Kaplan, Goodglass, & Weintraub, 1983), or the Test of Word Finding (German, 1986). For those with word recall (naming) scores significantly below the level expected on the basis of their age or, if it is available, their Performance IQ, intervention is recommended.

It has been proposed that word finding problems in SLI children are related to: (1) lack of elaboration of the lexicon—that is, a sparse network of associations in lexical memory—and (2) difficulty with retrieval from memory (Kail, Hale, Leonard, & Nippold, 1984; Kail & Leonard,d 1986). Kail and Leonard showed that both of these effects are present in SLI children. The authors have proposed that these children may also have difficulty with initial learning of new words—that is, with storing them in short-term memory and transferring them to long-term memory.

Two different approaches to intervention have been proposed, based on the Kail and Leonard findings. The first is to provide for elaboration of lexical representation, usually for noun words, for example, by categorizing the noun as an article of food or clothing; to give the child a number of exemplars from the category in question and to discuss similarities and differences; and to point out the particular lexical features (e.g., customary location of the object represented). The second is to draw the child's attention to the form of the target word (e.g., number of phonemes, number of syllables, and initial consonant phoneme). These two approaches have been assessed by McGregor and Leonard (1989) who emphasized the semantic aspects of training on recall of familiar words and found it to be effective. The results of the present study suggest that facilitation of storage and retrieval of the phonetic and syllabic structure of words is also important. It may be important first to increase the child's awareness of these aspects. Such intervention could make use of some of the procedures discussed by Mann (Chapter 4, this volume) before SLI children are required to learn to read. Modifications would be necessary for the kindergarten or preschool SLI child.

First, words that rhyme with a target word may be emphasized. The child may be asked to identify words that do and do not rhyme with that word, thus borrowing from an intervention technique used successfully by Bradley (1988). The child can also be encouraged to make up nonsense rhymes for a target word (e.g., for *man—ban, wan, san,* etc.)

Next, the initial or final consonant of a target word might be brought to the child's awareness. Consonants should first be presented in isolation and in association with common objects or events. For example, the /m/ consonant can be associated with appreciative sounds made in response to tasty foods, the /s/ sound with the hissing of a snake or the sound of running water. The child can later progress to a play activity in which he decides if the good-taste sound, /m/, or the water running sound, /s/, does or does not occur at the beginning or end of spoken words in a selected set. Frequently, it is easier for the child to listen for the initial consonant first. Vowels can be dealt with in a similar manner—for example, by associating the vowel /u/ with an expression of surprise. It is suggested, however, that it is best to work with consonants before introducing this approach with vowels.

If such an approach is used, then, when graphemes are introduced, it is helpful to associate them with the objects or events chosen to represent the consonant phoneme earlier in auditory training. Thus, /s/ might be depicted as a snake in the shape of the letter *s* if the hissing sound was selected earlier, and /m/ as a three-legged cookie monster who continually expresses gustatory satisfaction by means of the /m/ sound.

Both of these techniques (lexical categorization and elaboration, and emphasis on phonetic aspects of form) should be considered. However, it is not suggested that intervention should focus directly on increasing rate of production. Instead, production of new words should be attempted at a comfortable rate, and they should be presented in many familiar contexts and activities and with high frequency of occurrence.

It will also be important to continue efforts to study the responses of SLI and developmentally dyslexic children to the rapid syllable production task. The relationship of timing in motor control and of sequencing errors in production to auditory short-term memory is an important area of experimentation. Careful investigation of the effects of intervention may help us to a better understanding of this relationship.

REFERENCES

American National Standards Institute. (1969). *Standard specifications for audiometers.* New York: American National Standards Institute.

Baddeley, A., Thomson, N., & Buchanan, M. (1975). Word length and the structure of short-term Memory. *Journal of Verbal Learning and Verbal Behavior, 14,* 575–589.

Benton, A. (1964). Developmental aphasia and brain damage. *Cortex, 1,* 40–52.

Bradley, L. (1988). Rhyme recognition and reading and spelling in young children. In R. L. Masland & M. W. Masland (Eds.), *Prevention of reading failure* (pp. 143–162). Parkton, MD: York Press.

Catts, H. W. (1989). Speech production deficits in developmental dyslexia. *Journal of Speech and Hearing Disorders, 54,* 422–428.

Denckla, M. B., & Rudel, R. C. (1976). Rapid "automatized" naming: Dyslexia differentiated from other learning disabilities. *Neuropsychologia, 14,* 471–479.

Elliott, L. L., & Hammer, M. A. (1988). Longitudinal changes in auditory discrimination in normal children and children with language learning problems. *Journal of Speech and Hearing Disorders, 53,* 467–474.

Elliott, L. L., Hammer, M. A., & Scholl, M. E. (1989). Fine-grained auditory discrimination in normal children and children with language learning problems. *Journal of Speech and Hearing Research, 32,* 113–119.

Gardner, M. F. (1991). *Expressive One-Word Picture Vocabulary Test.* Novato, CA: Academic Therapy Publications.

Gathercole, S. E., & Baddeley, A. D. (1990). Phonological memory deficits in language disordered children: Is there a causal connection? *Journal of Memory and Language, 29,* 336–360.

Gathercole, S. E., Willis, C., Emslie, H., & Baddeley, A. D. (1991). The influence of number of syllables and wordlikeness on children's repetition of nonwords. *Applied Psycholinguistics, 12,* 349–367.

German, D. J. (1986). *Test of Word Finding.* Allen, TX: DLM Teaching Resources.

Hulme, C., Thomson, N., Muir, C., & Lawrence, A. (1984). Speech rate and the development of short-term memory span. *Journal of Experimental Child Psychology, 38,* 241–253.

Johnston, R., Stark, R. E., Mellits, E. D., & Tallal, P. (1981). Neurological status of language-impaired and normal children. *Annals of Neurology, 10,* 159–163.

Kail, R., Hale, C., Leonard, L. D., & Nippold, M. (1984). Lexical storage and retrieval in language impaired children. *Applied Psycholinguistics, 5,* 37–49.

Kail, R., & Leonard, L. B. (1986). Word finding abilities in language impaired children. *ASHA Monographs, 25.*

Kamhi, A., & Catts, H. W. (1989). *Reading disabilities: A developmental language perspective.* Boston: Little, Brown.

Kaplan, E., Goodglass, H., & Weintraub, S. (1983). *Boston Naming Test.* Philadelphia: Lea & Febiger.

Katz, W., Curtiss, S., & Tallal, P. (1991). *Rapid automatized naming and gesture by normal and language-impaired children.* Paper presented at the Second International Symposium on Specific Speech and Language Impairment in Children, Harrogate, United Kingdom.

Kelso, J. A. S., & Tuller, B. (1983). "Compensatory Articulation" under conditions of reduced afferent information: A dynamic formulation. *Journal of Speech and Hearing Research, 26,* 217–224.

Lindblom, B. E. F., Lubker, J. F., & Gay, T. (1979). Formant frequencies of some fixed-mandible vowels and model of speech motor programming by predictive stimulation. *Journal of Phonetics, 7,* 147–161.

McGregor, K. K., & Leonard, L. B. (1989). Facilitating word finding skills of language-impaired children. *Journal of Speech and Hearing Disorders, 54,* 141–147.

Robbins, J., & Klee, T. (1987). Clinical assessment of oropharyngeal motor development in young children. *Journal of Speech and Hearing Disorders, 52*(3), 271–277.

Semel, E., Wiig, E., & Secord, W. (1987). *Clinical Evaluation of Language Fundamentals — Revised.* San Antonio, TX: Psychological Corporation, Harcourt Brace Jovanovich.

Siegel, S. (1956). *Nonparametric statistics for the behavioral sciences.* New York: McGraw-Hill.

Smith, A. (1992). The control of orofacial movements in speech. In *Critical reviews in oral biology and medicine, 3,* 233–267.

Smith, A., & Luschei, E. (1983). Assessment of oral motor reflexes in stutterers and normal speakers: Preliminary observations. *Journal of Speech and Hearing Research, 26,* 322–328.

Smith, A., McFarland, D., Weber, C. M., & Moore, C. A. (1987). Spatial organization of human perioral reflexes. *Experimental Neurology, 90,* 489–509.

Stark, R. E., Bernstein, L. E., Condino, R., Bender, M., & Tallal, P. (1984). Four-year follow up study of language impaired children. *Annals of Dyslexia, 34,* 49–68.

Stark, R. E., & Tallal, P. (1981). Perceptual and motor deficits in language-impaired children. In R. W. Keith (Ed.), *Central auditory and language disorders in children,* Houston: College Hill Press.

Stark, R. E., & Tallal, P. R. McCauley (Ed.). (1988). *Language, speech and reading disorders in children: Neuropsychological studies.* San Diego: College-Hill Press.

Stark, R. E., Tallal, P., & Mellits, E. D. (1983). Behavioral attributes of language disorders in children. In C. Ludlow (Ed.), *Genetic aspects of speech and language disorders* (pp. 37–51). New York: Academic Press.

Tallal, P., & Piercy, M. (1974). Developmental aphasia: Rate of auditory processing and selective impairment of consonant perception. *Neuropsychologia, 13,* 83–93.

Tallal, P., & Piercy, M. (1975). Developmental aphasia: The perception of brief vowels and extended stop consonants. *Neuropsychologia, 13,* 69–74.

Tallal, P., Sainburg, R. L., & Jernigan, T. (1991). The neuropathology of developmental dysphasia: Behavioral, morphological, and physiological evidence for a temporal processing disorder. *Reading and Writing, 3,* 363–378.

Tallal, P., & Stark, R. E. (1981). Speech acoustic-cue discrimination abilities of normally developing and language impaired children. *Journal of the Acoustical Society of America, 69,* 568–574.

Tallal, P., Stark, R. E., & Mellits, E. D. (1985). Identification of language-impaired children on the basis of rapid perception and production skills. *Brain and Language, 25,* 314–322.

Wechsler, D. (1974). *Wechsler Intelligence Scale for Children — Revised.* New York: Psychological Corporation.

Wolff, P., Michel, C. F., & Ovrut, M. (1990). The timing of syllable repetitions in developmental dyslexia. *Journal of Speech and Hearing Research, 33,* 281–289.

Wood, J. L., & Smith, A. (1991). Oral motor reflexes in normal-speaking and articulation-disordered children. *Developmental medicine and child neurology, 33,* 797–812.

▶ 7

Morphological Awareness, Spelling, and Story Writing

Possible Relationships for Elementary-Age Children with and without Learning Disabilities

JOANNE F. CARLISLE
Northwestern University

Abstract

This chapter presents a study of the interrelations of morphological knowledge, spelling ability, and aspects of story-writing capabilities. Second- and third-grade learning-disabled (LD) poor spellers were compared to LD and non-LD good spellers on tasks assessing oral and written production of morphological words and on a story-writing task. LD poor spellers showed less morphological awareness on both oral and spelling tasks than did their LD and non-LD good speller peers. On the story-writing task, LD poor spellers differed from controls on the number of words they wrote, the imaginative quality of their stories, and the percentage of misspelled words, but did not differ in incorrect use of morphologically complex words. These results suggest tht LD poor spellers have difficulties in learning rule-based linguistic systems and that their difficulties affect their ability to write stories as well as their peers do. The chapter concludes by considering the assessment of linguistic knowledge as one part of a comprehensive assessment of children's writing capabilities.

Until very recently, there has been a curious lack of interest in the writing problems of learning-disabled (LD) students, if we can judge from the number of research studies published on this topic. In reviewing the papers published in an issue of *Exceptional Children* devoted to writing, Newcomer, Nodine, and Barenbaum (1988) found only 18 references to studies focused on the writing of exceptional children. They expressed the concern that practitioners must decide on instructional strategies for children with writing problems when the nature of these problems is poorly understood (Newcomer et al., 1988); this concern has been echoed by others (see Lynch & Jones, 1989).

A number of research studies on the writing of LD children have focused on descriptive characteristics, often comparing LD and non-LD children on the length of compositions, complexity of sentences, and the like (see, for instance, Houck & Billingsley, 1989; Johnson & Grant, 1989). These studies represent a start, in that we can see that LD children do generally differ from their peers in the quality and quantity of their writing; but it may not help us understand the underlying causes of writing difficulties or the interrelations of the many sources of knowledge and mental processes that are needed for proficient written expression. Reviewers have suggested that researchers turn to studies of the process of writing (Lynch & Jones, 1989) and of the effectiveness of different types of instruction (Graham, Harris, MacArthur, & Schwartz, 1991) in order to improve our understanding of the writing of LD children. Another approach, one that may help us understand some possible causes, involves investigations of relations between oral language and written language skills. Writing is, after all, an expressive language function and depends on understanding the linguistic structure of words. If we do not investigate capabilities in these areas, we may recommend forms of remediation that are inappropriate. For example, efforts to make children more productive writers or more conscious of their own writing processes (Graham et al., 1991; Moran, 1988) may be inappropriate if a child has expressive language difficulties.

Attempts to assess children's language capabilities through examining their spontaneous writing samples can be confusing. We are apt to encounter the kinds of errors found in the story written by a second-grade girl shown in Figure 7-1. With only the story to go on, it is impossible to tell whether the girl lacks knowledge of inflected word forms (e.g., *set*), has significant difficulties with spelling, is prone to "production" failures (i.e., gets bogged down by the act of writing and inaccurately represents what she wants to say), or is experiencing a combination of these problems. It would help us understand the nature of her problem if we could compare this child's oral and written production of morphologically complex words. Such information should help her teachers decide whether or not she needs language training in the area of morphology.

The focus of this chapter is elementary-age LD children with significant spelling problems; the questions concern both the possible causes of these problems and their possible effects on written expression. One question is whether the spelling problems of these children might be due to underlying deficits in linguistic or metalinguistic knowledge. The second is whether spelling problems

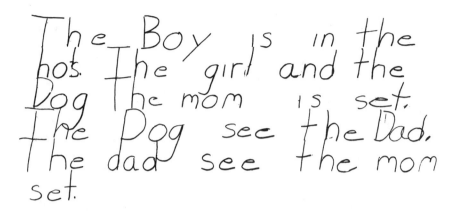

FIGURE 7-1 **PSLT (Picture Story Language Test) story written by a second-grade LD girl**

in the elementary years affect children's story-writing capabilities. These questions were investigated in a study of second- and third-grade LD poor spellers and LD and non-LD good spellers. The first part of this chapter will present a discussion of the rationale and background for the study, the method, and the results. The results suggest relationships between morphological knowledge, spelling ability, and aspects of story writing (namely productivity, the imaginative quality of stories, and spelling) for LD and non-LD children in elementary school. The second section of this chapter discusses how assessment of linguistic capabilities constitutes one part of a comprehensive assessment of children's writing capabilities.

LANGUAGE CAPABILITIES AND POOR SPELLING

Links between Oral and Written Language

To express their ideas in writing, children must have the words and linguistic structures needed to convey their ideas. Thus, assessment of a child's proficiency in oral language would provide a sense of what he or she might be able to achieve in writing. For LD children, comparisons of oral and written language capabilities have been used in some areas of research, such as knowledge of story grammar (see Nodine, Barenbaum, & Newcomer, 1985). Surprisingly little has been done to examine the kinds of linguistic knowledge children use in spelling. Several research studies have suggested that even as early as the elementary years, children are drawing on various kinds of linguistic knowledge to spell words – letter-sound correspondences, orthographic patterns, word-specific knowledge, and morphological knowledge (Schwartz & Doehring, 1977; Waters, Bruck, & Malus-Abramowitz, 1988), but these researchers have based these judgments on tasks involving dictation spelling and recognition spelling. For LD poor spellers, we would have a better sense of the depth of the problem if linguistic knowledge were assessed with oral as well as written tasks. A study of this kind was conducted by Rubin (1987) in investigating the link between awareness of the morphological structure of words and the ability to spell these words for kindergarten and first-grade children. She found that the first-graders who demonstrated poor morphological knowledge on an oral task tended to omit the final consonant representing the inflectional marker (e.g., the /d/ in "pinned") in spelling. In this way, she linked a weakness in orthographic representation to a weakness in the learning of morphological rules.

The linguistic foundations for spelling need to be explored more fully for all school-age children, but such information may be particularly helpful to those who are trying to understand the writing problems of children with learning disabilities. In particular, studies of oral and written language capabilities might help us determine whether gaps in linguistic awareness and expressive language capabilities characterize the problems of at least some LD poor spellers.

Development of Morphological Knowledge

Children acquire implicit understanding of the morphological structure of words first through oral language. As children become readers and writers, morphological knowledge appears to be linked to the development of their vocabulary (Freyd & Baron, 1982; Nagy & Anderson, 1984), word recognition (Nagy, Anderson, Schommer, Scott, & Stallman, 1989), and spelling (Carlisle, 1987; Templeton & Scarborough-Franks, d1985). For LD poor spellers, one concern is whether the process and timing of the acquisition of morphological awareness is like that of their peers.

Different approaches to investigating the morphological knowledge of children have yielded different views of when and how children learn morphological forms. One approach has been to study the productive knowledge of morphology, particularly inflected forms, using nonsense word stems so that knowledge of real words does not aid a child's performance (Berko, 1958; Selby, 1972). Preschoolers' and first-graders' performances on such a task suggested to Berko (1958) that the learning of inflected forms is distinct from the learning of derived forms. She concluded that inflected forms are almost completely mastered before derived forms are learned. First-graders are able to use compounding (e.g., a person who "zibbed" for a living is called a "zibman") but not derivation (e.g., responding "a zibber" to the same sentence stem). On the other hand, studies of children's learning and use of new words provide evidence that some principles of derivation are learned in the preschool years (Bowerman, 1981; Clark, 1982). Borrowing a model of the process of understanding or producing morphologically complex words from MacWhinney (1979), we can suppose that morphological learning depends on the child's mastery of the phonology, the syntax, and the semantics of the language. The speech stream is analyzed in order to identify and extract morphemes from different contexts. Synactic and semantic analysis accompany the development of lexical representation and the identification of morphemes. For example, the child learns to distinguish the prefix *un-* in *undo* from the syllable *un-* in *under*. Whereas morphological knowledge in a narrow sense means knowing morphemes and combinatory principles, in a broader sense it is acquired by identification of phonologically similar elements and an understanding of semantic relations and syntactic roles. Presumably, deficits in any of these components of language would affect the manner and the pace with which a child learns morphological forms.

Inflectional and derivational expression might be seen as falling along a continuum (Bybee, 1985). At one end is the kind of inflectional expression that combines morphemes in obligatory ways (e.g., to express plurality, one must use the marker /s/). At the other end are those derivational expressions that are idiosyncratic in formation or meaning (e.g., *crux* and *crucial*). The derivational constructions that younger children learn first are regular and productive (e.g., *er* attached to verbs to make agentives like *teacher*); the semantic and syntactic relations are relatively simple. The less transparent forms of derivational expression often require more sophisticated knowledge of semantic and syntactic roles and phonological relations. It is, therefore, not surprising that productive use of many derived forms may develop slowly.

The sometimes complex phonological transformations from base to derived forms (e.g., *divide* and *division*) may make awareness of morphological relations less apparent or accessible. Tyler (1986) has presented evidence that children between the fourth and eighth grades learn "neutral" suffixes (e.g., "-ness") and readily decomposable forms (e.g., *happiness*) before they learn the "nonneutral" forms that entail sound shifts in words (e.g., *invade, invasion*). Difficulties in mastering phonological changes are also evident from an analysis of students' errors when they were asked to finish sentences that required producing derived forms. Given a base word, such as *produce,* and a sentence stem, such as "The play was a grand _____," fourth- to eighth-graders who were unsure of the correct answer tended to give responses that avoided phonological changes (e.g., *producement* instead of *production*) (Carlisle, 1988).

As the foregoing discussion suggests, children normally use inflected forms before they use many derived forms, but it seems likely that they are learning principles that govern construction of both inflected and derived forms. Of the derived forms, they learn first morphological relations with transparent elements (e.g., *happiness*), but awareness of morphological relations that entail phonological shifts may not emerge until the middle school years (Carlisle, 1988). Certainly, investigations of the knowledge of derivational morphology among elementary-age children are needed to understand developmental patterns of morphological learning more fully.

Researchers have found LD children to be significantly weaker than their peers on tasks of morphological knowledge (Vogel, 1977; Wiig, Semel, & Crouse, 1973). As noted earlier, it is not surprising that problems learning morphological forms often co-occur with difficulties in learning the syntax and phonology of the language. Older LD children have a similar pattern of understanding of derivational relations that undergo phonological and orthographic changes to that of their non-LD peers, but their performance is comparable to that of younger children (Carlisle, 1987). If this pattern holds true for elementary-age children, we might expect the LD children to have a less comprehensive knowledge of morphological forms than their peers.

Spelling Morphologically Complex Words

In the past, the most common way to categorize or describe disabled spellers (and sometimes the spelling of all children) has been on the basis of their ability to spell phonetically regular and irregular words (see Boder, 1971; Finucci, Isaacs, Whitehouse, & Childs, 1983; Nelson, 1980). Phonetically regular words are those that can be constructed using phoneme–grapheme correspondence "rules," and irregular words are those that contain one or more elements (phoneme or syllable) that cannot be so constructed (such as the *eo* in *people*). Such words can be described as requiring "word-specific" knowledge. There are problems with this model in terms of the phonological structure of words, the validity of the rules, and the discreteness of the dichotomy (see Henderson, 1982). A major flaw of this system is that it does not accurately represent the English language, which is morphophonological in nature.

Learning phoneme–grapheme correspondences only partially represents the challenge of learning to spell English words. Learning the orthographic representation of morphemes may stabilize awareness of the structure of words and have a positive impact on spelling ability (Templeton & Scarborough-Franks, 1985). From the beginning of their experience writing stories, children try to represent morphologically complex words because they use such words in formulating their ideas. Gradually, they learn that spelling often preserves the identity of morphemes orthographically, even when pronunciation varies. A vivid example is the ease with which most children learn the spelling of the past tense *-ed,* even though it can be pronounced in three ways (e.g., /t/ in *stripped,* /d/ in *grabbed,* and /ed/ in *sledded*). To become accurate writers, children must learn the spelling of morphemes as well as phonemes.

A key ingredient in the linguistic-orthographic connection described here is the child's explicit awareness of the segments of words. Exposure to written language is believed to help children acquire an awareness of phonemes (Ehri, 1989), and the same may be true of morphemes. One reason may simply be that a notational system is helpful in any kind of abstract analytic learning, as Mattingly has suggested (1987). Awareness of and memory for the spelling of particular morphemes may be reinforced by their repetition in various words (e.g., *love, lovely, lovable, lover*). The frequency with which certain morphemes appear in the words children encounter may affect word recognition (Nagy et al., 1989) and knowledge of spelling patterns.

In addition to learning letter–sound correspondences and the spelling of specific morphemes, children are also learning orthographic patterns (such as when to use *-ge* or *-dge*) and positional constraints (such as the use of *-ck* to spell /k/ at the ends of words). Two studies have shown that all four kinds of knowledge—letter–sound correspondences, word-specific spellings, orthographic patterns, and morphemic units—are used by children from the elementary years on and that growth in the use of linguistic knowledge in spelling is evident between grades 2 and 6 (Schwartz & Doehring, 1977; Waters, Bruck, & Malus-Abramowitz, 1988). One particular aspect of both studies involved the mastery of morphological rules for spelling. In the Schwartz and Doehring (1977) study, good spellers performed better on orthographic than on morphological patterns, but the reverse was true for the poor spellers. In the Waters et al. (1988) study, children had the most difficulties with the morphological rules and the least difficulty with basic letter–sound correspondences; the poorer spellers at all ages followed this same pattern. These somewhat conflicting results may have to do with whether morphological knowledge is directly targeted (e.g., asking children to spell plurals and past tenses, as in Schwartz & Doehring, 1977) or implied (e.g., asking the children to spell *sign,* assuming that if they know *signal* they will think to end the word with an *n,* as in Waters et al., 1988). These studies suggest confusion about the developmental appropriateness of different types of morphologically complex words (inflected versus derived) and about the difference between obligatory rules that may be applied in a rote fashion (as with inflections) and high levels of morphological awareness or linguistic problem solving (as are likely to be required if *sign* is spelled by thinking about *signal*).

Morphological awareness appears to be a crucial element in the process of learning to spell morphologically complex words. In a study of the knowledge and spelling of morphologically complex words by fourth-, sixth-, and eighth-graders and LD ninth-graders (Carlisle, 1987), the results showed that the LD ninth-graders were more delayed in their mastery of the spelling of the morphologically complex words than in their oral productive knowledge of these words. Their performance on the oral task was slightly stronger than that of the sixth graders, but their spelling performance was like that of the fourth-graders. The LD students were less aware of the morphological structure of the words but also appeared to have specific difficulties remembering the spelling of base morphemes and suffixes.

It is not clear when and why such gaps in knowledge develop. It is possible that LD poor spellers are generally slower in developing metalinguistic capabilities, even in the elementary years. If this is true, morphemic awareness might be delayed on oral as well as written language tasks. On the other hand, poor spellers' problems may relate more specifically to difficulties in learning other aspects of linguistic knowledge that affect spelling, such as letter–sound correspondences, which may make awareness of the morphological structure of words less apparent than it is to their peers. To test these two possibilities, we need to investigate not only elementary-age children's productive knowledge of inflected and derived forms, but also their ability to spell these forms. If elementary-age LD poor spellers follow the pattern of the older LD poor spellers, they will know more about morphology than they use in their spelling, but delays will be evident in both areas. This pattern would suggest that LD poor spellers have deficits in both the basic linguistic skills used in spelling and in the development of general metalinguistic capabilities.

Contrived and Spontaneous Writing Tasks

Most studies of poor spellers assess spelling on tests of dictation, using real and/or nonsense words, sometimes accompanied by tests of spelling recognition (for examples, see Finucci et al., 1983; Hoff, 1990; Schwartz & Doehring, 1977; Waters et al., 1988). It has not been common practice to compare children's spelling on tests of dictation with their spelling in their own writing (one notable exception is Sterling, 1983). One problem with the use of tests of dictation is the possibility that children are asked to spell words they themselves do not use in their own writing and have never attempted to spell. For this reason, comparison of spelling on dictation tests and spontaneous writing tasks would be useful. Such comparisons should also provide information about the relationship between children's spelling problems and their writing problems, more broadly conceived.

It might be reasonable to expect that children with spelling problems would be less fluent and productive writers. In addition, the quality of their ideas may be affected by their need to devote so much of their mental energies to the process of getting words onto the page accurately. A few studies have provided results that indirectly may support these intuitions. Juel (1988) reported that one-third of the poor writers in the fourth-grade group she was studying had poor ideas but good spelling, and one-third had good ideas but poor spelling. Nonetheless, for some children, poor spelling seemed to inhibit the process of writing, so that the quality of the composition was affected in ways other than the poor spelling itself. Juel remarked that some first-graders were unwilling to try to write words because they could not spell them; she found that spelling had more of an impact on first-grade writing than on fourth-grade writing. Specifically, spelling accounted for 29 percent of the variance in story writing (after controlling for the influence of ideas) for the first grade, but only 10 percent of the variance for the fourth grade.

The results of Juel's study make one wonder about LD children with poor spelling abilities. Are they, like the first-graders, unwilling to write down ideas because of awareness of their spelling difficulties? Graham and his colleagues (1991) found that LD children were more productive when they were allowed to dictate their stories, in comparison to writing them by hand. This study, however, does not focus specifically on the writing of LD poor spellers. We might wonder whether all LD children are less productive when writing by hand than when dictating a story. Analysis of the productivity and quality of the story writing, as well as the number of spelling errors made by LD poor spellers and by LD and non-LD good spellers, might help us answer these questions.

It is possible that some children with spelling problems choose to use words they feel they can spell correctly. If this were the case, then LD poor spellers might write relatively short stories but might not make significantly more spelling errors than their peers. A second possibility is that some LD poor spellers might write fluently, without much awareness of or regard for the accuracy of their spelling. If this were the case, we might find that LD poor spellers write stories that are about as long as those of their peers but that they make significantly more spelling errors in them.

Finally, performances on contrived tasks, where children are asked to generate and then spell morphologically complex words, may provide a useful comparison to the children's spontaneous writing performances. Having determined whether LD poor spellers differ from their peers in producing and spelling words on request, we might learn whether children use morphologically complex words accurately in their own stories and whether word form errors are more prevalent for LD poor spellers than for LD and non-LD good spellers.

Certainly, deficiencies in spontaneous writing may stem from many different problems. After all, for young children, few if any aspects of the writing process have been sufficiently learned and practiced to become automatic in execution. Scardamalia (1981) suggests that we consider the many different aspects of writing young children need to concentrate on at one time. Unlike adults, they must give conscious and fairly constant attention even to basic components like handwriting. LD poor spellers clearly lack automaticity in spelling, and their pronounced difficulties with spelling may affect the ease with which they can formulate ideas, compose sentences, and monitor their own writing processes. Thus, even though we may uncover specific problems that children are experiencing through the use of contrived tasks, these may not necessarily tell the whole story.

DESIGN OF THE STUDY

The study reported here is one part of a larger investigation undertaken by a group of researchers seeking to understand developing linguistic and graphomotor skills in relation to spelling and story writing for LD and non-LD children in the primary grades. One aspect of this project centered on the children's morphological knowledge, spelling ability, and story writing. One purpose was to determine whether LD poor spellers have trouble specifically with spelling, or whether there are other aspects of rule-based language learning that also are sources of difficulty (in particular, their learning of rules for producing morphologically complex words). A second purpose was to investigate the development of metalinguistic abilities, specifically looking at whether LD poor spellers in the elementary years have adequate morphological knowledge but are not able to (or do not think to) use this knowledge in spelling complex words. A third purpose was to determine whether poor spellers differed from their peers in the quality of their written stories or in the accuracy with which they were written. Specifically, the research questions were as follows:

1. Do LD poor spellers differ from LD and non-LD good spellers in their knowledge of morphological forms?
2. Do they differ in their ability to spell morphologically complex words that they know orally?
3. Do LD poor spellers differ in the length and complexity of their written stories?
4. Do LD poor spellers differ in the proportion of spelling errors and morphological errors in their written stories?

Subjects

Eighty-five students in grades 2 through 3 will be discussed in this report — 36 learning-disabled (LD) children and 42 non-LD children. The LD students who participated in this project came from six different educational settings in a midwestern suburban region. The non-LD children all attended the same elementary school. While some of the LD students attended this school, the decision was made to include LD students from neighboring schools in order to assemble a large enough group to allow us to make comparisons of LD and non-LD students across grade levels. A breakdown of the LD and non-LD groups by grade level and gender, found in Table 7-1, shows a fairly even ratio of boys

TABLE 7-1   **Breakdown of LD and Non-LD Groups by Grade and Gender**

	Grade 2 Males, Females	Grade 3 Males, Females
LD poor spellers ($n = 20$)	7,3	4,6
LD good spellers ($n = 16$)	2,3	7,4
Non-LD good spellers ($n = 42$)	14,11	9,8

to girls in the LD and non-LD groups, collapsed across grade levels and types of LD students.

The LD children had been previously identified as having specific learning disabilities, following the regulations of the state of Illinois, and all were receiving special education services at the time of the testing. Only second- and third-graders with average or above-average receptive vocabulary scores were included (at or above a standard score of 85 on the Peabody Picture Vocabulary Test – Revised); as a result, 6 LD children who had participated in the project were eliminated from the analyses described here. Two groups of LD children and one group of non-LD children were formed. Performances on the Wide Range Achievement Test, Spelling subtest (WRAT-R; Jastak & Wilkinson, 1984), were used to form an LD group with below-average spelling performance (e.g., below a standard score of 85) (henceforth called LD poor spellers), a second LD group with average to above-average spelling performances (henceforth called LD good spellers), and a group of non-LD good spellers, also with WRAT-R Spelling scores of 85 or above. Table 7-2 shows the mean standard scores for the LD and Non-LD groups on the Peabody Picture Vocabulary Test – Revised (PPVT-R; Dunn & Dunn, 1981), the WRAT-R Spelling subtest, and the Developmental

TABLE 7-2   **Mean Standard Scores (and SDs) of LD Good and Poor Spellers and Non-LD Good Spellers on the PPVT-R, WRAT-R Spelling, and VMI-R**

	PPVT-R	WRAT-R Spelling	VMI-R
LD poor spellers ($n = 20$)	105.2 (9.5)	77.6 (7.7)	88.7 (9.3)
LD good spellers ($n = 16$)	111.3 (14.8)	97.6 (8.3)	93.4 (11.2)
Non-LD good spellers ($n = 42$)	106.8 (11.8)	106.0 (11.6)	105.7 (12.7)

Test of Visual Motor Integration — Revised (VMI-R; Beery, 1982). Analysis of variance for each of these measures indicated that overall group differences were not significant on the PPVT-R ($p > .05$) but were for the WRAT-R, $F(2,73) = 49.076$, $p < .001$, and for the VMI, $F(2,73) = 16.307$, $p < .001$. For both of these analyses, paired comparisons (Tukey HSD, $p < .05$) showed that the LD poor spellers differed from the LD good spellers and the non-LD good spellers. For the LD poor spellers, the mean difference between PPVT-R and WRAT-R Spelling standard scores was 28.9 (7.8 SD); for the LD good spellers, the mean difference between these same scores was 13.7 (15.6 SD); and for the non-LD children, the mean difference between these scores was 0.7 (12.0 SD).

Materials

As noted previously, the children were administered the PPVT-R and the WRAT-R. The PPVT-R, a test of receptive vocabulary, was administered to assess the children's verbal comprehension. The WRAT-R, Level 1, Spelling subtest, is a test of dictated words; it was used as a general measure of productive spelling ability.

Two additional tests were administered to answer the research questions:

1. The Picture Story Language Test (Myklebust, 1965) requires each child to write a story based on a picture of a boy playing with toys. The analyses of the children's protocols that will be discussed include two of Myklebust's scales — Productivity (total number of words the child wrote) and the Abstract-Concrete Scale (a measure of the writer's ability to distance himself or herself from the concrete image(s) in the picture and to tell a story that is imaginative). Two additional analyses were included for this project — Misspellings (words misspelled as a proportion of total words) and Word Form Errors (omissions or substitutions of morphological markers as a proportion of total words).

2. An experimental test called the Word Forms Test, Oral and Spelling subtests, was also administered. The purposes of this test are to assess productive knowledge of inflected and derived word forms (Oral subtest) and to assess children's ability to spell the word forms they are able to generate (Spelling subtest). The task for the Oral subtest entailed deciding on the right word form to end a sentence, after listening to the base word, followed by a sentence with its last word missing. For example, having heard the examiner say, "Farm. My uncle is a _____," the child would correctly respond, "Farmer." The target words on the test included five inflected forms (e.g., *taller* and *jackets*), six derived forms that involved no phonological change, hereafter referred to as *transparent* (e.g., *quickly* and *driver*), and five derived forms that involved a phonological change (e.g., *invention* and *magician*). The words were presented in a fixed random order. An effort was made to use words that would be familiar to the children; the base and derived words of the three types described here did not differ significantly in frequency (Standard Frequency Index) of use in written texts used by school children (Carroll, Davies, & Richman, 1971).

The task for the Spelling subtest entailed writing the word on a blank line following the sentence. The base form was not given. Because the children had just heard the base form and had just produced the morphologically complex response, the task was thought to present the children with the best possible opportunity to be aware of the morphological structure of each word as they spelled it. The child's spelling of a word was only considered if he or she gave the correct oral response to the sentence; the total score on the Spelling subtest is the number of correct spellings as a proportion of correct oral responses. In this way, the child's Spelling subtest score represented his or her ability to spell correctly words that he or she produced, given the sentence prompt.

Procedures

In addition to the tests discussed above, the children were administered the VMI-R and a computer-based test of figure drawing and word writing executed on a graphics tablet to assess the development of their graphomotor skills (Meeks, Kuklinski, & Hook, 1990). However, these two aspects of the project will not be discussed in this chapter.

Each student was tested in two sessions, at least a week apart, in the winter and early spring; each session lasted about one-half hour. In the first session, the VMI-R, the PPVT-R, and the graphomotor test were administered. In the second session, the WRAT-R, PSLT, and Word Forms Test were administered.

RESULTS AND DISCUSSION

Morphological Knowledge, Oral and Spelling

The first question asked whether the LD poor spellers differed from the LD and non-LD good spellers in their ability to produce morphologically complex words orally. The percentage correct on each word type on the Word Forms Test, Oral subtest, was calculated. A repeated-measures analysis of variance showed that there were significant differences between the groups, $F(2,74) = 7.177$, $p < .001$, and the three word types, $F(2,148) = 43.550$, $p < .001$. The interaction was not significant. As Figure 7-2 shows, each group did better on inflected than transparent derived forms, and better on transparent derived forms than on phonological change derived forms. The relative difficulty of these word types is about comparable for the LD poor spellers and the LD and non-LD good spellers.

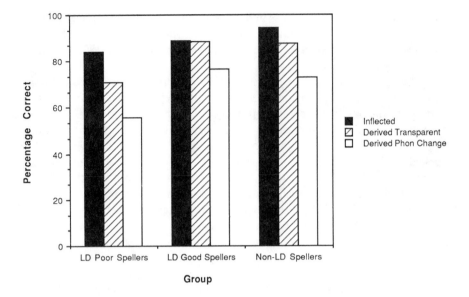

FIGURE 7-2 **Performances on the three word types of the Word Forms Test (Inflected, Transparent Derived, and Phonological Change Derived forms)**

Therefore, a one-way analysis of variance was carried out for each word type. These analyses showed that the LD poor spellers were significantly weaker than their non-LD peers on each of the word types and that they were significantly weaker than the LD good spellers on all but the inflected forms. (Here and throughout this discussion, Tukey HSD, $p < .05$ was used as a post hoc test of differences in group means.) Thus, even though the LD poor spellers did not differ from the LD good spellers on receptive vocabulary, their mastery of the system by which derived words are formed is significantly weaker. The relative weakness of the poor spellers' morphological knowledge may stem from difficulties with rule-based language learning, including difficulties with phonological processing, as well as a deficiency in metalinguistic skills.

In general, the pattern of performance on the word types shows the relative difficulty of the three types. Even the LD children did quite well on the inflected forms; the transparent derived forms appear to be an area of active learning, whereas all of the children had trouble with the phonological change forms. These results suggest that mastery of these forms may be slow in emerging because the complex phonological shifts make the semantic and morphological relations harder to appreciate.

The second question asked whether the LD good and poor spellers and the non-LD good spellers differed in their ability to spell the morphologically complex words on the Word Forms Test (WFT), Spelling subtest. Of interest also was whether there was an interaction between their performances on the two subtests — Oral and Spelling. A repeated-measures analysis of variance was carried out; the results showed a significant difference between the groups, $F(2,74) = 23.167$, $p < .001$, and for the subtests, $F(1,74) = 233.061$, $p < .001$. The interaction was also significant, $F(2,74) = 6.65$, $p < .01$. As Figure 7-3 shows, the LD poor spellers had greater difficulty spelling the words correctly (on average, only 15 percent were correct) than the LD or non-LD good spellers, who spelled about 50 percent of the words correctly. It is important to remember that the score on the Spelling subtest is the percentage correct of those words each child gave correctly on the Oral subtest. Thus, of the words they knew, the LD poor spellers were able to spell correctly fewer than half as many words as their LD and non-LD good speller peers.

Further insight into the nature of the problems of the LD poor spellers came from additional analysis of the children's spellings of the words on the WFT, Spelling subtest. This analysis was accomplished by creating a complete corpus of the written versions of each word, correct or incorrect. The number of times children spelled or misspelled a word a given way were then tabulated. From

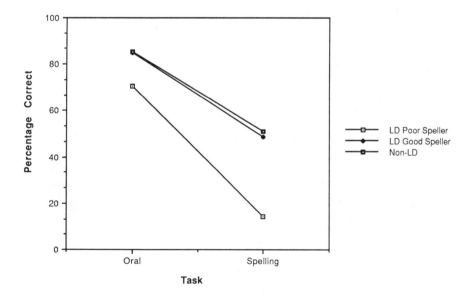

FIGURE 7-3 **Performances on the Oral and Spelling subtests of the Word Forms Test**

this analysis, it seemed that the LD poor spellers had a relatively immature understanding of the way "traditional" spelling is accomplished. There were some incidents of preconventional phonetic spellings (Moats, 1983), such as *jiver* for *driver*. Furthermore, vowels were commonly omitted or misrepresented (e.g., *hrmfl* for *harmful*). Finally, the LD poor spellers seemed to be learning the correct spellings of inflectional and derivational suffixes more slowly; thus, for example, a non-LD first-grader might spell *sleepy* as *slepe*; this error was found for LD but not for non-LD second-graders.

It is not surprising that all three groups of children were less able to spell the morphologically complex words than to say them. As was noted earlier, spelling requires not only awareness of the internal structure of the word but also knowledge of letter–sound correspondences, orthographic patterns, and nonphonetic elements (word-specific spellings). This same pattern of stronger oral than spelling performance was evident on a similar test administered to fourth- through eighth-graders and LD ninth-graders (Carlisle, 1987). One important difference was that for the elementary children, the oral and spelling responses came one right after the other, in order to heighten the children's awareness of the morphological structure of the words they were spelling; for the older students, administration of the oral and spelling tasks took place on separate days. We might expect older students and LD ninth-graders to understand the need to override the process of spelling by letter–sound correspondence when suffixes are added to words, but we might not have the same expectation for the younger children, as metalinguistic skills are less well developed in the elementary years. Nonetheless, the good spellers in this study showed more sensitivity to the spellings of certain suffixes (e.g., *-tion*) than did the LD poor spellers. As a result, gaps in metalinguistic skills appear to be more pronounced for the poor spellers than the good spellers, even in these early school years.

Story Writing, Morphological Knowledge, and Spelling

The third research question asked whether the LD poor spellers differed from the LD good spellers and the non-LD good spellers on their story writing. The children were given the Picture Story Language Test (PSLT). Several aspects of the scoring system of the test were included in this study, namely a measure of productivity (the total number of words the child wrote) and a measure of the imaginative quality or thematic sophistication of the story (the Abstract-Concrete scale) (Myklebust, 1965).

Because one purpose of this project was to investigate LD poor spellers' knowledge and spelling of morphologically complex words, two additional analyses were carried out. These involved tabulations of Misspellings and Word Forms Errors (WFE), which were then converted to a proportion of the total number of words each child wrote. Misspellings were simply words that were not spelled correctly. WFEs were those words for which a morphological marker was omitted or incorrectly chosen (e.g., "The boy play with his doll," instead of *plays* or *played*). An incorrect spelling of the marker did not constitute a WFE; thus, "He had two dollz" would not count as a WFE. However, both a Misspelling and a WFE were counted when both were clearly present (e.g., "He had two dall," where the Misspelling is the *a* in *doll* and the WFE is the omission of the plural *s*). These measurements were intended to indicate whether LD and non-LD children differed in the accuracy of their use of morphologically complex words and in their ability to spell the words they chose to use.

As Table 7-3 shows, the LD poor spellers performed quite differently in story writing than their LD and non-LD peers. Analysis of variances showed a significant group difference on Productivity, $F(2,68) = 6.770, p < .01$; the LD poor spellers differed significantly from the LD and the non-LD good spellers. Analysis of variance also showed significant group differences on the Abstrct-Concrete scale, $F(2,68) = 7.390, p < .001$; again, the LD poor spellers differed significantly from the other two groups. These results suggest that not all LD children may differ from their non-LD peers in story writing. While other studies have reported that LD students write shorter and less complex stories than their non-LD peers (Graham et al., 1991; Houck & Billingsley, 1989; Johnson & Grant, 1989; Nodine, Barenbaum, & Newcomer, 1985), these results were found only for the LD poor spellers in this study. The stories written by LD good spellers were like those of the non-LD children in length and complexity.

As Table 7-3 also shows, the analysis of Misspellings and WFEs of the LD showed that the LD poor spellers misspelled a greater percentage of the words

TABLE 7-3 **Scores of LD Poor Spellers and LD and Non-LD Good Spellers on PSLT Story Writing, Including Number of Words (Productivity), Imaginative Quality (AC), Word Form Errors (WFE), and Spelling Errors (SE)**

	Picture Story Language Test			
	Productivity	**AC**	**WFE**[a]	**SE**[a]
LD poor spellers	29.6	8.1	3.0	14.8
($n = 20$)	(17.4)	(4.5)	(5.5)	(13.6)
LD good spellers	63.3	15.3	2.3	6.0
($n = 16$)	(37.8)	(5.8)	(6.6)	(4.6)
Non-LD good spellers	60.6	13.6	0.8	4.9
($n = 42$)	(31.6)	(5.4)	(1.5)	(5.0)

Note: Standard deviations in parentheses.
[a]Errors as proportion of total words written.

they wrote than their LD and non-LD peers and that the two LD groups showed a greater percentage of WFEs than the non-LD children. Analysis of variance indicated that the groups differed significantly on the Misspellings, $F(2,68) = 9.662$, $p < .001$; the LD poor spellers differed significantly from the other groups. In contrast, analysis of variance indicated that the groups did not differ significantly on the WFEs. It is perhaps noteworthy that for all three groups the percentage of WFEs was very small, with a great deal of variation in each group. It is also true, however, that since WFEs were calculated as a percentage of total words, we need to remember that the LD poor spellers wrote significantly fewer words and simpler compositions than the children in the other groups. They therefore may have had fewer opportunities to use or misuse morphologically complex words.

Elementary children who are having trouble with writing of any kind may make errors in spelling or in the representation of word forms because their attentional capacities must be shared by so many aspects of the writing process. Thus, the girl whose story is shown in Figure 7-1 wrote *set* for *sitting* and *see* for *sees*; these may indicate a deficient knowledge of inflection markers, but it is also possible that the errors represent the child's difficulties in remembering the wording of ideas as she writes them down. Earlier, the possibility was raised that particular difficulties with lower level skills (e.g., spelling) would limit poor spellers' ability to generate and formulate ideas. The results of this study suggest that they do, in fact, have trouble writing as long and as mature stories as their peers. If their attention is focused on the accuracy of their spelling, however, it does not result in more accurate spelling in their stories. The spelling difficulties they show on tests of dictated spelling are also present in their written stories. It is true, however, that although the LD poor spellers were weaker than their peers in morphological knowledge, this weakness did not result in significantly more word form errors in their story writing.

SUMMARY AND RECOMMENDATIONS FOR FUTURE STUDIES

The results of this study suggest that LD poor spellers have trouble understanding the morphological structure of words and that lack of awareness affects their spelling of morphologically complex words. The difference between the LD poor and good spellers in morphological awareness is particularly striking because these groups did not differ in their receptive vocabulary. It may be that the language-learning difficulties of poor spellers are specific to rule-based systems; this is certainly a topic that needs further investigation.

The severity of the poor spellers' spelling problems indicates gaps in other aspects of the linguistic knowledge used in spelling. These gaps were not formally analyzed in this study, but they certainly constitute another area of elementary-age writing that needs further investigation. Similarly, more work needs to be done to understand the relationship between developing linguistic and metalinguistic abilities. In particular, it seems important to determine whether basic problems in acquiring various kinds of linguistic knowledge used in spelling affect children's development of morphological awareness.

Performance of the LD poor spellers in story writing indicated that they wrote shorter and less mature stories and made more spelling errors than their LD and non-LD good speller peers. These results suggest that in the elementary years, at least, the writing process is hindered by difficulties with spelling. If the poor spellers are devoting attention to their spelling as they write, such attention does not result in spelling that is as accurate as that of their peers. It is also important to note that the LD children with adequate spelling capabilities did not differ from their peers in the aspects of story writing measured for this study. A suggestion that might be made on the basis of this finding is that, in future studies of the writing of LD children, subgroups of children with different spelling and language capabilities be compared further. In particular, it would be interesting to see how LD poor spellers would perform if asked to dictate stories rather than write them by hand. If LD poor spellers have average to above-average receptive vocabularies, it is possible that their storytelling capabilities would be superior to their story-writing capabilities.

COMPREHENSIVE-WRITING ASSESSMENTS

At present, assessment of writing seems to consist primarily of analysis of written products, whether scoring is done holistically or by analysis of separate skills and kinds of knowledge. Although holistic scoring of writing samples has been popular for some time, several recent studies recommend assessment of instructionally relevant aspects of writing because they are sensitive to children's progress and are more useful to teachers (Parker, Tindal, & Hasbrouck, 1991; Tindal & Hasbrouck, 1991). The one common addition to analysis of writing samples is tests of dictated spelling and sometimes recognition spelling. Such approaches to writing assessment seem to lack recognition of the link between oral expressive language capabilities and writing performance, as well as the complexity of the interrelations among the component processes of writing. Further, simple characterizations of the writing problems of LD children are unlikely to be helpful for teachers who need to decide how to help children with their writing problems. For all these reasons, comprehensive assessments of writing problems should go beyond analysis of writing samples and spelling errors. They might also include evaluation of oral language capabilities, particularly expressive language, reading, and handwriting capabilities.

The results of this study point to several ways in which writing assessments might be augmented. One way is through the use of tasks that allow for comparisons of different oral and written language capabilities. Such tasks need to be designed to help determine whether or not children's writing problems stem from oral language learning. Morphology is not the only area of language learning that might profitably be used in oral–written language assessments. Children's expressive vocabulary and their understanding or use of sentence structure are also important to assess. Phonological awareness is another area in which comparison of oral and written language performances is fruitful.

A second way is through comparing performances on contrived and spontaneous writing tasks. Contrived tasks are those designed to measure specific kinds of knowledge or skill that are thought to have an impact on success in writing. One standardized test that includes both contrived and spontaneous tasks is the Test of Written Language – 2 (Hammill & Larsen, 1988), but contrived tasks may best be designed for a given child in order to probe specific areas of weakness. In the study reported in this chapter, the Word Forms Test provided information about the children's knowledge and spelling of complex word forms. Other contrived tasks might involve knowledge of spelling principles or rules, knowledge of mechanics, knowledge of grammatical structures, and so on. So little of the writing process is fluent and automatic for young children that we can sometimes best understand what they really know by examining one source of knowledge at a time.

The examiner might also want to consider ways to determine the extent to which a child lacks the metalinguistic or metacognitive skills needed to coordinate different kinds of knowledge in writing. It is possible that certain children have the knowledge they need but either do not think to use it in writing or get bogged down by the many aspects of the writing process that require their attention, as we have seen. There are a number of different ways to investigate the difficulties of a child who is unable to orchestrate the many subprocesses of writing (such as remembering one's ideas and sentences while writing them down and, in the middle of all this, trying to remember the spellings of words). One suggestion is to focus the child's attention to one part of the process at a time, so that breakdowns in knowledge or skills become evident. For instance, in a study of good and poor reader/spellers, Bailet (1990) asked children to spell a base word before they were asked to spell the derived form; this system resulted in better performances than asking them to spell the derived forms only and indicated that the children did not spontaneously analyze the morphemic structure of words. A second method is to use a talk-aloud procedure. This can be accomplished by having the child explain his or her own thinking processes as he or she writes. This system may suggest ways in which children do not attend to their own writing. However, young children may have difficulty in explaining why they are doing what they are doing, and they may find this procedure disruptive. A third system involves an informal interview immediately after the child has completed writing a story or composition. Langer (1986) has shown that middle school children can be quite articulate about what they think is hard or easy about writing. How true this is for younger children and LD children is worth exploring. Interviews can inform the examiner about what the child intended and how he or she feels about his or her own writing abilities and products. Whichever method is used, the general goal is to arrive at a sense of the child's strengths and weaknesses, coping strategies, and motivation.

Finally, gathering background information concerning the child's development, educational history, and physical and psychological well-being may provide important insights into writing problems. Particularly important is investigating the writing curriculum to which the child is exposed. In some elementary school classrooms where whole language approaches are being used, little instruction or guidance in spelling is given. Typically, however, the children in these classrooms have many opportunities to write. In other classrooms, basic instruction in spelling accompanies basic instruction in word recognition, but there may or may not be a deliberate attempt to involve the children in writing activities, stories or otherwise. As is true of reading acquisition, both guidance and experience are important to the development of fluent and accurate writing capabilities. Similarly, the feedback children get from their parents and teachers may affect their willingness to attempt to express themselves in writing.

In short, a comprehensive assessment of writing acknowledges the many facets of cognitive, linguistic, educational, and psychological growth that lead children to develop competence in this complex means of communication.

REFERENCES

Bailet, L. L. (1990). Spelling rule usage among students with learning disabilities and normally achieving students. *Journal of Learning Disabilities, 23*(2), 121–128.

Beery, K. E. (1982). *Revised administration, scoring, and teaching manual for the Developmental Test of Visual–Motor Integration.* Cleveland: Curriculum Press.

Berko, J. (1958). The child's learning of English morphology. *Word,* 14, 150–177.

Boder, E. (1971). Developmental dyslexia: Prevailing diagnostic concepts and a new diagnostic approach. In H. R. Myklebust (Ed.), *Progress in learning disabilities* (Vol. 2, pp. 293–321). New York: Grune and Stratton.

Bowerman, M. (1981). The child's expression of meaning: Expanding relationships among lexicon, syntax, and morphology. *Annals of the New York Academy of Sciences, 379,* 172–189.

Bybee, J. L. (1985). *Morphology.* Philadelphia: John Benjamins.

Carlisle, J. F. (1987). The use of morphological knowledge in spelling derived forms by learning-disabled and normal students. *Annals of Dyslexia, 37,* 90–108.

Carlisle, J. F. (1988). Knowledge of derivational morphology and spelling ability in fourth, sixth, and eighth graders. *Applied Psycholinguistics, 9,* 247–266.

Carroll, J. B., Davies, P., & Richman, B. (1971). *Word frequency book.* New York: American Heritage.

Clark, E. V. (1982). The young word maker: A case study of innovation in the child's lexicon. In E. Wanner & L. Gleitman (Eds.), *Language acquisition: The state of the art* (pp. 391–425). Cambridge: Cambridge University Press.

Dunn, L. M., & Dunn, L. M. (1981). *Peabody Picture Vocabulary Test — Revised.* Circle Pines, MI: American Guidance Service.

Ehri, L. C. (1989). The development of spelling knowledge and its role in reading acquisition and reading disability. *Journal of Learning Disabilities, 22*(6), 356–365.

Finucci, J. M., Isaacs, S. D., Whitehouse, C. C., & Childs, B. (1983). Classification of spelling errors and their relationship to reading ability, sex, grade placement, and intelligence. *Brain and Language, 20,* 340–355.

Freyd, P., & Baron, J. (1982). Individual differences in acquisition of derivational morphology. *Journal of Verbal Learning and Verbal Behavior, 21,* 282–295.

Graham, S., Harris, K. H., MacArthur, C. A., & Schwartz, S. (1991). Writing and writing instruction for students with learning disabilities: Review of a research program. *Learning Disability Quarterly, 14,* 89–114.

Hammill, D., & Larsen, S. (1988). *Test of Written Language — 2.* Austin, TX: Pro-Ed.

Henderson, L. (1982). *Orthography and word recognition in reading.* New York: Academic Press.

Hoff, L. K. (1990). Comparison of spelling abilities in reading disabled and nondisabled children. *Learning Disabilities, 1*(3), 137–142.

Houck, C. K., & Billingsley, B. S. (1989). Written expression of students with and without learning disabilities: Differences across the Grades. *Journal of Learning Disabilities, 22*(9), 561–567, 572.

Jastak, S., & Wilkinson, G. S. (1984). *Wide Range Achievement Test — Revised.* Wilmington, DE: Jastak Associates.

Johnson, D. J., & Grant, J. O. (1989). Written narratives of normal and learning disabled children. *Annals of Dyslexia, 39,* 140–158.

Juel, C. (1988). Learning to read and write: A longitudinal study of 54 children from first through fourth grades. *Journal of Educational Psychology, 809*(4), 437–447.

Langer, J. A. (1986). *Children reading and writing: Structures and strategies.* Norwood, NJ: Ablex.

Lynch, E. M., & Jones, S. D. (1989). Process and product: A review of the research on lD children's writing skills. *Learning Disability Quarterly, 12,* 74–86.

MacWhinney, B. (1979). *The acquisition of morphology.* Monographs of the Society for Research in Child Development, Serial No. 174, Vol. 43, Nos. 1–2.

Mattingly, I. G. (1987). Morphological structure and segmental analysis. *Haskins Laboratories Status Report on Speech Research,* SR-92, 107–111.

Meeks, M. L., Kuklinski, T. J., & Hook, P. E. (1990). *How normal and learning-disabled children draw a geometrical pattern.* Presentation for Learning Disabilities Association Conference, Chicago.

Moats, L. C. (1983). A comparison of the spelling errors of older dyslexic and second-grade normal children. *Annals of Dyslexia, 33,* 121–139.

Moran, M. R. (1988). Rationale and procedures for increasing the productivity of inexperienced writers. *Exceptional Children, 54*(6), 552–558.

Myklebust, H. R. (1965). *Development and disorders of written language,* Vol. 1. New York: Grune & Stratton.

Nagy, W. E., & Anderson, R. (1984). How many words are there in printed school English? *Reading Research Quarterly, 19*(3), 233–253.

Nagy, W. E., Anderson, R. C., Schommer, M., Scott, J. A., & Stallman, A. C. (1989). Morphological families and word recognition. *Reading Research Quarterly, 24*(3), 262–282.

Nelson, H. (1980). Analysis of spelling errors in normal and dyslexic children. In U. Frith (Ed.), *Cognitive processes in spelling* (pp. 475–493). New York: Academic Press.

Newcomer, P., Nodine, B., & Barenbaum, E. (1988). Teaching writing to exceptional children: Reaction and recommendations. *Exceptional Children, 54*(6), 559–564.

Nodine, B. F., Barenbaum, E., & Newcomer, P. (1985). Story composition by learning disabled, reading disabled, and normal children. *Learning Disability Quarterly, 8,* 167–179.

Parker, R. I., Tindal, G., & Hasbrouck, J. (1991). Progress monitoring with objective measures of writing performance of students with mild disabilities. *Exceptional Children, 58*(1), 61–73.

Rubin, H. (1987). The development of morphological knowledge in relation to early spelling ability. *Haskins Laboratories status report on speech research* SR-89/90, 121–131.

Scardamalia, M. (1981). How children cope with the cognitive demands of writing. In C. H. Frederikson & J. F. Dominic (Eds.), *Writing: The nature, development, and teaching of written communication* (pp. 81–103). Hillsdale, NJ: Erlbaum.

Selby, S. (1972). The development of morphological rules in children. *British Journal of Educational Psychology, 42,* 293–299.

Schwartz, S., & Doehring, D. G. (1977). A developmental study of children's ability to acquire knowledge of spelling patterns. *Developmental Psychology, 13*(4), 419–420.

Sterling, C. M. (1983). Spelling errors in context. *British Journal of Psychology, 74,* 353–364.

Templeton, S., & Scarborough-Franks, L. (1985). The spelling's the thing: Knowledge of derivational morphology in orthography and phonology among older students. *Applied Psycholinguistics, 6,* 371–390.

Tindal, G., & Hasbrouck, J. (1991). Analyzing student writing to develop instructional strategies. *Learning Disabilities Research and Practice, 6,* 237–245.

Tyler, A. E. (1986). *Acquisition and use of English derivational morphology: An experimental investigation.* Doctoral dissertation, University of Iowa.

Vogel, S. A. (1977). Morphological ability in normal and dyslexic children. *Journal of Learning Disabilities, 10,* 35–43.

Waters, G. S., Bruck, M., & Malus-Abramowitz, M. (1988). The role of linguistic and visual information in spelling: A developmental study. *Journal of Experimental Child Psychology, 45,* 400–421.

Wiig, E. H., Semel, E. M., & Crouse, M. A. B. (1973). The use of English morphology by high-risk and learning disabled children. *Journal of Learning Disabilities, 6,* 59–67.

▶ 8

Differential Calculation Abilities in Young Children at Risk
Linking Research with Assessment and Instruction

NANCY C. JORDAN
Rutgers, The State
University of New Jersey

SUSAN COHEN LEVINE
JANELLEN HUTTENLOCHER
The University of Chicago

Abstract

This chapter describes our current research program on the development of calculation abilities in young children. In particular, we are concerned with children's abilities to add and subtract on nonverbal and verbal calculation tasks. We examine calculation abilities in preschool, kindergarten, and first-grade children, including those from middle- and low-income families. We also present preliminary data on the calculation performance of children with specific language weaknesses. Overall, our findings indicate that young children who are at risk for learning disabilities in school (e.g., low-income children and children with specific language impairments) may have underlying calculation competencies that are not uncovered by conventional arithmetic tests. That is, they may have difficulty solving verbally presented calculation problems, despite adequate performance on a nonverbal calculation task. Implications for assessment and instruction are discussed.

We gratefully acknowledge the Spencer Foundation, the Smart Family Foundation, and The Rutgers University Research Council for their generous support of the research presented in this paper. We also thank Angela O'Donnell for her helpful comments on an earlier version of this manuscript.

Mathematics difficulties are a pervasive problem among U.S. schoolchildren. Research suggests that levels of mathematics achievement in the United States are substantially lower than those of other industrialized nations and that the quality of U.S. children's mathematical knowledge is inadequate (Steen, 1987; Stigler & Perry, 1988). As demands for quantitative literacy grow in our increasingly technological society, difficulties in mathematics are becoming far more significant. Mathematics failure can have negative impacts on vocational opportunities, self-esteem, and quality of everyday life (Garnett, 1989; Johnson & Blalock, 1987). Many of the children who fail are from economically disadvantaged backgrounds, making them even more at risk for lifelong underachievement (Ginsburg & Allardice, 1984). Unfortunately, however, mathematics has received surprisingly little attention in the literature on learning problems (Garnett & Fleischner, 1987), in contrast, to the large body of research conducted on reading disabilities over the past deveral decades.

In this chapter we describe our current research program on the development of early mathematical abilities, with an eye toward the assessment and treatment of children who are having difficulties with mathematics. Our research is concerned specifically with the development of children's abilities to add and subtract on a nonverbal calculation task as well as on two kinds of verbal calculation tasks, namely story problems and number-fact problems. This area of study is particularly important, as basic calculation skills are emphasized in the early elementary grades and provide a foundation for higher level mathematical learning (Siegler & Jenkins, 1989). Our studies focus primarily on children in preschool, kindergarten, and first grade. By examining children at an early age, we can determine the mathematical abilities they have developed prior to and at the beginning of formal instruction in school. This information, in turn, can help educators take advantage of the abilities children bring to the school setting in making decisions about how mathematics should be taught most effectively to young children.

The chapter is divided into three sections. In the first section, we summarize our previous work. The initial phase of our research examined the development of calculation abilities in 4- to 6-year-old children, using both verbal and nonverbal tasks. The second phase of our research used the same tasks to examine calculation abilities in kindergarten and first-grade children who come from families that live in poverty. These children are particularly at risk for Adelman's (see Adelman, Chapter 1, this volume) Type I learning problems, which are caused primarily by environmental factors. In the next section, we present some new data on the relation of young children's performance on verbal and nonverbal calculation tasks to their performance on language measures (i.e., syntax and vocabulary). In this study, we examine children without environmental disadvantages who display specific weaknesses in language. These children are at risk for Adelman's Type III learning problems, which are caused primarily by organic factors within the child. Although many studies have demonstrated that specific language weaknesses are concomitants of reading problems, the relation between language deficits and the development of mathematical abilities is less clear. In the final section, we link our cumulative research findings with practical issues in mathematics assessment and instruction.

DEVELOPMENT OF CALCULATION ABILITIES IN 4- TO 6-YEAR-OLD CHILDREN

Prior to our research, no studies had directly compared young children's abilities to calculate on verbal problems relying on conventional number words to their abilities to calculate on nonverbal problems that do not rely on conventional number words. It had been suggested, however, that the amount of verbal understanding required by the task and the availability of object referents can affect a young child's performance on mathematics problems (Gelman & Gallistel, 1978). In an initial study, we gave two verbal calculation tasks and one nonverbal calculation task to 60 children between the ages of 4 and 6 years who were attending preschools and kindergartens in the Chicago area (Levine, Jordan, & Huttenlocher, 1992).

The two verbal calculation tasks were presented orally, one in the form of story problems and one in the form of number-fact problems. The story problems referred to object sets that were not physically present (e.g., "Mary has 3 marbles. She got 2 more marbles. How many marbles did she have altogether?"), whereas the number-fact problems did not refer to or provide object sets (e.g., "How much is 3 and 2?"). On both verbal problem types, the child was required to respond with a number word. In contrast to the story and number-fact problems, the nonverbal problems provided object sets with no accompanying verbal information. On the nonverbal task, the child was shown a set of disks that was then hidden with a cover. The hidden set of disks was transformed either by adding one or more disks to the covered set or by removing one or more disks from the covered set. Children were not allowed to view simultaneously the initial set and the set to be added or removed. This ensured that they would need to perform a calculation to arrive at a correct solution. After the addition or subtraction transformation, the child was asked to indicate how many disks were under the cover by laying out the appropriate number of disks. The experimenter did not provide verbal labels (i.e., number words) for either term of the problem, nor was the child asked to generate them. The procedure for the nonverbal calculation task allowed us to compare children's performance on problems presented in a completely nonverbal format to verbally presented story and number-fact problems. Identical addition and subtraction problems were used for each task. All problems had sums or minuends no larger than 6.

Levine et al.'s (1992) results showed that children as young as 4 years of age can calculate on nonverbal problems involving relatively small number sets (i.e., sums or minuends of 4 or less) and that their performance on larger number sets increases steadily throughout the preschool and kindergarten years. In contrast, children were not successful with even the simplest story problems or number-fact problems until 5 to 6 years of age.

Several factors may contribute to children's ease with the nonverbal calculation task relative to their performance on the story and number-fact problems. First, the nonverbal calculation task does not require knowledge of number words and relational terms. To solve story problems and number-fact problems, on the other hand, children must understand and generate verbal labels for numbers, understand words for operations, and comprehend various synactic structures. A lack of any of these verbal skills might mask a child's underlying ability to calculate on the verbally presented tasks. Second, the nonverbal calculation task uses physical props to represent object sets, making the numerosities involved in the original set and the set added or removed more readily available. The ordering of problem type difficulty for the group of children as a whole supports the importance of object referents in children's calculation success. That is, children performed best on nonverbal problems that provided physical representations of object sets (i.e., disks), at an intermediate level on story problems that referred to object sets that were not physically present, and worst on number-fact problems that made no reference to object sets. Moreover, an analysis of children's problem-solving strategies indicated that use of fingers to represent numerosities increased as the availability of object referents decreased (i.e., children used their fingers most often on number-fact problems, at an intermediate level on story problems, and least often on nonverbal problems). On the nonverbal calculation task, the physical representations of the relevant object sets obviated the use of fingers to represent numerosities.

In sum, Levine et al.'s study (1992) shows that children can perform calculations on the nonverbal task before they can perform calculations on conventional verbal tasks. The findings suggest that the child's earliest ability to calculate is based on his or her experiences in combining and separating sets of objects in the world. The findings also suggest that children bring rich informal knowledge of addition and subtraction operations to the school situation before they are taught algorithms and conventional computational procedures in kindergarten and first grade. As Ginsburg and Allardice point out (1984), this informal knowledge serves as a cognitive foundation for mathematical learning in school.

It should be noted that the subjects in Levine et al.'s study were from middle-class backgrounds. We next asked whether the verbal and nonverbal calculation tasks are differentially sensitive to environmental influences. In other words, is the ability to solve nonverbal problems less affected by social class than the ability to solve more conventional story and number-fact problems?

SOCIOECONOMIC VARIATION AND THE DEVELOPMENT OF CALCULATION ABILITIES

Prior research examining the relation between the home environment and cognitive abilities has found that variables such as the quality of language use of parents and the number of "thought-provoking" toys and games available to the child correlate more highly with performance on verbal cognitive tasks than with performance on tasks involving low verbal content (Kellaghan, 1977). Studies also report that performance on verbal tasks, such as vocabulary, is affected more by environmental factors than is performance on spatial tasks (MacArthur & Elley, 1963; Walberg & Marjoribanks, 1973). Thus, it is likely that verbal calculation tasks that rely on language and conventional procedures would present particular problems for children from low-income families, even though these children may have underlying competencies in addition and subtraction. In contrast, low-income children may perform as well as middle-income children on the nonverbal calculation task, which does not depend on verbal understanding and conventional arithmetic knowledge.

To address this question, we compared the performance of 42 middle- and 42 low-income kindergarten children in central New Jersey on addition and subtraction calculations presented as nonverbal problems, story problems, and number-fact problems (Jordan, Huttenlocher, & Levine, 1992). The sums or minuends of the calculation problems were 7 or less, and the problems were identical for each condition. The low-income children attended inner-city schools that served families residing in government-subsidized housing projects. The middle-income children attended schools in middle-class neighborhoods and did not reside in government-subsidized housing projects. None of the children had received formal arithmetic instruction in school.

As expected, the middle-income children performed better than the low-income children on both types of verbal problems (story problems and number-fact problems). However, there were no differences between the two groups on the nonverbal problems (see Figure 8-1). Observations of calculation strategies indicated that children rarely used their fingers on the nonverbal calculation task, regardless of income group. In contrast, middle-income children used their fingers more often than low-income children on both the story and number-fact problems, and the use of this strategy was associated with higher levels of performance. When we adjusted for the frequency of finger usage in another analysis, however, the performance level differences between the two groups on the verbal calculation tasks were still large and statistically significant. That is, the middle-income children performed better than the low-income children on story and number-fact problems even when we took frequency of finger use into account. When we adjusted for language abilities (based on a standardized test of vocabulary and sentence comprehension), on the other hand, the

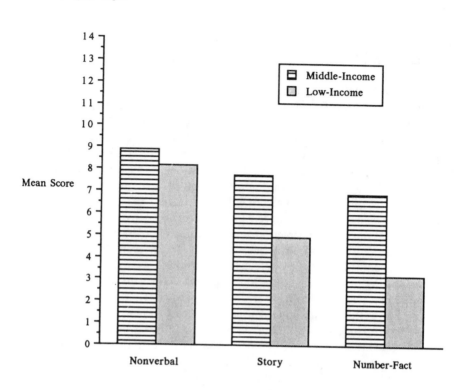

FIGURE 8-1 **Mean calculation scores of middle- and low-income children, by problem type**

difference between the two groups was eliminated on the story problems and greatly reduced on the number-fact problems. This latter finding indicates that the disparity between the middle-and low-income children on the verbal calculation tasks is strongly associated with verbal factors, such as word knowledge and syntax.

In a follow-up investigation, we reexamined the performance of the middle- and low-income children on the nonverbal and verbal calculation tasks in first grade, one year after the initial testing (Jordan, Levine, & Huttenlocher, in press). We were especially interested in the progress the children had made after formal calculation instruction in school. The nonverbal, story, and number-fact problems were readministered to each child. Because of the possibility of ceiling effects, however, several more difficult items involving larger numerosities were added to each condition. To assess children's first-grade mathematics achievement more generally, the mathematics subtests (Calculation, Applications) of the Woodcock-Johnson Tests of Achievement — Revised (WJTA-R; Woodcock & Johnson, (1989) were administered. The Calculation subtest required children to solve written number-fact problems, whereas the Applications subtest required children to solve various kinds of verbally presented problems.

The results showed that first grade middle- and low-income children still did not differ in performance on the nonverbal calculation task (mean = 79 percent correct for low-income versus 81 percent for middle-income). Moreover, the low-income children no longer lagged behind the middle-income children on number-fact problems (mean = 81 percent correct for low-income versus 87 percent for middle-income). Low-income children, however, once again performed more poorly than middle-income children on story problems (mean = 66 percent correct for low-income versus 81 percent for middle-income).

Interestingly, in first grade the middle- and low-income children did not differ in the number of trials on which they used their fingers for representation. That is, low-income children used their fingers to represent numerosities as often as middle-income children regardless of problem type. Recall that in Jordan et al.'s study (1992), the low-income kindergarten children rarely used finger strategies on any problem type. For both income groups, children used their fingers most often on number-fact problems, at an intermediate level on story problems, and least often on nonverbal problems. Finger strategies were associated with accurate performance, regardless of income group.

Children's performance on the WJTA-R achievement test reflected their performance on the experimental calculation tasks. That is, the two income groups did not differ on the WJAT-R Calculation subtest, but the middle-income children performed significantly better than the low-income children on the Applications subtest, a measure that depends on verbal skills.

In sum, our research comparing middle- and low-income children suggests that the ability to add and subtract on the nonverbal calculation task is not sensitive to environmental factors. That is, children, regardless of social class, develop these skills at about the same time. Most likely, this early mathematical knowledge has been constructed directly from a child's own actions on objects as well as from his or her observations of the world (Piaget, 1971). On the other hand, mathematics tasks depending on conventional verbal knowledge (e.g., story problems) are highly sensitive to socioeconomic variation, even after formal instruction in school.

CALCULATION ABILITIES IN CHILDREN WITH SPECIFIC LANGUAGE WEAKNESSES: A PRELIMINARY STUDY

Language difficulties are common among children with learning disabilities. Over the past decade a large body of research has shown that children with language weaknesses also have difficulties learning to read (e.g., see Mann, Chapter 4, this volume; Mann & Brady, 1988; Scarborough, 1990; Vellutino, 1986). Far fewer studies have examined the relation between language weaknesses and mathematics difficulties. Previous research, however, does suggest that language plays an important role in aspects of mathematics learning (Badian, 1983). For example, neuropsychological investigations indicate that number processing depends partially on the intactness of the language areas of the left hemisphere of the brain (Holender & Peereman, 1987). Our research with low-income children suggests that language weaknesses can compromise children's development of certain mathematics skills, such as the ability to solve story problems, even though they may have an adequate grasp of the underlying quantitative representations (Jordan et al., 1992).

It seems likely that the language skills of the low-income children in Jordan et al.'s (1992) sample were influenced by their environments. In the study described next, we examine the calculation abilities of children who show specific language weaknesses despite an adequate home and school environment. We predicted that language weaknesses would negatively affect the ability to solve story problems and number-fact problems but not the ability to solve nonverbal problems.

The subjects were 49 kindergarten children in a suburban Chicago school district serving a middle-class population. The children had just begun to receive formal instruction in addition and subtraction in school. All of the children were given identical addition and subtraction calculations presented as nonverbal problems, story problems, and number-fact problems ($N = 12$ problems for each condition, sums or minuends no greater than six). The order of presentation was counterbalanced across subjects. The specific materials and procedures for the experimental calculation tasks were the same as the ones used in our previous work (Levine et al., 1992; Jordan et al., 1992) and described earlier in this chapter. Children also were given the verbal subtest of the Primary Test of Cognitive Skills (PTCS; Huttenlocher & Levine, 1990). The PTCS verbal subtest is a standardized measure of syntax and vocabulary skills. Specifically, the test examines children's understanding of various words and syntactic constructions, which are presented orally.

The mean calculation scores for the group as a whole were 5.7 for the nonverbal problems, 4.4 for the story problems, and 2.8 for the number-fact problems. These mean differences were significant, $F(2,96) = 27.27, p < .0001$, indicating that nonverbal problems are easier than story problems, which in turn are easier than number-fact problems. The data showed that the scores on the verbal calculation tasks were more highly correlated with language skills than were the scores on the nonverbal calculation task. The correlation between scores on the PTCS verbal subtest and story problems was significant ($r = .52$, $p < .001$) as was the correlation between the scores on PTCS verbal subtest and number-fact problems ($r = .54$, $p < .001$). In contrast, the correlation between scores on the PTCS verbal subtest and the nonverbal problems was smaller and less significant ($r = .28, p < .05$). This correlation was significantly smaller than the correlations involving story problems and number-fact problems ($p < .05$ in each case).

We were especially interested in the calculation performance of the children who showed specific language weaknesses on the PTCS verbal subtest. Therefore, we identified the children who performed below the 10th percentile on the PTCS verbal subtest (based on national norms). To rule out general cognitive delays, the spatial reasoning subtest of the PTCS was administered to the children. This subtest measures children's thinking in a nonverbal context. Among the 15 children who exhibited language weaknesses, 8 showed relative strengths on the PTCS spatial reasoning subtest (mean = 43rd percentile). These eight children made up our sample of children with specific language weaknesses (low language/adequate spatial reasoning). Five of the 8 children also had been identified by the school system as being at risk for learning disabilities.

The mean calculation scores of the children who showed specific language weaknesses are graphically displayed in Figure 8-2, along with the mean calculation scores of the kindergarten children without language weaknesses ($n = 34$). Overall, the data support our prediction. That is, whereas the children with specific language weaknesses performed almost as well as the control group on the nonverbal calculation task (average difference in scores = 0.8), they performed more poorly than the control group on story problems (average difference in scores = 2.05) and number-fact problems (average difference in scores = 3.0). An analysis of variance showed an interaction between group (specific language-impaired and nonimpaired) and problem type (nonverbal, story, and number-fact problems) that approached significance, $F(2,80) = 2.6$, $p < .07$. There appeared to be no difference between the two groups on the nonverbal problems but relatively large differences favoring the nonimpaired children on both the story problems ($p < .05$) and the number-fact problems ($p < .01$). This performance pattern is similar to that found with low- and middle-income children (Jordan et al., 1992).

Although the findings should be interpreted cautiously because of the small number of subjects, they suggest that young children with specific language impairments may have difficulties with verbally presented calculation problems even though they have a good understanding of addition and subtraction. In another study, we compared the nonverbal calculation performance of preschool children with general cognitive deficits (who are in special education classrooms) with that of normal preschool children without general cognitive deficits (Huttenlocher, Jordan, & Levine, under review). Unlike the children with specific language impairments, who seemed to have language-specific problems with calculation, we found that the children with general cognitive deficits performed worse than the children without general cognitive deficits on the nonverbal

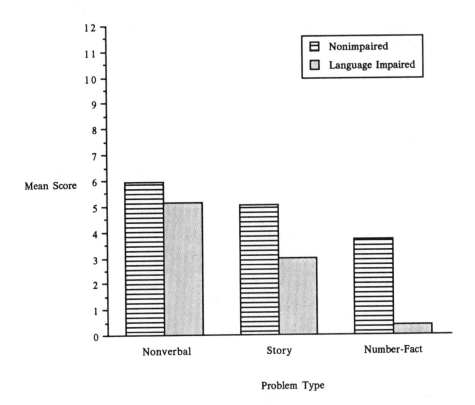

FIGURE 8-2 **Mean calculation scores of children with specific language weaknesses and without impairments, by problem type**

calculation task. This finding suggests that the ability to calculate on the nonverbal task is highly related to intellectual competence.

SUMMARY OF RESEARCH FINDINGS

We have conducted a series of studies on the development of calculation abilities in young children. In particular, we systematically examined children's performance on addition and subtraction problems that were presented verbally as well as on problems that were presented nonverbally. The verbal calculation tasks (i.e., story problems and number-fact problems) required conventional arithmetic knowledge, whereas the nonverbal calculation task did not. Our findings show that children as young as 4 years of age can perform simple addition and subtraction calculations on the nonverbal calculation task. In fact, a more recent study (Huttenlocher et al., under review) indicates that even 2½- to

3-year-old children have some success in solving nonverbal problems involving small numbers.

The research suggests that the acquisition of calculation skills does not depend on knowledge of conventional procedures or language and that children develop the ability to transform sets by adding and subtracting objects before formal instruction in school. Our finding that low-income children perform more poorly than middle-income children on the verbal calculation tasks but as well as middle-income children on the nonverbal calculation task supports this hypothesis. Furthermore, we found that children with specific language impairments perform more poorly than children without specific language impairments on the verbal calculation tasks but not on the nonverbal calculation task.

IMPLICATIONS FOR ASSESSMENT AND INSTRUCTION

More practically, our findings suggest several important directions for early mathematics assessment and instruction. First, the findings indicate that children's mathematics abilities, such as calculation, should be assessed on a variety of tasks to determine individual strengths and weaknesses. As Gelman and Gallistel (1978) maintain, "Failure on a single task should not be accepted as proof of the null hypothesis under any circumstances. By definition any nontrivial cognitive structure will play a role in a variety of contexts. Before concluding that a particular structure is absent, we should at the very least test for it with a variety of different tests, in each of which the structure plays a role" (p. 3). Such an approach would be especially important for children who are at risk for learning disabilities, such as low-income children or children with specific language impairments. The mathematics abilities of these children in particular may be masked by conventional tasks that depend on language.

The nature and amount of verbal understanding required by the task and the availability of object referents are two factors that should be considered when assessing the mathematical abilities of young children. Systematic variation of verbal demands and availability of object referents makes it possible to pinpoint more precisely where the child is having difficulty. For example, if a child is having difficulty with conventional addition and subtraction tasks in school, he or she might be asked to solve problems in nonverbal, story, and number-fact problem formats. Such a differential assessment would help to clarify whether the child has a fundamental problem with set transformation, or whether the child understands the operations of addition and subtraction but has difficulty with formal tasks involving language and conventional mathematical symbols.

A comparison of calculation performance across tasks also might reveal whether a child can make connections between story problems that use a meaningful verbal context with object referents, and number-fact problems that involve decontextualized language and abstract quantities. For example, we found that some young children responded correctly to a story problem such as, "Mary had 4 pennies. She got 2 more pennies. How many pennies did she have altogether?" but had difficulty with the parallel number-fact problem, "How much is 4 and 2?" The meaningful context of the story problems as well as the references to objects appeared to help these young children reach correct solutions even though they had not learned the number facts.

Conversely, some of the children we tested were successful with many number-fact problems, but had difficulty with story problems involving the same addition or subtraction calculations. Interestingly, we observed this pattern (i.e., better performance on number-fact problems than on story problems) most often in first-grade children who had received some formal arithmetic instruction. In some cases, formal instructional methods may have encouraged children to use rote procedures (e.g., memorizing number facts) for solving problems rather than applied calculation knowledge (Baroody, 1987). In fact, some of the difficulty children experience during the early grades in solving mathematical problems may be attributable to shifting away from the use of the rich informal knowledge developed during early childhood to relying on algorithms memorized by rote (Carpenter & Moser, 1982; Ginsburg & Allardice, 1984). When children learn facts and procedures with minimal understanding, their mathematics concepts become increasingly detached from their own experiences (Baroody, 1987). Such approaches may constrain their flexibility and can create later problems with practical applications (Carpenter & Moser, 1982; Levine & Jordan, 1987; Kamii, 1985).

If a basic calculation problem is still present early on, as revealed by performance on a nonverbal calculation task, instruction might provide extended practice with concrete objects to help children find sums or differences. Initially, children might be encouraged to use their fingers or other available objects to represent numerosities. If the child shows a good understanding of addition and subtraction on tasks using object referents but has difficulty with story or number-fact problems or both, verbal problems could be linked with everyday activities making use of object referents. Such experiences would encourage children to incorporate rather than abandon their informal knowledge.

Investigations are beginning to examine how concrete objects can be used most effectively to help children acquire various mathematics concepts. There is some evidence that children benefit more from a highly structured approach using a single form of object representation than from an approach that encourages spontaneous discovery with a variety of representations (Tang, 1991). This finding is important, as practices in U.S. classrooms tend to make use of a variety of concrete representations. Future research should investigate how to facilitate the transition from using concrete objects in problem solving to using the formal symbols of mathematics.

Finally, an assessment procedure should involve careful observation of children's solution strategies on different mathematics tasks. Our studies indicate that calculation strategies vary across problem type (e.g., fingers are used more often on number-fact problems than on story problems, low-income kindergarten use their fingers less often than middle-income kindergarten children on verbally presented problems). Further, Siegler and Jenkins (1989) report that children as young as 4 years of age use a wide range of strategies while they are acquiring addition and subtraction skills (e.g., counting with fingers, counting without fingers, using fingers without counting, counting up from the augend in addition or down from the minuend in subtraction, retrieving an answer from memory, guessing, etc.). In many instances, children used a particular strategy on problems for which it is most advantageous. For example, they retrieved answers from memory on easy problems involving small numerosities and counted on their fingers on more difficult problems involving larger numerosities. Siegler and Jenkins (1989) observe that such flexibility allows children to balance speed and accuracy when solving calculation problems.

Research has shown, however, that some children with learning problems apply strategies less flexibly than their normally achieving peers (Fleischner, Garnett, & Shepard, 1982; Goldman, Pelligrino, & Mertz, 1988; Russell & Ginsburg, 1984). In a recent study, Geary (1990) compared the strategy choices of first- and second-grade children with and without persistent mathematics difficulties. Children were asked to solve a series of addition number-fact problems, and their strategies and solution times were recorded on a trial-by-trial basis. The study showed that children with persistent mathematics difficulties made poor strategy choices, made frequent counting and memory retrieval errors, and displayed a variable rate of information processing compared to children without mathematics difficulties. The results suggest that invaluable information might be obtained by observing the type of strategies or procedures children employ on a set of problems (e.g., finger counting, tapping, counting aloud without fingers, etc.), the effectiveness of these strategies ("Did the child use his or her fingers on all of the problems, regardless of difficulty level?") and how flexibly and quickly children employ the strategies (e.g., "Did the child use his or her fingers on all of the problems, regardless of difficulty level?"). Siegler (1987, 1989) reports that children's own explanations of how they solved problems can reliably supplement information gained by direct observation. For example, the examiner might ask children to explain how they solved a particular problem immediately after the task is completed. To encourage more reflection, children also might be asked to "think aloud" during the problem-solving process (e.g., "Tell me everything you are thinking"; see Ginsburg, Jacobs, & Lopez, 1993; Ginsburg & Baroody, 1990).

In sum, our research as well as the research of others suggests that young children who are at risk for learning problems may have underlying competencies that are not uncovered by conventional tests of mathematical understanding (e.g., number-facts tests). We propose that mathematical skills or constructs should be assessed on a variety of tasks to determine the abilities children have as well as the abilities they lack. The verbal requirements of the task and the availability of object referents are two critical variables that should be considered when assessing early mathematical functioning. Moreover, an assessment should consider the strategies and procedures a child uses to reach solutions to problems. By examining mathematics performance and strategy use in different situations or contexts, assessments can describe individual performance patterns, uncover abilities (and disabilities), and help children take advantage of the rich mathematical knowledge they may have developed before formal instruction. This, in turn, may help prevent or reduce the cumulative mathematics failure that many children experience as they proceed through school.

REFERENCES

Badian, N. A. (1983). Arithmetic and nonverbal learning. In H. R. Myklebust (Ed.), *Progress in learning disabilities* (Vol. 5, pp. 235–264). New York: Grune & Stratton.

Baroody, A. J. (1987). *Children's mathematical thinking: A developmental framework for preschool, primary, and special education teachers.* New York: Teachers College Press.

Carpenter, T. P., & Moser, J. M. (1982). The development of addition and subtraction problem-solving skills. In T. P. Carpenter, J. M. Moser, & T. A. Romberg (Eds.), *Addition and subtraction: A cognitive perspective* (pp. 9–24). Hillsdale, NJ: Erlbaum.

Fleischner, F. E., Garnett, K., & Shepard, M. (1982). Proficiency in arithmetic basic fact computation in learning-disabled and nondisabled children. *Focus on Learning Problems in Mathematics, 4,* 47–55.

Garnett, K. (1989). Math learning disabilities. *The Forum* (publication of the New York State Federation of Chapters of the Council for Exceptional Children), *14,* 11–14.

Garnett, K., & Fleischner, J. (1987). Mathematical disabilities. *Pediatric Annals, 16,* 159–176.

Geary, D. C. (1990). A componential analysis of an early learning deficit in mathematics. *Journal of Experimental Child Psychology, 49,* 363–383.

Gelman, R., & Gallistel, C. R. (1978). *The child's understanding of number.* Cambridge, MA: Harvard University Press.

Ginsburg, H. P., & Allardice, B. S. (1984). Children's difficulties with school mathematics. In J. Lave & B. Rogoff (Eds.), *Everyday cognition: Its development in social context* (pp. 194–219). Cambridge, MA: Harvard University Press.

Ginsburg, H. P., & Baroody, A. J. (1990). *The test of early mathematics ability,* 2nd ed. Austin, TX: Pro-Ed.

Ginsburg, H. P., Jacobs, S. F., & Lopez, L. (1993). Assessing mathematical thinking and learning potential. In R. B. Davis & C. Maher (Eds.), *Schools, mathematics, and the world of reality* (pp. 237–262). Boston: Allyn and Bacon.

Goldman, S. R., Pelligrino, J. W., & Mertz, D. L. (1988). Extended practice of basic addition facts: Strategy changes in learning-disabled students. *Cognition and Instruction, 5,* 223–265.

Holender, D., & Peereman, R. (1987). Differential processing of phonographic and logographic single-digit numbers by the two hemispheres. In G. DeLoche & X. Seron, *Mathematical disabilities: A cognitive neuropsychological perspective* (pp. 43–85), Hillsdale, NJ: Erlbaum.

Huttenlocher, J., Jordan, N. C., & Levine, S. C. (under review). A mental model for arithmetic in young children.

Huttenlocher, J., & Levine, S. C. (1990). *Primary Test of Cognitive Skills.* Monterey, CA: CTB/McGraw-Hill.

Johnson, D., & Blalock, J. (1987). *Adults with learning disabilities: Clinical studies.* Orlando, FL: Grune & Stratton.

Jordan, N. C., Huttenlocher, J., & Levine, S. C. (1992). Differential calculation abilities in young children from middle- and low-income families. *Developmental Psychology, 28,* 644–653.

Jordan, N. C., Levine, S. C., & Huttenlocher, J. (in press). Development of calculation abilities in middle- and low-income children after formal instruction in school. *Journal of Applied Development Psychology.*

Kamii, C. K. (1985). *Young children reinvent arithmetic: Implications of Piaget's theory.* New York: Teachers College Press.

Kellaghan, T. (1977). Relationship between home environment and scholastic behavior in a disadvantaged population. *Journal of Educational Psychology, 69,* 754–760.

Levine, M. D., & Jordan, N. C. (1987). Learning disorders: The developmental underpinnings. *Contemporary Pediatrics, 4*(8), 16–43.

Levine, S. C., Jordan, N. C., & Huttenlocher, J. (1992). Development of calculation abilities in young children. *Journal of Experimental Child Psychology, 53,* 72–103.

MacArthur, R. S., & Elley, W. B. (1963). The reduction of socioeconomic bias in intelligence testing. *British Journal of Educational Psychology, 33,* 107–119.

Mann, V. A., & Brady, S. (1988). Reading disability: The role of language deficiencies. *Journal of Consulting and Clinical Psychology, 56,* 811–816.

Piaget, J. (1971). *Biology and knowledge.* Chicago: University of Chicago Press.

Russell, R. L., & Ginsburg, H. P. (1984). Cognitive analysis of children's mathematics difficulties. *Cognition and Instruction, 1,* 217–244.

Scarborough, H. S. (1990). Very early language deficits in dyslexic children. *Child Development, 61,* 1728–1743.

Siegler, R. S. (1987). The perils of averaging over strategies: An example from children's addition. *Journal of Experimental Psychology: General, 116,* 250–264.

Siegler, R. S. (1989). Hazards of mental chronometry: An example from children's subtraction. *Journal of Educational Psychology, 31,* 497–506.

Siegler, R. S., & Jenkins, E. (1989). *How children discover new strategies.* Hillsdale, NJ: Erlbaum.

Steen, L. A. (1987). Mathematics education: A predictor of scientific competitiveness. *Science, 237,* 251–252, 302.

Stigler, J. W., & Perry, M. (1988). Mathematics learning in Japanese, Chinese, and American classrooms. In G. B. Saxe & M. Gearhart (Eds.), *Children's mathematics* (pp. 27–54), *New Directions for Child Development,* no. 41. San Francisco: Jossey-Bass.

Tang, S. (1991). *Structure versus variety in concrete representation in early mathematical education.* Unpublished doctoral dissertation, University of Chicago.

Vellutino, F. (1986). Dyslexia. *Scientific American, 256,* 34–41.

Walberg, H. J., & Marjoribanks, K. (1973). Differential mental abilities and home environment: A canonical analysis. *Developmental Psychology, 9,* 363–368.

Woodcock, R. W., & Johnson, M. B. (1989). *Woodcock-Johnson Psycho-Educational Battery-Revised.* Allen, TX: DLM Teaching Resources.

▶ 9

Testing Linked to Teaching

JEANNE S. CHALL
Harvard University

Abstract

The article describes a new instrument to assess the reading and related language skills and abilities of students functioning at the first- to twelfth-grade reading levels. The instrument includes both formal and informal measures and is designed for use by classroom teachers, reading and special education teachers, and clinicians. The informal assessments — trial teaching strategies — are based on results of the formal tests. They are designed to find, with the collaboration of the student, those methods and materials from which he or she can learn. Profiles of students' scores illustrate how the test scores may be used to assess the strengths and weaknesses in reading and related language areas and how to plan an optimal instructional program.

A HISTORICAL VIEW OF CAUSES AND TREATMENTS OF READING DISABILITY

An overview of the history of reading disability shows repeated enchantments with different causes, diagnoses and treatments. During the past fifty years alone, the preferred causes have been successively defined as visual factors, emotional-social factors, and, more recently, neurological factors (for more detail, see Chall & Petersen, 1986; Chall & Curtis, 1992). Although most reading and learning disabilities specialists acknowledge that more than one factor is usually involved, the professional literature and particularly the writings for parents and teachers show a preference for the particular factor in vogue at a particular period of time, and the diagnoses and treatments tend to be based on these "causes."

Thus, during the period when visual factors were thought central, in the 1930s and 1940s, diagnoses in hospital and university clinics and in remedial reading centers in schools included various tests of visual processing. During the time when emotional-social factors received the major causal focus, the Rorschach, Thematic Apperception Test (TAT), and other projective tests were used in the diagnosis of reading disability. Beginning around the 1960s, the emphasis on neurological factors as the cause of reading disability led to the wider use of various neurological and neuropsychological tests.

These different causal emphases also tended to result in different preferred treatments. Those favoring visual factors, popular in the 1930s and 1940s, focused on visual training to speed up word, phrase, and sentence recognition. Those who viewed reading disability as part of the emotional-social development of the learner usually recommended play or psychotherapy as treatment. The treatment preferred by those who view reading disability as neurologically based has tended to focus on medication and on the training of the weaker underlying psychological factors (e.g., visual or auditory perception).

Of course, there were reading disability specialists who held minority views of causation during the various "consensus" periods and others who held fast to a multifactor causal theory (Roswell & Natchez, 1989). But I do not think I overstate the facts by noting that we have tended to go on a perpetual search for the one underlying cause with its matching diagnostic procedures and treatments. Indeed, although on the surface these broad "causes" differ, they have one common feature: They put major focus on the factor that is considered to be the underlying cause of the reading problem. Most tend to show only minor concern for the reading problem itself. Indeed, the reading problem has often been viewed as a "mere symptom" that will disappear when the underlying cause is treated. Yet the existing research on these issues, as well as the experience of clinics and schools, seems to indicate otherwise. Indeed, when the results of treating underlying factors have been compared to those of treating the problem through reading instruction, reading instruction has usually won out (Chall, 1978; Chall & Curtis, 1992).

To date, the treatment of the "underlying factors" has not done as well as direct treatment of the reading problem. Thus, the old visual training technology—the tachistoscopes and metronoscopes—has gathered dust, been stored in closets, or been thrown out. Psychotherapy and play therapy, although they helped some children's social and emotional development, seemed to be effective for reading only when reading instruction was also provided. More recently, research on the effectiveness of training "underlying" modalities found that students who received reading instruction instead of modality training achieved better in reading. Further, various attempts to improve the reading of learning-disabled students by matching their modality strengths and weaknesses to the methods used to teach reading did not fulfill the optimistic expectations. For example, using a sight approach for those strong in visual perception and phonics for those strong in auditory factors failed to improve their learning (Chall & Stahl, 1983). Thus, given that both research and clinical practice to date indicate that the more potent form of treatment for reading difficulties is reading instruction, a greater focus on the reading of the student with disability would seem to be indicated — a focus on assessment and teaching.

ASSESSMENT OF READING AND RELATED LANGUAGE SKILLS

The remainder of this chapter is concerned with such a diagnostic assessment and teaching program — one that evolved over many years. It was first used at the City College Reading Center in New York, later at the Harvard Reading Laboratory, and more recently in the Harvard Adult Literacy Center. The program was designed to be of assistance to classroom teachers, to reading and learning disability specialists, to psychologists, and to others responsible for the development of reading in children, young people, and adults.

For many years, a variety of published diagnostic and achievement measures were used in our assessments (see Roswell & Natchez, 1989; Chall & Curtis, 1987, 1990). During the past ten years, Florence Roswell and I have developed and tried out a separate instrument that takes less time and is easy to use and interpret (Diagnostic Assessments of Reading with Trial Teaching Strategies [DARTTS]; Roswell & Chall, 1992). The discussion that follows refers mainly to this assessment instrument, although it holds as well for the use of other published tests (see, in this connection, Chall & Curtis, 1987, 1990). The assessment is linked to an instructional program as well, and is appropriate for students functioning at reading grade levels 1 through 12. It consists of both formal and informal measures, with materials and instructions designed to help teachers assess and teach reading, particularly to those who have reading difficulty. It is the kind of testing program that psychologists and schools are currently looking for because the assessments lead directly to instruction (i.e., the tests are linked to teaching). For lack of space, I will discuss mainly the assessment part of the DARTTS.

The assessments are individually administered and concentrate not on any possible underlying causes of the reading problem, but on where the student is in reading — his or her strengths and weaknesses in various components of reading and language and what can be done to improve them.

The DARTTS has two parts. The first, the Diagnostic Assessments of Reading (DAR), contains a set of measures that are quantified. This portion gives an estimate of reading potential through a measure of vocabulary as well as estimates of strengths and weaknesses on various components of reading and language. The second part, the Trial Teaching Strategies (TTS), is an informal set of trial lessons that serve to confirm qualitatively the findings from the formal assessments for optimal levels of instruction and also for finding the methods and materials that work and are acceptable to the student. The formal assessment takes about thirty minutes or less and tests five to six components of reading and related language skills. Not all of these need to be given at the same time. The teacher selects the tests to be given based on his or her knowledge of the student's strengths and weaknesses from daily work or from standardized test scores that are available.

The DARTTS uses scoring that is criterion-referenced, norm-referenced and qualitative. The DAR (the formal assessment) is criterion- and norm-referenced. The items for each of the tests (Word Recognition, Word Analysis, Oral Reading, Silent Reading Comprehension, Spelling, and Word Meaning) are arranged in an order of increasing difficulty in terms of familiarity, frequency, readability, and curricular placement on the basis of widely used word lists. These criterion placements were confirmed by two validation studies of several thousand students — those in the first study reading at grave level and the second study functioning a year or two below grade level. The scoring, on the Trial Teaching Strategies is qualitative.

The theoretical basis for the DARTTS (and for the battery of standardized tests that can be used in its place) comes from two areas of knowledge about reading (see Chall & Curtis, 1990). First, reading is developmental and continuous. Following Chall's reading stages (1983), reading is viewed as changing as it develops, making different demands on readers — linguistic, cognitive, and specific reading demands — as they become more proficient. Also, the reading tasks and uses to which reading is put change from beginning to mature, skilled reading.

Thus, in the preschool years (Stage 0) the child's reading is essentially global, with the child attempting to "read" stories on the basis of memory and picture clues. The child also learns the letters of the alphabet and attempts to write his or her name and the names of other important people in the environment, words on signs, and the like. In grade 1 and part of grade 2 (Stage 1), the task usually shifts to recognizing words in print and to acquiring the alphabetic principle (i.e., learning the associations between letters and sounds in order to recognize and analyze in print the approximately 6,000 words most children already know at age 6). At grades 2 and 3 (Stage 2), the task is to coordinate the various ways of recognizing and understanding text — the quick recognition of high-frequency words, the ability to decode new words, and the ability to read meaningful connected text fluently and accurately.

At grades 4 through 8 (Stage 3), the reading task shifts to the reading of materials that go beyond the familiar and that usually contain more expository material. The ideas, vocabulary, and syntax of the reading materials become more complex and are used mainly for "learning the new." In grades 9 through 12 (Stage 4), the texts become ever more demanding, more difficult. They are more technical and abstract, and they depend on extensive vocabularies, background knowledge, and cognitive ability. In college and beyond (Stage 5), ever more background knowledge and cognitive abilities are required, along with judgment and critical abilities.

Second, reading is composed of various components and the relative importance of these components changes as the student achieves higher levels of development. Although all components — language, cognition, and reading skills — influence reading at all levels, at the beginning, word recognition and phonological aspects of language seem to play the stronger role. Beginning around grade level 3 or 4, when fundamental aspects of word recognition and analysis are usually mastered, word meaning and cognition become more important in reading development (Carroll, 1977).

Some of the other principles behind the DARTTS program are as follows:

1. The importance of active participation of the student. The teacher and student work together actively during assessment and teaching.
2. The use of challenging materials. Materials should be selected at the level at which the student learns well with the help of the teacher or a more knowledgeable peer. This is similar to Vygotsky's Zone of Proximal Development (Vygotsky, 1978). However, easier materials are used to develop fluency and automaticity and for independent reading.
3. A varied instructional program — focusing not only on weaknesses but also on strengths and on bringing the student up to ever higher reading development. Thus, for beginning reading, word recognition and oral reading (not silent reading) are generally emphasized. In grades 2 and above, greater time is given to silent reading.
4. The use of interesting and authentic materials that inform, inspire, and excite — expository as well as narrative.
5. Upgrading of the instructional program regularly as gains are made. Thus, regular assessments are encouraged, with new instructional plans made on the basis of new assessment profiles.

A Test of Word Meanings

A special feature of the formal assessment is the word meaning test, which *does not* require reading. A test of vocabulary has traditionally been found to be a useful measure of language and cognitive development when a longer test of verbal abilities cannot be administered (Wechsler, 1974). The Word Meaning Test can serve as an estimate of "reading potential" and of whether there is a problem with reading. Generally, if the student's Word Meaning score is appropriate for his or her grade placement or age, he or she is considered to have sufficient ability to function on level or above in reading and related areas. However, when a student has had a reading problem for many years (or has had insufficient verbal stimulation or is not fully proficient in English), the

Word Meaning score may be lower because the student may not have read widely, an important means of vocabulary development. Thus, it is suggested that, for older students, the Word Meaning score be viewed as an underestimate of the student's potential. Also, the Word Meaning score should not be viewed as absolute and unchangeable. Vocabulary can be developed, and the Trial Teaching Strategies of DARTTS and the DARTTS guidebook give many suggestions for doing so.

Others have used a listening comprehension test as a measure of reading potential (see Sticht, Beck, Hawke, Kleiman, & James, 1974). We considered using such a measure but decided that the many other factors involved in listening comprehension (e.g., the concentration of the student, the content appropriateness of the selections, and the difficulty of the passage) would make it less reliable than a test of word meanings. Vocabulary measures have been used for many years as measures of language and intelligence on such tests as the Weschler and the Stanford-Binet.

Tests of Reading Components

The remaining five subtests in the quantitative assessments measure the basic components of reading—word recognition and analysis, including spelling, and oral reading and silent reading comprehension, which are tested by questions and by oral and written summaries. Figure 9-1 reproduced from the DAR (Roswell & Chall, 1992), presents the different tests included in the formal assessment.

As will be illustrated later, the scores on these six components are used to assess a student's status and his or her strengths and weaknesses. First, the word meaning score indicates whether there is potential for higher functioning. Second, when reading scores are below the student's observed potential, the performance on the other subtests indicate what might be behind the lower functioning—that is, whether it is a problem of word recognition and analysis, of accuracy and fluency in oral reading of connected text, of silent reading comprehension, or of several or all of these.

Trial Teaching Strategies

Whatever the student's strengths and weaknesses, what can be done to improve his or her reading? To help answer this question and to help plan an appropriate instructional program, the teacher or clinician administers, either immediately after the formal assessments or on another day, the Trial Teaching Strategies. These are mini-lessons designed to determine the most useful methods and materials—the optimal level and content—that will help and motivate the student to learn. Similar to the formal assessment, they are designed to be given quickly (the entire Trial Teaching Session should take about thirty minutes or

Student _____ Date of Birth ____ / ____ / ____ Grade _____

DAR Administrator _____ Teacher _____ Date of DAR ____ / ____ / ____
(if different from teacher)

DAR Test	DAR Level
Word Recognition	
Word Analysis (Check if mastery is achieved.) _____ Consonant Sounds _____ Consonant Blends _____ Short Vowel Sounds _____ Rule of Silent *E* _____ Vowel Digraphs _____ Diphthongs _____ Vowels with *R* _____ Polysyllabic Words Prereading Subtests: _____ Naming Capital Letters _____ Naming Lowercase Letters _____ Matching Letters _____ Matching Words	
Oral Reading	
Silent Reading Comprehension	
Spelling	
Word Meaning	

1. For Word Recognition, Oral Reading, Silent Reading Comprehension, Spelling, and Word Meaning, enter the highest level for which the student achieved mastery.
2. For Word Analysis, check the subtests for which the student achieved mastery.

Source: Reproduced from Response Record with Directions for Administration, *Diagnostic Assessments of Reading with Trial Teaching Strategies* by F. G. Roswell and J. S. Chall with permission of The Riverside Publishing Company, © 1992, p. 45.

Note: See the TTS *Teacher's Manual,* especially "Part 2: Introduction to the Trial Teaching Strategies" and "Part 3: Preparing for Teaching," for information on reporting DAR results to students and using results to plan and implement the TTS session with the student.

FIGURE 9-1 **DAR interpretive profile**

less, and it can be given in more than one sitting). The Trial Teaching Strategies may also be used with results from other tests or teacher estimates.

The Trial Teaching Strategies give the teacher confirmation of what will be an optimal instructional program for the student as a start: what will give optimal challenge, the kind of instructional and recreational reading materials the student prefers, and optimal method(s) for learning word analysis, spelling, study skills, and writing.

Perhaps the most important outcome of the Trial Teaching Strategies is that the student discovers that he or she can learn — not from the teacher's assertions, but by experiencing progress. No matter how difficult a problem the student has in reading, writing, or spelling, he or she finds during the Trial Teaching that there is a way for him or her to learn. Of equal importance, the teacher learns from the formal and informal assessments what the student needs to learn and how it can be learned. This clarifies the student's reading problem and gives guidance and confidence to the teacher.

With some modifications, the DARTTS program can also be used to assess the needs of groups of students. Two of the subtests can be given in group settings: spelling and silent reading comprehension, including written summaries. Although the other four tests are given individually, the teacher can give them when there is time.

ILLUSTRATIVE USES OF THE ASSESSMENT INSTRUMENT: BEGINNING TO ADVANCED LEVELS

The following section illustrates the use of the assessment program with students who range in reading ability from beginning to advanced levels of reading. The focus is on the patterns of strengths and weaknesses obtained from the formal assessments and what they suggest for instruction. Generally, each student has a unique pattern of strengths and weaknesses on the formal tests, and these are used for planning the Trial Teaching Strategies and for planning an instructional program. However, some common patterns tend to be found among students who are functioning on similar levels of reading development.

Beginning and Primary Readers: Word Meaning Higher than Word Recognition

We find that students in the elementary grades who function at the lowest reading levels usually have difficulty with decoding, rather than with the meanings of words. Non-English-speaking individuals who have early reading difficulty may have weaknesses with word meaning as well as with word recognition and word analysis.

Table 9-1 presents a pattern for a second-grader who is functioning at about a middle level 1 on all components that require reading — Word Recognition, Word Analysis, Oral Reading, and Spelling. These are below both the student's grade placement and the level achieved on the Word Meaning test. Word Meaning is, in fact, higher than the student's grade placement. This pattern of scores suggests the need for Trial Teaching of word recognition, analysis, and oral

TABLE 9-1   **DAR Scores: A Second-Grader with Reading Difficulty in Word Recognition Skills and Strengths in Word Meaning**

Word Recognition	Level 1–2
Word Analysis	Mastery of consonant sounds; knowledge of some short vowels
Oral Reading	Level 1–2
Silent Reading Comprehension	Not administered
Spelling	Level 1–2
Word Meaning	Level 3 or higher

reading to determine how best he or she can learn these, and the optimal level for oral reading.

The profile (Table 9-1) indicates that the student's strengths are in Word Meaning, with weaknesses in Word Recognition and Analysis, Oral Reading, and Spelling. With Word Meaning at level 3, one level above the student's current grade placement of 2, there is much potential for improvement on the other reading components, with appropriate instruction.

A Third- or Fourth-Grader with Difficulty in Word Recognition

Table 9-2 presents a pattern that is often found among third- or fourth-grade students who have reading difficulty. This pattern, with its relatively high Word Meaning score, suggests that the student's potential for reading achievement is above his or her present reading achievement. Both this pattern and

TABLE 9-2   **DAR Scores: A Third- or Fourth-Grader with Difficulty in Word Recognition Skills and Strength in Word Meaning**

Word Recognition	Level 2
Word Analysis	Mastery of consonant sounds and blends and short vowels
Oral Reading	Level 2
Silent Reading Comprehension	Not administered
Spelling	Level 1–2
Word Meaning	Level 4 or higher

the one for the second-grader (see Table 9-1) reveal that weakness lies in word recognition and analysis, probably not in language and cognition. For both patterns, the low scores for Spelling confirm the extreme difficulty with word recognition and analysis. The profile suggests that Trial Teaching Strategies should focus on word recognition and analysis, spelling, and oral reading.

A Fifth-Grader with Good Word Meaning and Poor Reading

Table 9-3 presents a pattern common among many students in the fifth or sixth grades who function on about a third-grade reading level. The pattern suggests that the low reading comprehension score stems from weakness in word recognition and analysis, as well as from inaccuracy and lack of fluency in oral reading. The on-level Word Meaning score suggests that the student's ability to comprehend language is adequate and that, with proper instruction, both oral and silent reading comprehension levels will be on the same level.

An Eleventh-Grade Student Behind in Silent Reading Comprehension

Table 9-4 presents a pattern for an eleventh-grade student in high school who tested on grade level in Word Meaning but below grade level on Silent Reading Comprehension—a weakness that may be due to low word recognition (shown also in poor spelling) as well as to inaccuracy and lack of fluency in reading connected texts (Oral Reading below Word Meaning). Weaknesses in Word Recognition may also be contributing to a slower rate.

TABLE 9-3 **DAR Scores: A Fifth-Grader with Difficulties in Word Recognition and Silent Reading Comprehension, and Strength in Word Meaning**

Word Recognition	Level 3
Word Analysis	Mastery of all subtests except vowel diphthongs, vowels with *r*, and polysyllabic words
Oral Reading	Level 3
Silent Reading Comprehension	Level 3
Spelling	Level 2
Word Meaning	Level 5 or higher

TABLE 9-4 **DAR Scores: An Eleventh-Grader Behind in Silent Reading Comprehension**

Word Recognition	Level 8
Word Analysis	Not administered
Oral Reading	Level 9–10
Silent Reading Comprehension	Level 8
Spelling	Level 7
Word Meaning	Level 11–12

These profiles of scores suggest hypotheses regarding the student's strengths and weaknesses and the instructional plans that will help them. The Trial Teaching Strategies help confirm or disconfirm these hypotheses. Depending on the student's age and maturity, the Trial Teaching session begins by engaging the student in an analysis of his or her relative strengths and weaknesses on the DAR. (The reading levels are not mentioned to the student, only the relative positions on the different tests.) The student is then asked to respond to the results and to his or her reading problem. The student is also asked to respond to the methods and materials tried in the Trial Teaching Strategies session.

The DARTTS program also includes, in the manuals and in a guidebook, suggested teaching procedures for the various components (Word Recognition, Word Analysis, Oral Reading, Silent Reading Comprehension, Spelling, and Word Meaning), at beginning, intermediate, and upper levels. Case studies are presented in the assessment manuals and the teaching guide, with specific suggestions for interpreting the patterns of scores and translating them into teaching plans and instructional procedures.

USE OF DARTTS TO STUDY READING DEVELOPMENT

The DARTTS has also been used in a research study of the development of reading and related language abilities of children from low-socioeconomic-status (low-SES) families in grades 2 to 7 (Chall, Jacobs, & Baldwin, 1990). We examined whether these children decelerate in reading as they progress through the grades, as reported in many studies (e.g., Coleman et al., 1966) and in school and district reports. If they do decelerate, we wished to know when it starts, on what aspects of reading, and how these interact.

Table 9-5 from this study presents the scores on five reading components

TABLE 9-5 **Mean Test Scores and Differences from Norms on Reading Battery, Total Population Tested at End of Grades 2, 4, and 6**

Grade	Word Recognition	Oral Reading	Silent Reading	Spelling	Word Meaning
Grade 2	2.7	3.5	2.9	2.9	3.1
Difference from 2.8[a]	(−0.1)	(+0.7)	(+0.1)	(+0.1)	(+0.3)
Grade 4	4.5	4.9	5.5	4.6	4.3
Difference from 4.8[a]	(−0.3)	(+0.1)	(+0.7)	(−0.2)	(−0.5)
Grade 6	6.1	6.7	6.6	6.1	4.4
Difference from 6.8[a]	(−0.7)	(−0.1)	(−0.2)	(−0.7)	(−2.4)

Source: Reprinted by permission of the publishers from *The Reading Crisis: Why Poor Children Fall Behind* by Jeanne S. Chall, Vicki A. Jacobs, and Luke E. Baldwin, Cambridge, Mass.: Harvard University Press, copyright © 1990 by Jeanne S. Chall.
[a]Expected grade equivalents, or norms, for May of the school year.

for a group of 30 low-income children in grades 2 to 6. It indicates that the scores on all five tests were close to expectation in the early grades, closer than they were in the later grades. At grade 2, the children scored on level or higher on all the components—Word Recognition, Oral Reading, Silent Reading, Spelling, and Word Meaning. At grade 4, however, the scores began to slip below expected levels; the greatest slip was on Word Meaning, but there were also slips on Word Recognition and Spelling. On Oral Reading and Silent Reading Comprehension, the fourth-graders still scored on expected levels or higher. Yet by grade 6, scores on most of the subtests were below grade expectations. The greatest slip was in Word Meaning, almost two and one-half years below the norm. The next larger slips were in word recognition and spelling, with students scoring more than one-half year below expectations. Deceleration was lowest in oral and silent reading, where the students scored only slightly below norms.

Our interpretation of these patterns of strengths and weaknesses was that essentially these children had the language and cognitive abilities to progress as expected (the grade-appropriate scores in silent reading comprehension from grades 2 to 6). What they lacked, starting about grade 4, was knowledge of the meanings of words—the more uncommon, difficult, literary, abstract, and technical words. Children who were in classes in the intermediate grades where a greater emphasis was placed on word meanings and who read more widely showed greater gains in Word Meaning. Thus, the pattern of scores on the DAR could be used to suggest emphases in reading programs for those who tend to have difficulties with reading.

Perhaps the strongest evidence of the value of such an approach to diagnosis and treatment comes from the results we have gotten at the Harvard Reading Laboratory (which works with students in grades 1 to 12, college students, and adults) over a period of twenty-five years. First, the graduate students (mostly on a master's level with some teaching experience) were able to use the diagnostic program to develop effective instructional plans that produced, on average, gains of one and one-half to two years in reading in one year — a total of about 40 hours of instruction per year.

Our Adult Reading Center, a separate laboratory started in 1986 for adults who need assistance with their reading, has averaged a one-year gain in reading for one semester of work (about 20 hours of contact per semester) with about half of the teachers having prior teaching experience and the other half having no prior teaching experience.

The standardization data for the DARTTS are still being analyzed. The data on an earlier version indicated that testing the various components separately has merit because the tests tend to be correlated differently at different levels of development. Thus, Word Meaning and Word Recognition have a very low correlation in grade 1; are moderately related in grades 2, 3, and 4; and are highly related in grade 5 and above — as would be expected (see Chall, 1967/1983).

CONCLUSION

The value of the assessment program is that it helps those who plan and those who teach to know where the student is on a continuum of various components of reading development. It helps the teacher know what the student has already learned and what he or she still needs to learn in order to make continued and greater progress. Instead of focusing assessment on underlying causes — whether neurological, psychological, or visual — that may be needed for other purposes, it focuses on the students' reading and related language abilities, disentangles them, and suggests what the teacher can do to improve them.

REFERENCES

Caroll, J. B. (1977). Developmental parameters of reading comprehension. In J. T. Guthrie (Ed.), *Cognition, curriculum, and comprehension* (pp. 1–19).

Chall, J. S. (1967/1983). *Learning to read: The great debate.* New York: McGraw-Hill.

Chall, J. S. (1978). A decade of research on reading and language disabilities. In S. J. Samuels (Ed.), *What research has to say about reading instruction* (pp. 31–42). Newark, DE: International Reading Association.

Chall, J. S. (1983). *Stages of reading development.* New York: McGraw-Hill.

Chall, J. S., & Curtis, M. E. (1987). What clinical diagnosis tells us about children's reading. *The Reading Teacher, 40,* 784–788.

Chall, J. S., & Curtis, M. E. (1990). Diagnostic achievement testing in reading. In R. C. Reynolds & R. W. Kamphaus (Eds.), *Handbook of psychological and educational assessment of children: Intelligence and achievement* (pp. 525–551). New York: Guilford Press.

Chall, J. S., & Curtis, M. E. (1992). Teaching the disabled or below average reader. In A. Farstrup & S. J. Samuels (Eds.), *What research has to say about reading instruction,* 2nd ed. (pp. 253–276). Newark, DE: International Reading Association.

Chall, J. S., Jacobs, V. A., & Baldwin, L. E. (1990). *The reading crisis: Why poor children fall behind.* Cambridge, MA: Harvard University Press.

Chall, J. S., & Peterson, R. W. (1986). The influence of neuroscience upon educational practice. In S. L. Fredman, K. A. Klavangton, & R. W. Peterson (Eds.), *The brain, cognition and education* (pp. 287–318). San Diego, CA: Academic Press.

Chall, J. S., & Stahl, S. A. (1983). Reading. In H. Metzel (Ed.), *Encyclopedia of educational research,* 5th ed. (pp. 1535–1559). Washington, DC: American Educational Research Association.

Coleman, J. S., Campbell, E., Hobson, C., McPartland, J., Mood, A., Weinfeld, F., & York, R. (1966). *Equality of educational opportunity.* Washington, DC: U.S. Government Printing Office.

Roswell, F. G., & Chall, J. S. (1992). *DARTTS: Diagnostic assessments of reading with trial teaching strategies.* Chicago: Riverside.

Roswell, F. G., & Natchez, G. (1989). *Reading disability.* New York: Basic Books.

Sticht, T., Beck, L. J., Hawke, R. H., Kleiman, G. N., & James, J. H. (1974). *Auding and reading.* Alexandria, VA: Human Resources Research Organization.

Vygotsky, L. S. (1978). *Mind in society.* Cambridge, MA: Harvard University Press.

Wechsler, D. (1974). *Manual for the Wechsler Intelligence Scale for Children — Revised.* New York: Psychological Corporation.

▶ 10

Integrating Curriculum-Based Measurement with Instructional Planning for Students with Learning Disabilities

LYNN S. FUCHS
George Peabody College of Vanderbilt University

Abstract

This chapter explains what curriculum-based measurement is and how it can be used to inform instructional planning for students with learning disabilities. Following a definition and explanation of curriculum-based measurement, major advantages of curriculum-based measurement over other ongoing assessment methodologies are reviewed. Next, specific procedures for integrating curriculum-based measurement with teacher planning activities are described, and the relevant research base supporting each strategy is explained. Finally, future directions for research and development are discussed.

The research described in this chapter was supported in part by Grants #G008530198 and G008730087 from the U.S. Department of Education, Office of Special Education, to Vanderbilt University.

177

As conceptualized by Deno (1989), the problem-solving process within education comprises five interrelated decision-making phases: (1) identifying the problem, (2) certifying the problem, (3) exploring potential solutions, (4) evaluating those solutions, and (5) solving the problem. The first two phases within this model represent norm-referenced decisions, which entail social comparisons between individuals to define and verify that a meaningful, important learning problem exists.

Over the past two decades, assessment within the field of learning disabilities has focused in a concentrated fashion on these first two phases of the problem-solving process. Definitions of learning disabilities have been debated (e.g., Hammill, 1990; Harris, Gray, Davis, Zaremba, & Argulewicz, 1988; Siegel, 1988; Silver, 1990); research investigating differential characteristics of students with learning disabilities has proliferated (e.g., Arffa, Fitzhugh-Bell, & Black, 1989; Grolnick & Ryan, 1990; Morris & Levenberger, 1990; Waldron & Saphire, 1990); strategies for reliably diagnosing the presence of learning disabilities have been compared and critiqued (e.g., Adelman, Lauber, Nelson, & Smith, 1989; Evans, 1990; Fletcher, Espy, Francis, Davidson, Rourke, & Shaywitz, 1989).

By contrast, less attention has been directed at the final three stages of the decision-making process, which address how the assessment process can inform and enhance the process of solving the learning problems of students with learning disabilities. For example, an analysis conducted for the purpose of writing this chapter revealed the following: Among data-based, primary research reports published over the past several years in the *Journal of Learning Disabilities,* only approximately 15 percent focused on interventions to effect better academic outcomes for students with learning disabilities. Of these studies, only a handful were devoted to studying how assessment can be designed to improve the instructional programs and academic outcomes of this population of learners. Given that the field most commonly defines learning disabilities in terms of poor academic achievement relative to an individual's intellectual capacity, this lack of attention to how assessment can inform academic planning and problem solving is disconcerting.

Recently, however, research on dynamic assessment (e.g., Campione, 1989; Feuerstein, 1980; Haywood, 1988) and curriculum-based measurement (e.g., Fuchs & Deno, 1991) has begun to address the intersection between assessment and instructional planning for students with learning disabilities. The purpose of this chapter is to provide an overview of how one of these strategies, curriculum-based measurement (CBM), can be linked meaningfully to the instructional decision-making and problem-solving process. First, I define CBM and explain how it differs from other well-known ongoing assessment methods. Then, I review three major advantages of CBM over other ongoing assessment methodologies. Next, I explain three strategies for how CBM can inform the instructional process, and I provide a description of the research base supporting each use. Finally, I discuss directions for future research and development.

DEFINITION OF CURRICULUM-BASED MEASUREMENT

CBM is a set of procedures for indexing student progress in the curriculum through repeated measurement. CBM differs from other well-known ongoing curriculum-related assessment methodologies because of two distinguishing features: (1) throughout the year, repeated measurements are conducted on tests of equal difficulty, representing the desired end-of-year outcomes, and (2) the measurement is standardized to produce reliable, valid descriptions of student progress.

Measurement of Year-End Outcomes

With CBM, the teacher specifies the critical features of the year's curriculum; these critical features determine the parameters of the testing materials. For example, in mathematics, the teacher reviews the content to be taught during the upcoming year, specifies key types of problems, and weighs the importance of those types of problems. Once these dimensions of the annual curriculum are determined, alternate forms of CBM tests are generated, each of which contains all of the critical problem types, in proportion to the weights assigned by the teacher. Each test is a parallel form, developed according to a sampling plan designed to reflect the annual curriculum.

In reading, the teacher determines the type and difficulty of passages she expects the student to read proficiently by year's end; these passages become the measurement materials. All passages employed for testing are roughly equivalent and represent the material of type and difficulty that teachers expect students to read well by year's end.

In spelling, the teacher lists the entire set of words to be addressed instructionally over the academic year; this list becomes the pool of words from which twenty-word spelling tests are randomly sampled. Again, each test is a parallel form, sampling and representing the annual curriculum in the same way.

Consequently, each CBM test indexes student proficiency on what the teacher will teach over the entire year, and *all tests administered over the course of the year are of approximately equal difficulty.* We would, therefore, expect the test to be relatively difficult for the student at the beginning of the year, when little of the upcoming year's curriculum has been taught. As the teacher covers (and as the student presumably learns) the material, we expect to see the student's proficiency gradually improve. We can attribute increasing scores to the student's improved proficiency, not to changes in the test instrument.

Improved proficiency is represented in Figure 10-1, which shows a student's progress in the fourth-grade math curriculum over one year. In October, when the student was competent on few types of problems covered in the fourth-grade curriculum, he achieved a relatively low CBM score of 20 digits. Over the

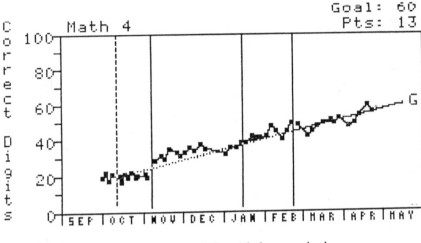

FIGURE 10-1   **Sample CBM graph showing student progress in mathematics operations**

course of the year, however, he became competent on most of the problem types in the curriculum, and his overall CBM score gradually increased to approximately 60 digits.

The CBM score (i.e., total number of digits correct on the test) is an overall indicator of the student's proficiency in the curriculum. It does not communicate which portions of the curriculum have and have not been mastered. Nevertheless, because every type of problem incorporated within the fourth-grade curriculum is tested on each CBM test administered over the year, we can analyze the student's tests during any time frame to get a profile of which skills currently are and are not mastered.

As shown in Figure 10-2, computer applications can facilitate this type of analysis. Figure 10-2 shows a skills analysis of the student's performance for the half-month interval between April 1 and April 15. The top portion of this analysis categorizes each skill represented in the curriculum into a mastery category and, for each skill, shows (1) the ratio between the number of attempted and the number of possible items of that problem type, and (2) the percentage of correct digits on the attempted problems. The bottom portion of this analysis depicts a graphic history of the student's performance over time. Each row represents a different type of problem; each column, a half-month interval. Boxes are coded. A white box signifies Not Attempted; striped, Nonmastered; checked, Partially Mastered; black, Mastered. Thus, increasingly dark boxes represent increasing mastery.

MASTERY STATUS FOR Warren Jones
APR 1-APR 15 (2 probes)

		Attempts	Accuracy
MASTERED			
A1	+ multidigit w/regrouping	6/6	93%
M1	× basic facts, factors to 9	12/12	100%
M3	× by 1- or 2-digit w/regrouping	6/8	100%
D1	• basic facts, divisors 6-9	8/8	100%
.1	+ / – mixed decimals to hundredths	4/4	92%
PARTIALLY MASTERED			
S1	– two 4-digits w/ regrouping	2/2	83%
M2	× two 2-digits no regrouping	2/2	67%
D2	– 3- by 1-digit no remainder	2/2	60%
D3	– 2- or 3- by 1-digit w/ remainder	2/2	71%
F1	+ / – simple or mixed no regrouping	6/6	56%

NONMASTERED

NOT ATTEMPTED

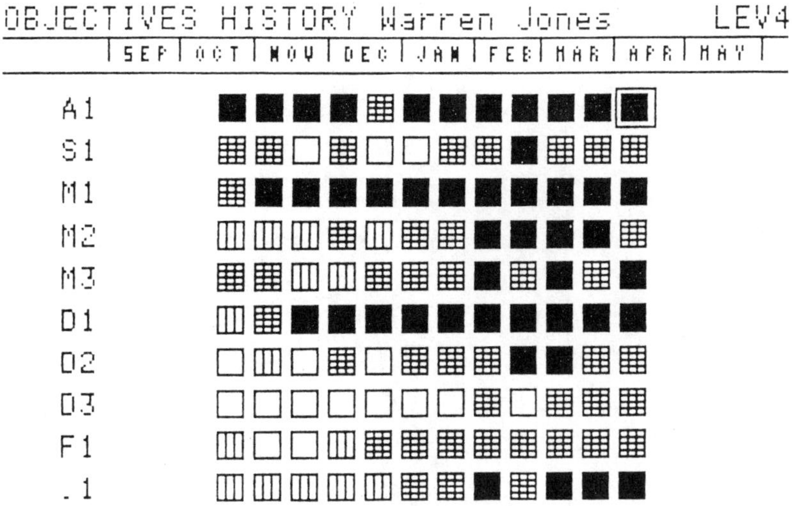

FIGURE 10-2 **Sample CBM skills analysis**

CBM's test inclusiveness and equivalency over the year differ dramatically from those of other ongoing measurement systems, such as mastery measurement or precision teaching. With these specific subskill mastery measurement models, the test domain is restricted to the current instructional topic (e.g., when multiplication of fractions is taught, the test domain is restricted to multiplication of fractions). Moreover, the test domain frequently shifts as the instructional content changes. When we see student scores increase or decrease, therefore, we must determine whether it is the student's performance or the test that has changed. A typical mastery measurement graph is shown in Figure 10-3. The student worked on multidigit addition for the first three or four weeks of the school year; as he worked on this skill, the ongoing testing system was restricted to multidigit addition problems. When the student had achieved the predetermined mastery criterion of eight problems correct on three consecutive days, the teacher shifted instruction to the next skill in the hierarchy, multidigit subtraction, and the testing domain simultaneously shifted to multidigit subtraction. The student worked on multidigit subtraction for the next six weeks until

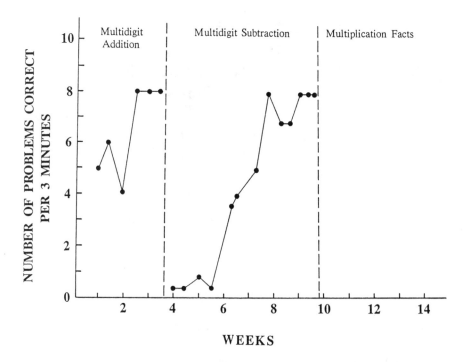

FIGURE 10-3 **Sample graph within a specific subskill mastery measurement system**

mastery was achieved, and instruction and measurement simultaneously shifted to the next skill in the hierarchy.

Standardized Measurement

It is important to note that, although the teacher's specific annual curriculum determines the CBM testing materials, no other measurement feature within CBM is determined by the teacher. This brings us to the second distinguishing feature of CBM: standardized measurement. Once the parameters of the curriculum are specified to determine how the test materials are sampled, the teacher relies on a standardized set of methods for determining how to sample the tests and how to administer and score the tests. These standardized procedures are based on empirical investigations of the psychometric and edumetric characteristics of alternative testing procedures, when materials are sampled across different curricula.

CBM relies on standardized, empirically derived procedures for determining (1) what behavior to measure (e.g., what should the student do in response to the passage — read words aloud, answer questions, or complete a maze task? What should we score — number or percentage correct?) and (2) what measurement conditions to employ (e.g., How long should the student read? Should self-corrections be scored as correct or incorrect?). Consequently, teachers can have confidence that the scores derived from CBM are accurate, meaningful representations of a student's proficiency and progress in the curriculum.[1]

This stands in stark contrast to other ongoing curriculum-related assessment methods, where teachers determine not only the testing materials but also the measurement methods. With idiosyncratic testing methodologies, it is not possible to determine whether derived information is accurate or meaningful.

ADVANTAGES OF CURRICULUM-BASED MEASUREMENT OVER OTHER ONGOING ASSESSMENT METHODOLOGIES

CBM differs from other major forms of ongoing assessment in that CBM employs standardized measurement that focuses on the annual, long-term goal. These distinguishing features of CBM give it four advantages over other major forms of ongoing curriculum-related assessment, which focus on specific subskill mastery. Next, I explain each of these advantages.

1. *Instructional hierarchies.* CBM does not require teachers to specify instructional hierarchies before measurement can occur. To initiate CBM, teachers must identify the content they want the student to know by year's end. Instead of focusing on sequential subskills for mastery, CBM focuses on the broader final task required at the end of the year. Thus, because it measures long-term goal outcomes, CBM focuses the teacher's attention (and the evaluative criteria for judging program success) on the broader desired outcomes of instruction. This results in the following advantages: (a) it increases social validity; (b) it is more compatible with notions of learning that attend to teaching integrated outcomes; (c) it avoids the onerous (and often incorrectly completed) task of decomposing and compartmentalizing the curriculum into steps of an hierarchy; and (d) it allows the teacher to use the measurement system to evaluate the effects of any instructional method (e.g., ordering the sequence of skills in different ways or avoiding a focus on individual skills altogether or supplementing instruction with sand trays or whatever approach the teacher wishes to try; see Fuchs & Deno, 1991, for a more complete discussion).

2. *Retention and generalization.* Because CBM structures measurement to include the multiple skills represented in the annual curriculum, it automatically assesses retention and generalization. Consequently, as the teacher provides instruction on multidigit subtraction with regrouping, the teacher can use CBM to assess simultaneously the student's performance on (a) acquisition of subtraction, (b) retention of the previously taught multidigit addition with regrouping, and (c) generalization to multidigit subtraction with regrouping involving decimals. By contrast (as reflected in Figure 10-3), the teacher has no automatic index of maintenance and generalization with specific subskill mastery measurement systems. Given the well-documented problems students with learning disabilities experience with retention of previously learned material (White, 1984), a measurement system that automatically reflects retention and generalization, as CBM does, offers important advantages.

3. *Measurement shifts.* With CBM, teachers can monitor student development across a school year without altering the testing parameters. As reflected in Figure 10-1, the difficulty of the test remains constant; when the scores go up or down, we can attribute these changes to improving or deteriorating performance. By contrast, as shown in Figure 10-3, scores on specific subskill mastery measurement systems often change because the testing content shifts — as the instructional content shifts. These shifts make it difficult to summarize student growth over extended time periods. By maintaining the difficulty of the test over the year, CBM can be used to summarize growth over time and to compare student growth at different periods during the year, with different instructional components, or under different service delivery systems.

4. *Test construction.* As already discussed, another advantage of CBM is its well-documented technical features. With known reliability and validity, teachers can have confidence that the data they collect are accurate and meaningful representations of student performance and progress. By contrast, with the idiosyncratic testing methods employed with specific subskill mastery measurement, little is known about the psychometric or edumetric features of measurement.

As demonstrated by Tindal, Fuchs, Fuchs, Shinn, Deno, and Germann (1985), it is not safe to assume that teacher-made or textbook-embedded mastery tests demonstrate adequate reliability and validity.

STRATEGIES FOR INTEGRATING CURRICULUM-BASED MEASUREMENT WITH INSTRUCTION

Over the past decade, considerable attention has been focused on how teachers can use CBM to help inform and enhance their instructional decisions. Next, I discuss three strategies: (1) using the graphed performance indicators to judge program success and adjust programs as necessary, (2) using the graphed performance indicators to monitor and adjust student goals, and (3) using the skills analysis to determine specific strategies for strengthening the program.

Using Graphed Performance Indicators to Adjust Programs

CBM structures the instructional decision-making process in the following ways. First, as the teacher identifies the measurement domain or level, she specifies the point within the curriculum where the student is expected to be proficient by year's end. Second, when setting the performance criterion (i.e., the score she hopes the student will achieve on the measurement level), the teacher selects the criterion against which the student's progress will be compared. That is, the student's current score, at any time during the year, can be compared to the score the teacher has established as the end-of-year goal.

As shown in the top panel of Figure 10-4, the teacher is monitoring the student's progress toward proficiency in the fourth-grade reading curriculum. At the beginning of the year, the student's performance was approximately 8 words correct on the CBM maze reading test, which requires pupils to read 400-word passages and restore every seventh word. Normative information about typical fourth-graders' improvement on the CBM maze measure indicates an increase of approximately 0.5 words per week (Fuchs, Fuchs, Hamlett, Walz, & Germann, 1993). Thus, the teacher sets a goal of 23 words correct as the expected score 30 school weeks later (i.e., 8 + [30 weeks × 0.5 words] = 23). This goal is represented by the "G" on the student's graph. In addition, a "moving goal" (see the broken diagonal line) indicates the rate at which the student will have to improve (0.5 words per week) in order to attain the goal.

When the student's progress is less steep than this moving goal line, the teacher judges the student's progress to be inadequate and adjusts the instructional program in an effort to stimulate better progress (see top panel of Figure 10-4). Consequently, the CBM performance indicators can be used to evaluate

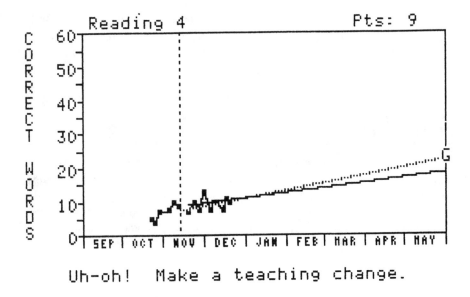

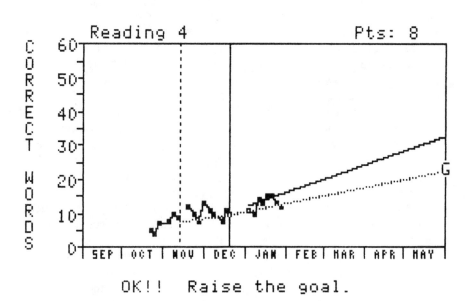

FIGURE 10-4 **Sample CBM reading graphs. Top panel shows inadequate student progress with a recommendation for a teaching change. Bottom panel shows better student progress with a recommendation for a goal increase.**

the student's program formatively, so that necessary improvements can be introduced during the school year.

A series of studies indicates the importance of this "instrumental" use of CBM. In a meta-analysis of systematic formative evaluation studies, Fuchs and Fuchs (1986) found that the decision rules can stimulate teachers' use of the data in decision making and result in better achievement. Fuchs (1988) found a relation between achievement and compliance with decision rules requiring instructional adjustments when student rates of progress were inadequate compared to the goal line.

Moreover, in a post hoc analysis of teachers' use of CBM in reading among students with learning disabilities, Fuchs, Fuchs, and Hamlett (1989b) identified differential patterns of achievement associated with teachers' instrumental use of CBM to formatively develop their students' instructional programs. Twenty-nine teachers were assigned randomly to a control or a CBM group. After the study, the graph of each CBM student was inspected to create two CBM implementation groups: the measurement-alone group and the measurement-with-evaluation group. *Measurement* was defined as administering, scoring, and graphing the curriculum-based tests on a routine basis. *Evaluation* was defined as the teacher introducing at least one instructional adjustment in response to the data and maintaining that adjustment for at least 2.5 weeks. Maintenance of the adjustment was included to ensure that an instituted instructional component was in effect long enough to influence student performance.

Consequently, students were placed in the measurement-alone group when their graphs indicated that, although measurement had occurred, the CBM database had not been used to evaluate the effectiveness of the program, and no instructional adjustments had been introduced to enhance learning. For these students, only one viable, unchanging instructional phase had been implemented over the fifteen-week study. Fifteen students were in this group.

The remaining 21 students were placed in the measurement-with-evaluation CBM group. These students' graphs showed that CBM had been collected and that teachers had used the database to evaluate and enhance the instructional program. Among these students, 6 had three viable, different instructional phases, each implemented for at least 2.5 weeks, and 15 had two viable, different instructional components, each implemented for at least 2.5 weeks.

Results indicated that although teachers in both implementation groups set up their measurement systems and actually measured student progress using CBM comparably well, as indexed on fidelity of implementation measures, important differences were associated with the CBM implementation groups. On the Stanford Achievement Test, Reading Comprehension subtest, administered before and after the study, students in the measurement-with-evaluation group achieved better than the control group students, whereas the achievement of the students in the measurement-alone condition did not surpass that of the control group. The effect size for the measurement-with-evaluation CBM group was twice as large as that of the measurement-alone group.

Consequently, findings support the importance of using CBM to determine when adjustments in students' instructional programs are required to enhance learning. Using CBM in this way, teachers can determine when student rates of progress are less than adequate and when program changes are warranted. Moreover, research indicates that (1) using CBM in this way relates to better achievement outcomes for students with learning disabilities, and (2) although teachers can experience these evaluation methods as time-consuming (Fuchs, Hamlett, Fuchs, Stecker, & Ferguson, 1988), computer applications (Fuchs, Hamlett, & Fuchs, 1990) that run on easily available hardware reduce teachers' time commitments almost entirely.

Using CBM Performance Indicators to Monitor and Adjust Goals

As clarified in the preceding discussion, the ambitiousness of the student's goal (i.e., the performance criterion or desired end-of-year goal) determines how frequently CBM decision rules recommend that teachers introduce instructional adjustments. For example, if a teacher selects a very low performance criterion, then the student's actual progress is unlikely to fall short of the moving goal line; hence, no teaching adjustments will be recommended. Consequently, for potential CBM effects to be realized, it is important for teachers to select appropriately ambitious CBM goals.

CBM research indicates that unambitious goal setting does, in fact, relate to poor student achievement. Fuchs, Fuchs, and Deno (1985) conducted a post hoc analysis of a database in which teachers, along with their four students with mild to moderate disabilities, had been assigned randomly to either a CBM or a control group for a four-month study in the area of reading (Fuchs, Deno, & Mirkin, 1984). We inspected student graphs after the study to sort the 58 CBM students into three goal ambitiousness conditions: highly, moderately, or low ambitious goals. Students also were divided into two goal mastery conditions: those who had achieved and those who had not achieved their goals.

On a variety of measures administered before and after the study, we found that the ambitiousness of the goal was associated positively with achievement. Further, no effects were related to actual mastery condition. It was the level of goal ambitiousness, not goal attainment, that was associated with achievement.

Consequently, it appears that the selection of an appropriately ambitious performance criterion may be critical within CBM decision making. Nevertheless, few satisfactory strategies for identifying appropriate performance criteria have been formulated. One potential solution to the goal-setting problem, referred to as *dynamic goal setting,* illustrates how the CBM performance indicators can be used to develop instructional programs.

With dynamic goal setting, when the student's progress is steeper than the moving goal line or four consecutive scores fall above the moving goal line, the goal is judged to be inappropriately unambitious. The CBM recommendation is to increase the goal (see bottom panel of Figure 10-4). Consequently, this dynamic goal-setting strategy for using CBM informs the academic planning process by helping teachers monitor the appropriateness of the goals they set.

Fuchs, Fuchs, and Hamlett (1989a) conducted a study to test the effectiveness of CBM dynamic goal setting. Participants were 30 special education teachers, each of whom selected two students with mild disabilities. Most of these students had an identified learning disability and all had IEP math goals. Teachers were assigned randomly to three groups: dynamic CBM goal setting, static CBM goal setting, and control (i.e., no CBM).

Within the static CBM goal-setting condition, when the student's actual rate of progress exceeded the rate established in the moving goal line, the decision was, "O.K.! Collect more data." The CBM pattern suggested that the student's rate of progress was acceptable with respect to goal attainment and that the corresponding program looked effective. Thus, the message was for the teacher to maintain the current instructional program and continue data collection. Teachers were always free to increase their goals, but, they were never directed to do so through the CBM decision-making system.

Using dynamic CBM goal setting, when the student's actual rate of improvement exceeded the rate established in the moving goal, the decision was, "O.K.! Raise the goal to N," where N equaled the student's predicted performance at the end of the study, based on the student's current rate of actual progress. Again, the CBM pattern suggested that the student's progress was acceptable with respect to goal attainment. The message, however, commented on the established goal criterion. The assumption was: If the student currently is exceeding the standards established in the goal, then the goal probably is inappropriately unambitious.

By raising the goal, the teacher accomplished two things. First, she always adjusted the goal to correspond to the student's actual rate of progress or better; the goal was not permitted to reflect a rate of progress lower than that which the student already had demonstrated could be achieved. Second, by adjusting the goal upward, the teacher was establishing a more ambitious criterion for subsequent decisions concerning the adequacy of student progress and the instructional program. With the goal increase, the likelihood of a subsequent recommendation to adjust the instructional program increased.

Two outcomes of this study are especially important. First, with respect to teachers' use of goals, teachers in the dynamic goal CBM group made more goal increases than teachers in the static goal CBM group. With the dynamic goal condition, teachers made an average of 0.60 goal increases; they increased goals for more than one of every two pupils. In the static goal group, only one teacher, for one of her pupils, spontaneously increased a goal in response to the student's CBM data.

This finding is important because it suggests that despite the potential importance of ambitious goals, special educators appear to underestimate many students' potential. Teachers in this study established initial goals freely, in line with their professional judgment about individual student potential. With these initial goals, teachers in the dynamic goal group were required to increase goals for more than 50 percent of their students. This need to revise teachers' goals upward has been corroborated in subsequent studies that incorporated the dynamic goal-setting procedure. Additionally, because teachers in the static goal-setting condition failed to raise goals in response to students' CBM data, findings suggest that, without systematic prompting to raise goals, practitioners cannot be expected to do so.

The second major outcome of interest in this study concerns student achievement. Students in the dynamic goal CBM group achieved better than control group during posttesting on a standardized math test (pretest performance was controlled statistically). The achievement of the static CBM goal group, however, did not reliably exceed that of controls. The effect size associated with dynamic goal CBM procedures was 0.52.

Using Skills Analysis to Identify Specific Strategies for Strengthening the Program

CBM performance indicators can be used to help teachers identify (1) when student progress is unsatisfactory and program adjustments are required and (2) when student progress is adequate but the goal requires adjustment upward. Research indicates that when the CBM performance indicators are used in these ways, student achievement increases. Nevertheless, those graphed displays provide less information to help teachers determine specific strategies for how to adjust the instructional program (see Casey, Deno, Marston, & Skiba, 1988, for information on how the graphed performance indicators can be used to judge the relative effectiveness of alternative instructional components in order to develop more successful components and delete unsuccessful components, which space limitations prevent me from discussing in this chapter).

Although the graphed performance indicators provide relatively few clues for how to adjust student programs, the CBM database does contain information about how the student performs on the different aspects of the curriculum within any time frame. Because the student is required to perform skills representing the entire year-long curriculum on each CBM test, information can be aggregated across tests to formulate a skills analysis of the student's performance on the year's curriculum. Such a skills analysis was provided in the area of math operations in Figure 10-2.

During the 1987–1988 academic year, Fuchs and associates undertook a series of studies investigating teachers' use of the CBM skills analysis. One study was conducted in math, one in reading, and one in spelling. In each study, there was a control group (i.e., no CBM); a CBM group that relied only on the graphed performance indicators to assist in their instructional planning; and a CBM group that relied on both the graphed performance indicators and the CBM skills analysis to formulate decisions about their students' instructional programs.

In all three academic areas, results indicated that teachers who employed both the CBM graphed performance indicators and the CBM skills analysis planned more effective programs — and, of course, with more effective programs, their students achieved better than those in the CBM group that relied solely on performance indicators, and also better than the control group. (For additional information on method and findings, see Fuchs, Fuchs, & Hamlett, 1989c, for reading; Fuchs, Fuchs, Hamlett, & Allinder, 1991a, for spelling; and Fuchs, Fuchs, Hamlett, & Stecker, 1990, for math.)

DIRECTIONS FOR FUTURE CBM RESEARCH AND DEVELOPMENT

Expert Systems to Enhance Instructional Decision Making with CBM

Using CBM to inform instructional decision making, a teacher relies on the CBM database for information about the student's progress in the curriculum in response to the instruction that has been provided. Then, the teacher considers additional information about the student's learning history, about previous instructional programs, and about her curricular priorities, and integrates these sources to formulate a decision about how to adjust the instructional program. Of course, as in any profession, regardless of the quality of the assessment or diagnostic data such as CBM, the quality of the decision varies with the ability and expertise of the professional.

In our work on CBM, we have begun to explore the use of expert systems (i.e., computer programs that attempt to reproduce the advice that experts might provide) to improve the quality of instructional decisions across teachers. We have developed expert systems in reading, spelling, and math, and have run studies to investigate how these programs affect teachers' instructional decisions and student achievement.

In all three academic areas (*reading:* Fuchs, Fuchs, Hamlett, & Ferguson, 1992; *spelling:* Fuchs, Fuchs, Hamlett, & Allinder, 1991b; *math:* Fuchs, Fuchs, Hamlett, & Stecker, 1991), we found that expert systems helped teachers plan more diverse instructional programs that incorporated a greater variety of instructional design features. In a related way, without expert systems, instructional decisions were linked closely to tips that the assessment systems provided.

Without expert system in math, for example, teachers tended to reteach problem types with which students experienced difficulty, but they failed to vary their instructional methods for reteaching. Using Glaser's (1977) scheme, this type of teaching adjustment falls at a low level of instructional adaptation. By contrast, with expert systems, teachers addressed a greater variety of problem types in their instruction and used alternative strategies for reteaching previously covered material.

In terms of achievement, findings varied by academic area. In math, achievement was reliably better among students whose teachers planned with the assistance of expert systems; this reliable difference was of strong practical importance. In reading, the achievement of students whose teachers who relied on CBM tended to exceed that of control teachers, whether or not expert systems were employed. However, on certain key reading measures that related to the types of instructional decisions expert systems tended to make, the achievement of expert system students was reliably stronger. In spelling, there were no differences between the achievement of CBM students, whether or not expert systems were employed. Moreover, some patterns in the data suggested that teachers who planned without the assistance of the expert system may have been more successful: Their reliance on the CBM data, without the additional considerations of the expert system, appeared sound.

Consequently, our work suggests the potential for expert systems to assist teachers in their instructional decision making. Nevertheless, as may be clear from this brief description of findings, additional work in developing expert systems and studying how they mediate instructional decision making clearly is warranted.

Methods for Facilitating Classwide Decision Making with CBM

Systematic use of CBM in instructional decision making has great potntial for enhancing student achievement. The graphed performance indicators can inform teachers about the overall success of their programs and the need to adjust the program or increase the goal; the analysis of the separate skills assessed can help teachers identify areas that require additional instruction and how they might plan instruction to help students maintain and generalize information; expert systems may assist teachers in broadening the sources of information they consider as they formulate adjustments in their programs.

Nevertheless, a persistent critical problem plagues the successful implementation of CBM: Given the large class sizes within both special and general education settings, it is difficult, if not impossible, for teachers to respond to individual students' CBM profiles—which produce different instructional decisions for different pupils at different times. Consequently, in our recent work on CMB, we have begun to focus on how teachers (with the assistance of computer management systems) can simultaneously consider the many students in their classes to formulate classwide decisions that are sensitive to individual needs but that are feasible for teachers to implement within their large-group settings (see Fuchs, 1992, for a description of classwide decision making in math). Additional work in classwide decision making is necessary to make CBM a usable technology in today's large-group instructional settings.

Expanding CBM Systems

As acknowledged by its developers (e.g., Deno, 1985; Fuchs & Deno, 1991; Shinn, 1989), well-developed CBM systems focus on basic skills. CBM, however, does provide an assessment model appropriate for addressing other domains of information and skills. Broadening CBM to address other domains of information, skills, and applications represents an important agenda for future related work. In fact, some more recent work (e.g., Fuchs, 1991) has expanded CBM to incorporate a more comprehensive mathematics curriculum, including operations, measurement, geometry, applied computation, problem solving, and applications. Additional work may focus on humanities and science content or on complex, applied problem solving.

NOTE

1. CBM's standardized method are described in numerous published materials (e.g., Fuchs, Hamlett, & Fuchs, 1990; Shinn, 1989). For additional information on materials and workshops on CBM, contact the author.

REFERENCES

Adelman, H. S., Lauber, B., Nelson, P., & Smith, D. C. (1989). Toward a procedure for minimizing and detecting false positive diagnosis of learning disabilities. *Journal of Learning Disabilities, 22,* 234–244.

Arffa, S., Fitzhugh-Bell, K., & Black, F. W. (1989). Neuropsychological profiles of children with learning disabilities and children with documented brain damage. *Journal of Learning Disabilities, 22,* 635–640.

Campione, J. C. (1989). Assisted assessment: A taxonomy of approaches and an outline of strengths and weaknesses. *Journal of Learning Disabilities, 22,* 151–165.

Casey, A., Deno, S. L., Marston, D., & Skiba, R. (1988). Experimental teaching: Changing teacher beliefs about effective instructional practices. *Teacher Education and Special Education, 11,* 123–132.

Deno, S. L. (1985). Curriculum-based measurement: The emerging alternative. *Exceptional Children, 52,* 219–232.

Deno, S. L. (1989). Curriculum-based measurement and special education services: A fundamental and direct relationship. In M. R. Shinn (Ed.), *Curriculum-based measurement: Assessing special children* (pp. 1–17). New York: Guilford Press.

Evans, L. D. (1990). A conceptual overview of the regression discrepancy model for evaluating severe discrepancy between IQ and achievement scores. *Journal of Learning Disabilities, 23,* 406–412.

Feuerstein, R. (1980). *Instrumental enrichment: An intervention program for cognitive modifiability.* Baltimore, MD: University Park Press.

Fletcher, J. M., Espy, K. A., Francis, D. J., Davidson, K. C., Rourke, B. P., & Shaywitz, S. E. (1989). Comparisons of cutoff and regression-based definitions of reading disabilities. *Journal of Learning Disabilities, 23,* 334–338.

Fuchs, L. S. (1988). Effects of computer-managed instruction on teachers' implementation of systematic monitoring programs and student achievement. *Journal of Educational Research, 81,* 294–301.

Fuchs, L. S. (1991). *Expanding curriculum-based measurement to incorporate a comprehensive math curriculum.* Unpublished manuscript.

Fuchs, L. S. (1992). Classwide decision making with computerized curriculum-based measurement. *Preventing School Failure, 2,* 30–33.

Fuchs, L. S., & Deno, S. L. (1991). Paradigmatic distinctions between instructionally useful measurement systems. *Exceptional Children, 57,* 488–501.

Fuchs, L. S., Deno, S. L., & Mirkin, P. K. (1984). Effects of curriculum-based measurement and evaluation on pedagogy, student achievement, and student awareness of learning. *American Educational Research Journal, 21,* 449–460.

Fuchs, L. S., & Fuchs, D. (1986). Effects of systematic formative evaluation on student achievement: A meta-analysis. *Exceptional Children, 53,* 199–208.

Fuchs, L. S., Fuchs, D., & Deno, S. L. (1985). The importance of goal ambitiousness and goal mastery to student achievement. *Exceptional Children, 52,* 63–71.

Fuchs, L. S., Fuchs, D., & Hamlett, C. L. (1989a). Effects of alternative goal structures within curriculum-based measurement. *Exceptional Children, 55,* 429–438.

Fuchs, L. S., Fuchs, D., & Hamlett, C. L. (1989b). Effects of instrumental use of curriculum-based measurement to enhance instructional programs. *Remedial and Special Education, 10*(2), 43–52.

Fuchs, L. S., Fuchs, D., & Hamlett, C. L. (1989c). Monitoring reading growth using student recalls: Effects of two teacher feedback system. *Journal of Educational Research, 83,* 103–111.

Fuchs, L. S., Fuchs, D., Hamlett, C. L., & Allinder, R. M. (1991a). The contribution of skills analysis to curriculum-based measurement in spelling. *Exceptional Children, 57,* 443–452.

Fuchs, L. S., Fuchs, D., Hamlett, C. L., & Allinder, R. M. (1991b). The effects of expert system advice within curriculum-based measurement on teacher planning and student achievement in spelling. *School Psychology Review, 20,* 49–66.

Fuchs, L. S., Fuchs, D., Hamlett, C. L., & Ferguson, C. (1992). Effects of expert system consultation within curriculum-based measurement using a reading maze task. *Exceptional Children, 58,* 436–450.

Fuchs, L. S., Fuchs, D., Hamlett, C. L., & Stecker, P. M. (1990). The role of skills analysis in curriculum-based measurement in math. *School Psychology Review, 19,* 6–22.

Fuchs, L. S., Fuchs, D., Hamlett, C. L., & Stecker, P. M. (1991). Effects of curriculum-based measurement and consultation on teacher planning and student achievement in mathematics operations. *American Educational Research Journal, 28,* 617–641.

Fuchs, L. S., Fuchs, D., Hamlett, C. L., Walz, L., & Germann, G. (1993). Indexing academic progress: standards for judging improvement over time. *School Psychology Review, 22,* 27–48.

Fuchs, L. S., Hamlett, C. L., & Fuchs, D. (1990). *Monitoring Basic Skills Progress.* Austin, TX: Pro-Ed.

Fuchs, L. S., Hamlett, C. L., Fuchs, D., Stecker, P. M., & Ferguson, C. (1988). Conducting curriculum-based measurement with computerized data collection: Effects on efficiency and teacher satisfaction. *Journal of Special Education Technology, 9*(2), 73–86.

Glaser, R. (1977). *Adaptive education: Individual diversity and learning.* New York: Holt, Rinehart and Winston.

Grolnick, W. S., & Ryan, R. M. (1990). Self-perceptions, motivation, and adjustment in children with learning disabilities: A multiple group comparison study. *Journal of Learning Disabilities, 23,* 177–184.

Hammill, D. D. (1990). On defining learning disabilities: An emerging consensus. *Journal of Learning Disabilities, 23,* 74–85.

Harris, J. D., Gray, B. A., Davis, J. E., Zaremba, E. T., & Argulewicz, E. N. (1988). The exclusionary clause and the disadvantaged: Do we try to comply with the law? *Journal of Learning Disabilities, 21,* 581–583.

Haywood, H. C. (1988). Dynamic assessment: The Learning Potential Assessment Device. In R. L. Jones (Ed.), *Psychoeducational assessment of minority group children: A casebook* (pp. 39–63). Berkeley, CA: Cobb & Henry.

Morris, M., & Levenberger, J. (1990). A report of cognitive, academic, and linguistic profiles for college students with and without learning disabilities. *Journal of Learning Disabilities, 23,* 355–361.

Shinn, M. R. (Ed.). (1989). *Curriculum-based measurement: Assessing special children.* New York: Guilford Press.

Siegel, L. S. (1988). Definitional and theoretical issues and research on learning disabilities. *Journal of Learning Disabilities, 21,* 264–273.

Silver, L. B. (1990). Attention deficit–hyperactivity disorder: Is it a learning disability or a related disorder? *Journal of Learning Disabilities, 23,* 394–397.

Tindal, G., Fuchs, L. S., Fuchs, D., Shinn, M. R., Deno, S. L., & Germann, G. (1985). Empirical validation of criterion-referenced tests. *Journal of Education Research, 78,* 203–209.

Waldron, K. A., & Saphire, D. G. (1990). An analysis of WISC-R factors for gifted students with learning disabilities. *Journal of Learning Disabilities, 23,* 491–498.

White, O. R. (1984). Descriptive analysis of extant research literature concerning skill generalization and the severely/profoundly handicapped. In M. Boer (Ed.), *Investigating the problem of skill generalization: Literature review* (pp. 1–19). Seattle: University of Washington, Washington Research Organization.

▶ 11

Mainstream Assistance Teams

Three Years of Research and Development on Prereferral Intervention and School Consultation

DOUGLAS FUCHS
George Peabody College of Vanderbilt University

Abstract

Enrollments in special education are burgeoning. One apparent reason is that classroom teachers are identifying many difficult-to-teach students and are referring them for psychological testing and possible special education placement. Prereferral intervention is a strategy aimed at helping teachers with their difficult-to-teach pupils and, presumably, lessening the likelihood of teacher referral. This chapter describes Mainstream Assistance Teams (MATs), a unique consultant-driven prereferral intervention, developed over several years during which it was implemented in more than 100 classrooms in a large metropolitan school system. Results from several MAT evaluation studies are presented, and the approach is contrasted to more conventional approaches to school consultation.

Preparation of this chapter was supported in part by Grant No. G008530158 from the Office of Special Education Programs in the U.S. Department of Education, and by Core Grant HD15052 from the National Institute of child Health and Human Development. This chapter does not necessarily reflect the position or policy of the funding agencies, and no official endorsement by them should be inferred.

I wish to thank the Nashville–Davidson County Metro Public Schools, without whose cooperation and support this research could not have been conducted. Special thanks are extended to Ed Binkley, Pat Cole, Morel Enoch, Richard Hooper, Elizabeth Ann Jackson, Cornell Lane, Hoyte Snow, Judy Stubbs, Barbara Thomas, and Jim Zerface.

INCREASING NUMBERS OF MILDLY HANDICAPPED STUDENTS

Since the U.S. Department of Education's first child count in 1976-1977, the number of students served under the Individuals with Disabilities Education Act and Chapter 1 has grown each year, with an increase of 978,707 children, or 26.4 percent, from 1976-1977 to 1988-1989 (see U.S. Department of Education, 1991, Figure 1.1, p. 5). In 1989-1990, 4,687,620 children and youth with disabilities from birth through 21 years of age were enrolled in special education programs (U.S. Department of Education, 1991).

To some degree, this burgeoning number reflects more than fifteen years of legal, legislative, and professional initiatives directed toward assuring handicapped youth a free and appropriate public education. There is growing sentiment, however, that special education's current size also reflects an overidentification of students with disabilities (e.g., Gerber & Semmel, 1984; Shepard & Smith, 1983; U.S. Department of Education, 1984). There are numerous and obvious reasons for concern. Erroneous placement can cause labeling, separation, and stigmatization (e.g., Jones, 1972; Reynolds & Balow, 1972), disruption of schooling (e.g., Will, 1986), and additional costs for school districts (e.g., Singer, 1988).

Two factors are often cited as further explanation for rising special education enrollments. First, general educators are referring more and more hard-to-teach pupils for evaluation and possible special education placement (e.g., Fuchs & Fuchs, 1988; Gottlieb, Alter, & Gottlieb, 1991; Research for Better Schools, 1986, 1988). Second, the evaluation process is insufficiently discriminating (e.g., Heller, Holtzman, & Messick, 1982; Shepard, Smith, & Vojir, 1983; Ysseldyke, Thurlow, Graden, Wesson, Algozzine & Deno, 1983). The other is that children with mild and moderate disabilities in many special education programs infrequently are transitioned into less restrictive environments, including regular classrooms, where they may be decertified (e.g., Anderson-Inman, 1987; Biklen, Lehr, Searl, & Taylor, 1987; Gottlieb, 1985; Weatherly & Lipsky, 1977). Although each explanation appears important for understanding why special education enrollments are expanding, this chapter focuses on the phenomenon of increasing teacher referrals.

Frequency of Teacher Referrals

It has been estimated that, from 1977-1978 to 1978-1979, the average number of referrals initiated by classroom teachers increased nearly 50 percent, from 2.2 to 3.0 students (Ysseldyke & Thurlow, 1983). Furthermore, evidence indicates that referral by a teacher often leads to identification of a pupil as handicapped. Algozzine and Ysseldyke (1981) reported that over a three-year period 92 percent of referred students were placed in special education. Similarly, Foster,

Ysseldyke, Casey, and Thurlow (1984) found that 72 percent of students referred were placed in special education, and most were placed in the special education category for which they had been referred.

Arbitrariness and Precipitousness of Teacher Referrals

Despite the apparent confidence that diagnosticians and special educators place in classroom teachers' referrals, empirical evidence indicates that their referrals often are arbitrary, if not biased (Kelly, Bullock, & Dykes, 1977; Lietz & Gregory, 1978; Tobias, Cole, Zibrin, & Bodlakova, 1982; Tucker, 1980; Ysseldyke & Thurlow, 1984; Zucker & Prieto, 1977). Investigations have found that minority pupils, boys, and siblings of children identified as learning-disabled are overrepresented when referrals are initiated by teachers as compared with those otherwise initiated by objective measurement (see Marston, Mirkin, & Deno, 1984). Additionally, in contrast to the reasons typically cited on referral forms, classroom teachers frequently refer students primarily because of disturbing behaviors (Algozzine, 1977), which tend to be defined idiosyncratically (Gerber & Semmel, 1984) and often represent situation-specific problems rather than enduring student characteristics (Balow & Rubin, 1973). In addition to findings that teachers' referrals often are arbitrary, evidence suggests that teachers frequently make referrals in a precipitous manner. It seems that many classroom teachers typically make few, if any, substantial programmatic changes prior to initiating referral (Ysseldyke, Christenson, Pianta, Thurlow, & Algozzine, 1983; Ysseldyke & Thurlow, 1980). The frequently observed result is that (1) a high percentage of teachers' referrals fails to meet local eligibility criteria (Marston, Mirkin, & Deno, 1984), and (2) many pupils certified as LD do not match legal definitions or definitions presented in the professional literature (Shepard et al., 1983).

The findings of arbitrariness and precipitousness in referral-related decision making suggest that many classroom teachers do not attempt to accommodate difficult-to-teach students. This hypothesis is corroborated by a related research literature demonstrating that teachers deliver qualitatively and quantitatively different and inferior instruction to lower achieving than to higher achieving pupils (e.g., Allington, 1980; Mosenthal, 1984).

PREREFERRAL ASSESSMENT AND INTERVENTION

Traditional Assessment versus Prereferral Assessment

Analysis of the referral-to-placement process highlights the importance of modifying conventional practices in educational assessment to permit prereferral assessment and intervention in general education classrooms. Such activity aims to enhance general educators' capacity to instruct and manage difficult-to-teach pupils, thereby reducing the number of students referred for formal assessment and possible placement in special education programs.

According to Salvia and Ysseldyke (1985), the traditional purposes of educational assessment are to specify and verify students' problems and to formulate decisions about referral, classification, instructional planning, and program modification. The referral and classification phases constitute an identification process in which pupils' performance on nomothetic aptitude and/or achievement measures typically are compared to identify "outliers" who warrant placement in special programs. In contrast, the instructional planning and program modification phases together represent a process by which assessment is relatively idiographic and related to the content and methods of instruction.

The concept of prereferral assessment requires that we reconceptualize the nature of educational assessment in at least two important ways. First, prereferral assessment explicitly refers to activity that is preliminary or preparatory to teacher referral, and that formalizes the decision whether to refer. Second, and in contrast to activity conventionally associated with the referral and classification phases of assessment, preferral assessment represents an opportunity to collect data helpful to the development and evaluation of classroom interventions. Toward this end, it is often necessary to gather information about instructional and social dimensions of the classroom and students' curriculum-related performance and/or social behavior. In addition to its potential contribution to the creation of classroom interventions, prereferral assessment signals an effort to fine-tune or validate these interventions. Thus, prereferral assessment typically is conceptualized as intervention-oriented, thereby necessitating the collection of data that are *sensitive to classroom ecology* and *curriculum-based*. Moreover, such data may be used formatively to fashion classroom-based modifications that permit general educators to accommodate greater student diversity.

Characteristics of Prereferral Intervention

Prereferral intervention may be described in terms of five basic characteristics, two of which already have been discussed. First, it is consonant with the *least restrictive* doctrine set forth in P.L. 94-142, which requires that educators attempt to accommodate difficult-to-teach students' instructional and social needs in the most "normal" setting possible. Second, it is meant to be preventive. According to Graden, Casey, and Christenson (1985), prereferral intervention focuses, first, on obviating inappropriate referral and placement of students in special programs and, second, on reducing the likelihood of future students' problems by enhancing general educators' capacity to intervene effectively with diverse groups of children.

Third, prereferral intervention typically is "brokered" by one or more special service personnel (e.g., school psychologists and special educators) acting as consultants. Usually working indirectly with targeted pupils through consultation with the classroom teacher, these consultants often employ a *problem-solving* approach borrowed from behavioral consultation to design, implement, and evaluate interventions (Curtis, Zins, & Graden, 1987). Fourth, prereferral intervention represents assistance to pupil and teacher, because support is provided at the point at which the teacher contemplates referral. Finally, it encourages an *ecological* perspective that identifies teacher, physical setting, and instructional variables as well as the individual learner's characteristics as possible causes of student difficulties. In other words, rather than assume the source of student problems resides within the child, the prereferral intervention approach challenges educators to investigate a larger context to determine the source(s) of and solution(s) to pupil difficulties.

There are many ways to implement a prereferral intervention program. One involves special service personnel such as school psychologists, special educators, and guidance counselors working alone or as part of multidisciplinary teams to assist classroom teachers (see Cantrell & Cantrell, 1976; Fuchs & Fuchs, 1989; Graden, Casey, & Bonstrom, 1985; Ritter, 1978). Chalfant and colleagues (Chalfant & Pysh, 1989; Chalfant, Pysh, & Moultrie, 1979) have used a contrasting approach that mobilizes teams of teachers to help other teachers.

Mainstream Assistance Teams

For several years, my associates and I have experimented with a number of the salient dimensions of prereferral intervention. At various times we incorporated all of the aforementioned well-known characteristics of the approach, including an ecological perspective and a collaborative problem-solving version of consultation. We also borrowed important programmatic features developed by other investigators. Following the pioneering work of Cantrell and Cantrell (1976), for example. we constructed Mainstream Assistance Teams (MATs) to reflect a behavioral approach to consultation and classroom intervention.

MATs, however, have not merely reiterated others' prereferral intervention programs. Our version is distinctive in at least three ways. First, we have attempted to be pragmatic rather than ideologically pure. No procedure has been sacrosanct, as evidenced by a continuous tinkering with the process of consultation and nature of classroom interventions developed for teachers. Second, and related to the first point, we have tried to be empiricists. Much effort and resources have been expended to test our various procedures empirically. We purposely have used both multiple methods of data collection (checklists, rating scales, open-ended interviews, direct systematic observation procedures, and standardized achievement tests) and multiple sources (teachers, students, and consultants).

Third, our version of prereferral intervention aims to be both effective and practical. Practicality is pursued in three ways:

1. MAT members follow written scripts that presumably contribute to efficient and proper use of behavioral consultation.
2. We have conducted component analyses of three increasingly inclusive versions of behavioral consultation to identify a most effective and economical process.
3. We developed classroom interventions that are managed almost entirely by students, thereby reducing teachers' involvement.

Following is a more detailed description of the components of our prereferral intervention approach.

MATS: BASIC DIMENSIONS

Behavioral Consultations

We have based much of the process of our MAT activity on a model of behavioral consultation (BC) because the process appears straightforward and there is at least limited support for its effectiveness (e.g., Tombari & Davis, 1979).

Definition and Character

BC, like alternative well-known consultation models of mental health and organizational development, involves a triadic network of persons (consultant, teacher, and pupil) and indirect service. Unlike other models, BC has roots in the learning theory tradition of Watson, Skinner, and Bandura. Not surprisingly, it emphasizes the role of environmental factors in modifying behavior. That is, BC encourages exploration of antecedents and consequences of behavior in naturalistic settings to permit identification of variables influencing the frequency, rate, intensity, and/or duration of problem behavior. Behavioral consultants employ respondent, operant, and modeling procedures to change disturbing behavior.

Additionally, BC is conducted within four well-defined, interrelated stages: problem identification, problem analysis, plan implementation, and evaluation. It depicts the consultee, and often the student, as a problem solver who participates as a coequal with the consultant in designing intervention strategies. Also, the nature and implementation of these intervention strategies are based on empirically validated laws of behavioral change. Finally, evaluation of the success of these planned interventions must be data-based; effectiveness is judged in terms of whether student and/or teacher behavior has been modified sufficiently to meet previously set goals.

Evidence of Effectiveness
The effectiveness of BC has been evaluated experimentally more often than the importance of alternative consultation models (Alpert & Yammer, 1983). Although some of this efficacy research suffers from conceptual and methodological limitations (Alpert & Yammer, 1983; Meyers, Pitt, Gaughan, & Freidman, 1978), there is a steadily growing corpus of school-based investigations indicating BC's success in increasing pupils' attention, study behavior, completion of homwork assignments, and mathematics and compositional response rates, and in reducing lateness, out-of-seat behavior, general disruptiveness, stealing, chronic absences, and digit reversals (e.g., Tombari & Davis, 1979).

Identifying Essential Components of BC

Stages of BC
As mentioned, BC is conducted during a series of four interrelated stages: problem identification, problem analysis, plan implementation, and problem evaluation. The consultant, typically a school psychologist or special educator, guides the teacher through a majority of these stages in a succession of structured interviews in which specific objectives must be accomplished before consultation can proceed to subsequent stages. The major objectives of the first stage, problem identification, are to define the problem behavior in concrete, observable terms; obtain a reliable estimate of the frequency or intensity of the behavior; and tentatively identify the environmental events surrounding the problem behavior.

In the second stage, problem analysis, the goal is to validate the existence of a problem, discover classroom factors that may influence problem solution, and develop with the teacher an intervention plan that directly addresses the problem. During the third stage, plan implementation, the consultant makes certain the agreed-on intervention plan is implemented and is functioning properly. Although plan implementation is primarily the responsibility of the teacher, the consultant monitors details, including the degree of implementation. The goal of the final stage, evaluation, is for the consultant and teacher to collaborate in evaluating the effectiveness of the implemented intervention and, if necessary, to determine how it should be modified.

Rationale for Component Analysis
An apparent basic and widespread presumption in the literature on BC is that all four stages of the model are important; none are indispensable (e.g., Gresham, 1982). Although Bergan and associates (e.g., Bergan & Tombari, 1976;

Tombari & Davis, 1979) have indicated that the initial stage, problem identification, may be the most important to consultation outcomes, we are unaware of any systematic attempt to determine the relative value of the various stages or components of the BC model, or whether all are necessary.

The absence of component analyses (i.e., an effort to determine which parts are important or unimportant) seems to reflect a more general dearth of process-outcome research in the consultation literature (e.g., Alpert & Yammer, 1983; Medway, 1982; Meyers et al., 1978; Witt & Elliott, 1983). This is unfortunate, because process-outcome research, including component analyses, can help identify dispensable elements of the consultation process and lead to processes that are simultaneously effective and efficient: effective in that they are responsible for meaningful desirable change; efficient in the sense that they require a minimum of time, effort, and resources. To this end, as well as to contribute to the pertinent research literature, we undertook component analyses of the BC model in Years 1 and 2 of the MAT project.

Description of Component Analysis
We decided to explore the importance of the various components of the BC model by creating three increasingly inclusive versions of it. In the least inclusive variation, BC 1, the consultant and teacher worked collaboratively on problem identification and analysis, but the consultant did not help the teacher implement the intervention developed during the problem analysis stage. Moreover, the consultant and teacher did not evaluate intervention effects in any formative fashion, precluding an opportunity to modify or fine-tune the intervention. In other words, our first version of the model incorporated only the first two of the model's four stages (i.e., problem identification and problem analysis).

BC 2 also included the first two stages. Additionally, it required the consultant to make a minimum of two classroom visits, during which the consultant (1) observed the teacher implementing the intervention and (2) provided corrective feedback to the teacher. Like BC 1, however, this second variation of the model did not include a formative evaluation stage. Thus, BC 2 comprised the first three of the four stages of BC. Finally, BC 3, our third and most inclusive version, required consultant and teacher to formatively evaluate intervention effects, thereby incorporating all four stages of the BC model.

Written Scripts and Fidelity of Treatment

Three of four BC stages (1, 2, and 4) are implemented during the course of formal interviews or meetings. Stage 3, plan implementation, typically is conducted in the classroom. Gresham (1982) has provided one of the more comprehensive descriptions of the substance to be covered during these meetings. Because my colleagues and I believe that prereferral interventions should be embedded in a well-structured and time-efficient consultation process, we recast

Gresham's materials into written scripts that guided much of our consultants' verbal behavior.

The scripts, based loosely on the Cantrells' Heuristic Report Form (Cantrell & Cantrell, 1977, 1980), provided consultants with an efficient means to (1) create rationales and overviews for the meetings; (2) establish structure and maintain a logical and quick-paced flow; (3) obtain succinct descriptions of the classroom environment, qualitative and quantitative evaluations of the most difficult-to-teach students, and logistical information, such as days and times when the target child could be observed and tested; and (4) check, and systematically double-check, that key information, such as descriptions of the target pupil's behavior, was sufficiently elaborate and precise to permit easy identification during the consultant's classroom observations.

In addition to promoting efficiency, we believe scripts enhance fidelity of treatment. That is, assuming that the scripts accurately reflected the BC model and that consultants faithfully followed them, we could be confident that the model was implemented as intended. This issue of fidelity to treatment has been especially important to us, because a majority of our consultants have lacked formal consultation training and experience. Finally, in Years 1 and 2, each of our three versions of BC had its own script (see Fuchs & Fuchs, 1989, for an unabridged copy of Meeting #1 [Problem Identification], which is the only meeting whose script is the same across the three treatments).

YEAR 1

Setting and Participants

Four experimental schools were identified. Then five control schools were selected that matched the experimental schools on seven factors: (1) location (inner city); (2) level (middle school); (3) proportion of black students; (4) annual percentage of pupils referred for psychological evaluations; (5) average reading and math scores on the Stanford Achievement Test and a locally designed criterion-referenced test; (6) a composite index of a school staff's likelihood of referring students for psychological evaluations; and (7) percentage of pupils receiving free lunch (see Table 1 of Fuchs & Fuchs, 1988, for means, standard deviations, and statistical values).

Subjects were 48 teachers, their 48 most difficult-to-teach nonhandicapped students, and 12 school consultants. Consultants were 10 school-based support staff associated with the four experimental schools: 5 special education resource teachers, 2 school psychologists, and 3 pupil personnel specialists, a newly created position requiring the assessment skills of a psychologist, the advising capacity of a school counselor, and the family-work experience of a social worker. Two graduate students with special and general education experience also served as consultants. Each was deployed in two different schools, where they worked with the same number of teachers as the school-based consultants. In experimental schools, consultants recruited 24 fifth- and sixth-grade teachers. In control schools, principals and project staff recruited an equal number of fifth- and sixth-grade teachers who, like the experimental teachers, had a difficult-to-teach, nonhandicapped pupil and agreed to participate in the MAT project.

The 48 difficult-to-teach students were largely boys (71 percent), mostly black (65 percent), and approximately one grade below expectations in reading and math. Each was chosen by one of his or her general educators. Additionally, 58 percent were described as difficult-to-teach primarily because of "off-task" or "inattentive" behavior; 23 percent because of "poor academic work" despite an ability to perform better; 4 percent because of "poor interpersonal skills with adults"; 4 percent because of "poor interpersonal skills with peers"; and 2 percent because of "intrapersonal characteristics" (see Bahr, Fuchs, Stecker, & Fuchs, 1991, for a more detailed description of these students).

Half the experimental teachers were randomly and evenly assigned to one of three BC versions; the remaining 24 teachers were controls. The duration of the intervention ranged from six to eight weeks, depending largely on the version of BC.

Findings

Findings appeared contradictory. Teacher ratings of the severity, manageability, and tolerability of the difficult-to-teach students' classroom behavior indicated that the students in the more inclusive and most inclusive versions of the model (BC 2 and BC 3) displayed greater social or academic improvement than did those in the least inclusive BC 1 and control groups. Direct observation of their classroom behavior, however, failed to produce similar between-group differences. Such inconsistency produced many, and sometimes conflicting, interpretations (see Fuchs & Fuchs, 1989).

Another disquieting finding involved the second stage of BC, in which MAT consultants participated as members of a multidisciplinary team composed of the regular teacher and other building-based support staff. Its purpose was to engage in collaborative problem solving to develop effective interventions. To better understand Year 1 outcomes, we scrutinized the nature of these collaboratively developed interventions. This analysis, reported in Table 1 of a previous article (Fuchs & Fuchs, 1989, p. 269), revealed that all but one of the 24 interventions involved some type of student reinforcement. Disturbingly, however, a majority of these planned interventions did not call for teachers to monitor or maintain written records of student performance, which presumably should have been the basis for determining whether, and if so when, reinforcement was appropriate. In short, whereas some interventions were planned and implemented carefully, most reflected weak designs or were conducted inconsistently (see Fuchs & Fuchs, 1989).

YEAR 2

Poorly conceptualized or executed interventions in Year 1 argued for a second component analysis of BC. They also forced us to rethink the nature of the activity. We decided to modify our prereferral interventions by selecting a limited set of interventions supported by research and by developing prescriptive instructions and materials to guide their use. By requiring MAT consultants and teachers to select among a small group of carefully detailed interventions, we sacrificed some consultation-teacher autonomy and collaboration to help ensure accurate implementation of judiciously chosen interventions. In keeping with this more directive aproach, the importance of the multidisciplinary team diminished, and it was eliminated in Year 2 (see Fuchs, Fuchs, Bahr, Fernstrom, & Stecker, 1990).

We asked another important question in Year 2 — namely, whether teacher–student contracts associated with teacher monitoring were as effective as those connected with student self-monitoring.

Setting and Participants

Five project schools participated, three of which had served as project schools during the first year. Two of five control schools in Year 1 also continued their involvement in the project. These seven schools were inner-city middle schools that were alike in terms of Stanford Achievement Test reading and math scores, student enrollment, proportion of black students enrolled, and yearly rate of student referrals for psychological evaluations (see Fuchs et al., 1990).

There were 8 school-based consultants: 5 special educators, 2 school psychologists, and, at the insistence of a principal, 1 school librarian. Four graduate students also served as consultants, bringing to 12 the number of consultants in the five project schools. Consultants in the project schools helped recruit 31 teachers in fifth and sixth grades. In the control schools, principals and project staff recruited another 12 fifth- and sixth-grade teachers. Each of the 43 teachers was requested to identify a most difficult-to-teach, nonhandicapped pupil. These students were 77 percent male, 40 percent black, and approximately one grade below expectations in reading and math. Additionally, 53 percent of the subjects were described as difficult-to-teach students primarily because of "off-task" or "inattentive" behavior; 21 percent because of "poor interpersonal relations with adults"; 19 percent because of "poor academic work" despite capability to perform better; 2 percent because they "lacked academic skills"; 2 percent because of "poor motivation"; and 2 percent because of "intrapersonal characteristics."

The 43 general educators (and each of their most difficult-to-teach non-disabled students) were assigned randomly to three BC groups, representing least (BC 1), more (BC 2), and most (BC 3) inclusive variants of BC, and one control group. While blocking for membership in BC groups, the 31 teachers were assigned randomly to either a student- or teacher-monitoring group. Sixteen were directed to monitor student performance; 15 were trained by consultants to instruct their students to monitor themselves.

Teacher–Student Contracts

A teacher–student contract was selected as an intervention component for several reasons. First, a majority of teacher–consultant pairs independently decided to use it during Year 1. Second, recent surveys (e.g., Martens, Peterson, Witt, & Cirone, 1986) have indicated that many classroom teachers view it positively. Third, much research has demonstrated that a salient feature, the setting of specific challenging goals, positively affects student performance (e.g., Locke, Shaw, Saari, & Latham, 1981). The contract stipulates six dimensions of treatment: (1) the type and degree of desired change in the target behavior, (2) the classroom activity to which the contract applies, (3) the strategy by which the target behavior will be monitored, (4) the nature of the reward, (5) when and by whom it will be delivered, and (6) whether the contract can be renegotiated (see Fuchs, 1991, for an example of the contract).

To enhance the salience of these rewards, consultants encouraged teachers to base the nature of the reward on student interest and to award reinforcers as soon as possible following a demonstration of the desired behavior. Each contract was good for only one day. Teachers were required to use them for at least three weeks: every day during the first week and a minimum of two times during the second and third week. Thus, across the three weeks, as well as across BC groups (see below), teachers were to use the contracts for a minimum of nine days.

Teacher and Student Monitoring

Borrowing from others' work (e.g., Broden, Hall, & Mitts, 1971; Hallahan, Lloyd, Kosiewicz, Kauffman, & Graves, 1979; Sagotsky, Patterson, & Lepper, 1978), and mindful of the teacher-identified difficult-to-teach pupils with whom we had worked during the previous year, we developed two monitoring procedures. *Interval recording* was defined as a monitoring technique used to record whether a social behavior does or does not occur during a predetermined period or interval. Consultants recommended use of interval recording when student behavior was primarily disruptive to the teacher's or classmates' work or well-being (such as disturbing noise or inappropriate touching of others). *Product inspection* was defined as evaluation of academic work at the end of a predetermined duration. This form of monitoring was used for behaviors that primarily interfered with the student's own academic work (such as inattentiveness and frequent getting out of seat). For product inspection as well as interval recording, teachers and students were required to adhere to specific guidelines, and special monitoring sheets were created to facilitate record keeping.

Findings

Results from the component analysis suggested that the more inclusive versions of BC 2 and BC 3 promoted more positive student change than the least inclusive variant, BC 1 (see Fuchs et al., 1990). Preobservations and postobservations of classroom behavior buttress this view. In comparison to difficult-to-teach students in BC 1 and control groups, BC 2 and BC 3 pupils significantly reduced initial discrepancies between themselves and their peers regarding percentage of problem behavior. BC 1 and control students did not differ in this respect. Moreover, these results were unchanged at follow-up, three weeks after termination of formal interventions. Corroborating these data were responses to the Revised Behavior Problem Checklist (Quay & Peterson, 1983), indicating that BC 2 teachers perceived significantly greater reductions of conduct disorders than did other teachers.

Adding incisiveness to the component analysis were fidelity-of-treatment data. They substantiated that students and teachers in BC 1, BC 2, and BC 3 implemented the interventions with similar frequency, thoroughness, and accuracy; they also strengthened the conclusion that group differences in difficult-to-teach students' classroom behavior and their teachers' perceptions of conduct disorders were due to variation in the consultative process, not in quantitative or qualitative differences in classroom interventions.

In addition, observations of difficult-to-teach pupils' classroom behavior and teacher responses to various rating scales indicated that student monitoring and teacher monitoring were superior to controls, and that there were no important differences between the two monitoring groups (see Bahr, Fuchs, Fuchs, Fernstrom, & Stecker, in press).

YEAR 3

Despite strong evidence for the effectiveness of the relatively directive MAT interventions in Year 2, problems remained. Teachers claimed that improved behavior did not generalize, prescribed treatments were too complex, and the interventions still demanded too much time. Thus, in Year 3, we again modified MAT activity. We designed an experiment that simultaneously explored the efficacy of several generalization strategies and interventions of shorter and longer duration. Next we describe the second of these dimensions.

Setting

This experiment took place in the same metropolitan school system in which previous MAT activity had been conducted, one that recently had adopted a districtwide testing policy and more stringent standards for grade promotion (see Fuchs, Fuchs, & Bahr, 1990). These standards resulted in more frequent student retentions, which, in turn, prompted many teachers to ask for help with difficult-to-teach children without disabilities. Concerned about such requests as well as by increasingly large enrollments in special education, the district's director of pupil personnel requested large-scale implementation. He identified the district's 23 elementary guidance counselors, each located in a different school, as consultants. Because of our interest in departmentalized schools, including grades 3, 4, 5, or 6, we eliminated 5 schools from the director's list. The principal of another school refused to participate, leaving us with 17, or 26 percent of all elementary schools in the district.

Participants

Consultants

School-based consultants were 17 guidance counselors. Shortly after project startup, 1 counselor dropped out, but her school remained in the study. Six graduate students in special education, referred to as research assistants (RAs), also served as consultants. They were assigned to from two to four schools.

Teachers

Mainstream classroom teachers were assigned randomly to one of three roles: experimental teachers, in whose classes the MAT project initially was implemented; transfer teachers, whose classrooms became the site of MAT transfer or generalization activity; or control teachers. No teacher served in more than one role, and all were recruited by the school-based consultants. The consultants recruited 92 teachers, 48, 32, and 12 of whom were assigned randomly to experimental, transfer, and control conditions, respectively.

The 16 counselors worked with 28 experimental teachers; 12 consulted with two each, while 4 worked with one teacher. The 6 RAs were paired with 20 additional experimental teachers. Between 2 and 5 teachers were assigned to each RA, with a median and mode of 3 teachers each.

Difficult-to-Teach Students

Experimental and control teachers identified their single most difficult-to-teach student without disabilities. Of 60 experimental and control students, 42 (70 percent) were boys and 29 (48 percent) were black. Their mean age was 10.13 years (SD = 1.16), with 24 (40 percent), 21 (35 percent), 8 (13 percent), and 7 (12 percent) in grades 3, 4, 5, and 6, respectively. On the Stanford Achievement Test, administered systemwide by the district just before project startup, they earned a mean normal curve equivalent of 41.70 (SD = 15.00) in reading and 44.42 (SD = 17.43) in math. Twenty-three (38 percent) had been retained at least once.

Consultation Process

In light of Year 2 findings, MAT participants conducted all four phases of behavioral consultation (i.e., BC 3) in Year 3. They also used written scripts and teacher–student contracts similar to those employed in the previous year. On the basis of Year 2 findings, monitoring procedures were modified whereby students were trained to conduct virtually all monitoring activity.

Student Self-Monitoring

In Year 3, product inspection and interval monitoring were implemented in six phases. The first two were complex; successive phases became increasingly simple. The purpose of this progressive simplification was to reduce monitoring responsibility so that it would become increasingly feasible in the initial setting (and in transfer classrooms).

To ensure understanding of procedures, teachers monitored students in Phase 1. Students self-monitored in the remaining phases. The most complex Phases, 1 and 2, subsumed the following activities. For product inspection monitoring, the teacher first set a daily goal (e.g., "John will complete 90 percent of his math assignment with a minimum of 75 percent correct"). Second, the teacher monitored (in Phase 1) or the student self-monitored (in Phase 2) for a prespecified time, and then recorded and charted performance. Third, using these data, the student and teacher collaboratively decided on a summary or global rating of "1" (poor) to "4" (excellent).

Next, the student wrote a "self-talk question," reflecting the nature of the target behavior (e.g., "Did I do good work in math today?"), and wrote an answer pegged to the global rating. A rating of "1" dictated an answer like, "No, I did not do good math work today. I'll do better tomorrow." A rating of "4" deserved an answer like, "I did great math work today!" If the rating was a "3" or "4," the teacher rewarded the student in accordance with the teacher–student contract. Figures 11-1 and 11-2 display student-monitoring sheets for Phases 1 and 3, respectively. (For more information on product inspection monitoring, see Fuchs, Fuchs, Bahr, et al., 1990; for a complete description of interval recording, see Fuchs, Fuchs, Gilman, et al., 1990.)

PHASE 1: STUDENT MONITORING SHEET

STUDENT NAME: _____   DATE: _____

PART A: GOALS

AMOUNT Goal: _____   Items Completed

ACCURACY Goal: _____   Items Correct

TIME Limit: _____   Minutes

PART C: GLOBAL RATING

Student Rating: 1   2   3   4

Chart

4		Better Than Goal
3		Met Goal
2		Needs Some Improvement
1		Needs Big Improvement

Teacher Rating: 1   2   3   4

_____ Check after giving verbal feedback

PART B: CHARTING

25			25		
20			20		
15			15		
10			10		
5			5		

Items COMPLETED   Items CORRECT

PART D: SELF TALK

Question: _____
_____
_____
_____
_____
_____

Answer: _____
_____
_____
_____
_____
_____

STAPLE TODAY'S WORK SAMPLE TO THIS SHEET

FIGURE 11-1   **Student self-monitoring sheet for Phase 1 of product inspection**

    Unlike the first four phases, Phases 5 and 6 were conducted concurrently. Phase 5 was the last and most streamlined version of self-monitoring in the initial classroom; Phase 6 indicated that Phase 5 monitoring was occurring simultaneously in a transfer setting.

```
┌─────────────────────────────────────────────────────────────────┐
│              PHASE 3: STUDENT MONITORING SHEET                    │
│  STUDENT NAME: _____   DATE: _____       │
├─────────────────────────────────┬───────────────────────────────┤
│  PART A: GOALS                   │  PART C: GLOBAL RATING         │
│                                  │                                │
│  AMOUNT Goal:    Items Completed │  Student Rating:  1  2  3  4   │
│               ____               │                                │
│  ACCURACY Goal:  Items Correct   │                                │
│               ____               │  Teacher Rating:  1  2  3  4   │
│  TIME Limit:     Minutes         │                                │
│               ____               │                                │
│                                  │  ____ Check after giving       │
│                                  │       verbal feedback          │
├─────────────────────────────────┼───────────────────────────────┤
│  PART B: CHARTING                │  PART D: SELF TALK             │
│                                  │  Question:                     │
│         Eliminated               │  _____   │
│                                  │  _____   │
│                                  │  _____   │
│                                  │  _____   │
│                                  │  _____   │
│                                  │  _____   │
│                                  │  Answer:                       │
│                                  │  _____   │
│                                  │  _____   │
│                                  │  _____   │
│                                  │  _____   │
│                                  │  _____   │
│                                  │  _____   │
├─────────────────────────────────┴───────────────────────────────┤
│         STAPLE TODAY'S WORK SAMPLE TO THIS SHEET                  │
└─────────────────────────────────────────────────────────────────┘
```

FIGURE 11-2 **Student self-monitoring sheet for Phase 3 of product inspection**

Long versus Short Conditions

Whereas teachers always monitored twice in Phase 1, the number of times students self-monitored in Phases 2 through 6 depended on whether they were in the short or long group. In the short condition, students monitored in each phase for five days or until the daily goal was achieved three times, whichever came first. Pupils in the long condition self-monitored in each phase for six days or until the daily goal was met four times. The range in total number of monitoring sessions was 14 to 22 in the short condition, 18 to 28 in the long version.

Findings

Findings indicated that MAT teachers were significantly less likely to refer difficult-to-teach pupils to special education than were control teachers (see Fuchs, Fuchs, & Bahr, 1990). Their preratings to postratings of the severity, manageability, and tolerability of students' target behavior became more positive than control teachers' ratings. In addition, on two scales of the Revised Behavior Problem Checklist, short-group teachers exhibited a significantly positive shift from preintervention to postintervention in comparison to controls. On the other hand, whereas MAT pupils' target behavior decreased in frequency to the same level of their peers, control students also reduced their problem behavior, with a result that preobservation to postobservation comparisons between the groups were not significant.

We are at a loss to explain the improved behavior among controls, and we are disappointed that the observations failed to corroborate the teacher ratings. Nevertheless, the lack of congruence between our observation and teacher ratings data does not necessarily represent a major contradiction or cancellation of findings. As we have suggested elsewhere (e.g., Fuchs & Fuchs, 1989), the observations and teacher ratings may address different dimensions of behavior: Whereas observations generated frequency data, teacher ratings represented in part judgments about severity, manageability, and tolerability of behavior—judgments that very possibly were more influenced by the (unassessed) intensity and duration of behavior than by its frequency.

Results also suggested the short version of MAT was at least as effective as the long. The two groups' preintervention to postintervention changes were similar for teachers' severity, manageability, and tolerability ratings; for students' observed classroom behavior; and for teachers' rates of referral for testing and possible special education placement.

DISCUSSION

MAT Prescriptiveness

Three years of MAT research suggests the effectiveness of a relatively prescriptive approach to prereferral intervention and school consultation. By *prescriptive,* we mean a process that is guided by written scripts and that includes interventions, such as teacher–student contracts and monitoring procedures, decided by us, not by school personnel. MAT prescriptiveness differs from a currently popular view that consultation should be "collaborative," representing a reciprocal arrangement "that enables people with diverse expertise to generate creative solutions to mutually defined problems" (Idol, Paolucci-Whitcomb, & Nevin, 1986, p. 1). Thus, we suspect our directive approach may be viewed as an oddity by some researchers and practitioners with interest in consultation-related school activity.

Nevertheless, we did not set out to implement prescriptive prereferral interventions. During Year 1, MAT consultants received intensive training in collaborative consultation (see Fuchs, 1991; Fuchs & Fuchs, 1988, 1989). Despite expectations for success, in-class interventions were largely unimpressive. Further, during project implementation and subsequent debriefing interviews, many teachers complained they had insufficient time for the give-and-take nature of collaborative problem solving. In contrast, during debriefings and on questionnaires administered after more directive Year 2 and Year 3 activity, teachers from the same school district expressed satisfaction with the MAT interventions and consultation process. No one described the project experience as coercive or implicitly denigrating of his or her knowledge or skill.

Our MAT experience suggests that the form and substance of consultation should be consonant with the specifics of the situation. In schools in which stress is high, expertise is low, and consultation time is nonexistent, prescriptive approaches appear better suited for success than collaborative ones. My colleagues and I have no doubt that, in different situations, more collaborative approaches may represent a better choice. Moreover, situations change. As teachers and support staff as well as school administers become more experienced, confident, and positive regarding consultation-related activity, prescriptive approaches might give way to more collaborative efforts. We endorse a pragmatic approach that posits that the nature of consultation activity should be determined more by the circumstances in which consultants find themselves than by an a priori belief system.

Important Features of Prereferral Intervention

Following several years of experimentation, my associates and I believe that a number of salient features of prereferral intervention can be identified.

1. School systems interested in implementing prereferral intervention must build such activity into the job descriptions of support staff selected as consultants. School psychologists typically will *not* be capable of fulfilling such a role on top of a busy schedule of testing. Likewise, resource room teachers cannot be expected to provide direct service to a full caseload of students and also function as consultants.

2. A consultant or team of consultants should be responsible for the overall direction of the prereferral effort.

3. Consultants must receive adequate training (a) in the process of consultation, (b) in understanding completely the classroom intervention(s) to be used, and (c) in how to implement such interventions so as to cause the least disruption and burden to the teacher and classmates of the targeted pupil.

4. The consultation process must be efficient. Because school time is precious, the process must be carefully structured to include only activity that is essential to achieve desired outcomes, and the participants should always be time-conscious.

5. As to the previous point, however, consultants cannot cut corners with the process. That is, lack of time may not be used as an excuse to eliminate essential aspects of consultation such as (a) defining problem behavior; (b) setting explicit goals for students and/or teachers; (c) collecting reliable and valid data on performance observed before, during, and after implementation of the intervention; and (d) conducting systematic formative evaluation of intervention effectiveness.

6. The classroom interventions must be acceptable to teachers, which, first and foremost, means they should be feasible. This very important characteristic cannot be defined in the absolute, because what is feasible to one teacher may not be feasible to another. Thus, the consultant must define and redefine *feasibility* with each and every teacher.

7. There must be provision for ensuring the fidelity of the classroom interventions. In other words, consultants must be certain that teachers and students implementing the interventions do so according to the manner in which they were instructed.

8. As indicated, data on student or teacher behavior should be collected at multiple points during the consultation process, and these data should be socially valid. One means of accomplishing this is to obtain consumer satisfaction information; teachers, students, and consultants should be encouraged to express their comprehension, thoughts, feelings, and overall evaluation of the process. They should also be asked to make recommendations for improving the effort.

REFERENCES

Algozzine, B. (1977). The emotionally disturbed child: Disturbed or disturbing? *Journal of Abnormal Child Psychology, 5,* 205–211.

Algozzine, B., & Ysseldyke, J. E. (1981). Special education services for normal children: Better safe than sorry. *Exceptional Children, 48,* 238–243.

Allington, R. (1980). Teacher interruption behavior during primary grade oral reading. *Journal of Educational Psychology, 72,* 371–377.

Alpert, J. L., & Yammer, D. M. (1983). Research in school consultation: A content analysis of selected journals. *Professional Psychology, 14,* 604–612.

Anderson-Inman, L. (1987). Consistency of performance across classrooms: Instructional materials versus setting as influencing variables. *Journal of Special Education, 21,* 9–29.

Bahr, M. W., Fuchs, D., Fuchs, L. S., Fernstrom, P., & Stecker, P. (in press). Effectiveness of student versus teacher monitoring during prereferral intervention. *Exceptionality.*

Bahr, M. W., Fuchs, D., Stecker, P., & Fuchs, L. S. (1991). Are teachers' perceptions of difficult-to-teach students racially biased? *School Psychology Review, 20,* 599–608.

Balow, B., & Rubin, R. (1973). Factors in special education placement. *Exceptional Children, 39,* 525–532.

Bergan, J. R., & Tombari, M. L. (1976). Consultant skill and efficiency and the implementation and outcomes of consultation. *Journal of School Psychology, 14,* 3–14.

Biklen, D., Lehr, S., Searl, S. J., & Taylor, S. J. (1987). *Purposeful integration: Inherently equal.* Syracuse, NY: Center on Human Policy.

Broden, M., Hall, V. R., & Mitts, B. (1971). The effects of self-recording on the classroom behavior of two eighth-grade students. *Journal of Applied Behavior Analysis, 4,* 191–199.

Cantrell, R. P., & Cantrell, M. L. (1976). Preventive mainstreaming: Impact of a supportive services program on pupils. *Exceptional Children, 42,* 381–386.

Cantrell, R. P., & Cantrell, M. L. (1977). Evaluation of a heuristic approach to solving children's problems. *Peabody Journal of Education, 54,* 168–173.

Cantrell, R. P., & Cantrell, M. P. (1980). Ecological problem solving: A decision making heuristic for prevention-intervention education strategies. In J. Hogg & P. J. Mittler (Eds.), *Advances in mental handicap research* (Vol. 1). New York: Wiley.

Chalfant, J. C., & Pysh, M. V. (1989). Teacher assistance teams: Five descriptive studies on 96 teams. *Remedial and Special Education, 10,* 49–58.

Chalfant, J. C., Pysh, M. V., & Moultrie, R. (1979). Teacher assistance teams: A model for within-building problem solving. *Learning Disability Quarterly, 2,* 85–96.

Curtis, M. J., Zins, J. E., & Graden, J. L. (1987). Prereferral intervention programs: Enhancing student performance in regular education settings. In C. A. Maher & J. E. Zins (Eds.), *Psychoeducational interventions in schools: Methods and procedures for enhancing student competence* (pp. 7–25). Elmsford, NY: Pergamon Press.

Foster, G. G., Ysseldyke, J. E., Casey, A., & Thurlow, M. L. (1984). The congruence between reason for referral and placement outcome. *Journal of Psychoeducational Assessment, 2,* 209–217.

Fuchs, D. (1991). Mainstream Assistance Teams: A prereferral intervention system for difficult-to-teach students. In G. Stoner, M. R. Shinn, & H. M. Walker (Eds.), *Interventions for achievement and behavior problems* (pp. 241–267). Washington, DC: National Association of School Psychologists.

Fuchs, D., & Fuchs, L. S. (1988). Mainstream assistance teams to accommodate difficult-to-teach students in general education. In J. E. Graden, J. E. Zins, & M. J. Curtis

(Eds.), *Alternative educational delivery systems: Enhancing instructional options for all students* (pp. 49–70). Washington, DC: National Association of School Psychologists.

Fuchs, D., & Fuchs, L. S. (1989). Exploring effective and efficient prereferral interventions: A component analysis of behavioral consultation. *School Psychology Review, 18,* 260–281.

Fuchs, D., Fuchs, L. S., & Bahr, M. W. (1990). Mainstream Assistance Teams: A scientific basis for the art of consultation. *Exceptional Children, 57,* 128–139.

Fuchs, D., Fuchs, L. S., Bahr, M. W., Fernstrom, P., & Stecker, P. M. (1990). Prereferral intervention: A prescriptive approach. *Exceptional Children, 56,* 493–513.

Fuchs, D., Fuchs, L. S., Bahr, M. W., Reeder, P., Gilman, S., Fernstrom, P., & Roberts, H. (1990). Prereferral intervention to increase attention and work productivity among difficult-to-teach pupils. *Focus on Exceptional Children, 22,* 1–8.

Fuchs, D., Fuchs, L. S., Gilman, S., Reeder, P., Bahr, M., Fernstrom, P., & Roberts, H. (1990). Prereferral intervention through teacher consultation: Mainstream Assistance Teams. *Academic Therapy, 25,* 263–276.

Gerber, M. M., & Semmel, M. I. (1984). Teacher as imperfect test: Reconceptualizing the referral process. *Educational Psychologist, 19,* 137–148.

Gottlieb, J. (1985). *Report to the Mayor's Commission on special education on COH practices in New York City.* Unpublished paper.

Gottlieb, J., Alter, M., & Gottlieb, B. W. (1991). Mainstreaming academically handicapped children in urban schools. In J. W. Lloyd, N. N. Singh, & A. C. Repp (Eds.), *The regular education initiative: Alternative perspectives on concepts, issues, and models* (pp. 95–112). Sycamore, IL: Sycamore.

Graden, J. L., Casey, A., & Bonstrom, O. (1985). Implementing a prereferral intervention system: Part II. The data. *Exceptional Children,* 487–496.

Graden, J. L., Casey, A., & Christenson, S. L. (1985). Implementing a prereferral intervention system: Part I. The model. *Exceptional Children, 51,* 377–384.

Gresham, F. M. (1982, March). *Handbook for behavioral consultation.* Unpublished manuscript, Louisiana State University.

Hallahan, D. P., Lloyd, J., Kosiewicz, M. M., Kauffman, J. M., & Graves, A. W. (1979). Self-monitoring of attention as a treatment for a learning disabled boy's off-task behavior. *Learning Disability Quarterly, 2,* 24–32.

Heller, K. A., Holtzman, W. H., & Messick, S. (Eds.). (1982). *Placing children in special education: A strategy for equity.* Washington, DC: National Academy Press.

Idol, L., Paolucci-Whitcomb, P., & Nevin, A. (1986). *Collaborative consultation.* Austin, TX: Pro-Ed.

Jones, R. L. (1972). Labels and stigma in special education. *Exceptional Children, 38,* 553–564.

Kelly, T. J., Bullock, L. M., & Dykes, M. K. (1977). Behavioral disorders: Teachers' perceptions. *Exceptional Children, 43,* 316–318.

Lietz, J. J., & Gregory, M. K. (1978). Pupil race and sex determinations of office and exceptional educational referrals. *Educational Research Quarterly, 3,* 61–66.

Locke, E. A., Shaw, K. N., Saari, L. M., & Latham, G. P. (1981). Goal setting and task performance: 1969–1980. *Psychological Bulletin, 90,* 125–152.

Marston, D., Mirkin, P. K., & Deno, S. L. (1984). curriculum-based measurement of academic skills: An alternative to traditional screening, referral and identification. *Journal of Special Education, 18,* 109–117.

Martens, B. K., Peterson, R. L., Witt, J. C., & Cirone, S. (1986). Teacher perceptions of school-based interventions. *Exceptional Children, 53,* 213–233.

Medway, F. J. (1982). School consultation research: Past trends and future directions. *Professional Psychology, 13,* 422–430.

Meyers, J., Pitt, N. W., Gaughan, E. J., & Freidman, M. P. (1978). A research model for consultation with teachers. *Journal of School Psychology, 16,* 137–145.

Mosenthal, P. (1984). The problem of partial specification in translating reading researh into practice. *Elementary School Journal, 85,* 1–28.

Quay, H. C., & Peterson, D. R. (1983). *Revised Behavior Problem Checklist.* Coral Gables, FL: University of Miami.

Research for Better Schools. (1986). *Special education: Views from America's cities.* Philadelphia: Author.

Research for Better Schools. (1988). *Special education in America's cities: A descriptive study.* Philadelphia: Author.

Reynolds, M. C., & Balow, B. (1972). Categories and variables in special education. *Exceptional Children, 38,* 357–366.

Ritter, D. (1978). Effects of a school consultation program upon referral patterns of teachers. *Psychology in the Schools, 15,* 239–242.

Sagotsky, G., Patterson, C. J., & Lepper, M. R. (1978). Training children's self-control: A field experiment on self-monitoring and goal setting in the classroom. *Journal of Experimental Child Psychology, 25,* 242–253.

Salvia, J., & Ysseldyke, J. E. (1985). *Assessment in special and remedial education,* 3rd ed. Boston: Houghton Mifflin.

Shepard, L., & Smith, M. L. (1983). An evaluation of the identification learning disabled students in Colorado. *Learning Disability Quarterly, 6,* 115–127.

Shepard, L., Smith, M. L., & Vojir, C. P. (1983). Characteristics of pupils identified as learning disabled. *American Educational Research Journal, 20,* 309–331.

Singer, J. D. (1988). Should special education embrace the Regular Education Initiative? Lessons to be learned from the implementation of P.L. 94-142. *Educational Policy, 2,* 409–424.

Tobias, S., Cole, C., Zibrin, M., & Bodlakova, V. (1982). Teacher–student ethnicity and recommendations for special education referrals. *Journal of Educational Psychology, 74,* 72–76.

Tombari, M., & Davis, R. A. (1979). Behavioral consultation. In G. D. Phye & D. J. Reschly (Eds.), *School psychology: Perspectives and Issues* (pp. 281–307). New York: Academic Press.

Tucker, J. A. (1980). Ethnic proportions in classes for the learning disabled: Issues in nonbiased assessment. *Journal of Special Education, 14,* 93–105.

U.S. Department of Education, Special Education Programs. (1984). *Sixth annual report to Congress on the implementation of Public Law 94-142: The Education for All Handicapped Children Act.* Washington, DC: Author.

U.S. Department of Education, Special Education Programs. (1991). *Thirteenth annual report to Congress on the implementation of the Individuals with Disabilities Education Act.* Washington, DC: Author.

Weatherly, R., & Lipsky, M. (1977). Street level bureaucrats and institutional innovation: Implementing special education reform. *Harvard Educational Review, 47,* 171–197.

Will, M. (1986). Educating children with learning problems: A shared responsibilty. *Exceptional Children, 52,* 411–415.

Witt, J. C., & Elliott, S. N. (1983). Assessment in behavioral consultation: The initial interview. *School Psychology Review, 12,* 42–49.

Ysseldyke, J. E., Christenson, S., Pianta, B., Thurlow, M. L., & Algozzine, B. (1983). An analysis of teachers' reasons and desired outcomes for students referred for psychoeducational assessment. *Journal of Psychoeducational Assessment, 1,* 73–83.

Ysseldyke, J. E., & Thurlow, M. L. (Eds.). (1980). *The special education assessment and decision making process; Seven case studies* (Research Report No. 44). Minneapolis: University of Minnesota Institute for Research on Learning Disabilities.

Ysseldyke, J. E., & Thurlow, M. L. (1983). *Integration of five years of research on referral* (Research Report No. 143). Minneapolis: University of Minnesota Institute for Research on Learning Disabilities.

Ysseldyke, J. E., & Thurlow, M. L. (1984). Assessment practice in special education: Adequacy and appropriateness. *Educational Psychologist, 19,* 123–136.

Ysseldyke, J. E., Thurlow, M. L., Graden, J., Wesson, C., Algozzine, B., & Deno, S. L. (1983). Generalizations from five years of research on assessment and decision making. *Exceptional Education Quarterly, 4,* 75–93.

Zucker, S. H., & Prieto, A. G. (1977). Ethnicity and teacher bias in educational decision. *Instructional Psychology, 4,* 2–5.

▶ 12

Parent–Child Attribution Training

TANIS BRYAN   JAMES BRYAN
ELIZABETH DOHRN
University of Illinois at Chicago

Abstract

A large corpus of research has shown that people who perceive their successes and failures to be the result of personal characteristics (i.e., ability, effort) will be willing to choose cognitively challenging tasks and persevere when confronted by adversity. Research on children with LD, however, finds them more likely than achieving students to believe their successes and failures to be the result of factors outside their personal control; hence, they are less likely to persevere when faced with cognitively challenging tasks. This chapter reviews laboratory, classroom, and parent training studies that show that children's beliefs can be altered. When attribution training is combined with learning specific task strategies, children show increases in achievement and positive changes in their self-referent thoughts. Although there are limitations of this research, responding to children's performance with adaptive interpretations seems a viable addition to our therapeutic arsenal.

PURPOSE

The purpose of this chapter is to convince you of the following:

1. Self-referent thoughts (self-concept, self-efficacy, self-esteem, attributions) drive the decisions we make in life.
2. People who acquire adaptive self-referent thoughts — that is, who have self-confidence and believe they can control the events in their lives — make

different decisions than people who lack self-confidence and do not believe they have much influence over their destinies.

3. Children with learning disabilities tend to develop maladaptive self-referent thoughts; that is, they tend not to take credit for the good things that happen to them and they tend to blame themselves for their failures.

4. Recent research shows that we can help children interpret their successes and failures in ways that build self-efficacy.

5. What is most striking is that when we combine this training with specific problem-solving strategies, children feel better about themselves, and show markedly better achievement progress in the strategy area.

In order to build this case, we have done the following. First, we define attribution theory. The interventions that have been most effective in helping children acquire adaptive self-referent thoughts are nested in this theory. Second, we summarize what we know about the attributions of children with learning disabilities and describe how teachers' behaviors, the organization of the classroom, class placement, and the home shape and maintain children's beliefs about themselves. Third, we summarize the research that has been done in laboratories to help children acquire adaptive attributions. This is followed by a description of how we are translating this work to help parents help their children acquire beliefs in their self-efficacy.

OVERVIEW OF ATTRIBUTION THEORY

We know that children's ideas or beliefs about themselves can hinder learning and information processing (Kolligian & Sternberg, 1986). There is a reciprocal relationship between children's self-referent thoughts and their learning. Models of learning recognize the interactive nature of cognition, motivation or will, and affect.

Much of the effort to understand the relationships between children's self-referent thoughts and achievement has been nested in attribution theory. Attribution theory posits that an individual's interpretations of the causes of outcomes (successes and failures) influence future behavior. This is to say, it is the individual's cognitions about the causes for success and failure that affect future efforts and choices, not performance per se (Weiner, Frieze, Kukla, Reed, Rest, & Rosenbaum, 1971). Attribution theorists (Weiner et al., 1971) categorize people's cognitions or beliefs along three dimensions: stability, internality, and intentionality or control. *Stability* refers to the consistency of causes across time. For example, factors such as ability, task difficulty, and personality are considered to be stable causes, whereas effort, mood, or luck are seen as unstable. *Internality* refers to factors within the individual, such as ability, effort, and mood. External factors include such things as task difficulty and others' behavior. *Intentionality* refers to causes such as personal effort and interest, which are under a person's control, in contrast to ability and personality, which are not.

According to attribution theory, if people perceive that their successes are the result of their abilities, they will be likely to attempt similar tasks in the future because they will expect to do well and feel good about their performance. If they believe their successes on a task are due to factors not in their control (like luck or being given easy work), they will be less likely to persevere. In sum, although our views of ourselves are complex, it is clear that these opinions determine how we behave, how we think, and the emotional responses we experience in taxing situations. As Bandura (1982) maintains: "Self efficacy judgments, whether accurate or faulty, influence choice of activities and environmental settings. People avoid activities that they believe exceed their coping capabilities, but they undertake and perform assuredly those of which they judge themselves capable" (p. 123).

Research on children has found their responses to task difficulty to be correlated with their beliefs about the causes of outcomes. In a series of studies, Dweck and colleagues (Dweck, 1975; Diener & Dweck, 1978; Dweck & Repucci, 1973) showed that children who attribute failure to uncontrollable, invariant factors, such as lack of ability, show deterioration in performance following failure. In contrast, children who attribute failure to controllable, variant factors such as lack of effort do not show deterioration in performance and, indeed, often show improvement. Children who believe that failure is due to lack of ability focus on the cause of failure (i.e., their own shortcomings), whereas children who believe that failure is due to lack of effort focus on remedies for solving problems. In general, children confident of future success who believe that failure is surmountable are likely to persevere, expend effort, and select cognitively challenging tasks, in comparison to children who adopt alternative, less adaptive explanations.

SELF-CONCEPTS AND ATTRIBUTIONS AND ATTRIBUTIONS OF CHILDREN WITH LEARNING DISABILITIES

Although there is disagreement as to whether maladative self-referent thoughts (i.e., self-concept, self-esteem, low motivation, attributions) are a cause of learning disabilities or an outcome of experiencing learning problems (Kershner, 1990), there appears to be consensus that students with LD are at risk for holding self-referent thoughts that may interfere with their academic achievement progress. The results of a growing body of research demonstrate that children with LD are at risk for a variety of problems in the social domain that may not abate even though these children receive special education services (Gregory,

Shanahan, & Walberg, 1986) and experience increases in academic achievement (Thomas, 1980). These problems may play a role in the teacher referral process (Bay, 1987), are viewed as very important by parents (*Special Education Today,* 1985), and continue through high school (Gregory, Shanahan, & Walberg, 1986) and adulthood (Buchanan & Wolf, 1986; Polloway, Smith, & Patton, 1984; White, 1985).

Research on self-referent thoughts of children and adolescents with LD shows they are likely to have negative self-concepts, although this seems generally restricted to their ratings on cognitive abilities and academic achievement (Boersma, Chapman, & Maguire, 1978; Chapman, 1985; Hiebert, Wong, & Hunter, 1982; Margalit & Zak, 1984). Low self-concept in regard to academic performance may reflect realistic perceptions and honesty in responding; however, students with LD express lower academic self-concepts than achieving classmates in school subjects with which they have had little (Chapman & Boersma, 1980) or no experience (Butkowsky & Willows, 1980), and they feel less optimistic about the likelihood of future improvements in performance (Chapman & Boersma, 1980; Hiebert, Wong, & Hunter, 1982; Pearl, Bryan, & Herzog, 1983).

It may be that children with LD who adopt pessimistic self-concepts despite little or even contrary evidence have interpreted their academic experiences as an indication that they have no control over outcomes. Attribution studies support this interpretation. In general, children with LD are less likely to attribute success to ability and more likely to attribute failure to lack of ability (Butkowsky & Willows, 1980; Butkowsky, 1982; Licht, Kistner, Ozkaragoz, Shapiro, & Clausen, 1985; Palmer, Drummond, Tollison, & Zinkgraff, 1982; Pearl, 1982; Pearl, Bryan, & Donahue, 1980). Moreover, attributions of failure to lack of ability are negatively correlated with self-concept (Cooley & Ayres, 1988) and persistence on a reading task (Butkowsky & Willows, 1980).

It is important to consider how children with LD develop their self-perceptions. Obviously, the experience of school failure, especially if it comes early and is severe, plays an important role. But children's notions about themselves and causes are not generated from their experience alone. The words and deeds of significant others such as parents and teachers may alleviate or exacerbate the likelihood that these students will adopt maladaptive notions about their capabilities.

FACTORS THAT INFLUENCE CHILDREN'S SELF-CONCEPTS AND ATTRIBUTIONS

Subtle Teacher Behaviors

In the classroom there are various teacher behaviors, often implicit and subtle, that children "read" as signs that they are competent or not, and there is apparently early consensus among children as to the meaning of these clues (Weinstein & Middlestadt, 1979). Brophy (1983) summarized the teacher behaviors that communicate their expectations and judgments to students for whom teachers have high and low academic expectations: (1) waiting less time for low-expectation students to respond to questions, (2) providing low-expectation students with the answer or calling on someone else rather than trying to improve their responses, (3) more frequently criticizing low-expectation students than high-expectation students for failure, (4) less frequently praising low-expectation students than high-expectation students for success or praising them for minimal effort and performance, (5) paying less attention to low-expectation students and demanding less from them than they are capable of doing, (6) having fewer friendly interactions (less smiling and nonverbal indications of support) with low-expectation students, and (7) making less use of effective but time-consuming instructional methods with low-expectation students.

Classroom Organization

Classroom organizational structures also correlate with children's development of self-referent thoughts. This may be particularly true of structures that facilitate children's social comparisons and their judgments of their performances relative to that of their classmates. For instance, declines in children's perceptions of competence have been linked to receiving negative evaluative feedback that is very obvious to others (e.g., doing worksheet-type tasks or participating in whole-class teacher-directed lessons as opposed to small-group collaboration; Stipek & Daniels, 1988). A high frequency of graded, paper-and-pencil tasks and few opportunities for choice may make it easier for children to compare their performance with that of classmates (Rosenholtz & Rosenholtz, 1981). Public evidence of a lag in performance is interpreted by lower achievers as negative information about their competence. Because children increasingly define their competence in terms of social comparisons, normative evaluative feedback gives low achievers negative information about their competence that cannot be overcome by effort (Stipek & Daniels, 1988).

Furthermore, once students believe they lack competence, they are relatively more likely to respond to chance events or poor instruction in self-blaming ways. A study of nonhandicapped students underscores how the experience of failure can negatively influence students' beliefs in their competence, irrespective of its causes. Lepper, Ross, and Lau (1986) assessed the perseverance of erroneous self-assessments among high school students exposed to highly effective or useless filmed instruction that led to their consequent success or failure. Some students received no assistance in recognizing the relative effectiveness of their instructions, while others were shown the obvious differences in instructional quality. All subjects recognized the effectiveness or ineffectiveness of their instruction. Nevertheless, students exposed to the useless instruction drew unwarranted inferences in line with their failures about their personal capacities. Thus, even when students who had failed were explicitly shown that their failures were the result of inadequate instruction, they continued to see themselves as incompetent and to express relatively little liking for or optimism regarding subsequent course work that might tap the abilities in question. In reality, environmental factors that might contribute to students' poor performance are seldom if ever made explicit. The likelihood that children or adolescents could accurately identify and discriminate between self and situational variables that influence their achievement is highly unlikely.

The same principle has been demonstrated with educationally handicapped students and students with LD using the interrupted-task paradigm. Keogh, Cahill, and MacMillan (1972) interrupted 9- and 12-year-old educationally handicapped boys doing a task and provided the boys with different reasons for the task interruption. The 9-year-olds' placement of blame for interruption varied with experimenter feedback, but the 12-year-olds were self-blaming regardless of what they had been told. Similar results were obtained by Palmer et al. (1982), who found that students with LD were more likely than nondisabled students to judge a lack of ability to be the cause of failure to complete a task.

Class Placement

Another classroom factor found related to the self-concept of children with LD is class placement. Several studies demonstrate that children with LD in resource rooms or in segregated classrooms may maintain their self-esteem, in contrast to children fully mainstreamed (Rogers & Saklofske, 1985; Ribner, 1978; Strang, Smith, & Rogers, 1978; Rogers, Smith, & Coleman, 1978; Battle & Blowers, 1982; Schneider, 1984). Children compare their levels of achievement to those of their classmates; in this way, they construct a vision of themselves. Children with LD in regular classrooms inevitably compare themselves with classmates who are making greater academic progress and with greater ease; children in segregated settings can compare themselves with others of similar academic competence.

Specific Teaching Strategies

Yet another classroom factor has been found to be related to children's attributions and achievement. In this case, the factor is the teacher's strategies for teaching a particular content area. Bendell, Tollefson, and Fine (1980) compared the spelling performance of male adolescent students with LD who were internal and external in their attributions. Half of each group were assigned to a low-structure treatment in which they studied a set of spelling words any way they wanted (5 cents was used as a reward); the other half were in a high-structure condition in which they followed precise directions on how to study the words. The results were that the internal males learned more spelling words in the low-structure treatment than in the high-structure treatment. The opposite effect was found for external students. Essentially the same results were found by Pascarella and Pflaum (1981) and Pflaum and Pascarella (1982). In two studies, children with and without LD from the same reading groups were taught to use context cues in oral reading as a way of determining error seriousness and ways to self-correct. In a low-structure training condition, students, after responding, were directed by teachers to study the sentence context to determine for themselves what was a correct response. In a high-structure training condition, teachers indicated whether or not students' responses were correct. The instructional program contained 24 lessons taught over a twelve-week period. Twelve of the lessons were on how to decide about error seriousness, and 12 were lessons on how to self-correct. Teachers were given complete scripts detailing how to respond to students' errors in the two conditions. Results in both studies found a significant interaction effect. Students initially high in internal control made greater reading achievement progress under the condition in which they were encouraged to determine the correctness of their responses. Students initially low in internality made greater reading progress in the highly structured condition in which the teacher determined the correctness of their responses. An attempt to "wean" the low-internal students from the high to the low teaching structures was not successful in improving performance or changing attributions (Pascarella, Pflaum, Bryan, & Pearl, 1983).

Mothers' Attributions

The home may be the most important social force in shaping and maintaining a child's beliefs in himself or herself. Thus, we consider the research on parents' attributions regarding the capabilities of children with LD. A number of studies have found that mothers of children with LD and nondisabled children differ in their beliefs about the causes of their children's successes and failures. By and large, the beliefs of the mothers mirror those of the children. Pearl and Bryan (1982) found that mothers of elementary-age students with LD, compared to mothers of nondisabled children, attributed success less to ability and more to luck, while attributing failure more to a lack of ability and less to bad luck. In addition, mothers of LD students were more likely than mothers of nondisabled students to attribute success at home less to their own ability and failures at home more to their lack of ability than did mothers of nondisabled children. Bryan, Pearl, Zimmerman, and Matthews (1982) found that mothers described children with LD as having fewer academic and behavioral strengths and more weaknesses than did mothers of nondisabled children. Chapman and Boersma (1979) reported that mothers of LD males held lower expectations for academic success than did mothers of achieving males. Hiebert, Wong, and Hunter (1982) found that parents of adolescents with LD had lower academic expectations for their children than did parents of normally achieving adolescents.

A few studies considered mothers' attributions and mother–child interactions. In addition to finding that mothers of LD males held lower expectations for their sons than mothers of normally achieving males, Chapman and Boersma (1979) found they reported more negative and fewer positive reactions. Tollison, Palmer, and Stowe (1987) reported that in comparison to mothers of achieving boys, mothers of boys with LD held lower expectations for their sons' performance, were more likely to attribute their sons' failures to lack of ability, and provided more negative nonverbal responses. When given success feedback, mothers of boys with LD interpreted their son's ability as important; when given failure feedback, mothers of boys with LD perceived that their sons' lack of ability played an important role. Mothers of nondisabled boys viewed ability as important in determining success, but unimportant in determining failure. However, mothers' lower expectations for sons with LD were associated with higher performance on an achievement task.

Mothers appear to be aware of their children's lack of self-confidence; they may compensate as well as they can yet be less certain of their child's and their own ability than are mothers of nondisabled children. Given the reciprocal interactive nature of parent–child relationships (Bell, 1968), these few studies indicate that further examination of parents' perceptions of and interactions with their children may be helpful in furthering our understanding of children with LD and the complex milieu in which we expect them to prosper. At this point, we turn to studies that have focused on helping children acquire more adaptive self-referent thoughts.

ATTRIBUTION RETRAINING STUDIES

Laboratory Studies

Given the importance of attributions in affecting learning, it is not surprising that interest has arisen in attribution retraining. Various studies have tried to increase children's willingness to persist on difficult tasks by changing their beliefs about the causes for their failures (and sometimes successes). A seminal study in this area was conducted by Dweck (1975). Children aged 8 to 13 who exhibited learned helplessness (i.e., tended not to attribute failure to lack of effort but, rather, to external causes or a lack of ability) were given 25 days of training on arithmetic problems of increasing difficulty. In an attribution training condition, the experimenter responded to the child's errors with an effort attribution ("You should have tried harder"). In a second condition, children received positive reinforcement for their correct responses, and failures were ignored. In a subsequent posttest, children in the attribution condition increased their effort attributions and showed improved performance reltive to children in the "success-only" condition. Thus, children in the attribution training condition responded much better to difficult math problems than children who did not get this training.

The Dweck study led to a spate of attribution training studies that focused on teaching subjects to attribute outcomes to effort (Forsterling, 1985). In general, the results have found attribution training methods to influence a variety of dependent variables, including cognitions about causes, task persistence, and performance accuracy in the desired directions.

Research on children with learning disabilities also has had encouraging findings. In one study (Shelton, Anastopoulous, & Linden, 1985), fourth- and fifth-grade students participated in six attribution training sessions. During these sessions, students read aloud 16 sentences that varied in difficulty levels. At the beginning of the first two sessions, they heard a tape recording of a child saying things like: "I got it right. I tried hard and did a good job. . . . No, I didn't get that quite right, but that's O.K." During the sessions the trainer exhorted children to practice making such statements to themselves, and to do so in their classrooms, and the trainer gave the children attribution feedback. Across the sessions, children were reminded to use the attribution statements and to verbalize them. Results found students receiving attribution training were significantly more persistent on the reading task and increased their effort attributions.

A series of studies was conducted by Schunk (1981, 1982, 1983, 1984). In these studies, children with poor math achievement participated in a series of exercises to improve their math. In addition, in different studies they were given effort feedback ("You've been working hard"), or ability feedback ("You're good at this and you've been working hard"). Schunk found that children who received ability feedback developed higher ability attributions, self-efficacy, and subtraction skills than did students who received effort feedback. Schunk's results are very important for us. They suggest that, "As children solve problems during training, they perceive that they are becoming more competent and begin to develop a sense of efficacy for continued success . . . telling them early in the course of skills development that ability is responsible for their successes supports these self perceptions" (1984, p. 1166).

Borkowski and colleagues (Borkowski, Weyhing, & Turner, 1986; Borkowski, Weyhing, & Carr, 1988; Reid & Borkowski, 1987) developed an instructional model that integrated attribution training with strategy training in the area of reading. In this work, attribution training included: (a) a discussion about beliefs regarding the causes of failure, (2) an opportunity to perform a previously failed item successfully using a series of specific steps, and (3) a reflection on long-standing beliefs about the causes of success. Children were given program-specific attribution feedback about the reasons for correct and incorrect performance on several learning tasks. In addition, students were taught specific strategies for reading. Results showed that students who received attribution training plus reading strategies performed better on paragraph summaries at the end of training and two weeks later than children who were only taught the reading strategy. These results provide powerful support for the integration of attribution feedback and teaching children specific task strategies.

Classroom Studies

So far, we have discussed laboratory studies that showed how children's beliefs about outcomes can be altered and how these alterations are related to achievement gains. This raises the important question of whether attribution training can be conducted in classrooms. One study (Andrews & Debus, 1978) had a sixth-grade teacher direct children to use effort attributions after failure. Students were told to say, "Students fail because they do not try hard enough." Children were reinforced, or not, with tangible reinforcers following their attribution statements. This procedure was found to be effective in increasing performance and effort attributions irrespective of whether or not tangible reinforcers were used. In another study (Thomas & Pashley, 1982) special education teachers conducted the program in classes for learning-disabled students, following their participation in an extensive training program. In one condition, children were engaged in increasingly difficult novel nonacademic tasks like tangram puzzles, mazes, and number patterns as well as spelling. As the materials became more difficult students had the opportunity to practice making effort attributions. A second group of students with LD participated in similar effort-attribution training but were given materials at their mastery level; that is, they were in a success-only condition. Results showed that students with LD in both training conditions increased their persistence, time spent on task, and number of attempts at a difficult puzzle relative to a control group who received no training.

Peer Tutoring Studies

Another approach to attribution training in classrooms used peer tutoring as a framework. There is an impressive body of data showing that children participating in peer tutoring as tutors and as tutees make significant academic gains. In a review of 24 research studies that employed children with LD, Scruggs and Richter (1988) found a majority reported academic benefits favoring peer tutoring. Oral reading, spelling, and math gains among elementary and high school students who served either as tutors or as tutees have been found. Reports that peer tutoring also yields improvements in social skills (Argyle, 1976), self-esteem (Strodtbeck, Ronchi, & Hansell, 1976), and attitudes toward school (Feldman, Devin-Sheehan, & Allen, 1976) make peer tutoring an attractive mode for classroom-based attribution training.

Bryan, Dohrn, and Bryan (1993) conducted a peer tutoring study in which older students with LD, grades 5 to 7, tutored younger children in grades 1 to 4 on how to use a calculator to solve math problems. The notion was that if the tutors were trained to respond to younger children's performance with attributions to effort and ability, the tutors would come to adopt these beliefs for themselves. The hypothesis was based on two well-established findings in the adult literature. One is reactance theory, the observation that people will resist influence attempts (Brehm, 1981). The second, from the persuasion literature, is that people are more likely to be persuaded if they make a public commitment to a position.

The general procedure conducted across a five-week period was to have graduate assistants meet weekly with the tutors. During these sessions, the tutors practiced the lesson they were to teach to 100 percent accuracy. Students, randomly assigned to one of two treatments, also were taught to make either attribution or encouragement statements in response to tutees' correct and incorrect answers. In the attribution condition, they made ability attribution statements in response to tutees' correct answers (e.g., "You seem smart to me," "You have the skills it takes to do this"), and effort attribution statements to tutees' incorrect responses (e.g., "You should try a bit harder," "You need to practice more"). In the encouragement condition, they responded to both correct and incorrect answers with encouragement statements (e.g., "You're doing a great job," "Don't worry too much about this"). Within a day or two of the training sessions, the tutoring sessions took place, with graduate assistants present to monitor the program.

Analysis of results found that the only effect of training was found in the encouragement condition. Children in this condition were more likely to make effort attributions for success than were children in the attribution condition. There were no condition effects for children's ability attributions. Failure to find results could not be explained on the basis of failure to induce children to use the attribution statements. Observations made during the peer tutoring sessions indicated that children's statements to their tutees were influenced by the type of training they received. Children in the attribution condition made significantly more ability and effort attributions to their tutees, whereas children in the encouragement condition were more likely to model the encouraging statements in response to correct and incorrect responses from tutees.

In a second study (Bryan, Dohrn, & Bryan, 1993), currently being analyzed, peer tutoring focused on teaching children vocabulary. In the attribution condition, children were coached to make ability attributions in response to tutee's correct answers and to make strategy statements in response to tutee's incorrect answers. Analyses to date show that tutors and tutees learned significantly more words in the attribution-plus-strategy-training condition than they did in the strategy-only condition.

In sum, in two studies we have found that peer tutoring helps students with learning disabilities perceive themselves as working hard, helping others, and becoming more proficient at math or reading. In the first study, children's attributions about ability did not change. Indeed, children in the control condition increased their effort attributions. In the second study, the differences between attribution training and the control (strategy-only) condition were increased. But we are waiting to see if increasing training differences makes a difference in children's attributions in the second study. Meanwhile, it is notable that the second study found significantly better performance on the achievement variable of reading vocabulary. This replicates and underscores Borkowski's (Borkowski, Weyhing, & Carr, 1988) finding that attribution training plus a specific task strategy produces better achievement gains than only teaching the task strategy.

Parent–Child Studies

The last two studies we are going to describe are Parent–Child Attribution Training studies. In these studies, we focused on training mothers to model attribution statements in response to their child's performances. The rationale for this approach is based on three sets of important attitudes. Depending on how old the child is, these attitudes are: (1) attitudes about intelligence, or being smart; (2) attitudes about the self relative to classmates; and (3) reasons that the child does well or poorly in school. In these studies, we explore the feasibility of using parents as models of ability and strategy responses to their children's performances. Let us consider these attitudes.

Many children (and adults) believe that intelligence is God-given—that, no matter what, intelligence is fixed and unchanging throughout life (like the color of one's eyes—barring contact lenses). Many people believe that intelligence is a static characteristic, one we are born with and thus are "stuck with." Children who experience difficulty in school come to believe that they are stupid, that they lack intelligence. Because they believe they are stupid, they come to believe they will never overcome their learning problems. Belief that intelligence does not change leads many children to become discouraged and give up trying to master what is difficult for them to learn.

In fact, intelligence is a dynamic characteristic. There is variability in IQ scores across time. This means people get smarter as they learn new things. Therefore, we built into our program the principle that parents should respond to their child's successes as an indication that being smart is something that is learned and that they are getting smarter as they learn new things.

The second principle, particularly important for older children, has to do with how children judge their work. Children, like adults, compare themselves with their peers. Children who see that they are doing poorly in comparison to their classmates may be pained by this observation. These comparisons provide additional "proof" that they are "dumb." Daily reminders that one is "dumber" than one's classmates can be very discouraging. These comparisons can contribute to children's unwillingness to tackle school challenges. This leads children to avoid schoolwork, which in turn leads to worse performance. Children then get information that they are dumb, and around it goes.

What can we do to stop or reverse this cycle? The main idea is that when children make self-disparaging comparisons, we train parents to redirect their evaluations to their own progress. For example, when a child complains that everyone does better, or that everyone takes less time, a parent might say: "Lots of kids think they're dumb because other kids do better. But there is always someone who does things better than you, or me. What's important is that you get better at what you work at. See how well *you* are doing — don't worry about what other kids are doing."

The third set of ideas may be the most important of all. This has to do with the child's beliefs about what makes him or her successful or unsuccessful. Children's thoughts about why they do well make a big difference in their willingness to work. The effort they put forth, their persistence when learning is difficult, their continued attempts in the face of challenge — are related to their beliefs about causes.

How should parents interpret the causes of children's successes and failures? As in the peer tutoring, we trained parents to encourage children to believe that their successes are due to their own ability and effort. When children fail, when they get something wrong, we trained parents to redirect their children to a strategy that would help them solve the problem.

STUDY 1

Method

Design
This study was conducted in a private day school located in a Chicago suburb that enrolls students with learning disabilities from Chicago and the surrounding suburbs. Mothers who volunteered to participate and were able to attend weekly sessions were assigned to an attribution-plus-strategy-training condition. A group of mothers who were interested in the program but unable to commit to attending the sessions served as a no-treatment control group. The effectiveness of the program was assessed through pre- and posttest measures administered to both groups of mothers and their children.

Subjects
Subjects initially included 18 students and their mothers. Of the 18, 6 indicated willingness to attend ten weekly sessions. These mothers constituted the experimental training group. After two sessions, one dropped out because her son had to attend basketball practice. Data analysis was based on the five mothers and their children who had attended each of the sessions. Thirteen

mothers who indicated interest in participating in the program were unable to schedule the weekly meetings. These mothers agreed to complete the pre- and posttest measures and served as the no-treatment contgrol group. Nine mothers completed the pretest measures, and 4 completed the posttest measures.

Students in the attribution training group included four males and one female, ages 7.3 to 12.3 years (mean = 10.4 years). Their IQs ranged from 80 to 110 (mean = 95). Reading comprehension scores, based on the Stanford Achievement Test, ranged from grade level 2.2 to 7.1 (mean = 3.6). Math application scores, based on the Stanford Achievement Test, ranged from grade level K.9 to 6.9 (mean = 3.4). Students in the no-treatment condition included 3 females and 8 males, ages 9.2 years to 18.0 years (mean = 12.4). Their IQs ranged from 78 to 115 (mean = 96). Reading scores ranged from grade level 1.4 to 9.2 (mean = 4.3). Math scores ranged from 1.5 to 8.2 (mean = 4.2). Students in both conditions were predominantly white (one student was an Arab, and another was Hispanic). All but two (one in each condition) were from two-parent middle-class homes.

Measures

Parents in the experimental group were administered the following measures during the first and last of ten sessions. Parents in the control group were mailed the questionnaires at the same time. Students in the experimental and control groups were administered the various measures during the school day. Following is a description of the measures administered to parents and students.

Parent attributions about the child.   This is a 32-item questionnaire in which the mother rates the importance of ability, effort, task difficulty, and luck on a four-point scale for successful and unsuccessful outcomes in reading, doing math, and getting along with others. For example, mothers are asked, "When your child does good work in reading, how important would — being smart in reading — be?

Child attributions about self.   Children indicate on a four-point scale, portrayed with circles increasing in size, how important ability, effort, luck, and task difficulty are when they do well or poorly on reading, math, puzzles, and getting along with classmates.

Forced choice attributions.   Children are given a series of six questions about doing well or poorly on reading, puzzles, and getting along with others. Children have to choose between one of two reasons (ability, effort, task difficulty, or luck) for successful or unsuccessful outcomes.

Child social comparisons.   Children are shown three vertical rows of smiling faces and told that the face at the top represents the child in the class who is best at reading (doing puzzles, getting along with others), and the face at the bottom is the child who is doing worst. Children are asked to circle the face that shows how well they are doing.

Parent attribution and strategy statements. To estimate the parents' application of the training, a tape recorder was set up at one of the family math stations. Parents were taped while working with their child at this station. This was done during four of the sessions.

Family Math Activities
The math activities were chosen from *Family Math* (Stenmark, Thompson, & Cossey, 1986). This program was designed to provide parents with math materials that they could use at home with their child. The focus of the activities is to develop problem-solving skills and to build an understanding of mathematics utilizing hands-on materials. The activities involved estimation, measurement, word problems and logical reasoning, numbers and operations, probability and statistics, time and money, geometry and spatial thinking, patterns and number charts, and calculator use. The Venn diagrams station provides an example of an activity that involved logical reasoning combined with sorting and classifying. The dyads were to make a Venn diagram on a large piece of paper and choose characteristics that people will and will not have alike. They then signed their name in the circle that was true for them (e.g., "I live in California" in the outer circle and "I live in San Francisco" in the inner circle). Another station, Perfect People, involved the exploration of measurement. The dyads were instructed to cut a piece of string to exactly the height of their partner. They used their own string to find out if they were a "tall rectangle," a "short rectangle," or a "perfect square." The directions explained how to measure, and the parent and child recorded their responses on a chart. The activity then explored distance around (circumference of) different body parts. Calculator Paths has a series of game boards for addition, subtraction, multiplication, and division. The parent and child decided which game board to use, and the object of the game was to choose correctly, by estimating, numbers that will make a path from one side to the opposite side. The dyads used a calculator to check their estimation. The winner was the person who had a connected line of numbers from one end of the game board to the other. All the activities in the *Family Math* program can be adapted to different age and ability levels. The materials include items that can be found around the home or school or that can be purchased inexpensively.

Procedures. Each session began with a fifteen-minute period in which the mother and child met separately with two graduate assistants. The mothers reviewed the activities to be done that day and were coached on how to make attribution statements in response to their child's accuracy on the task and strategy statements in response to their child's having difficulty getting the correct answer or doing the task.

The attribution statements included:

"You are smart."
"You're doing great."
"I can tell you're talented at this sort of thing."
"You're really trying hard."
"You're really getting smart because you're working hard."

The strategy statements included:

"Can you think of another way to do this?"
"Try to read the word aloud; it might help you."
"Let's go one by one."
"Let's go over it again."
"This word is hard, try to look for a clue."
"You almost got it."

Mothers were given folders containing the materials to be used that day and a list of the attribution and strategy statements as reminders. While the mothers were meeting, their children had a snack and worked with a graduate assistant on various math activities and using a calculator to solve math problems.

Parents and children were then united in a room set up with six work stations. A different math activity was at each station. The dyads spent twenty minutes working at each station, rotating and completing three of the activities per session. The graduate assistant circulated among the stations, answering questions and modeling attribution and strategy statements for the parents. A tape recorder was set up at one station to audiotape the dyad's interaction.

At the end of each training session, the dyads were provided with treats and the children worked on calculator skills while the parents had a brief wrap-up meeting. The trainer discussed with parents the number of times they used the attribution and strategy statements and how they might increase their use of these statements. Mothers were verbally reinforced for their attempts to use the attribution and strategy statements.

Results

Parents' Attributions about Child

There were no group differences on the pretest. On the posttest, mothers in the training group perceived their children as growing better on academics (mean = 11.0) than did mothers in the control group (mean = 8.8, t = 2.26,

$p < .05$). Mothers in the training group also perceived their children as growing better on social skills (mean $= 11.5$) than did mothers in the control group (mean $= 8.8$, $t = 2.02$, $p < .08$). Mothers in the training group perceived their children as growing better in their behavior (mean $= 10.5$) than mothers in the control group (mean $= 7.8$, $t = 2.39$, $p < .05$).

Children's Attributions about Self
Children in the attribution training group were more likely than children in the control condition to attribute failure to ability (mean $= 14.0$, mean $= 11.0$, respectively, $t = 1.96$, $p < .07$).

Children's Forced-Choice Attributions
Children in the attribution condition tended to attribute their successes to their ability more than did children in the control condition (mean $= 6.2$, 3.6, respectively, $t = 2.05$, $p < .06$). Children in the attribution training were more likely to attribute failure to lack of effort than children in the control condition (mean $= 5.4$, 3.2, respectively, $t = 2.8$, $p < .01$).

Social Comparisons
There were no significant differences on the posttest. An assessment of pre- to posttest difference scores, however, suggests that the children in the attribution group compared to children in the control group rated themselves as doing better relative to their classmates in math, reading, and getting along with others.

Parent Statements
The number of attribution and strategy statements made by mothers was tallied. Mothers made 29 attribution statements and 96 strategy statements.

STUDY 2

The purpose of this study was to replicate the first study using at-risk children in an inner-city school. In addition, this study expanded the design to assess the relative impact of attribution plus strategy training versus strategy training, and a no-treatment control.

Method

Subjects
Subjects included 13 students, 10 mothers, and 1 father. Of the 11 parents, 7 were able to attend the sessions. They were randomly assigned to the attribution-

plus-strategy or the strategy-only condition. The parents unable to attend were assigned to the no-treatment control group. Eleven parents completed the pretests, but only the parents in the two training conditions completed the posttests.

The children in the attribution training group included 1 male and 3 females. Students' grades ranged from third to seventh (mean = 4.2). Reading achievement scores ranged from 1.6 to 5.2 (mean = 3.3), and math achievement scores ranged from 2.7 to 6.1 (mean = 4.0). In the strategy-only group, there were 2 males and 3 females. Students' grades ranged from first to fifth (mean = 3.6). Reading achievement grade-equivalent scores ranged from K.8 to 2.9 (mean = 2.2) and math achievement grade-equivalent scores ranged from 1.2 to 5.5 (mean = 3.4). In the control group there were 2 males and 2 females. Students' grades ranged from third to fourth (mean = 4.2). Reading achievement scores ranged from 1.3 to 5.1 (mean = 3.5), and math achievement scores ranged from 1.5 to 4.8 (mean = 3.7).

Measures
The same measures were used in this study as in Study 1.

Procedures
Procedures in the attribution-plus-strategy-training condition were the same as described above. In the strategy-only condition, parents were coached to respond to their child's accurate responses with statements like, "That's correct, you got it right," and to their child's errors with statements like, "Let's go one by one, can you think of another way to do this?"

Results

The first set of analyses examined pretest differences between the parents in the three groups. There were no group differences. Analyses of posttests are based only on the parents in the two training groups because parents in the no-treatment control condition failed to complete the questionnaires.

Parents' Attributions about the Child
Results found parents in the attribution-plus-strategy-training group perceived their child as doing better than did parents in the strategy-only condition. They rated their children higher in athletic ability (mean = 10.4, mean = 8.4, $t = 1.89$, $p < .09$), physical appearance (mean = 11.8, 9.8, $t = 1.84$, $p < .10$), and behavior (mean = 10.2, 7.5, $t = 2.39$, $p < .04$).

Children's Attributions about Self
Children in the attribution-plus-strategy group perceived their successes to be due to effort significantly more than did children in the strategy-only and

control conditions (mean = 15.6, 15.5, 13.5, respectively, $F(2,7) = 4.14$, $p < .05$). Newman-Keuls post hoc comparisons indicated the main effect was due to differences between the strategy-only condition and the control $Q(3,8) = 1.83, p < .05$). Children in the strategy-only condition attributed their failures more to their ability than did children in the attribution-plus-strategy or control conditions (mean = 11.0, 6.3, 10.7, $F(2,8) = 3.97$, $p < .06$). Newman Keuls post hoc comparisons indicated that significant differences occurred between the attribution-plus-strategy condition and the control $Q(3,7) = 2.25, p < .05$) as well as between the strategy condition and the control $Q(3,7) = 2.25, p < .05$).

Children's Attributions – Forced Choice
There were no significant group differences.

Social Comparisons
There were no significant main effects.

Parent Attribution Statements
Parents in the attribution-plus-strategy condition made 12 attribution and 15 strategy statements. Parents in the strategy-only condition made 3 attribution and 11 strategy statements.

CONCLUSIONS AND IMPLICATIONS

So far the results of our preliminary research on attribution training for children with LD have been reasonably encouraging. Attribution training is a practical and easy-to-carry-out procedure. All we are asking parents to do is to respond to their children's successes with interpretive statements about how learning new things means getting smarter. And we want parents to help children become task-strategic when they experience difficulty. Although the samples in our research studies were small, we think the results show that parents can play a significant role in helping their children acquire adaptive beliefs. Parents serve as role models when they voice opinions about why things happen to them. Parents influence children by giving them feedback about their performance. This feedback communicates to children parents' evaluations of their children's self-worth and ability.

An important aspect of our research was having parents and children interact while doing a specific task – in our case, family math activities. During the parent training sessions, parents sometimes expressed reservations about their children's ability to do the tasks. Encouraged by us to try anyway, parents then were able to see their children successfully performing math tasks that were challenging and fun for both of them. In both studies, parents' perceptions of their children became more positive, and children increased their expression of personal responsibility for their successes and failures. To reiterate, we think attribution training is likely to be successful in changing children's and parents' perceptions only if done in conjunction with performing or learning tasks that both parents and children deem reasonably challenging or worthwhile.

With these positive outcomes in mind, some limitations and complications also must be considered. This is not to discourage you from adopting the use of the ability, effort, and strategy responses to children, but to acknowledge that other factors do play a part. Sometimes children cannot do a task because they do not have the ability. Exhorting more effort when the child lacks the background skills to do a task would be very discouraging. Clearly, only when one is sure that the child's failure is the result of failure to apply some strategy, or to try hard, can one exhort the child to try harder and to use a strategy. When you are not sure why a child is doing poorly, the wisest course is to encourage the child while also providing task strategies so the child can solve the problem.

It also is important to recognize that there are developmental changes during childhood and differences in capacities for processing and integrating information (Ruble, 1980). Attribution theory seems to assume that there are unequivocal standards of success and failure; the theory ignores the possibility that there may be situational influences on the definition of success (Blumenfeld, Pintrich, Meece, & Wessels, 1982). Definitions of success are not held constant: Different children are held to different standards of success, and children are held to different standards in different situations. Our concern is that teachers and parents be of one mind in providing feedback regarding performance. There should be some agreement on expectations and standards for performance. Both parents and teachers should contribute to the child's development of self-efficacy by responding in constructive ways to the children's performance. It is also important to understand that other motivational factors, such as values or perceived consequences for success and failure, may be more crucial in determining the degree and quality of effort exerted and the subsequent level of achievement than causal attributions (Nicholls, 1979; Covington & Omelich, 1979). Clearly, when home and school are consistent in setting standards and expectations, and share common values that support academic achievement, the child has the best chance for thriving intellectually and socially. Our objective must be to establish environments in school and at home that support children's intellectual initiations and effort, that enhance the likelihood that children will perceive themselves to be competent. It is both cost-effective and moral for adults to make the effort to help children acquire a belief in themselves.

REFERENCES

Andrews, G. R., & Debus, L. (1978). Persistence and the causal perception of failure. *Journal of Educational Psychology, 70,* 154–166.

Argyle, M. (1976). Social skills theory. In V. L. Allen (Ed.), *Children as teachers* (pp. 57-71). New York: Academic Press.

Bandura, A. (1982). Self-efficacy mechanism in human agency. *American Psychologist, 37*, 122-147.

Battle, J., & Blowers, T. (1982). A longitudinal comparative study of the self-esteem of students in regular and special education classes. *Journal of Learning Disabilities, 15*, 100-102.

Bay, M. (1987). *Student factors that influence teacher's referral decisions.* Unpublished doctoral dissertation, University of Illinois at Chicago.

Bell, R. Q. (1968). A reinterpretation of the direction of effects in studies of socialization. *Psychological Review, 75*, 81-95.

Bendell, D., Tollefson, N., & Fine, M. (1980). Interaction of locus of control orientation and the performance of learning disabled adolescents. *Journal of Learning Disabilities, 13*, 32-35.

Blumenfeld, P. C., Pintrich, P. R., Meece, J., & Wessels, K. (1982). The formation and role of self perceptions of ability in elementary classrooms. *Elementary School Journal, 82*, 401-420.

Boersma, F. J., Chapman, J. W., & Maguire, T. O. (1978). The Student's Perception of Ability Scale: An instrument for measuring academic self-concept in elementary school children. *Educational and Psychological Measurement, 39*, 1035-1041.

Borkowski, J. G., Weyhing, R. S., & Carr, M. (1988). Effects of attributional retraining on strategy-based reading comprehension in learning-disabled students. *Journal of Educational Psychology, 80*, 46-53.

Borkowski, J. G., Weyhing, R. S., & Turner, L. A. (1986). Attributional retraining and the teaching of strategies. *Exceptional Children, 53*, 130-137.

Brehm, S. S. (1981). Oppositional behavior in children: A reactance theory approach. In S. S. Brehm, S. M. Kassin, & F. X. Gibbons (Eds.), *Developmental social psychology,* (pp. 96-121). New York: Oxford University Press.

Brophy, J. E. (1983). Research on the self-fulfilling prophecy and teacher expectations. *Journal of Educational Psychology, 75*, 631-661.

Bryan, T., & Bryan, J. (1993). *The effects of attribution training nested in peer tutoring on teachers' and students' causal attributions and self perceptions.* Unpublished manuscript.

Bryan, T., Pearl, R., Zimmerman, D., & Matthews, F. (1982). Mothers' evaluations of their learning disabled children. *Learning Disability Quarterly, 16*, 149-160.

Buchanan, M., & Wolf, J. S. (1986). A comprehensive study of learning disabled adults. *Journal of Learning Disabilities, 19*, 34-38.

Butkowsky, I. S. (1982). *The generality of learned helplessness in children with learning difficulties.* Paper presented at the Annual Convention of the American Psychological Association, Washington, DC.

Butkowsky, I. S., & Willows, D. M. (1980). Cognitive-motivational characteristics of children varying in reading ability: Evidence for learned helplessness in poor readers. *Journal of Educational Psychology, 72*, 408-422.

Chapman, J. W. (1985). *Self-perceptions of ability, learned helplessness and academic achievement expectations of children with learning disabilities.* New Zealand: Massey University, Education Department.

Chapman, J. W., & Boersma, F. J. (1979). Academic self-concept in elementary learning disabled children: A study with the Student's Perception of Ability Scale. *Psychology in the Schools, 16,* 201–206.

Chapman, J. W., & Boersma, F. J. (1980). *Affective correlates of learning disabilities.* Lisse: Swets & Zeitlinger.

Cooley, E. J., & Ayres, R. R. (1988). Self-concept and success–failure attributions of nonhandicapped students and students with learning disabilities. *Journal of Learning Disabilities, 21,* 174–178.

Covington, M. V., & Omelich, C. L. (1979). Effort: The double-edged sword in school achievement. *Journal of Educational Psychology, 71,* 169–182.

Diener, C. I., & Dweck, C. S. (1978). An analysis of learned helplessness: Continuous changes in performance, strategy, and achievement cognitions following failure. *Journal of Personality and Social Psychology, 36,* 451–461.

Dweck, C. S. (1975). The role of expectations and attributions in the alleviation of learned helplessness. *Journal of Personality and Social Psychology, 31,* 674–685.

Dweck, C. S., & Repucci, N. D. (1973). Learned helplessness and reinforcement responsibility in children. *Journal of Personality and Social Psychology, 25,* 109–116.

Feldman, R. S., Devin-Sheehan, L., & Allen, V. L. (1976). Children tutoring children: A critical review of research. In V. L. Allen (Ed.), *Children as teachers* (pp. 235–249). New York: Academic Press.

Forsterling, F. (1985). Attributional retraining: A review. *Psychological Bulletin, 98,* 495–512.

Gregory, J. F., Shanahan, T., & Walberg, H. J. (1986). A profile of learning disabled twelfth-graders in regular classes. *Learning Disability Quarterly, 9,* 33–42.

Hiebert, B., Wong, B., & Hunter, M. (1982). Affective influences on learning disabled adolescents. *Learning Disability Quarterly, 5,* 334–343.

Keogh, B. K., Cahill, C. W., & MacMillan, D. L. (1972). Perception of interruption by educationally handicapped children. *American Journal of Mental Deficiency, 77,* 107–108.

Kershner, J. R. (1990). Self concept and IQ as predictors of remedial success in children with learning disabilities. *Journal of Learning Disabilities, 23,* 368–374.

Kolligian, J., & Sternberg, R. J. (1986). Intelligence, information processing, and specific learning disabilities: A triarchic synthesis. *Journal of Learning Disabilities, 20,* 8–17.

Lepper, M. R., Ross, L., & Lau, R. R. (1986). Persistence of inaccurate beliefs about the self: Perseverance effects in the classroom. *Journal of Personality and Social Psychology, 50,* 482–491.

Licht, B. G., Kistner, J. A., Ozkaragoz, T., Shapiro, S., & Clausen, L. (1985). Causal attributions of learning disabled children: Individual differences and their implications for persistence. *Journal of Educational Psychology, 77,* 208–216.

Margalit, M., & Zak, I. (1984). Anxiety and self-concept of learning disabled children. *Journal of Learning Disabilities, 17,* 537–539.

Nicholls, J. G. (1979). Quality and equality in intellectual development. *American Psychology, 34,* 1071–1084.

Palmer, D. J., Drummond, F., Tollison, P., & Zinkgraff, S. (1982). An attributional investigation of performance outcomes for learning-disabled and normal-achieving pupils. *Journal of Special Education, 16,* 207–219.

Pascarella, E. T., & Pflaum, S. W. (1981). The interaction of children's attribution and level of control over error correction in reading instruction. *Journal of Educational Psychology, 73,* 533–540.

Pascarella, E. T., Pflaum, S. W., Bryan, T. H., & Pearl, R. (1983). Interaction of internal attribution for effort and teacher response mode in reading instruction: A replication note. *American Educational Research Journal, 20,* 269–276.

Pearl, R. A. (1982). LD children's attributions for success and failure: A replication with a labeled LD sample. *Learning Disability Quarterly, 5,* 173–176.

Pearl, R., & Bryan, T. (1982). Mothers' attributions for their learning disabled child's successes and failures. *Learning Disability Quarterly, 5,* 53–57.

Pearl, R. A., Bryan, T., & Donahue, M. (1980). Learning disabled children's attributions for success and failure. *Learning Disability Quarterly, 3,* 3–9.

Pearl, R., Bryan, T., & Herzog, A. (1983). Learning disabled and nondisabled children's strategy analysis under conditions of high and low success. *Learning Disability Quarterly, 6,* 67–74.

Pflaum, S. W., & Pascarella, E. T. (1982). Attribution retraining for learning disabled students: Some thoughts on the practical implications of the evidence. *Learning Disability Quarterly,* 422–426.

Polloway, E. A., Smith, J. D., & Patton, J. R. (1984). Learning disabilities: An adult development perspective. *Learning Disability Quarterly, 7,* 179–186.

Reid, M. K., & Borkowski, j. G. (1987). Causal attributions of hyperactive children: Implications for teaching strategies and self-control. *Journal of Educational Psychology, 79,* 296–307.

Ribner, S. (1978). The effects of special class placement on the self-concept of exceptional children. *Journal of Learning Disabilities, 11,* 319–323.

Rogers, C. M., Smith, M. D., & Coleman, J. M. (1978). Social comparison in the classroom: The relationship between academic achievement and self-concept. *Journal of Educational Psychology, 70,* 50–57.

Rogers, H., & Saklofske, D. H. (1985). Self-concepts, locus of control and performance expectations of learning disabled children. *Journal of Learning Disabilities, 18,* 273–278.

Rosenholz, S. J., & Rosenholz, S. H. (1981). Classroom organization and the perception of ability. *Sociology of Education, 51,* 132–140.

Ruble, D. N. (1980). Developmental perspective on the theories of achievement motivation. In L. J. Fyans, (Ed.), *Achievement motivation: Recent trends in theory and research,* (pp. 225–245), New York: Plenum.

Schneider, B. H. (1984). LD as they see it: Perceptions of adolescents in a special residential school. *Journal of Learning Disabilities, 17,* 533–536.

Schunk, D. H. (1981). Modeling and attributional effects on children's achievement: A self-efficacy analysis. *Journal of Educational Psychology, 73,* 93–105.

Schunk, D. H. (1982). Effects of effort attributional feedback on children's perceived self-efficacy and achievement. *Journal of Educational Psychology, 74,* 548–556.

Schunk, D. H. (1983). Ability versus effort attributional feedback: Differential effects on self-efficacy and achievement. *Journal of Educational Psychology, 75,* 848–856.

Schunk, D. H. (1984). Sequential attributional feedback and children's achievement behaviors. *Journal of Educational Psychology, 76,* 1159–1169.

Scruggs, T. E., & Richter, L. (1988). Tutoring learning disabled students: A critical review. *Learning Disability Quarterly, 8,* 274–286.

Shelton, T. L., Anastopoulos, A. D., & Linden, J. D. (1985). An attribution training program with learning disabled children. *Journal of Learning Disabilities, 18,* 261–265.

Special Education Today. (1985). Volume 2, No. 5. Set Press, Ltd.

Stenmark, J. K., Thompson, V., & Cossey, R. (1986). *Family math.* Berkeley: University of California Press.

Stipek, D. J., & Daniels, D. H. (1988). Declining perceptions of competence: A consequence of changes in the child or in the educational environment? *Journal of Educational Psychology, 80,* 352–356.

Strang, L., Smith, M. D., & Rogers, C. M. (1978). Social comparison, multiple reference groups and the self-concepts of academically handicapped children before and after mainstreaming. *Journal of Educational Psychology, 70,* 487–497.

Strodtbeck, F. L., Ronchi, D., & Hansell, S. (1976). Tutoring and psychological growth. In V. L. Allen (Ed.). *Children as teachers* (pp. 199–218). New York: Academic Press.

Thomas, A., & Pashley, B. (1982). Effects of classroom training on LD students' task persistence and attributions. *Learning Disability Quarterly, 5,* 133–144.

Thomas, J. W. (1980). Agency and achievement: Self-management and self-regard. *Review of Educational Research, 50,* 213–240.

Tollison, P., Palmer, D. J., & Stowe, M. L. (1987). Mothers' expectations, interactions, and achievement attributions for their learning disabled or normally achieving sons. *Journal of Special Education, 21*(3), 83–93.

Weiner, B., Frieze, I., Kukla, A., Reed, L., Rest, S., & Rosenbaum, R. (1971). *Perceiving the causes of success and failure.* New York: General Learning Press.

Weinstein, R. S., & Middlestadt, W. E. (1979). Students perceptions of teacher interactions with male high and low achievers. *Journal of Educational Psychology, 71,* 421–431.

White, W. J. (1985). Perspectives on the education and training of learning disabled adults. *Learning Disability Quarterly, 86,* 231–236.

▶ 13

"Now I'm a *Real* Boy"

Zones of Proximal Development for Those at Risk

JOSEPH C. CAMPIONE
ANN GORDON
ANN L. BROWN
University of California, Berkeley

MARTHA RUTHERFORD
JILL WALKER

Abstract

We describe a learning environment, developed over the past five years, designed to provide a setting in which reading, writing, and computer use are integrated in the service of learning scientific content. The program, implemented with fifth- and sixth-graders, involves new roles for students and teachers, and a curriculum fashioned to foster higher order thinking. In this chapter, we consider specifically the ways in which the environment supports the inclusion of students with learning problems. We illustrate, via a series of case studies, how "special needs" students were able to become involved in the program and to benefit from it. We argue that two aspects of the classroom organization are important: the valuing and exploitation of students' particular expertise, and the existence of a number of recurring collaborative activity structures that provide all students with zones of proximal development in which to practice and hone their emergent skills.

Portions of this research were supported by grants from the James S. McDonnell and Andrew W. Mellon Foundations. We would also like to acknowledge the considerable support of the teachers and principals at the John Swett School in Oakland, California, and Margaret Hauben, Assistant Superintendent for Curriculum of the Oakland Unified School District. Last, of course, we wish to acknowledge the students who have made the work possible.

For the past two decades we have conducted research on children's thinking. The work has moved gradually from an emphasis on laboratory-based research to a focus on classroom research. Throughout, we have been concerned with the development and facilitation of learning and comprehension skills in both normally achieving and academically delayed children (e.g., Brown, 1974, 1975; Brown, Bransford, Ferrara, & Campione, 1983; Brown & Campione, 1986; Brown & Day, 1983). One major strand of this work has focused on metacognitive factors in children's learning and in instruction (Brown, 1978; Brown & Campione, 1986; Brown et al., 1983; Campione, 1984). We have also been concerned with theories of intelligence and individual differences, assessment (Brown & Campione, 1986; Campione, 1989; Campione & Brown, 1978, 1990), and the design of remedial instructional programs (Brown, 1978; Brown & Campione, 1978, 1986; Campione, 1984; Campione & Armbruster, 1984).

During the last ten years or so, an increasing proportion of our work has taken place in classroom settings, and we have designed and implemented successful school-situated interventions based on this prior theoretical and empirical work (Brown & Campione, 1990, in press; Brown & Palincsar, 1982, 1989; Campione, Brown, & Jay, in press; Palincsar & Brown, 1984). The classroom research has progressed from the design of a program, reciprocal teaching, aimed at improving text comprehension skills in poor readers, to the construction of a more general and powerful learning environment. This community of learners (Brown & Campione, 1990) features a focus on intentional learning—or learning to learn—set within a curriculum devised to integrate the basic enabling literacies (reading, writing, mathematics) with the learning of scientific content.

We have come to treat the work as a large-scale "design experiment" (Brown & Campione, in press; Collins, in press), in which we simultaneously aim to change the design of classroom practices and to study the effects of those changes. Within the overarching experiment, a number of more specific research questions are also raised, including the following: (1) analyses of the mechanisms involved in successful learning (Brown, 1991), (2) the nature of a curriculum that supports intentional learning (Ash, Rutherford, & Brown, 1992), (3) the role of technology (Campione et al., in press), and (4) the process of teacher change. In this chapter, we focus on the extent to which this classroom learning environment is responsive to students with "special needs." In our classrooms, the incidence of such students is increasing dramatically, as schools are required to serve larger numbers of students, from more varied ethnic, linguistic, and cultural backgrounds, and encompassing many who are, for assorted reasons, relatively unprepared to enter an academic community.

STUDENTS WITH LEARNING PROBLEMS

Traditionally, poorly prepared or underachieving students have been served by special education programs. These programs vary along two, not independent, dimensions, which involve the contexts and contents of the instructional programs.

By *context* we refer to the extent to which the students are served, on a full- or part-time basis, in special day classes divorced from the regular classroom situation, versus a more fully mainstreamed program, in which all instruction takes place in the regular classroom. We conceive of three main points along this continuum:

1. Exclusionary approaches, in which much instruction takes place in special settings
2. Nonexclusionary practices, in which students remain physically in a regular classroom but are nonetheless treated differently
3. Inclusionary programs, which afford all students opportunities to learn in regular classrooms

By *content,* we refer to the fact that the curriculum can range from instruction that emphasizes "basic" skills to one that focuses primarily on "higher order" thinking skills.

Although in principle these two could vary independently, it is probably safe to assume that exclusionary programs focus more on basic skills, whereas the presumed targets of regular classroom settings include a greater emphasis on higher order skills. This covariation reflects the assumption that, for students with learning problems, basic skills must be in place before these students can benefit from exposure to higher level skills. This emphasis is then thought to be best served in a context outside the regular classroom. Then, when students "catch up," they can be returned to a mainstreamed setting.

Simply placing students with learning problems in the regular classroom, however, does not guarantee that they will be afforded equivalent instruction. There are clearly occasions, which we term nonexclusionary, on which they are treated differently from peers who are seen by their teacher as academically more capable. In classes in both reading (Brown, Palincsar, & Purcell, 1985; Collins, 1980) and mathematics (Petitto, 1985), for example, teachers tend to engage students whom they see as capable in higher order thinking activities, whereas they restrict their interactions with less able students to a focus on lower order skills.

There is now considerable discontent with instructional practices, in either setting, that focus primarily on lower order skills (decoding rather than comprehending, punctuating rather than communicating, learning algorithms rather than problem-solving routines, etc.), and this discontent is becoming particularly striking when the target students are those with learning problems.

There is, however, an interesting tension involved in these conversations. On the one hand, there is the argument that students experiencing school difficulties should be exposed to the same kinds of curricular emphases extended to better performing students: They should not receive a watered-down curriculum, one that features increasing drill and practice activities aimed at basic skills, but, rather, the same "thinking curriculum" (Resnick, 1987) advocated for all students. On the other hand, a favorite axiom of those who study diverse populations is that instruction should be tailored to individuals' needs in order to "build on their strengths"—hence a tension between affording all students equivalent opportunities to acquire desired important academic skills, while simultaneously providing a range of treatments that support different students' learning styles, proclivities, or interests.

Our efforts over time have been to work toward a classroom learning environment hospitable to students with a variety of learning problems, while simultaneously focusing on higher order thinking. We began with a reading comprehension program (Brown & Palincsar, 1982, 1989; Palincsar & Brown, 1984) referred to as *reciprocal teaching.*

Reciprocal teaching is a form of guided coopertive learning that provides students practice in applying four concrete strategies (questioning, clarifying, summarizing, and predicting) to scaffold a discussion concerning the meaning of expository texts. These particular strategies both promote comprehension and provide the student with concrete methods of monitoring their understanding. All members of the group, in turn, serve as the learning leader, responsible for orchestrating the discussion, and as supportive critics, whose job it is to encourage the learning leader to explain the content and help resolve misunderstandings. The goal of the procedure is joint construction of meaning. It is the teacher's job to see that responsibility for the comprehension activities of the group is transferred to the students as soon as possible. As students master one level of involvement, the teacher increases her demands so that students are gradually called on to function at a more challenging levels, finally adopting the leader/critic roles fully and independently. The teacher then fades into the background and acts as a sympathetic coach, allowing the students to take charge of their own learning.

In the initial application, reciprocal teaching was conducted with special education students in a one-on-one intervention as part of a pull-out remedial program. It progressed through several stages until finally it was employed as part of a regular class reading program involving both "regular" and "remedial" students. In the next section of this chapter, we describe the integrated learning environment we have developed, proceed to sketch some of the main results achieved by students in these classrooms, and then turn to a set of case studies elaborating the way in which the environment proved supportive to students with a variety of learning problems.

THE LEARNING ENVIRONMENT

We have worked primarily with inner-city fifth–sixth-graders in a setting fashioned to integrate reading, writing, and computer use with the learning of scientific content. The choice of science, specifically environmental science, as the core of the curriculum was made for several reasons. One is simply that we wanted our students to be exposed to science during their grade school years, in an effort to whet their interests and forestall the typical finding that minority (and female) students tend not to enroll in science classes in junior and senior high school, thus restricting their career choices upon graduation. In addition, we wanted our students reading and writing both about coherent content and in the service of learning. That is, we wished to avoid the typical classroom organization in which reading and writing are practiced as separate activities, divorced from each other and from the rest of the curriculum. Finally, we wanted topics that were of interest to the students.

We also have come to include a technology component, again for a number of reasons. As with the case for scientific content, one reason is simply that we want our students exposed to computers and other forms of technology. Computers are becoming ubiquitous in many workplace settings, and inner-city students are less often afforded access to them than students from more affluent districts, a "rich get richer" phenomenon. More substantively, as will be described, we believe that computers can play an important role in facilitating learning.

The environment we are currently exploring was designed as a vehicle for introducing change into all aspects of traditional instruction. It resulted from an analysis of the reasons educational practice has not been as successful as one would like. In this analysis, traditional education has these features:

1. A *didactic teaching style,* with the teacher teaching and the students functioning as passive recipients of incoming information
2. A *basic literacies curriculum* (reading, writing, and arithmetic) aimed at instilling basic before higher level skills
3. A *content curriculum* (history, geography, science) that emphasizes breadth over depth, with a resulting focus on factual information rather than understanding
4. A *fragmented curriculum,* in which the enabling literacies are taught as discrete strands separable not only from substantive content courses, but even from each other

To circumvent these problems, we aimed to alter: (1) the nature of the curriculum, (2) the role of the teacher, (3) the role of students, (4) the role of technology, and (5) the nature of assessment.

THE ROLE OF THE CURRICULUM[1]

With these goals in mind, we decided to examine the effect of exposing elementary school children to science in, to borrow Bruner's (1963) term, "an intellectually honest way"—that is, without oversimplifying the material until it is intellectually vacuous. In so doing, we assumed that in the process the students would increase their reading, writing, and thinking skills. One cannot think critically in a vacuum, and coherent scientific inquiry provides a fertile ground for promoting literacy skills in general.

As one major step in the process, we generated our own "science curriculum," specifically a year-long environmental science program based on the underlying themes of *interdependence* and *adaptation*. We decided that although we wanted depth over breadth in coverage, we did not want to introduce biochemical substrata to children this young. Instead, the students were invited into the world of the nineteenth-century naturalist and asked to do library research, conduct experiments, participate in field trips, and engage in various forms of data collection and analysis around central, repeating themes. These themes included notions of balance, change, adaptation, competition and cooperation, species and populations, and predator–prey relations that are central to an understanding of ecosystems.

We devised three main units, each with five subunits:

1. Changing populations (extinct, endangered, artificial, assisted, and urbanized)
2. Food (producing, consuming, recycling, distributing, and energy exchange)
3. Survival (reproduction, defense mechanisms, protection from the elements, ecological niches, and communities)

A representation of Unit 2, of which the central theme of food webs is the unifying concept, is shown in Figure 13-1. Each unit had five subunits to support the jigsaw activities, to be described, that are a central and recurrent feature of the classroom environment.

STUDENTS AS RESEARCHERS

Students are asked to function as researchers responsible for designing part of the curriculum. They work in cooperative groups based on the jigsaw method (Aronson, 1978). Students form five *research groups*[2] each assigned responsibility for one of five subtopics of a content area unit. They use computers to guide their research and to prepare booklets on their research topics. Next the students move into *learning groups* where one member of each group is an expert on one-fifth of the material. This expert then guides reciprocal teaching seminars on their area. All members of each group are thus experts on part of the material. In these classrooms, students are involved in: (1) *extensive reading* in order to research their topic; (2) *writing and revision* to produce booklets from which to teach as well as to publish in class books covering the

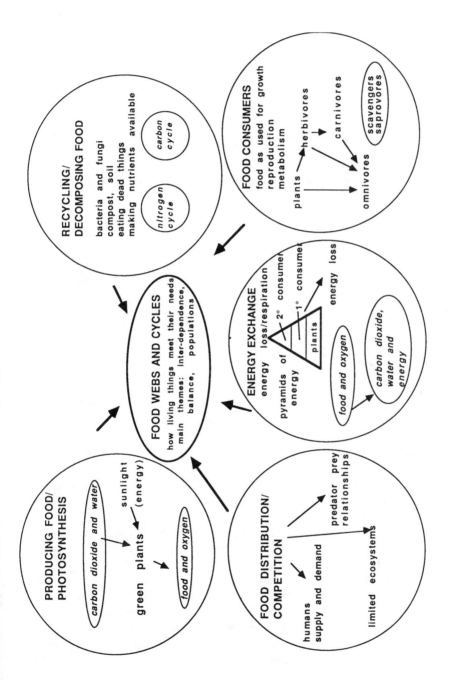

FIGURE 13-1 A representation of the constitution of Unit 2, including the jigsaw subtopics

251

entire topic; and (3) *computer use* to publish, illustrate, and edit their booklets. They read, write, and use computers in the service of learning. Students serve as teachers, editors, advisors, and mentors, making comments on one another's work and entering a network of learners with different areas of expertise in the domain. Their continuing task is to produce a class book summarizing the course itself. This text is then published and becomes a resource for students in later years. In addition to researching and teaching topics, students are also responsible for generating questions that form one-half of the class test on their subunit. Thus, the students play a role in selecting the information forming a part of the curriculum, teaching others what they believe to be important, and assessing the extent to which their teaching has been successful.

An essential part of the classroom is establishing a collaborative and cooperative atmosphere. Students are required to collaborate most directly in their research groups, but we also want them to discuss across those groups. For example, it is impossible to understand the notion of food webs without understanding all five subunits and the relations among them, so it is essential that each of the research groups provide its piece of the puzzle. In the course of doing research, students are bound to encounter information that would be helpful to other groups, and we encourage them to communicate those findings, verbally or electronically. Similarly, when students are working on their long-term projects, they are encouraged to provide feedback to one another, including both constructive criticism and suggestions about additional information sources.

THE ROLE OF THE TEACHER

We have used the term *guided discovery* to describe the form of adult teaching we wish to feature. There is considerable evidence that unguided discovery can be dangerous: Children in our initial classroom invented scientific misconceptions (Brown & Campione, in press). Didactic teaching, however, leads to passive learners. We know that challenging students' assumptions, providing them with counterexamples to their own rules — in general, being a Socratic teacher (Collins & Stevens, 1982) — can be effective. But how intrusive should the teacher be? When should she guide, when should she teach? How can she furnish guidance while fostering self-direction? This uncharted territory, midway between "pure" discovery learning and direct teaching, is where our teachers are asked to work.

When a teacher knows something the students do not, she must make judgment calls about when and where to intervene. How long should she let students flounder? She must decide whether the problem involves an important principle that needs work or only a trivial error that she can let pass for now. Alternatively, the teacher may not know the answer or may share the students' puzzlement. In this equally interesting case, she is required first to recognize this fact and then, after admitting uncertainty, to find ways to remedy it, for example by seeking help. In so doing, the teacher can be a role model of the learning crafts we wish to foster. Children can thus witness teachers learning, discovering, doing research, and using computers as tools for learning, rather than only lecturing, managing, assigning work, and controlling the classroom. This is not an easy role for many teachers: Guided learning is easier to talk about than to do. The successful teacher must continually engage in on-line diagnosis of student understanding. She must navigate the current zone of proximal development, involving not one student but many. We see this as an extension of our original reading work that was also conducted within a Vygotskian (1978) framework of a zone of proximal development, or region of sensitivity to instruction, where the student is ripe for new learning.

We also argue that teaching and learning is more effective on a need-to-know basis. In our environment, teachers certainly do a great deal of teaching, but the ideal is that they respond to a student's felt need. For example, when introducing students to the computer environment, we taught them only what they needed to get started. After that, additional features of the system were taught only when a student pointed out that she needed some new function, or noted that it would be nice if he could accomplish some other task. Students thus motivated learn rapidly and are encouraged to pass their new expertise on to others. This is the general model of teaching we are examining. The trick is to arrange the classroom context in such a way that students regularly recognize the need for additional resources.

COMPUTERS AND TECHNOLOGY

Although several extremely powerful computer environments have been developed (see particularly CSILE, Scardamalia & Bereiter, 1991), we chose (with one exception) to work with commercially produced and stable software available to any school and capable of running on "low-end," relatively inexpensive hardware. The general configuration and the associated software were designed to: (1) simplify student access to research materials, including books, magazines, videotapes, and videodiscs; (2) support writing, illustrating, and revising texts; (3) allow for data storage and management; and (4) enable easy communication within and beyond the classroom.

Two pieces of software are included to facilitate student access to research materials and to allow them to trade information, including one, Browser, we developed ourselves.

- *Appleshare* allows students to access files and documents on a classroom network (LAN) and on a wide area network (WAN). By having the information stored in one place, they can use any computer and not have to worry about storing information on a floppy disk or working at the same computer every day.

• *Browser* is a piece of software that serves several functions. First, it allows filing of documents by topics (e.g., Animal Defense Mechanisms) and themes (e.g., Camouflage, Mimicry). Given a topic and theme, Browser generates a list of titles and indicates the type (text, magazine, videotape, or videodisc) of each. Browser also supports some interesting student activities. For example, when students choose to publish some of their own work, they must generate key words in the form of a topic and theme, as well as a summary. Over time, the library becomes progressively more annotated by the students, with their entries providing important data about what they see as significant.

The system also contains three applications that allow students to compose reports and presentations. Again, all are commercially available:

• *Microsoft Works* is an integrated application that includes a word processor, database, and spreadsheet. This is the primary word processor that the students use to create reports. It allows database, spreadsheet, and graphical information to be included along with the text of any report. Students use the database and spreadsheet components to analyze data collected from hands-on experiments.

• *MacDraw* is a drawing package that can be used when precision is required and is most useful in producing charts or schematics.

• *MacPaint* is a graphics package that allows the children to create new pictures and/or customize artwork that has already been created (either scanned in or prepackaged clip art).

Finally, one piece of software is used to facilitate communication among students in the class, between students and their teacher, and between the classroom and the broader community, including the university:

• *QuickMail* is a program that allows students to send information electronically. It supports communications between members of the classroom (LAN) and the extended research community (WAN, including the university community).

MAIN OUTCOMES

Reading

One immediate outcome of the collaborative classroom is the development of a community of learners acquiring and sharing a common knowledge base. The nature of the reading/learning discussions reflects higher levels of reasoning than were apparent in a comprehension-based reading group covering the same material (to be discussed). Over time, we saw increasing incidence of comprehension-extending activities in the student teaching dialogues. A number of statistically significant changes were documented. For example, the conditions of spontaneous use of deep analogy changed dramatically over the course of the program. First, impasse-driven analogy occurred only in the face of breakdowns in comprehension. This was followed by the use of analogy to help resolve annoying inconsistencies. Finally, spontaneous analogy was used in the absence of obvious inconsistencies or misunderstandings, as learners continually monitored, revised, and deepened their understanding of complex causal mechanisms. The same pattern was found for causal explanations, which increased in explanatory precision and coherence over time. Argumentation formats developed, permitting comparisons of different points of view and defensible interpretations. Finally, the nature and importance of spontaneous prediction evolved, with students going beyond predictions of simple outcomes to considering possible worlds and engaging in thought experiments about them.

The results of reading comprehension outcome measures, where students read and answered, from memory, a series of ten questions on passages unrelated to the curriculum, are shown in Figure 13-2. The fifth- and sixth-grade students were assigned to easy (third-grade) or hard (sixth-grade) passages depending on their standardized reading scores and teacher recommendations. Students in the collaborative classroom (Research) were compared to three control groups: a group who studied the same science passages via reciprocal teaching (RTC); a read-only control (ROC), who read the target passages on their own; and a partial control group (PCont), which was treated identically to the main research group for the first unit but was then taught the final two units in a manner determined by their own (science) teacher — the PCont group did have access to the computers, the research materials, and the like that were used with the research group. The research students outperformed, though not significantly, the RTC group, even though the RTC groups were given at least twice as much practice in collaborative reading procedures. The research group showed significantly larger pretest to posttest improvements than both the ROC and PCont groups.

Writing

There were dramatic changes in the students' writing performance: They came to produce structures of increasing complexity. At the outset, they produced a perfect linear structure with 22 examples on 22 different cards; throughout the year, however, they progressed to hierarchical structures of several levels. Specific examples were now relegated to the fifth or sixth level and served as supporting details for the higher level organization. Comparing the microgenetic change of our best students over a year, we estimate tht they progressed from

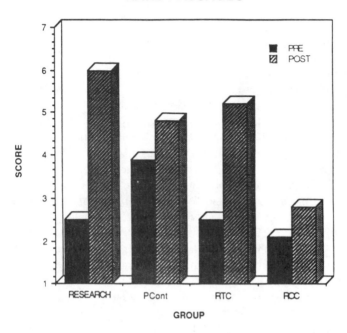

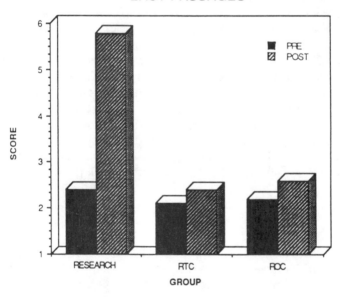

FIGURE 13-2 **Mean number of items correct on reading tests as a function of Group, Test Phase, and Difficulty Level (see text for explanation of groups)**

poor grade school levels to using organizational structures more typical of young adults.

Knowledge

The students also showed substantial gains on short-answer questions concerning the curricular content. These data are shown in Figure 13-3. Pre- and posttest measures were given for Units 1 through 3. A Groups × Units × Phase analysis of variance revealed significant main effects of Groups and Phase, as well as a Groups × Phase interaction. In Unit 1, where the partial PCont and research groups were treated identically, both groups showed substantial gain, whereas the ROC did not. In the remaining two units, the research group showed significantly larger pretest to posttest gains than the ROC and PCont groups, even though the latter had equal access to the materials and computers, spent the same amount of time on the subject, and pursued the same topics albeit under their own teacher's direction. Finally, in tests of application and transfer, the research children also outperformed control groups in their ability to apply biological principles to novel tasks, such as designing an animal to fit a habitat. Their answers involved significantly more biological principles, and the causal chains exhibited were more complex and more biologically accurate.

In general, in terms of both in-depth analyses of on-line processes (dialogues, planning, designing instruction) and outcome measures of basic literacy, the collaborative research classroom was defensible. The improvement in reading and writing scores when those activities were practiced in the service of learning scientific content is particularly important given the reluctance of administrators to permit "too much science" in grade school because of the need to improve reading scores. Such activities contribute to, rather than detract from, the acquisition of basic literacy.

STUDENTS WITH SPECIAL NEEDS

Up to this point, we have described the overall environment and shown some representative group outcome data. We are also concerned with the extent to which the classroom provokes multiple zones of proximal development for individual children. *Zone of proximal development* is a Vygotskian (1978) term that refers to the distance between what children can do working independently and what they can accomplish when working with others. In Vygotsky's view, this zone both represents the area in which teaching can be effective and affords a description of a students' current capabilities. It defines upper levels of ability, bandwidths of competence that students can navigate with aid (Brown & Reeve, 1987).

Students in the collaborative classroom are given considerable responsibility

KNOWLEDGE TEST. UNIT I

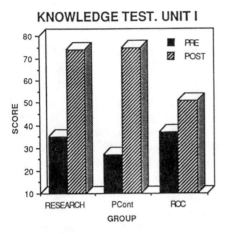

KNOWLEDGE TEST, UNIT II

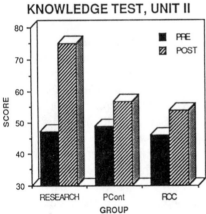

KNOWLEDGE TEST, UNIT III

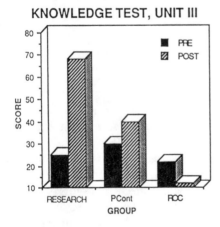

FIGURE 13-3 **Mean percentage correct on domain-specific knowledge tests as a function of Unit, Group, and Test Phase**

for their own learning. They select a portion of the curriculum, engage in extended reading and writing in order to research various areas of that curriculum, and have responsibility for teaching their expertise to others as well as devising tests of the knowledge they teach. The question is: In this setting, what happens to children with learning problems? What if someone is not a good reader or a sophisticated writer? In a classroom organized around discussion and dialogue, what happens to students whose English is weak or who do not have good discussion skills?

To investigate this feature, we have carried out a number of case studies. The data from these studies come from a variety of sources, including student logs, teacher logs, analyses of videotaped sessions, and the on-line reports of classroom observers. For the purposes of this chapter, we describe three students: the first, a student with a moderate to severe hearing impairment; the second, a classic dyslexic student; and the third, a student with limited English proficiency. One goal of the environment was to capitalize on the role of distributed expertise (Brown, Ash, Rutherford, Nakagawa, Gordon, & Campione, in press), wherein different members of the community could take responsibility, or ownership, for various aspects of the overall projects. In the community of learners environment, students "major" in different aspects of the environmental science curriculum — computer use, writing, illustrating, organizing research, becoming animal experts, and so on. The availability of numerous potential sources of ownership should maximize the likelihood that all students would be able to find a niche, one that would allow them to become a part of the classroom ethos. There are also a number of recurring rituals, involving small groups of students, that form a regular portion of the protocol, specifically reciprocal teaching sessions that students use to become familiar with their area of specialty and jigsaw sessions where they teach that expertise to their peers. These small groups, involving considerable social support, serve to initiate those less voluble into the community of discussion.

CASE 1: DAVID, OR "I'M A *REAL* BOY NOW!"

David arrived in the Bay Area from mainland China in 1984 at the age of 6. His limited use of language and his school test results prompted further medical evaluation. As a result, David was diagnosed as moderately to severely deaf. The use of hearing aids allowed David to hear at the level of the mildly hearing impaired, although at the cost of leaving him vulnerable to a corresponding increase in background noise. Because of the severity of his hearing loss, David was placed in special classes for the deaf and hard of hearing for seven full years. In the fall of 1990, he was mainstreamed full time into our experimental sixth-grade classroom.

By the time David was mainstreamed, he was able to communicate at home in Cantonese, at school in English, and in the deaf community in Signed American Sign language (a combination of signed English and American Sign language). His special education teacher (JW) described him as an unusually bright child, who was shy and originally spoke little. She further described David as somewhat of a social isolate who tended to separate himself from his peers. He listened well in group activities but then took over without regard for what had been said, and his level of academic performance remained far below the level his teacher thought appropriate. His strongest areas of achievement, apart from spoken language, could be found in the content, if not the quantity, of his writing and in his drawing. David's special education teacher saw him as a child "waiting for an opportunity to emerge."

"Now I am a *real* boy," said David upon entering the mainstreamed classroom. Succinctly, David both described the self-image he wished to acquire in his new environment and the damaged one he was ready to leave behind. In the following section we describe David's pattern of participation in the classroom and the effects of that participation on David's social and academic development.

Within the classroom structure, David was a member of a group of five boys of widely varying abilities, and one of their tasks was to understand the mechanisms underlying the endangerment of red wolves. The groups were expected to work collaboratively throughout the activity. Although David began by being very quiet at first, he quickly took on the role of drawing "expert" and in that role volunteered himself increasingly as consultant to his peers: David was a confident and experienced artist. The computers in the classroom, however, provided an opportunity for David to acquire and use an entirely new skill, computer graphics. His intense interest motivated him to allow a more skilled peer in his group to guide him through novel tasks, even when that peer tended to be rather overbearing and directive. As his own computer ability increased, David moved into a helping role with other members of the class. And as David became an increasingly active participant in the reciprocal teaching and whole-group discussions, he learned that his contributions were taken seriously and responded to by his peers. The frequent cycles of jigsaw groupings, in which each child's expertise was highlighted, also provided David opportunities to display, and be reinforced for, his newfound confidence and capabilities. The comfortable, repetitive participant structures of the classroom provided David with a basis for peer interactions in which he was sometimes teacher, sometimes learner, and sometimes partner.

Over the course of the program, David became more outwardly social. He learned to cooperate and made his first real friends. He found that he was liked for who he was, rather than as someone "special." David became more expressive both verbally and in writing, and he learned to question. In response to a story about the effects of the use of DDT in Borneo, he asked: "Why did the farmers use such [bad] judgment?" He went on to suggest an answer to this question in his field notes:

The farmers wants to protect their food crop and stop getting malaria by using DDT. They don't care about the other living thing. They don't want to get hungry. So that's why peole use DDT. They think DDT is important. They should [find] something else that culd kill mosquitoes. The farmer things the DDT is a only way to get rid of mosquitoes. DDT is too powerful. I think the farmer don't know what the consequences for using DDT.

As David became a more active and confident participant in the classroom, his overall academic performance began to be more commensurate with his apparent intelligence. The differences between David's performance on pre- and posttests of content material indicate that he acquired domain-specific knowledge at an impressive rate. His notes and research writing demonstrate the extent of content information that he essentially taught himself. For example, the central theme of interdependence was emphasized throughout the program, and the study of food chains was one vehicle for exploring this theme. On both pre- and posttest, the students were presented with an example of an incomplete food chain (e.g., Grasshopper—Robin—Wildcat). They were asked to respond to the statement, "There is something missing from this food chain," by marking "agree," "disagree," or "not sure." They then were asked to explain their answers. David's pretest explanations tended to be short, restricted sometimes to "I can't tell." He answered the food chain question by marking "disagree" but provided no reason for his answer. On the posttest, however, David marked "agree" and went on to write: "The grasshopper must eat something and the sun is always in the food chain because the sun is the main source." His new knowledge of the role of the sun was reflected in his response to the statement: "Most animals need to find food, but most plants live off food they make themselves." David answered: "The plant make food for themselves to eat so they could survive. They need sun and carbon dixoid that product were called photosynsite [photosynthesis]." David's responses to the explanation probes on all the posttest items were more elaborated and sophisticated than his corresponding responses on the pretest.

Entering junior high school in the fall of 1991, David was faced with a related question: "When a kind of plant dies out, other animals or plants are affected." David, apparently missing "a kind of" in the statement, marked "agree" and went on to say:

The food is always the second in the food chain or else the food chain is broken. All the hibervorious would died. Then the carniverous can't eat the hibervorious. Even the omivorious can't eat something.

This statement indicates the stability of David's growing knowledge base and the flexibility with which he can use his knowledge when faced with novel questions, while at the same time reflecting the kinds of reading comprehension problems he still faces. David's grasp of the notion of interdependence, his skilled use of a relatively newly learned (and yet well maintained) scientific vocabulary, his certainty, and his associated appreciation of cause-and-effect relationships, are impressive accomplishments. His special education teacher noted that these achievements should be considered as particularly impressive and unusual in light of the extent of David's hearing deficit. The collaborative classroom provided David with an environment that allowed him to move toward his potential — something tht neither his special education teacher nor David felt would have been possible had he remained in a self-contained resource room or in a special pull-out program designed for the hard of hearing. In a letter to the principal investigators (ALB and JCC) at the end of the year, David summed up his experience this way:

I would like to say that I like researching alot. At first I don't know alot about the wolves. That more you research, you know alot about the topic. I foret *[forget] to say that I was hard of hearing.*

At the end of the school year, we decided to have a summer "computer camp" for students who would be entering the sixth-grade program the following year. In addition to one staff person, we also wanted to include a program graduate as part of the teaching staff. David quickly volunteered for the position and played a prominent role in the camp activities. In addition to his having mastered the specific applications used throughout the year, it became apparent that he had also acquired considerable general facility with the Macintosh interface. He learned new features quickly, and he also turned out to be an extremely good tutor, working smoothly with a number of the new students. He spontaneously introduced his tutees to the computer through a variety of verbal suggestions of the type known to stimulate wider zones of proximal development ("You might try . . . ," "What do you think would happen if. . . ." "Try the edit menu," etc.). This approach stands in contrast to the modal technique (of both children and adults), which involves grabbing the mouse or taking over the keyboard to demonstrate a (usually unrememberable) sequence of points, drags, clicks, and keystrokes. Serving in this capacity strengthened David's self-confidence and helped him make the difficult transition from a relatively small and friendly elementary school to a much larger and more intimidating junior high school, where his computer expertise and tutoring experiences were again valued. It should be noted that David continued to be released from all special education services in his junior high placement.

CASE 2: CHRISTOPHER, OR "IT'S GREAT TO BE GIFTED AT SOMETHING!"

Our second case study concerns a fifth-grade student, Christopher, diagnosed as learning-disabled and reading at approximately the second-grade level. Christopher, at the beginning of the study, in many ways resembled Adam, the LD child studied by the Rockefeller group (Cole, Hood, & McDermott, 1978; Cole & Traupmann, 1980; McDermott, in press). His disability was not readily apparent to observers, as Christopher had become adept at manipulating his environment to hide his learning problems. His teacher aptly describes him as "wily," "extremely clever at avoiding demonstrations of his reading problem." At the beginning of the study, Christopher nonchalantly described himself as a nonwriter and refused all writing assignments because, as he put it, "I'm learning disabled, didn't you know?"

Within the community of learners environment Christopher discovered two strengths. Like David, Christopher was an accomplished artist. And, again like David, he rapidly mastered the software packages MacPaint and MacDraw. He emerged as a graphic artist of some skill, and it was in this capacity that he was called upon to illustrate his research group's initial written material. Further, as an avid viewer of television programs on environmental science and nature study, he was a storehouse of appropriate background knowledge. These twin strengths were valued in the community, and Christopher found his niche. But remember, Christopher could not read, and he had a low self-image at the beginning of the project.

During the first two reciprocal teaching sessions, when Christopher was in a new learning group, he rarely spoke. For example, on the second day the group was discussing the camouflage properties of chameleons. They had already covered seasonal color change, as in the case of the snowshoe rabbit, and were beginning to question the time span of the camouflage phenomenon.

S1: Could another animal change its color that quickly?

C. Well, the chameleon doesn't have to change during seasons. It changes anytime that it wants to or has to.

S2: Chameleon can turn every second really. How many times a day?

S3: Maybe five times.

S1: Probably as much as he wants.

C: As many times as it goes around into different surroundings. — Like if it doesn't leave his home more than twice he wouldn't change that many times really.

Christopher's verbal offerings were small, but not his conceptual contribution. He was the one who introduced the concept of immediate versus seasonal change and the constraint upon the number of changes, "as many times as it goes around into different surroundings" although it was also Christopher who introduced the teleological confusion of intent, "anytime that it wants to" — a little expertise comes at a cost.

On the third day, the topic was mimicry, and it was Christopher's task to be the expert. He was unable to read the teacher-provided text, but he knew the material. During the reciprocal teaching session, Christopher formulated questions with the help of the adult teacher but participated little in the discussion. However, when the students turned to a discussion of the student-provided text that he had illustrated, Christopher came into his own, for example when discussing the page shown in Figure 13-4.

C: Okay, now this example is a example of predatory — O.K., uh, this one right here is a beetle. And the other one is an ant. And, uh, the beetle mimics the ant so it can get in the anthill and get the ant eggs for food — like it's an easy meal. And, here's an anthill like and here's the imposter beetle.

S1: Is that supposed to be an ant farm or something?

C: It is.

S1: Did you guys make that by yourself?

C: Yeah.

S2: It's cool.

S3: Did you draw it, Christopher?

C: Yeah.

S1: Figures. (Reinforces Christopher's artwork.)

Christopher proceeded to discuss the illustration shown in the bottom of Figure 13-4.

C: Okay, now, this is another, this is an example of defenses which like we're learning about. O.K., this hoverfly that mimics the bumblebee and, um, it mimics the bumblebee 'cause the bumblebee can sting people and people don't really like to be stung. Um, so they stay away from it but — um — , but, there's a difference, because flies, they only have two wings, all flies. And all bees like in, you probably won't understand this, octarians have four wings.

S2: Okay, so if you really look closely you can tell which one's the bee —

C: Well, actually, you don't, sometimes you wouldn't be able to look that close because you wouldn't want to get stung.

He went on to discuss the next example, coral snakes and their mimic, milk snakes. He pointed out the color difference — the coral snake is red and

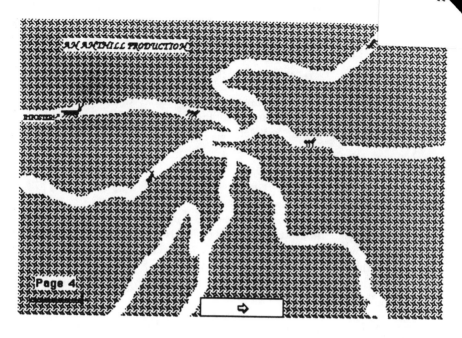

The wooly bear hoverfly mimics the stinging bumble bee so as to not be harmed by its enemies.
    The hoverfly is harmless while the bumblebee is dangerous.
    You can plainly see the difference between the two in the number of wings each has.

bumble bee ☞

wooly bear hoverfly

Page 5

FIGURE 13-4   **Christopher's artistic contributions to his group's research on mimicry**

yellow, the milk snake red and black — and then fielded a misunderstanding concerning the color of the milk snake (it is red and black, but the children's book incorrectly states red and white). Then he summed up:

C: Okay the red and black milk snake mimics the lethal coral snake. And um, the conclusion is about mimicry and people . . . like in spies. (Looks like he is reading from the book the couplet that he has memorized.)

C: When you see a snake
Red touches black, O.K. for Jack
Red touches yellow, kills a fellow.

By the second set of reciprocal teaching sessions, three months later, Christopher was well established as a leader in the group. In the following discussion, this group was revisiting the notion of camouflage. They were discussing adaptation in the context of the moths of Manchester, an example of generational change due to random selection, favoring dark over white moths in increasingly industrial Manchester.

S1: Why did the moths change color?

S2: Because of the factory smoke.

S3: Because of soot.

C: Did they just change?

S1: Some did, some didn't.

C: Do you mean a particular moth changed?

S1: No, no, no, no — they reproduced the black one.

S3: Like camouflage.

S2: No, not, not like that, not so quickly.

C: Camouflage doesn't have to be fast. It's not just camouflage, the white ones *were* best at first 'cause they blend in. Then it got sooty, and slowly — slowly — there got to be more black ones, cause they're the survivors now, cause they blend in to the soot.

S3: But the moths don't change color after they've been hatched.

S1: Right, it's diversity.

S3: How long did it take?

S4: Billions.

S3: Hundreds.

S1: Read, it says about thirty [years].

S4: That's not long for nature.

S3: I'm still not sure, were the white ones born white and then went black?

C: No, remember the 2,000 rats [reference to thought experiment from previous material] — lots of white and a few blacks. As it got darker, whites were spotted and eaten so they couldn't reproduce. Black ones survived and got to be many, and they had black ones like themselves.

It was also Christopher who introduced the thought experiment as an answer to a question, a ploy later picked up by other children in Christopher's group, but rarely in other groups, suggesting that Christopher was the role model for this particular activity.

S1: How long does it take man versus nature to make a species endangered?

C: If you're talking about endangered — well, say nature wanted to get rid of chameleons. The way nature would do it would be to change some of its colors so that chameleons couldn't fit in [couldn't disguise via camouflage]. And the chameleons would die out. But people can just go there and kill them in a day [destroy habitat]. But if nature cause it to die out, it would take many years because of all the changes.

Within the reciprocal teaching sessions, Christopher's expertise enabled him to participate fully, and he emerged as a domain expert, an expertise that was recognized by his peers and reflected in his status in the discourse. Others deferred to Christopher and rarely questioned one of his pronouncements, even when he was wrong. In part because of this newfound confidence, Christopher agreed to attempt to provide written products for the first time in his academic career; although his mechanics were imperfect, his writing did show a clear mastery of the material. In Figure 13-5 we show his answer to a transfer assessment item, in which he was asked to design an animal to fit an imagined habitat. Although his spelling and punctuation remained weak, Christopher succeeded in his task admirably, incorporating several relevant biological principles in his design. The notion of an animal being immune to its own poison is an original concept not discussed in class. The idea that eggs could mimic a snake and thus be protected is also a concept original to Christopher.

We argue that Christopher's skill at computer graphics won him recognition and respect from other members of his group. Both within his research group and among the class as a whole, he was consulted regularly as the resident computer expert. This in turn stimulated increased participation in the research/teaching sessions, despite his serious reading problems. Over the course of the year, Christopher's reading improved; he gained approximately two years on standardized reading scores and was a major gainer on the pre- to posttest criterion-referenced reading scores. Christopher became more of a risk-taker, eventually taking part in all class activities and ending up as one of the top students in the class. In addition, Christopher's parents, impressed by his

(My animal eats) Most insects some small fish and a canal rat her and thereand some crafish. There are small spikes all over the body and 4 long poison stingers on it tail that they are amun to so when they eat it they do not get poisined like there pray. It has a very strong noise and very sharp eye sight. It doesn't depend on other animals because its mean.

(It defends itself) There are small spikes all over the body and 4 long poison stingers on it tail that they are amun to so when they eat it they do not get poisined like there pray. It has a very strong noise and very sharp eye sight. Yes they are very aggersive if you bother it would try very hard to hurt you.

On the avarge year the female will have about 60 babys a year. they are bord under ground and the mother will get as many worms as possable.

If not for the very strange way of protection prey coule wipe out the whole litter in one atack. this strang way of proction is when they are born they do not have legs yet and it has allmost the exact pattern of a full groun corba.

FIGURE 13-5 **Christopher's response to a "design an animal" transfer probe**

Note: *amun = immune*

computer graphics, arranged for him to have art lessons. In the middle of one session, Christopher reported, "My art teacher thinks I am gifted. It's great to be gifted at something!" No doubt there were changes in Christopher's self-esteem.

CASE 3: LEE, OR "I CAN TEACH THE WHOLE CLASS!"

Lee, a sixth-grader, is trilingual, speaking Thai, Laotian, and English. She immigrated to this country when she was 4 years old, so all of her schooling has been in English, although she has been at this particular school for only the last three years.

Lee considers English to be her preferred language. During an interview, she expressed concern over forgetting her other languages. At home, Lee continues to speak to her parents and elders in Laotian and Thai, but, she has switched to conversing with her school-age siblings in English. By virtue of her high scores on the district language assessment measure, Lee was removed from any support services, including English as a Second Language (ESL) programs. The district test, an oral examination, focused exclusively on hypothetical events that might occur during a social exchange. Lee's written or verbal academic capabilities were never assessed formally prior to withdrawal of support services.

Though Lee was successful in school subjects, as evidenced by teacher comments and report cards over the years, prior to participating in this program, she had made no voluntary or spontaneous oral contributions to the classroom discussions. Lee was not a promising student to become a member of a community of discourse. Over time, with the introduction of this project, participation in the variety of small-group configurations provided Lee with a means of accessing a variety of discourse modes. The change in Lee occurred gradually, first in the safety of her own research group, later in the reciprocal teaching, and finally in the end-of-the-unit jigsaw sessions. Each step represented a bold departure for this child; each step was made slowly and cautiously.

Lee was in a self-selected research group of four Asian-American females. The smallness of the group enabled Lee to feel willing to take risks. In this arena, she was able to communicate with colleagues, thus creating opportunities for language learning. There was a chance to talk and expand ideas. Lee, reticent to talk in public, was more comfortable with her research companions and therefore able to explore the complexities of their research project. For example, when they were preparing the questions that they wanted to research, their discussion took them from concrete questions like, "How did whales get endangered?" "How much do whales eat?" "Do they live in warm places or cold places?" to Lee's more esoteric questions (e.g., "Are they [the whales] aware of the land outside of the water?").

The small-group research and reciprocal teaching settings offered a variety of benefits for Lee. First, the formulaic aspects of reciprocal teaching offered a way for Lee to anticipate demands that might be made on her during the course of the discussion. Initially, the routine of reciprocal teaching was restated at the beginning of each session, thereby allowing Lee to anticipate her role. Over the course of the first four reciprocal teaching sessions, Lee's participation increased dramatically. She spontaneously chose to answer questions that were addressed to the whole group. Table 13-1 illustrates the number of times in each session Lee chose to speak voluntarily, as compared to the number of times that the teacher elicited her input.

Increased participation in classroom discourse was not the only benefit

TABLE 13-1   Lee's Spontaneously Produced versus Teacher-Elicited
Comments over Successive Reciprocal Teaching Sessions

Spoke Voluntary		Requested to Speak by Teacher
RT #1	5 times	3 times
RT #2	8 times	1 time
RT #3	22 times	7 times
RT #4	37 times	2 times

of reciprocal teaching for Lee. Her apparent fluency in English, when she did speak, coupled with her quiet nature, made opportunities for close scrutiny of Lee's speech rare. Furthermore, like so many children learning a new discipline, in this case, science, Lee was eager to display competence and reticent to say anything wrong. Fortunately, the reciprocal teaching forum provided the teacher with opportunities to detect and avert misconceptions that might otherwise go unnoticed. In the following example, another second-language learner is trying to clarify a word meaning. Lee and her friend Yuan, both assumed to be competent speakers of English, attempt to define a word. At first, it appears that the girls are correct; as they continue to speak, however, it becomes apparent that they have misunderstood the word, with a resulting misunderstanding of the concept presented in the text:

Mi: What's "fewer"?

Lee and Yuan: Littler, smaller, less.

Teacher: Not as many.

Mi: [Reads the sentence] There have been fewer and fewer hungry chicks . . . [and asks what it means]

Lee and Yuan: They have been smaller and smaller.

Teacher: Smaller numbers, not as many.

Often, when students reach a certain level of verbal sophistication in a second language, it is assumed that they understand most of what is being said. Reciprocal teaching provides a much-needed system of checks and balances so that even the most subtle misconceptions can surface. Without this intervention, the children in the group would have assumed, erroneously, that peregrine falcons are having smaller rather than fewer chicks. The presence of the more experienced speaker allowed the subtleties of the text to be considered, and the students were able to ferret out the specific meaning and function of an ambiguous term.

Reciprocal teaching also provided a structure for revising writing. As a group, the children "RT'd" (their term) their completed writing. While examining Lee's contribution, they grappled with the complicated notion of how pollution enters into a whale's system through the food chain. In her first draft, she made the following argument:

> *Plution is also causing whales to die. Since the ocean is dirty it cause some of their food to die or their habit in the ocean being distroyed. It is also because the whales food chain is broken so the whales have less food to eat. Their are not enough food to go around for the whales.*

From discussion, it became clear that Lee had a greater understanding of the material than she had exhibited in her written piece. The members of her research group and the teacher questioned Lee about the meaning of her text. Clarification was sought on points that were unclear. At the end of the discussion Lee, with the help of a spell checker, made the following adjustments:

> *Pollution is also causing whales to die. Since the ocean is dirty it causes some of the whale's food to get dirty. For example, DDT gets on the algae and the krill eat the algae. When the whales eat the krill they might get sick because they will get DDT in their system. Remember that the whales eat a lot of krill.*

Clearly in her revision, Lee was better able to make herself understood. Without the discussion that had taken place, Lee's unaided writing would have suggested a lower level of understanding of the subject matter than was true.

By the end of the semester, Lee was a fully participating member of her reciprocal teaching group. She also was willing to offer comments in the more public forum of jigsaw, which in this class was a group of seven students from seven different research groups. For Lee, this meant conversing with people with whom she had little association. During the first half of the year, she would not have ventured into scientific discourse with these children, yet in the jigsaws she spoke spontaneously several times without the teacher's prompting, on occasion even making repeated attempts to make sure she would be heard.

Finally, in the last whole-class discussion of the year, Lee spoke for the first time in such a forum. She spoke softly and was not attended to. She took a deep breath and repeated her question in a firm voice. This time her bid for a turn was respected, and the class' discussion centered on Lee's point (about low-birthweight babies as a cause of endangerment). By this point, Lee's small research group had been reduced even further to two members. An observer (ALB) asked Lee how she would manage, with such a small group, to teach the entire class about whales. She responded: "It doesn't matter. I can teach the whole class." She surely could!

As a final comment, when Lee entered junior high school, she was originally assigned to a special education class on the basis of her presumed limited

English proficiency. Her parents objected to the placement. Using data from her sixth-grade class, it was possible to have her reassigned to a regular class, where she performed extremely well.

CONCLUSIONS

We have described the community of learners environment we have been refining over the past five years, indicated some of the motivation for its particular features, and illustrated the positive outcomes that have emerged. More particularly, we have presented evidence in the form of a number of case studies that the environment supports the teaching of students with a variety of "special needs." We argue that there are two primary features of the environment that make this happen. First, the classroom structure highlights collaboration, recognizes the role of distributed expertise (Brown et al., in press), and affords multiple opportunities for students to find their own niche (Christopher and David did this in good part through artistic and computer skills). This allows students to gain ownership of some feature of the class' diverse array of activities, which in turn enables them more readily to enter the community of learners we wish to establish. Second, there are a small number of repetitive participant structures—reciprocal teaching, jigsaw activities, computer work—that become familiar, ritualized, and relatively automated with practice, again affording those students with learning problems a supportive context for entering into the main activities. The repetitive supportive structures were particularly important for Lee's emergence as a discussion participant. In this environment, diversity—in terms of ability, cultural background, and learning styles—is valued. Each child can find a niche in which to develop independent talents.

NOTES

1. The sections on the nature of the environment and the main outcomes are adapted from Brown and Campione (in press).

2. The selection and constitution of groups is a major issue in itself, and we do not have space to describe the process in detail. Generally, students have input into the process in several ways: They get to nominate the topics in which they are to specialize and the other students with whom they are to work. When conflicts arise, however, as they almost always do, the teacher makes the final selections. Students whose priorities cannot be handled at the outset are given first priority on later occasions; thus, all students manage to have their choices honored at some point during the year.

REFERENCES

Aronson, E. (1978). *The jigsaw classroom*. Beverly Hills, CA: Sage.

Ash, D. B., Rutherford, M. E., & Brown, A. L. (1992, April). *Networks of related meanings: Themes in children's science discourse.* Paper presented at the Annual Meeting of the American Educational Research Association, San Francisco.

Brown, A. L. (1974). The role of strategic behavior in retardate memory. In M. R. Ellis (Ed.), *International review of research in mental retardation* (Vol. 7, pp. 55–111). New York: Academic Press.

Brown, A. L. (1975). The development of memory: Knowing, knowing about knowing, and knowing how to know. In H. W. Reese (Ed.), *Advances in child development and behavior* (Vol. 10, pp. 103–152). New York: Academic Press.

Brown, A. L. (1978). Knowing when, where, and how to remember: A problem of metacognition. In R. Glaser (Ed.), *Advances in instructional psychology* (Vol. 1, pp. 77–165). Hillsdale, NJ: Erlbaum.

Brown, A. L. (1991). *Explanation, analogy, and theory in children's spontaneous learning.* Kenneth Craik Memorial Lecture Series, St. John's College, Cambridge, October.

Brown, A. L. (1992). Design experiments: Theoretical and methodological challenges in creating complex interventions in classroom settings. *The Journal of the Learning Sciences, 2*(2), 141–178.

Brown, A. L., Ash, D., Rutherford, M., Nakagawa, K., Gordon, A., & Campione, J. C. (in press). Distributed expertise in the classroom. In G. Salomon (Ed.), *Distributed cognitions.* New York: Cambridge University Press.

Brown, A. L., Bransford, J. D., Ferrara, R. A., & Campione, J. C. (1983). Learning, remembering, and understanding. In J. H. Flavell & E. M. Markman (Eds.), *Handbook of child psychology,* 4th ed. *Cognitive development* (Vol. 3, pp. 77–166). New York: Wiley.

Brown, A. L., & Campione, J. C. (1978). Permissible inferences from cognitive training studies in developmental research. In W. S. Hall & M. Cole (Eds.), *Quarterly Newsletter of the Institute for Comparative Human Behavior, 2*(3), 46–53.

Brown, A. L., & Campione, J. C. (1986). Psychological theory and the study of learning disabilities. *American Psychologist, 41,* 1059–1068.

Brown, A. L., & Campione, J. C. (1990). Communities of learning and thinking, or A context by any other name. *Human Development, 21,* 108–125.

Brown, A. L., & Campione, J. C. (in press). Restructuring grade school learning environments to promote scientific literacy. In *Restructuring learning: Analysis and proceedings of the annual conference of the Council of Chief State School Officers.* San Diego, CA: Harcourt.

Brown, A. L., & Day, J. D. (1983). Macrorules for summarizing texts: The development of expertise. *Journal of Verbal Learning and Verbal Behavior, 22*(1), 1–14.

Brown, A. L., & Palincsar, A. S. (1982). Inducing strategic learning from texts by means of informed, self-control training. *Topics in Learning and Learning Disabilities, 2*(1), 1–17.

Brown, A. L., & Palincsar, A. S. (1989). Guided, cooperative learning and individual knowledge acquisition. In L. B. Resnick (Ed.), *Knowing, learning, and instruction: Essays in honor of Robert Glaser* (pp. 393–451). Hillsdale, NJ: Erlbaum.

Brown, A. L., Palincsar, A. S., & Purcell, L. (1985). Poor readers: Teach, don't label. In U. Neisser (Ed.), *The academic performance of minority children: A new perspective* (pp. 105–143). Hillsdale, NJ: Erlbaum.

Brown, A. L., & Reeve, R. A. (1987). Bandwidths of competence: The role of supportive contexts in learning and development. In L. S. Liben (Ed.), *Development and learning: Conflict or congruence?* (pp. 173–223). Hillsdale, NJ: Erlbaum.

Bruner, J. S. (1963). *The process of education.* Cambridge, MA: Harvard University Press.

Campione, J. C. (1984). Metacognitive components of instructional research with problem learners. In F. E. Weinert & R. H. Kluwe (Eds.), *Metacognition, motivation, and learning* (pp. 109–132). West Germany: Kuhlhammer.

Campione, J. C. (1989). Assisted assessment: A taxonomy of approaches and an outline of strengths and weaknesses. *Journal of Learning Disabilities, 22,* 151–165.

Campione, J. C., & Armbruster, B. B. (1984). An analysis of the outcomes and implications of intervention research. In H. Mandl, N. Stein, & T. Trabasso (Eds.), *Learning and comprehension of texts* (pp. 287–304). Hillsdale, NJ: Erlbaum.

Campione, J. C., & Brown, A. L. (1978). Toward a theory of intelligence: Contributions from research with retarded children. *Intelligence, 2,* 279–304.

Campione, J. C., & Brown, A. L. (1990). Guided learning and transfer: Implications for approaches to assessment. In N. Frederiksen, R. Glaser, A. Lesgold, & M. Shafto (Eds.), *Diagnostic monitoring of skill and knowledge acquisition* (pp. 141–172). Hillsdale, NJ: Erlbaum.

Campione, J. C., Brown, A. L., & Jay, M. (in press). Computers in a community of learners. In E. De Corte, M. Linn, H. Mandl, & L. Verschaffel (Eds.), *Computer-based learning environments and problem solving* (NATO ASI Series: F. Computer and Systems Series). Berlin: Springer-Verlag.

Cole, M., Hood, L., & McDermott, R. P. (1978). Concepts of ecological validity: Their differing implications for comparative cognitive research. In W. S. Hall & M. Cole (Eds.), *The Quarterly Newsletter of the Institute for Comparative Human Development, 2,* 34–37.

Cole, M., & Traupmann, K. (1980). Comparative cognitive research: Learning from a learning disabled child. In A. Collins (Ed.), *Minnesota symposium on child development* (pp. 125–154). Hillsdale, NJ: Erlbaum.

Collins, A. (in press). Toward a design science of education. In E. Scanlon & T. O'Shea (Eds.), *New directions in educational technology.* New York: Springer-Verlag.

Collins, A., & Stevens, A. (1982). Goals and strategies of inquiry teachers. In R. Glaser (Ed.), *Advances in instructional psychology* (Vol. 2, pp. 65–119). Hillsdale, NJ: Erlbaum.

Collins, J. (1980). Differential treatment in reading groups. In J. Cook-Gumperz (Ed.), *Educational discourse.* London: Heinemann.

McDermott, R. P. (in press). The acquisition of a child by a learning disability. In S. D. Chaiklin & J. Lave (Eds.), *Understanding practice.* New York: Cambridge University Press.

Palincsar, A. S., & Brown, A. L. (1984). Reciprocal teaching of comprehension-fostering and monitoring activities. *Cognition and Instruction, 1*(2), 117–175.

Petitto, A. L. (1985). Division of labor: Procedural learning in teacher-led small groups. *Cognition and Instruction, 2,* 233–270.

Resnick, L. B. (1987). *Education and learning to think.* Washington, DC: National Academy Press.

Scardamalia, M., & Bereiter, C. (1991). Higher levels of agency for children in knowledge building: A challenge for the design of new knowledge media. *The Journal of the Learning Sciences, 1*(1), 37–68.

Vygotsky, L. S. (1978). *Mind in society.* Cambridge, MA: Harvard University Press.

Name Index

Subject Index